THE
O.S.S.
IN
ITALY
1942-1945

THE
O.S.S.
IN
ITALY
1942-1945

A Personal Memoir

MAX CORVO

PRAEGER

New York
Westport, Connecticut
London

Library of Congress Cataloging-in-Publication Data

Corvo, Max.
  The OSS in Italy, 1942-1945 : a personal memoir / Max Corvo.
    p. cm.
  Bibliography: p.
  Includes index.
  ISBN 0-275-93333-4 (lib. bdg. : alk. paper)
  1. Corvo, Max. 2. United States. Office of Strategic Services.
3. World War, 1939-1945—Personal narratives, American. 4. World
War, 1939-1945—Secret service—United States. 5. World War,
1939-1945—Secret service—Italy. 6. Intelligence officers—United
States—Biography. I. Title.
D810.S7C64 1990
940.54'86'73—dc19   89-3801

Library of Congress Catalog Card Number: 89-3801
ISBN: 0-275-93333-4

First published in 1990

Praeger Publishers, One Madison Avenue, New York, NY 10010
A division of Greenwood Press, Inc.

Printed in the United States of America

The paper used in this book complies with the Permanent
Paper Standard issued by the National Information Standards
Organization (Z39.48—1984).

10 9 8 7 6 5 4 3 2 1

Contents

Photo section follows page 178.

DEDICATED TO THE MEN AND WOMEN
WHO FELL ON ITALIAN SOIL
IN THE QUEST OF FREEDOM

Preface

The events recounted in this volume took place over 40 years ago and until now have been withheld from public scrutiny because of the extreme secrecy which our government exercised through the original "Secret-Control" classification and other restrictive classifications. This account derives from the recently declassified documents of the Office of Strategic Services (OSS) covering U.S. operations in North Africa and Italy during World War II and from my personal papers which have gathered dust for the past four decades. It should help to shed light on some of the most successful and controversial secret intelligence operations conducted by the OSS during World War II. Some of these operations have been at the center of heated controversies triggered by books written without access to the authentic historical records to back up often subjective suppositions and theories.

This book will examine the monumental problems which the fledgling OSS faced in early 1943. Beset by the pressures and hostility of the traditional competing intelligence services, Director William J. Donovan was asked to have his organization perform veritable miracles in order to survive and eventually achieve acceptance in high military and diplomatic circles of the U.S. government. As the records show, in order to achieve success against the enemy, it was often necessary to wage equally vigorous struggles within the organization. The OSS was generously endowed with ambitious, well-connected, highly placed individuals, who were accustomed to giving unchallenged corporate-style and military orders.

Over the years, as some of these operations became controversial front-page stories, it was not possible to initiate a point-by-point challenge to the assertions or motivations behind the revelations. In most cases, documentary evidence which would have shed light on the events was still unavailable because of its secret classification.

The first official history of the Office of Strategic Services was undertaken on July 26, 1946, as the History Project of the War Department's Strategic Services Unit (successor to OSS). Kermit Roosevelt was chief historian and Serge Peter Karlow executive officer. The history was not completed until after Roosevelt's departure from the service in May 1947. All of the reports and supporting documents retained their top secret classification and were integrated within the OSS archives under the jurisdiction of the Central Intelligence Group (another interim successor of OSS).

Immediately after World War II, a number of articles on OSS operations were published in various national magazines, and several books were authored by former OSS people. It was not until 1972, however, that the first volume which attempted to reconstruct the history of the organization and some of the key people was written by R. Harris Smith and published by Berkeley University Press, under the title *OSS: The Secret History of America's First Central Intelligence.* Smith based his book on personal and telephone interviews, as well as written communications with a large number of former OSS persons. He had few, if any, official sources for historical references. Some of the individuals who provided general background information were still serving in the Central Intelligence Agency (CIA), where Smith had also been employed before writing the book. Smith's book spawned numerous historical controversies and many inaccuracies which have since become accepted as historical facts by other writers who have repeated the errors.

In 1976, the Walker Company published the partially censored two-volume history of the OSS under the title *The War Report of the OSS* with a "new introduction by Kermit Roosevelt." In the same year (1976) Anthony Cave Brown, a British author, published a volume entitled *The Secret War Report of the OSS,* using much the same material that had appeared in the Roosevelt edition. He plucked some material from Harris Smith's book and the U.S. Archives, further propagating the historical inaccuracies.

Also in 1976, an Italian team of leftist writers, Marco Fini and Robert Faenza, who were tied with the communist Giangiacomo Feltrinelli Foundation in Milan, published a volume in Italy entitled *The Americans in Italy.* It, too, repeated many of Smith's inaccuracies about the OSS. They were assisted in their research by Edward J. Becker and Mark Lynch of Ralph Nader's Center for the Study of Responsive Law. The preface of the book was written by G. William Dumhoff of the University of California, and the object of the book was to create a negative climate for U.S. foreign policies and CIA operations.

In 1970, Corey Ford wrote a biography of Bill Donovan (*Donovan of OSS*) using some unclassified material and anecdotes. The sales of the book were reported to be limited because, while Corey had access to a good deal of material, he respected the need to honor the still secret classification. A book on Donovan with a restricted in-house CIA circulation was written by Tom Troy in 1970. At that time, Troy was working for the CIA, and only recently has this book become available to the general public. Troy's book sticks to the facts and in the 1970's was considered required reading for new CIA recruits as background material.

General Donovan's personal archives contained thousands of classified documents relating to the OSS and other government operations. At the time of his death in 1959, these documents were stored with his New York law firm which jointly controlled them with his son David. Otto Doering, a partner in the law firm and a wartime assistant of Donovan's, reached an agreement with Cave Brown by which the Donovan papers were turned over to the British author, who was to write a definitive biography of Donovan and the OSS. The result was a tome entitled *The Last Hero: Wild Bill Donovan*. It was published by Times Books in 1982 and immediately provoked a spate of controversies and challenges about the author's historical accuracy.

At the time the book was published, it was criticized for depicting Donovan as the head of a failed corporation. Brown singled out and magnified a series of unsuccessful operations, and he interpreted a number of incidents on the basis of speculation rather than the historical facts which he should have taken time to research.

After Cave Brown's book was published, I decided that it was time to correct many of the misconceptions, distortions, and historical errors that had been written regarding OSS participation in the Italian campaign. The Italian effort was the most complex, the longest, and the most difficult of the organization's undertakings. It covered a span of time from July 1942 until the end of the war in 1945. It was during this period that I was in charge of the operations of the Italian Secret Intelligence Section of the OSS, a period during which I was intimately connected with plans, recruitment, and training in the United States. I also directed field operations in the Mediterranean Theater of war.

The OSS role in the Italian campaign was not restricted to secret intelligence, but also included the efforts of all other branches such as Special Operations, X-2, research and analysis, morale operations, maritime units, communications, parachute training, administrative units, and commando-type operational groups.

Donovan closely followed the work in Italy and visited the theater frequently, helping to shape many of the command and policy decisions.

This account is the story of the Italian Secret Intelligence Section of OSS, its relationship with other branches of the organization, and the evolution of U.S. policies which led to the establishment of the close relationship between Italy's postwar government and Washington. The forging of these links of friendship was tempered in countless underground battles waged against the Nazi-Fascist forces by OSS missions working in concert with Italian underground forces.

Italy was the testing ground for OSS tactics and strategic concepts. The lessons learned there were successfully applied to similar undertakings in other parts of the world.

THE
O.S.S.
IN
ITALY
1942-1945

Chapter 1

Prelude

Early in 1942, I was stationed at the Quartermaster Training Center at Camp Lee, Virginia, where, to my great disappointment, I had been assigned as a trainee for clerical duties. I had volunteered for service prior to the Japanese attack on Pearl Harbor because I felt strongly about the Fascist and Nazi regimes' persecutions in Europe and hoped to receive an assignment to a section of the Army intelligence services. By good fortune, the lieutenant who was my school instructor at Camp Lee took some interest in my background and, after a series of chats in which I explained some of my ideas regarding underground warfare in Italy, he arranged for me to be excused from his clerical course and assigned to the Camp S-2 and Public Relations office. I was given permission to be allowed time to put my ideas down on paper and develop an intelligence plan while awaiting an opportunity to transfer to an intelligence outfit. The lieutenant and I would meet again many times during the war and later in Washington and Spain. He was Angier Biddle Duke, chief of protocol of the State Department during the Kennedy administration and later ambassador to Spain.

In my new assignment at camp headquarters, I was given ample opportunity and freedom to put my ideas on paper and write extensively about the type of operation I envisioned. Both the officers and the men in the office made it possible for me to outline the tactics to be used to undermine the Fascist regime in Sicily and later in Italy.

The subject of anti-Fascism was hardly new to me, although at that time I was only twenty-one years old. I had been brought up in a highly anti-Fascist atmosphere. My father, Cesare Corvo, had gone into self-imposed exile from Sicily in 1923 after a spirited struggle against the

Fascist hierarchy in the province of Syracuse, one of the last holdout areas against the Fascist tide that had engulfed Italy. With the help of powerful friends in Palermo, he managed to secure a passport and to board a ship to the United States where, as a young man, he had lived for a few years as a member of a troupe of traveling Italian actors.

Leaving his wife and three children in the care of his mother, my father took up residence in Middletown, Connecticut, a town where many of his friends had settled. He kept in touch with fellow political expatriates in New York, Chicago, and other major cities of the United States where anti-Fascists made common cause with labor organizations such as Luigi Antonini's Local 89 of the International Ladies Garment Workers Union and Augusto Bellanca's Amalgamated Clothing Workers Union.

Language difficulties forced him to work in one of the local factories, but before long he founded an Italian-language weekly newspaper which achieved a wide circulation in Connecticut and which spoke out fiercely against abuses of power in Fascist Italy. At the same time, he continued to correspond with many friends in Italy who were prominent in the underground battle against the Mussolini regime.

In 1929, when our father became a citizen of the United States, he sent for us. Difficulties arose, however, when anonymous letters sent from the United States to the Opera Volontaria Repressione Antifascista, the Fascist Secret Police, charged him with overt anti-Fascist activities and withheld the family passport. Fortunately, one of his boyhood friends who had achieved prominence in the Fascist party, interceded, picked up the passport, and personally delivered it to my mother only one week before the family's scheduled departure. We arrived in New York on October 12, 1929, Columbus Day, just as the worst depression in the history of the United States began.

The warmth of the New England foliage greeted us as we drove to our new home, past the town green, which was carpeted with the golden harvest from the stately maples that dotted the park. A lonely sentinel, the weatherbeaten bronze statue of a Civil War soldier, stood atop a four-sided pedestal on which were inscribed the names of famous Civil War battles. This was a new and wonderful world for a young boy coming from the ancient, rocky soil of Sicily. Although I did not know a word of English, the mystery of this new experience and the desire to become a participant in what was happening were so great that they accelerated my capacity to communicate with my teachers and classmates in school.

In a very short time I managed to make it to the fifth grade where I met one of those rare teachers who leaves an indelible impression on her pupils. At the time she was almost at the end of her teaching career, but she had retained the vivacity and dynamism of youth. A product of a Victorian New England upbringing, Ida M. Keigwin was an active member of the local Methodist church and a member of the WCTU

(Women's Christian Temperance Union); an internationalist who imbued her young students with an irresistible desire to communicate with children of other nations; a pacifist who believed ardently in the League of Nations; and finally, an individual free of racial or ethnic prejudice.

The blackboards on two sides of her room were aflame with maps of China and other faraway lands about which she had written little ditties that synthesized their history and geography. The school, located in the very heart of the town's Little Italy, was a segregated school by today's standards. Almost 100 percent of the children enrolled were Italian-Americans whom she treated as the natural descendants of Dante, Raphael, Michelangelo, and other giants of the Renaissance. Who could fail to be influenced by such a teacher? At the distance of over half a century I still have her little mementoes tucked away in my desk and a portrait of Abe Lincoln (her favorite person) which she gave me upon graduation from her fifth grade class.

Less than a decade after graduating from Ida Keigwin's fifth grade, world conditions had made a shambles of the League of Nations; Manchuria had been incorporated as a part of Japan; huge areas of China had been conquered by the Imperial Japanese Army; Ethiopia had become part of the Italian Empire; Spain had been torn apart by civil war; France and the Lowlands had been overrun; Norway and Poland were occupied lands; massive battles in the Russian steppes were bleeding both Russia and Germany; and Britain's Eighth Army was on the defensive at the Egyptian-Libyan border, while Field Marshal Erwin Rommel was begging Hitler to provide additional sinews of war which would permit him to march victoriously to Alexandria.

Despite the negative news from almost all the world's battlefronts, in my mind there was no doubt about the final outcome of the war. Nor did I harbor any doubt that one of the key decisions would have to be made in the Central Mediterranean and that eventually both Sicily and Italy would be enveloped by battle. This thought kept me working long hours at my desk at the Camp Lee S-2 office. When I could obtain a three-day pass, I would hurry home and seek my father's advice or talk to some of his New York anti-Fascist friends to fill some of the gaps in my knowledge.

By May 1942, I had managed to formulate a plan which foresaw the advance of the Eighth Army in North Africa with the participation of the Free French drive northward from Fort Lami in the Chad territory.[1] The Eighth Army attack did not come until October 1942 when General Bernard Law Montgomery broke the back of the Afrika Korps at El Alamein and forced Rommel to retreat all the way to the Tunisian frontier. This military success and the Allied desire to assist beleaguered Russia through the creation of a Second Front triggered the combined British-American "Torch" operation against Morocco and Algeria in November 1942, bringing the war even closer to Sicily and the Italian homeland.

By June 1942, my plan for subversive warfare against Sicily was ready. In consultation with the officers in the S-2 office I decided to submit a copy of the plan to my immediate supervisor, Lieutenant Robert L. Kunzig, who endorsed it and sent it to the Camp S-2, Lieutenant Colonel E. L. Stewart (camp intelligence chief), who, in turn, endorsed it for the commanding general of the camp and forwarded it to the assistant chief of staff G-2, Third Corps Area, Baltimore, Maryland.

Papers sent through Army channels seldom get to their destination, tending to get lost on some desk or other. Aware of this reality, I took the precaution of making several copies of the plan and its enclosures. After thinking the matter over, I decided to write to Thomas M. Russell, vice-president of the corporation where I had worked briefly before volunteering for service. I explained to him what I wanted to do and asked his advice about contacting someone in Washington who could be of help. He immediately wrote to U.S. Senator John Danaher (R-Connecticut) asking him to give me an appointment. On July 2, 1942, I received a letter from Senator Danaher requesting that I contact his office and set up an appointment to see him.[2] I was elated. Things seemed to be moving rapidly. I had no trouble convincing my superiors to give me a three-day pass to go to Washington. By this time, they were completely amazed at my progress and were ready to believe that anything might be possible.

Chapter 2

On to Washington

The trip to Washington from Petersburg, Virginia, aboard an old Seaboard train crowded with soldiers and civilians going north was no picnic on a hot day. The old steam locomotive chugged along at a fast clip and belched black smoke which entered the coach in the form of thousands of particles of black soot, showing no respect for any passenger in the steaming coach. By the time the train arrived at Union Station in Washington, we were all thoroughly coated.

The confusion that reigned at Union Station with its thousands of passengers and hundreds of taxis at the exit was almost overwhelming. I finally prevailed on a cabby to take me to a hotel, who realized that I did not know the city and goodnaturedly teased me that I was probably on pass looking for a good time.

As soon as I got into my room, I picked up the phone to call Senator Danaher's office and inform his executive assistant of my arrival. He confirmed my appointment for the following morning. So much depended on my presentation of the plan to the senator that I decided to rehearse what I would say. Over and over again, I went through it, until I felt I had it all down pat.

The following morning I presented myself to the senator's assistant in full buck private's uniform to unfold my plan. Looking back, I still marvel at the senator's patience and obvious interest in what I had to propose. He allowed me to present my case without display of boredom or impatience. Apparently, he could see that I had put much thought and time into devising my psychological warfare plan for Sicily, and he interrupted only when he needed additional data.

When my presentation was over, in a kind, fatherly tone of voice, he stated that he was impressed with both the plan and my fervor in pursuit of it, and that he would try to help me by having his assistant make some appointments for me to present it. However, he advised me that the men to whom I would be talking were terribly busy men and that I should make my presentation brief and to the point in order not to lose listener interest.

He then pressed the buzzer, and his assistant came into the room. The senator told him that he wanted him to call the Senate military liaison officer, who at that time was Colonel Whelms. I could talk to him, and he in turn could decide whom I should talk to in order to promote my plan. The meeting with Colonel Whelms, whose office was nearby, was easily arranged; taking the senator's advice, I trimmed my presentation sharply.[1] The colonel displayed a good deal of interest and said he would make appointments for me to be interviewed by the intelligence people at the old Munitions Building on Constitution Avenue, which, at that time, was the headquarters of the War Department. There I was interviewed by a number of desk chiefs in G-2, including several colonels whom I was later to meet in the field and with whom I was to form lasting friendships.

All of them showed interest, but it soon became obvious to me that I was heading down a blind alley. While these men held high General Staff positions in the intelligence field, they had no program that seemed to fit the peculiar parameters of what I was proposing. All of them had words of encouragement and all of them duly jotted down my name, serial number, and Camp Lee assignment. But all they could promise was to keep their eyes open for some eventual opening.

It seemed to me that they were more interested in the theories I was advancing than the geographic area for which I was proposing the operations. (In retrospect, I can see why this attitude prevailed. At the time, early July 1942, military interest centered on the defense of Alexandria which Rommel was threatening from his positions around the Qattara Depression, and the Mediterranean problem was essentially a British one. Montgomery's successful offensive with the Battle of El Alamein did not take place until October 1942 and the joint British-American "Torch" operation was not kicked off until November 1942.)

The encounter with the various G-2 officers at the War Department was encouraging and helped sharpen my presentations at other scheduled meetings. When I had finished with my various appointments in the War Department and I went back to the Capitol, I learned that they had set up one more appointment on the following morning which was to be the final day of my three-day pass.

I was told to take a cab and go past the Marine Barracks, to almost the very end of Constitution Avenue. At this point, I was to look for a red flagpole on the right and to head for the building behind the flagpole: "Q" Building which was one of the cluster of buildings housing the newly created Office of Strategic Services. Once there I was to ask for a Dr. Stirling Callisen who would interview me. I was told that the OSS was a recently created organization that would understand proposals like mine and that might be interested in my project.

While waiting for the appointment at OSS, I carefully went over the events of the past two days and reluctantly came to the conclusion that, although I had met some militarily important people, I had made not much progress with my Sicilian project. Nevertheless, the important thing was that most of the G-2 officers I had met seemed genuinely interested in helping, and they insisted that I should keep them informed of my eventual progress.

Finally, the time came, and I flagged down a cab and gave the driver instructions to head for the flagpole at the end of Constitution Avenue. When I had finished giving the instructions, the driver smiled and said, "Isn't that the building where all those strange people go, Buddy? You sure you got the right place?"

"Yes, that's the place," I replied, mulling over what he could have meant by "strange people."

Driving down Constitution Avenue past the Navy and Munitions Buildings, past the Washington Monument on the left and the Marine Barracks on the right, suddenly I saw the flagpole. The driver knew where he was going and drove in the semicircular driveway, depositing me on the front stoop. A guard was at the front door and asked me if I had an appointment. When I nodded in assent, he pointed to the front Security Office where a young woman asked whom I wanted to see, gave me a paper to fill out, and when I had returned it to her, picked up the phone and called Dr. Callisen's office to inform him of my arrival. Then another young lady from the reception office asked me to follow her, and as we walked down the corridor I could see that the security in the building was heavy. At every intersection of the corridor there was a manned guard desk. I felt that at long last I must be in the right place.

When we arrived at Dr. Callisen's office my escort turned me over to a secretary who signed me in and asked me to take a seat. While waiting, my thoughts raced a mile a minute wondering what lay in store for me. Would this be the end of the project I had been laboring over for so many months, or had I found the right connection to breathe real life into it? The experiences of the past two days passed through my mind in kaleidoscopic sequence. The kindly, fatherly interest demonstrated by Senator Danaher; my interviews with the Senate military liaison officer Colonel Whelms, with colonels Carter, Roderick, Bakeless, and Rodrigo who headed geographic desks at G-2; all came to mind in a pleasant recollection of what little rank consciousness or age discrimination there had been in my discussions. I was wondering what the impending interview would be like, when the secretary gently announced, "Private Corvo, Dr. Callisen will see you now." As the door opened, a tall, stocky individual with a broad grin partly hidden behind a rather thick moustache appeared. Dr. Callisen extended his hand in a hearty handclasp and welcomed me to the interview.

By now, I had learned to trim my presentation to the necessary details. Dr. Callisen occasionally asked a question to clarify some aspect of my presentation. He saw that I was well documented as I kept pulling out one paper after another from my briefcase. Finally, after an interview that lasted some thirty minutes, he informed me that he was doing the preliminary interview and that the in-depth interview would be done by the head of the Italian Division and by an officer from one of the other divisions. He called for an escort who took me in tow, accompanied me to the door, and, with another handshake, wished me well.

We climbed one flight of stairs and ran into several other guard posts before we finally entered Room 2252 which was occupied by the Italian Division of Special Activities/Bruce (SA/B). They handled the intelligence phase of the OSS charter with David Bruce as head of the division. I was taken into a room that was completely empty except for several chairs and tables and was told to wait. In a few minutes, a stocky man of medium height and stern demeanor introduced himself as Earl Brennan, chief of the Italian Division, and asked me to follow him into the next room. There on one wall behind his desk was a huge wall map of Italy, and in a bookshelf next to his desk were a number of Italian books.

Obviously, Callisen had already briefed him on the preliminary interview because he started in businesslike fashion to question me about my background, my age, and my Army service. When he finished his preliminary questioning, he asked me to make my presentation.

From our discussion I could see that Brennan was well informed about the Italian situation and that he obviously spoke Italian. He followed the presentation with intense interest, occasionally interrupting me for clarification or amplification of a point; he questioned me as to the sources of my information and as to those persons who had collaborated in putting the plan together. He also inquired about my contacts in the anti-Fascist movement in New York. I could see his interest growing as our conversation continued.

He finally asked me when I was due to return to Camp Lee, and I told him I would have to catch a train that evening to get back to camp so that I would not be reported AWOL. By this time I could see how deeply interested he was in the project as he started speaking Italian, apparently testing my language capabilities. Then he picked up the phone and asked for a Lieutenant Frank Ball whom he invited to join us. I had no inkling of what was about to happen when Lieutenant Ball, a soft-spoken Virginian, came in and made small talk with Brennan, who then introduced us.

Brennan gave him a brief synopsis of our conversation and also explained to me that Ball belonged to another branch of OSS designated

SA/G (Special Activity/Goodfellow), which also had an interest in talking to me. Ball deferred to Brennan, explaining that they had already received the plan I had sent through Army channels and they were about to send someone to Camp Lee to interview me. The knowledge that the plan had traveled so swiftly was very encouraging, and this was confirmed when Brennan asked me if I could stay overnight. So that I would not be reported AWOL, Lieutenant Ball suggested that his office would contact the S-2 at Camp Lee and arrange for the necessary extension of my three-day pass. I agreed to stay, and we continued to talk.

Brennan asked more questions about my preparation of the plan. He wanted to know how long it had been since I had personally talked to some of my New York contacts and suggested that I should secure some information on the anti-Fascist activities in New York which would help to complete a situation picture for him. When I said that I could do so in three or four days, he asked Lieutenant Ball to secure a six-day extension to my pass. This was done quickly by telephone, and that same afternoon I took the train to New York, promising to be back as soon as I had secured the information he wanted. In the interim he promised to review the papers I was leaving with him and to give me a definite reply about a transfer on my return from New York.

At the time, I didn't have any inkling that he was suspicious of the entire project: he deemed it a perfect setup by Italian intelligence services, especially considering my age and lack of formal higher education. Later, I learned that he had asked the security people to keep tabs on me while I was in New York to make certain I was not an enemy plant.

Within five days I was back in Washington with the information he had requested. Pleased with the results I had obtained, he had me fill out expense vouchers with Dr. Franklyn Jones, his assistant. Before leaving his office, he gave me a set of personal security forms to fill out so that OSS could conduct a thorough security investigation on me. He promised that as soon as the security check was completed he would have Lieutenant Ball request my immediate transfer to OSS so that I could start working full-time on what later became known as the "Corvo Plan." Thus, the preliminary Washington phase was over, and I headed back to camp without any idea of how long it would take to complete my security investigation or to effect the transfer from Camp Lee to Washington.

On my arrival back at camp everyone inquired about my trip to the "top spheres" of the Washington military. I was circumspect in all my answers, knowing that anything I might say could find its way into the security investigation report. I therefore told everyone who asked that I had been sworn to secrecy. This helped create a greater aura of mystery, and everyone treated me with considerable deference which amused me enormously.

In order to pass the time, I decided to continue beefing up my intelligence plan for the infiltration of Sicily, despite the fact that the British were not doing so well in North Africa and Rommel was already on Egyptian territory. I was confident that the situation would change, however, and that the British, with U.S. help, would conquer Libya and eventually North Africa would become the jumping-off point for an invasion of Sicily. To this end, I worked constantly to gather intelligence material and put a plan together.

An occasional letter arrived from home informing me that a credit agency was seeking information about me and that the editor of the local daily newspaper and my parish priest had been confidentially interviewed by some undercover persons who, in the course of the inquiry, confided that I was being considered for a fairly important post in the service. The arrival of these tidbits of information assured me that the top secret security investigation was well under way, but I could scarcely imagine that the wheels of the Army were churning so rapidly.

Hardly a month had passed since my July trip to Washington when, on August 5, I was called into conference at camp headquarters where the Camp G-2, Major Lister, was waiting to talk to me. Entering the room, I mustered a sharp salute which he acknowledged, and then pointing to a chair, he asked me to sit down. As he made small talk, he kept turning and fingering a large manila envelope he held with both hands. Finally, he asked me about my trip to Washington. He wanted to know some details of what had happened during my visit. Imagining that something had gone wrong, I stated that I was not at liberty to discuss the matter because I had been sworn to secrecy.

He acted as though my words had hurt his feelings, but a moment later I saw a smile cross his face and he handed me the large official envelope, asking me to look inside. As I opened the envelope nervously, the only thing I could see was a piece of paper with a bright red border.[2] Sensing that I was still nervous, he told me to read the War Department order. I could hardly believe my eyes. It was an Immediate Action War Department Secret Order transferring me from the Quartermaster Replacement Training Center at Camp Lee to the Strategic Services Training Unit in Washington, D.C. The order read:

1. In accordance with instructions contained in secret telegram The Adjutant General's Office, dated August 4, 1942, you are hereby transferred in grade to the Strategic Services Training Unit, Room 2051, "Q" Building, Constitution Avenue near 26th St., N.W., Washington, D.C., and are directed to arrive there not later than August 6th, 1942.

2. You are advised that the contents of this letter will be treated as strictly secret and under no circumstances will you disclose its contents to any person or persons. You will receive your service record and allied papers from the

Regimental Personnel Officer and report to the above address on the date indicated.

By command of Brigadier General Rowe

I sat there speechless at the rapidity with which events were happening. The major congratulated me and added:

"Corvo, start moving. Go to Regimental Headquarters, get your personal papers and travel orders because they obviously want you in Washington right away. Remember, you'll never get into trouble if you keep your mouth shut as you did with me a little while ago." Then he added, "If you should ever need an assistant don't be afraid to recommend your old G-2," and he extended his hand in a final goodbye.

I ran all the way to the office of the Assistant Adjutant Captain James G. Ligon. My travel orders were already cut, and he suggested that I pack and leave the next morning, so that I could report for my new assignment.

Provided with a railroad ticket and a box lunch, I set off on the morning of August 6 for Washington, D.C.. Since payday had come and gone, some of my barracks friends got together and raised the munificent sum of $75.00 for which I duly issued a series of IOUs.

On my second arrival in Washington I almost felt like a native. I loaded my heavy barracks bag and other impediments on the back seat of the cab and set off for "Q" Building. Both Brennan and Lieutenant Ball were waiting for me to report for duty. I was escorted to Brennan's office where he introduced me to his staff, which included a secretary, Miss Rosenfeld, his assistant, Dr. Franklyn Jones, and Dale MacAdoo, who had been a student in Italy and had returned to the states just before war was declared. Dr. Jones had studied in Rome and had found his way to Washington and Brennan's office where he was placed in charge of administrative affairs; Miss Rosenfeld was a conscientious worker and excellent secretary who had come from a small town in the state of Washington and had been assigned to Brennan's office from the secretarial pool; and Dale MacAdoo affected foreign mannerisms, spoke fluent Italian, and truly loved Italy and Italian culture, but had not yet been given a definite assignment. These men made up the Italian Secret Intelligence (S.I.) Section of OSS on the afternoon of August 6, 1942, together with one recently arrived new recruit, Private Corvo, formerly of the Quartermaster Corps.

Not long after my arrival, MacAdoo took me to the Military Detachment headquarters where I presented my orders and signed in. As it turned out, the Detachment had no living quarters, and all the men roomed out with private families. A temporary solution was quickly found when it was suggested that I might use one of the rooms in an empty firehouse located at the rear of "Q" Building until I resolved my housing problem. It was pointed out that I would shortly be starting a training program which was mandatory for all OSS recruits.

I managed to make myself comfortable among the chairs, tables and furniture which were stored on the second floor of the firehouse, and scouting the area (which is presently occupied by the Watergate complex), I managed to find an old-fashioned diner within walking distance. Nearby was a skating rink and the famous Watergate Inn. The entire neighborhood was dominated by a brewery, a massive red brick building.

Because I was anxious to get started, I spoke to Brennan about skipping the training school. After a series of calls, however, it was determined that I had to go to the school, and we postponed any planning sessions until I finished the prescribed course.

Several days later I picked up my barracks bag, and after being handed a sealed envelope I was taken to Union Station and given a ticket to Sparks, Maryland. My instructions were contained in the sealed envelope which I was told to open once the train got underway. The instructions to reach the school were classified "Secret."[3] I was expected to follow them to the letter until I arrived at my destination where an officer was scheduled to meet the train. The train left for Baltimore at 2 p.m., and the connecting train to Sparks left Baltimore at 3:18 with arrival at Sparks scheduled for 4 p.m.

On the train I saw several faces that looked familiar, but I approached no one, for the secret instructions were clear that I should not show any signs of recognition. When the train arrived at Sparks, an officer was standing on the platform. I went up to him and inquired whether he might be Lieutenant Cohen. Answering in the affirmative, he told me to walk to the back of the station and climb aboard the Army truck there and wait. Before I got to the truck, I saw four or five other men heading in the same direction, and we each climbed aboard the truck without uttering a word.

Finally, the officer climbed into the cab, and the truck started moving. Soon we came to a hilly forest which seemed to reach out to the horizon in every direction, and the truck started bumping along a narrow winding road. When we came to a roadblock which was manned by military personnel, the truck stopped briefly, then continued along the bumpy road until we came to a clearing and a camp that must have been originally a Civilian Conservation Corps installation. We dismounted and were assigned to different barracks. Looking about and considering the general direction we had traveled, I figured out that we were in the Catoctin Mountains near President Roosevelt's famous "Shangri La" Camp (now known as Camp David). This was the Special Operations (SO) training camp which specialized in paramilitary instructions.

Some fifteen of us were taking this training course which was patterned on the British Commando program and had been set up with the help of Special Operations Executive (SOE) officers, among whom was a Major Fairbairn who had served with the Hong Kong police and was reputed to be the foremost expert in hand-to-hand combat. Each of the students was asked to use a cover name so that the others would not know his real identity. As I recall, no one tried to penetrate the real identity of his fellow students. We represented various national groups, including Norway, Denmark, Hungary, and Greece, and most of those being trained were sailors from Scandinavia who were destined to go back to their homeland. Among the group was a student who chose to call himself "Johnny," which, incidentally, was his true name, as I later found out when we went back to "Q" Building. He was a lieutenant J.G. in the Navy with whom I would strike up a lifelong acquaintaince. With the other members of the class I formed a transitory friendship, but most of them, especially the Scandinavian sailors, I would never see again.

The training program at the SO camp was mostly physical, and it was conceived to test endurance and courage. Long marches were the order of the day; running the obstacle course was another exercise; and night compass runs through the woods were staged to inculcate a sense of direction-finding and map reading.

The course on explosives, run by Lieutenant Cohen, taught not only the formula of successful destruction, but also discipline and inner control. The trainees were expected to ignite a stick of dynamite and walk with the stick, place it in the middle of a field, and walk (not run) coolly away, timing themselves so that they could be out of harm's way by the time the explosion occurred. This was no easy task for a rookie, but considering the dangerous work we were to perform, it helped to build sang froid.

I recall one particular episode while on a training exercise that involved crawling on one's stomach and attempting to seize a flag placed in the middle of an open space by outwitting the guard who stood watch to see that this would not happen. I had teamed up with one of the oldest members of our class, a giant of a man whose total lack of hair on his head made him stand out in any crowd. A Hungarian who had not been in the states very long, he had chosen "Martin" as his code name. We were crawling through high brush, and it had been decided that he would make some distracting noise to draw the attention of the sentinel while I would make a break and attempt to seize the flag. As I crawled along to the edge of the clearing, I suddenly heard a loud hum as though a car was racing on a distant road. Then it dawned on me that there was no such road in the area. Looking about me, I suddenly realized that I had disturbed a nest of enormous blackstriped bees. For a moment my mouth went dry and then, seized by a primordial urge for self-preservation, I started jumping up and down, screeching unintelligible gibberish in loud gutteral tones. "Martin," who was some three or four yards away from me, obviously startled by my cries, shouted, "Vat is the matter, Ravens?" I did not get a chance to tell him, for by this time I moved with the speed of greased lightning, still screeching, past him followed by a swarm of bees. Martin stood up as I ran past him and, realizing what was happening, started his own race in the opposite direction, followed by part of the swarm which seemed magically to detach itself and take off after him as he ran down the hill.

In the meanwhile, the sentinel who was watching the flag, hearing this fracas, became thoroughly confused by all the yelling and started running around to see what was happening. When I had run far enough that I felt safe from the threatening swarm, I stopped to take stock of the damage. By some miracle, although the bees had swarmed around me, my aboriginal behavior had saved me from any sting. I did not see Martin until some thirty minutes later. His shiny pink pate had obviously attracted a number of bee stings, which were most painful but, fortunately, not as serious as they could have been. The matter of the swarm dividing itself and going after Martin became a standing joke in the class and after a while, when it hurt a little less, even Martin got a chuckle out of it.

Although our instructors kept us busy most of the day and sometimes even nights, I began to feel some anxiety that I was losing valuable time. I simply could not see spending six weeks going through these commando exercises. I finally wrote Brennan a note asking that he should secure my release from the training camp at the end of the second week so that I could go ahead with the important work of refining the plan and implementing the preliminary phases of it. However he managed it, Brennan convinced David Bruce that I should return to "Q" Building to start working on the Sicilian project. At the end of the second week, I again packed my barracks bag and returned to my makeshift quarters at the firehouse in Washington. Earl Brennan was elated to see me back in the office, ready to go to work seriously because he was being pressured to get moving.

Chapter 3

In the Beginning. . .

Soon after my return to Washington, the two rooms which the Italian Section occupied were augmented by a third room which was located across the hall.

My housing problem was resolved through an arrangement with Dale MacAdoo, who lived in an apartment on New York Avenue, N.W. Dale had a good collection of books, mostly in Italian, which was scattered throughout the small apartment. What was more important to me, he owned a superb record player with a small selection of classical records which I enjoyed when I had a few moments to listen to them.

Since Brennan did not yet have an operational plan, we immediately launched a marathon session during which I outlined what I believed our immediate goals should be. Now began one of the most active periods in my recollection as we raced the clock against the events that were taking place in Europe, in particular in the Mediterranean theater of operations, which was still *the* British sphere of influence. The Army of the Nile (later redesignated the Eighth Army) was still on the defensive on the Egyptian-Libyan border, awaiting reinforcements from the Commonwealth and equipment from the United States.

The problem for the Italian SI Division (and for that matter, for the entire OSS) was to build up momentum by recruiting personnel and planning operations for a theater of operations that was almost totally under the jurisdiction of the British who were themselves in a defensive mode. The only assets which the OSS controlled in the area during this period were a number of Foreign Service officers who were working out of Tangiers and French North African cities under the direction of one of our foremost Arabists, Marine Colonel Bill Eddy. These men had their hands full as they operated without logistical support. They were often hampered by Vichy officials in Morocco, Algeria, and Tunisia. At this time, without knowing the specifics, these men were laying the groundwork for the combined British-U.S. invasion of North Africa, "Operation Torch." Uppermost on our agenda, therefore, was the recruitment of key personnel to supervise and undertake operations against Sicily and Italy. Mindful of the fact that the British Secret Intelligence Service (SIS) and SOE had attempted to recruit personnel for their Italian operations in the United States and that Emilio Lussu, a key anti-Fascist exile, had come to the United States and broached the matter to various socialist and labor leaders in the New York area, we followed the developments. I was told of one group that had been recruited by the British and reportedly sent to the Middle East. The group was said to have refused to play the game, and some of its members had been interned in a retention camp in India for the duration of the war.

I had no doubt that some of the key people in the anti-Fascist movement in New York City were closely affiliated with the British intelligence service. As a consequence, I felt that we should steer clear of this influence and try to set up a service that would reflect the principles expressed by our way of life. I explained to Brennan that we should carry out a national recruiting program by enlisting the aid of New York labor leaders and proven anti-Fascist activists. He approved the proposal and left me free to work out the timing and the details.

Dale MacAdoo participated in some of the meetings because he was acquainted with some of those who had left Italy in the late 1930s as a result of the 1938 anti-Jewish laws promulgated by Mussolini after he consolidated his alliance with Hitler. MacAdoo should have played a more important role in the work of the Italian section, but essentially he loved to conduct highly philosophical discussions over cocktails and was primarily a student of events. He was a civilian and wanted to retain his civilian status. Brennan believed that MacAdoo could have done a good job if he had been sent to Switzerland to maintain contacts with the Italian underground.

In order to get things moving, I set out on the first of many recruiting expeditions to New York where I sought out Vincenzo Vacirca, an old friend of my father's who had been contributing editor of *Il Nuovo Mondo*, the anti-Fascist daily published in New York. Vacirca had been a socialist member of the Italian Parliament representing the province of Siracusa, Sicily. With the advent of Fascism, he had gone into exile in Switzerland and finally settled in New York. His credentials were impeccable. He had been deprived of his Italian citizenship by Royal Decree No. 529 on March 26, 1926, and all his possessions had been confiscated by Mussolini "for having carried out activities against the Italian state in Switzerland and the United States and criticizing internal conditions in

Italy.[1] The OVRA constantly watched Vacirca's activities in the United States and never missed an opportunity to punish those who were in touch with him. Thousands of copies of his editorials were sent to Italy through the mails, and many recipients who circulated the articles wound up before the Special Tribunal, receiving sentences as long as three years.

When I arrived at Vacirca's house, I found that he had recently undergone surgery for skin cancer. Even though his face was taped and he was in constant pain, we exchanged views on the situation in Italy and on his contacts both there and in other countries. Vacirca was then in his fifties and was both a prolific writer and speaker who had a thorough grounding in the Sicilian situation. Despite his illness he promised to do a comprehensive background paper on Sicily and mail it to me, together with a set of security employment forms that I left with him so that we could start processing his employment by OSS as soon as he was well enough to come to Washington. Before I left he provided me with his personal views on many of the leaders in the anti—Fascist movement. My visit seemed to buoy his spirits.

I then took the train to Connecticut to interview candidates for possible staff positions. Among these was Attorney Vincent Scamporino, a Middletown labor attorney who was in his middle thirties, spoke Italian and some French, and whose experience, I felt, made him a possible top candidate as our overseas section chief. The other candidate, Louis Fiorilla, was a young man who, until 1937, had studied in a seminary in Sicily and had recently graduated from Middletown's Wesleyan University with outstanding scholastic achievements. Both were eager to join the organization, feeling they could make a positive contribution to the war effort and put their knowledge to work for Uncle Sam. I left them copies of the SA-1 Personal History statements to fill out and quickly returned to Washington to get on with other urgent matters.

Based on my conversation with Vacirca, I provided Brennan an overview of the situation in the New York Italian community. I urged the desirability of working with the wing of the Italian Socialist party that was outspoken anti - Communist and of enlisting their support in the effort to overthrow Mussolini and establish a democratic government in postwar Italy. This faction included Luigi Antonini, president of Local 89, ILGWU, AFL, and his associates, Girolamo Valenti, editor of the Socialist weekly, *La Parola*; Giuseppe Lupis, editor of the monthly magazine, *Il Mondo*; Augusto Bellanca, one of the leaders of the Amalgamated Clothing Workers of America, and some of his associates.

Cautioning that we should not close the door to anyone who wanted to collaborate in our effort, I urged that we establish contact with Don Luigi Sturzo, spiritual leader in the fight against Fascism. Having spent a long time in London, Sturzo was currently a guest in a private home in Brooklyn.

I volunteered to contact Colonel Randolfo Pacciardi, who had commanded the Garibaldi Brigade in the Spanish Civil War and had fought alongside the Loyalists against the Fascist forces, playing a prominent role in their rout at Guadalajara. Pacciardi resigned his command of the Brigade when it became obvious that the Communist Komissars had taken over the conduct of the war from the Socialist government. He had been interned in a French detention camp in North Africa and, finally, through the good offices of Antonini and other U.S. labor leaders had been released and was living in New York.

My overview did not neglect a discussion of the Mazzini Society which was then attempting to gain the support of all factions of the anti-Fascist movement under the guidance of Count Carlo Sforza, Alberto Tarchiani, Alberto Cianca, and other emigres who had escaped from Paris when the Germans took over the city and who had come to New York via London.

The Mazzini Society had managed to obtain the support of Antonini, Bellanca, and their associates and was on the way to achieving its goal of becoming the official conduit of the anti-Fascist movement. Something was lacking in its leadership, many of whose key men were reported to have contacts with the British intelligence service which was believed to support a postwar retention of the monarchy. Although most of the anti-Fascists respected Sforza, he was by no means a charismatic person. He projected the image of an old aristocrat, and he had a tendency to talk down to people, even to many of those who were close to him.

The reality of the situation was that, despite the feelings about the British, they had been fighting against great odds since 1939 and the see-saw battle in the arid wastes of North Africa would soon see the pendulum swing against Rommel. If any intelligence work was to be undertaken against Sicily, it could only be with British assistance. They controlled the transportation and training facilities, and without their support no operations could be mounted against Sicily and Italy. We knew that the British were having bad luck attempting to penetrate Sicily and that most of their agents were being picked up by the Italian counterespionage people.

I suggested to Brennan that he have a talk with Lieutenant Colonel Bickham Sweet-Escott of the SOE who was visiting Washington at that time to examine the possibility of working with SIS to land some of our agents in Sicily. The colonel promised to contact London headquarters. Sweet-Escott received word from London that "The Middle East organization will cooperate fully, but demands on aircraft and submarines are extremely heavy." The message went on to suggest that "OSS train and dispatch men to Middle East which will provide required facilities at the earliest possible opportunity." On review, it was determined that we would not be able to take advantage of the SIS offer because we had just started our recruiting program. It would be some time before the applicants would be cleared by security, trained in the meager facilities that existed in mid-1942 and documented sufficiently to give them a chance to survive in a hostile environment hundreds of miles from their base of operations.

At this time, Anglo-American strategy regarding the Mediterranean theater had not jelled. Our chief of staff, General George Marshall, as well as the Joint Chiefs of Staff, did not favor peripheral action against the Axis and sustained an unrealistic strategy of a cross-channel invasion of Europe in 1942. The British, still licking the wounds they had received at Dunkirk and the Dieppe raid, were more realistic and preferred a more gradual encroachment, which pointed to a series of Mediterranean campaigns.

In mi-1942, we at the OSS and Italian SI in Washington were making plans based on our own deductions rather than on any foreknowledge of impending military operations. For obvious reasons, we had to proceed on the assumption that the war would sooner or later come to Italy. Our role should therefore be to prepare plans for both military and political action and to give aid and encouragement to the Italian underground democratic forces to work with the United States in helping to liberate Italy. These goals provided the incentive to get on with the broad recruitment program which I had proposed to Brennan. At this point, it was decided that I return to New York to prod our contacts into action.

I got in touch with Girolamo Valenti, the editor of *La Parola*, a Socialist weekly newspaper with a decided anti-Communist policy. Valenti had a great sense of humor, a very pleasant personality, and was never at a loss for words. Born in a little town near Catania, Sicily, he was a militant anti-Fascist who had crisscrossed the United States attacking Mussolini wherever he could muster an audience. In almost any town he went to he could ferret out an Italian anti-Fascist who received his paper.

As he liked to discuss business over lunch, he invited me to meet him at a little restaurant on East 11th Street. When I arrived, he was already sitting at a table at the back of the room in the company of a dark-haired young woman whom he introduced as his secretary and companion. When I came in, he was carrying on a spirited discussion with an old white-mustachioed waiter called Eugenio who obviously shared his political views. In our exchange of ideas about the status of the anti-Fascist organizations in New York, I could sense that there was less than unity among the various groups and that this division was further exacerbated by a series of personality clashes that had not surfaced publicly. Nevertheless, they had all managed to get together to form the Mazzini Society, an amalgam of the various elements participating in the democratic struggle against Fascism.

Although some contacts had been established with the State

Department and with the British Foreign Office and intelligence organizations, little or no contact had been established with the Coordinator of Information (COI) - OSS, despite the fact that the OSS Foreign Nationalities Division was operating in New York. The opportunity to establish a close rapport with the Italian Section appealed to Valenti. When lunch was over, we adjourned to his newspaper office, which was only a few blocks away. Thoroughly convinced of his sincerity and dedication, I didn't waste any time in subtlety. I asked him directly if he would like to cooperate with OSS in the eventual overthrow of Mussolini and the establishment of a democratic regime in Italy. I knew beforehand what his reply would be, and immediately we made an agreement of collaboration that was utterly selfless on his part and that would provide great advantages for the OSS. He placed himself at our complete disposition, asking nothing in return. Valenti became one of our primary recruitment sources and unofficial liaison to ILGWU's Antonini and Amalgamated Clothing Workers of America's (ACWA) Bellanca. Both organizations provided us with a number of recruits.

During the next seven months, Valenti and I traveled throughout the United States, interviewing labor leaders, academicians, lawyers, and workers in our quest for volunteers who would be willing to put their lives on the line in the fight against Fascism. For this purpose, OSS provided me with blanket military orders to travel to any part of the continental United States at will.[3] All of these travels had to be accomplished while continuing with my primary work which was to shape policy and plans for future operations; creating a permanent staff; and training the recruits in the specific intelligence objectives in Italy, Sardinia, and Sicily. Through Valenti I gained easy access to Antonini, Bellanca, and most of the anti-Fascist labor leaders in the United States. The fact that these contacts were recognized anti-Communists in no way lessened their value to OSS in an era when the Dies Congressional Committee and J. Edgar Hoover were powerful forces in Washington. Many of these leaders came to know and trust Earl Brennan who established close ties with them.

The recruiting policy of Italian SI was based on establishing close contact with individual expatriates, proven anti-Fascist members of the labor movement, and qualified members of the U.S. armed forces. Part of that policy was the exclusion of known Communists or any members of the organized crime syndicate. The decision to prohibit all contact with anyone having ties with the crime syndicates was made at an early date when several efforts by OSS/Treasury sources were made to have me meet "Lucky" Luciano who, at that time, was at Dannemora and was offering to place his ostensible contacts in Sicily at the government's disposal. On those occasions I explained to Brennan that we could gain nothing from such a tie and that the relationship might prove to be embarrassing in the future. I pointed out that the Mafia had been practically stamped out by Mussolini who, after having used many of its elements to help him come to power in 1922, had decided to exterminate it in 1926. Mussolini appointed Cesare Mori special prefect with extraordinary powers to extirpate the Mafia from Western Sicily and the interior Massif.[4] The key Mafiosi and their assistants had been deported to the penal colonies on Lipari and other Tyrrhenian islands, while many hundreds more were scattered in "forced residence" in small towns in mainland Italy. The proponent of the meeting with Luciano was a Major White who had formerly served with the Treasury Department and was simply passing on the information for whatever interest we might have.

Among the early recruits enlisted through Valenti was Tony Camboni, a Chicago sales representative of Fairbanks-Morse, whose father was a Sardinian poet and Socialist leader. Tony helped us put together a team of Sardinian volunteers whose training received top priority in view of the rapid developments in the Mediterranean theater.

On September 9, 1942, on orders from Brennan I went to New York to hold a series of meetings with Valenti and to develop other contacts. While in New York I also wanted to talk to Mayor Fiorello LaGuardia to check the bona fides of a contact in Europe who had given the mayor as a reference. On this same trip I planned to talk with Lisa Sergio who had joined the staff of Radio Station WQXR as a commentator. She had been one of the key people in Rome Radio where, with her well-modulated voice and her impeccable English, she extemporaneously translated Mussolini's speeches for broadcasts beamed to the United States and other English-speaking countries. Miss Sergio had been held in high esteem, not only by the Duce, but also by many other high Fascist officials, including Count Galeazzo Ciano. When the anti-Semitic laws went into effect in 1938, she left Italy and came to New York where she joined the staff of WQXR. With her knowledge of the internal workings of the Fascist hierarchy, I felt she could make a positive contribution to our planning, and, on my arrival in New York, I arranged an appointment with her for September 11.

We met at one of the studios and had a general exploratory conversation that was restricted to the subjects of propaganda and psychological warfare and the problems they posed during wartime. During our conversation she expressed ideas and views that coincided with our own. Since I was limited as to what I could discuss with her, she asked that I send her a clarifying memorandum so that she could inform the station manager, who was "a trustworthy person," in order to get his consent to work part-time for us. I promised I would do so when I got back to Washington.

When I returned to the hotel that night, a rude surprise awaited me. Opening the door and snapping on the lights, I felt a gun being stuck in my stomach by a burly individual who asked me to come in. Looking around, I saw another man in the room also pointing a gun at me. My first thoughts were that these two thugs were Axis sympathizers. I was about to start shouting for help, but then I thought better of it and complied with their order to face the wall or be a "dead duck." After frisking me for weapons and finding I was not armed, they put their weapons away and took my briefcase. They asked me for identification, and I gave them what I believed was enough to identify me. After repeated requests from me that produced their own IDs, they identified themselves as Counter-Intelligence Corps (CIC) men who were part of a stakeout to capture me in the belief that I was a Fascist spy. They then made several calls to colleagues who obviously were participating in the stakeout to inform them that their mission had been accomplished. At that point, they unceremoniously invited me to go with them to the Federal Building at 90 Church Street where a lieutenant in civies took my briefcase and started examining all my papers. I could see that the men were convinced that they were on to something big, a real Fascist spy in New York.

Even though I gave them a telephone number in Washington as a reference, they refused to make the call. They then began a long interrogation during which I refused to answer some of their questions. My lack of cooperation infuriated them. Then the officer stepped out of the room, and the men took turns insulting me in an attempt to get a reaction from me. I decided to disregard their remarks, and when the officer returned I asked him about my release. This time he told me he thought he knew someone who could identify me, but he would not give me the person's name. As it was getting late, they brought in a cot and told me to sleep in the office. The next day I was confined to an empty office, Room B1707. When I asked to be allowed to make a phone call, they refused to budge.

The next morning they took me to breakfast but then brought me back to the empty room until 1:00 P.M. when one of the men came to escort me to the officer's room. There I found H. Gregory Thomas, a New York OSS employee, with whom I had a slight acquaintance. I remembered Thomas from a prior visit to the New York office as an oversized, balding individual who, despite his large size, had rather effeminate mannerisms. Thomas liked to refer to himself as a parfumiere with European connections. Among the books in his office I had spotted a volume of Federico Garcia Lorca's poems; in talking with him, I gathered that his sympathies during the Spanish Civil War had been with the Loyalists. This was the only positive factor I could attribute to Thomas.

From the tone he used to scold me in front of the CIC officer, I could tell that I had not exactly impressed him either. He was provoked that on my arrival in New York I had not called at his office and he told the lieutenant that I had endangered the entire organization because of the names I was carrying among my papers. I noted that they were the names of well known anti-Fascists who were listed in all OVRA and *Schutz Staffel* (SS) lists and about whom the enemy had all vital statistics.

After the episode was over, I returned to Washington where I filed a report and had to appear for disciplinary action at a pro forma summary proceeding. [5] My papers were later returned to Washington.

It was not until almost a year later, during the Sicilian campaign that I found out what had triggered the New York episode. A chance meeting with an Office of Naval Intelligence (ONI) officer, Lieutenant Gioachino Titolo, who had been stationed in New York, revealed that he had been in contact with Lisa Sergio who had become suspicious of my reasons for wanting to talk to her and had asked his advice. CIC had been called into the matter in the belief that the Servizio Informazioni Militare (SIM) (Italian military intelligence) was trying to contact her. That explained the caution the CIC people had exercised when they were waiting for me in my room. It also explained why Sergio had insisted on using the studio for our interview. Fortunately, there was no serious security infraction in my discussion with her because I had limited myself to the discussion of hypothetical generalities. As for Miss Sergio, I never felt any chagrin at her attempt to protect herself from the Fascists.

Chapter 4

Proposed: A Government in Exile

By the end of September 1942, I had the recruitment program well underway as the Security Office had pulled out all stops to investigate and clear a number of persons whom I had interviewed for both administrative and field work. Other personnel were coming in through military channels, and the office was gradually becoming a mecca for the Italian anti-Fascist movement in the United States.

By agreement with Lieutenant Frank Ball, our office was also looking out for potential personnel for the SO Division, and I was undertaking overall planning to cover almost all phases of OSS work for Sicily. It was anticipated that the first groups of recruits would be arriving in October. While the OSS schools provided general intelligence and operational training programs, there were no programs specializing in the problems which we would confront in Italian operations. In order to fill this void, I put together a special course for Italian intelligence operations which would familiarize our people with field conditions. This program was tacked onto the regular OSS intelligence training schedule and included intensive instructions in geography; studies of the structure of the Fascist bureaucracy; operational procedures of the Italian police systems; military counterespionage and the OVRA, as well as the most recent intelligence culled from available underground sources, British intelligence, and the Italian press, smuggled out through Lisbon, which had become a hotbed of espionage activities.

The lack of intelligence on Sicily and the almost total failure of British intelligence operations on the island convinced us that our office had to bring together a body of information for our own use and that of other sections. We therefore embarked on a crash program to seek out special information in the dusty files of the Library of Congress, the New York Public Library, the Beach Erosion Board, and the Veterans Administration. This effort produced a treasure trove of information which was to become highly useful in the field both to OSS and our allies.

We found eighteenth century British Admiralty charts containing a wealth of detail, including profiles of the complete coastline of Sicily; maps of Sicily on which every cave on the island was marked; and studies on beach erosion of the Italian and Sicilian coastlines. From the Veterans Administration, we secured complete lists of World War I veterans who had returned to Italy and had been receiving pensions from the U.S. government each month until December 1941 when Mussolini declared war on the United States. Since then, the funds had been set aside by the Veterans Administration. I planned to utilize these lists to establish contact with some of the veterans to facilitate our work. At the same time, together with Demetrios Stampados, who was a first-rate cartographer and a member of the Greek Section, we undertook a project to build a detailed relief map of Sicily[1] on which could be worked out most of the problems we would face. Such a map could also be useful to the Army in planning the invasion of the island.

While these details were being worked out, I was busy traveling around the country with Girolamo Valenti interviewing candidates to carry out plans to infiltrate Sicily, Sardinia, and Italy from North Africa, when those bases should become available. During those trips, we met with many of the anti-Fascist leaders in the country in order to coordinate their activities and to weld their efforts to future OSS plans. At the University of Chicago, we had a long and interesting exchange with Professor Giuseppe Borgese, one of the early exiles who had written a much quoted book on Fascism: *Goliath: The March of Fascism*. Borgese was a spellbinding speaker, even in private conversation, and had been an outspoken critic of Mussolini. At Harvard, we were in touch with Professor George LaPiana, as well as with Gaetano Salvemini, one of the giants of militant anti-Fascism who had written many books and articles urging the overthrow of Fascism and the Savoyard monarchy. Salvemini was republican in thought and deed. Many of his suggestions were eventually incorporated into the new constitution of the postwar Republic of Italy.

At this time, Vincenzo Vacirca was brought to Washington to start writing position papers and psychological warfare appeals for various segments of the Sicilian population. In addition, Vacirca was useful in bringing together a body of material that was needed for the specialized intelligence training of the various groups starting school.

Early on September 1 for the first time I met with Colonel Randolfo Pacciardi who was then living with his wife in Greenwich Village. From the beginning our relationship was very cordial, and I put him in direct touch with Brennan with whom he formed a long and deep friendship.

Pacciardi had participated with Sforza in Montevideo's Congress of Free Italians which was held on August 14, 15, 16, 1942. At that time, he was designated military leader for any action the anti-Fascist exiles might undertake. When I met him he was editing a newspaper, *La Legione*, in New York, and it was highly unlikely that he would ever lead a volunteer military expedition against Fascist forces. As a result of our meeting, he was delighted to establish a contact with OSS in order to participate in the events that were about to unfold in the Mediterranean. At one point, in order to bring him into closer collaboration, we offered him a commission in the U.S. Army, which he turned down in order to retain his independent standing.

In the early meetings with Pacciardi (whom we codenamed "Waverly" becaused he lived at Waverly Place), we sought his help in contacting some of the veterans who had served under his command in the Garibaldi Brigade during the Spanish Civil War.[2] Many of these men were in Vichy concentration camps in North Africa, and we knew that he and many of his trusted officers were staunchly anti-Communist. We discussed with Colonel Pacciardi the possibility of organizing an Italian Brigade made up of anti-Fascist exiles from Europe and North and South America, which could eventually be bolstered by Italian-American volunteers assigned to special service from our own armed forces.

By the end of October, 1942, as Montgomery's Eighth Army punctured its way across El Alamein, the probability of a rapid advance by British armor across Libya offered the possibility of creating operating bases from which military strikes could be conducted by specially trained OSS paramilitary units against insular and mainland Italy. This possibility gave impetus to the examination of forming this special assault force. We failed to gain the support of the Army, however, which was then beset by more important problems and had not yet developed a Mediterranean war game plan and instead was still concentrating on an early cross-Channel assault. Disappointed, Pacciardi nonetheless believed that postwar Italian democracy needed U.S. support to survive the rocky road ahead. He also maintained that the United States must have a major voice in Italian affairs in order to overcome the influence of British conservatism, which had already staked out Italy as one of its zones of influence.

As the success of the British Eighth Army in North Africa gained momentum, the British intelligence services, which were tuned in on the thinking of 10 Downing Street, were anxiously looking forward to the next phase of Mediterranean operations: delivering a knockout blow to Mussolini. In order to maintain a high degree of control and to monitor anti-Fascist activities in the United States, the British relied on their connections with the Mazzini Society, the New York-based assemblage of outstanding Italian refugees who had been living in Paris prior to the German occupation. They had come to the United States between 1938 and 1941 when, with the help of anti-Fascists already living in New York, they formed the Mazzini Society and elected Max Ascoli as the first president.

In August 1942, the Mazzini Society and its representatives played a leading role in the Montevideo Conference which chose Sforza as the leader of the "Free Italians" and Pacciardi as their sword bearer. The impact of the Montevideo Conference was short-lived because at this point the British were not prepared to underwrite the creation of an Italian legion that would play a leading role in the overthrow of the Savoy monarchy. However, the British did not abandon their efforts to indirectly control the activities of the anti-Fascist movement in New York.

British intelligence periodically sent emissaries to New York and Washington with well-devised plans calculated to win the approval of elements in the State Department and the White House. The most serious of these efforts was undertaken by Dino Gentili who came from London to New York and Washington during the latter part of 1942 with a plan that had the obvious matrix of British intelligence. Gentili, who was well known to Alberto Cianca, Alberto Tarchiani, and Max Ascoli as an anti-Fascist refugee, proposed that the leaders of the movement set up a government-in-exile headed by Count Sforza. This government would be allowed to set up shop in Tripoli once that city was captured by the British. The government-in-exile would be endowed with the necessary funding and would be given powerful radio transmitters that would be beamed to Italy in the hope of inciting and fomenting the overthrow of Mussolini.

On the surface, Gentili, who posed as a representative of British textile firms, peddled this plan as the expressed desire of the Italian underground leaders and the Italian political refugees in England and the United States. [3] Gentili successfully sold the plan to Antonini, head of powerful Local 89 of the ILGWU, who was president of the Italian-American Labor Council. Through Antonini and other contacts, Gentili was able to pursue his plan to win the support of State Department and White House contacts in getting the United States to fund the government-in-exile and to provide the necessary communications equipment to set up the radio station at Tripoli. This effort had the support of Ernest Cuneo who was in the OSS and was well connected in both the White House and State Department, but who at that time did not know the origins of the proposal.

The entire matter finally came to the attention of Brennan who met with Gentili and later with Ernie Cuneo. Alarmed at what he perceived to be a British plot to entrap both the OSS and the U.S. government in an operation that would be detrimental to long-term U.S. interests in Italy, Brennan called me in Chicago where I was on a recruiting trip. He informed me that the official announcement of the acceptance of the plan by the White House would be made in New York at a dinner being

sponsored by the Italian-American Labor Council, at which the principal
speaker was to be Attorney General Francis Biddle. The dinner was to
take place the next evening. I pointed out to Brennan that almost all of
the Italo-American labor leaders had an intense dislike for the ultra-
conservative British policy and that Antonini and Bellanca were
obviously not aware of the extent of British intelligence involvement in
the plan. The mere fact that Sforza and his group were to operate out of
Tripoli and that they were going to establish their radio station there was
indicative of the fact that SOE or SIS would ultimately control the
American-financed operation. After I told Brennan that I would grab the
next plane out of Chicago to New York and have a talk with Luigi
Antonini, I got Valenti on the phone and briefly explained to him what
was happening. I asked him to make an appointment with Antonini so
that I could alert him as to what was actually happening. I then rushed to
the airport to catch the plane to New York.

It was late in the afternoon by the time I met Valenti at Antonini's
Manhattan office. Antonini expressed amazement at our assessment of
the aims of the plan which (in my view) was calculated to turn
responsibility for policy matters over to the British and the British-
controlled group of Italian anti-Fascists. I pointed out the numerous
British efforts that had been made to establish controls over New York-
based activities, as well as the trips that Emilo Lussu and other London-
based leaders had made to New York. I then added that the Gentili trip
must have been sponsored by British intelligence because civilian travel
between Britain and the United States without government priority was
impossible. Valenti then added other pieces of information that had come
his way to make the case and pointed out that the acceptance of an Italian
government-in-exile would establish a long-range hegemony over
postwar Italy and totally diminish U.S. influence over events.

Convinced that our assessment was correct and hurt that he had been
"taken in," Antonini actively sought to destroy any possibility that the
British plan would be carried out. He promised me that he would take
care of the matter before the dinner honoring Biddle, or he would
threaten to go public with the information. Having lit the fuse, I rushed
to return to Washington before some of my other contacts learned I had
been in the city. On arrival in Washington, I briefed Brennan on what
had happened, and he made a number of telephone calls to alert contacts
at the White House and the State Department.

In New York, the project which had been so meticulously hatched in
London began to collapse; Antonini was reported to be like a raging bull,
talking on two phones at once and getting ready to go public with his
expose during his speech at the dinner. Someone had alerted the Federal
Bureau of Investigation (FBI), which normally exchanged information
with the British services but knew nothing of Gentili's mission to the
United States. Word got around that Gentili's steps were being carefully

traced, and, for some inexplicable reason, Gentili's presence was immediately requested elsewhere. He was absent from the scene when the project that had been so painstakingly put together collapsed under Luigi Antonini's vociferous attack and Earl Brennan's whispered telephone calls. Thus ended the last British effort in the United States to take control of the Italian refugee situation.

From this point on, the fortunes of the Mazzini Society went steadily downhill. Its importance diminished with the acceleration of events in North Africa and with the British shift of attention to the military actions that were being planned to bring down Fascism.

Chapter 5

The Cauldron

The results of the wide recruiting program I had undertaken in September began to be felt as volunteers who had been cleared through stringent security investigations began reporting to Washington to attend the special training courses that would prepare them for overseas operations.

Vincent Scamporino, brought in to undergo indoctrination as Brennan's overseas deputy, was in his middle thirties and, as noted earlier, had been practicing law in Middletown. He had worked his way through the University of New Hampshire, where he attended law school. During the summer vacations he often came home to Middletown, and, when he found time, he took Italian lessons from my father. He became proficient in Italian and also gained some fluency in French which he had studied in school. Because of his age, experience, background, and intelligence, Scamporino was a natural for the role, and although he had never been to Europe, he adapted easily to the demands of his position. Brennan immediately liked and trusted him. The European contacts were elated to deal with a man who spoke their language and understood their problems. "Scamp," as everyone came to call him, took over some of my duties and contacts, and I continued my recruiting drive and planning sessions.

At this time (mid-October 1942), Brennan was planning to send Dale MacAdoo to Switzerland under State Department cover so that the Italian SI desk could establish direct ties with the Italian underground leaders in Milan, but this effort ran into a number of obstructions. These obstructions were explained when Allen Dulles, head of the OSS New York office, was named to head the Swiss desk in Berne. Dulles had been offered a position in London under David Bruce who was scheduled to head OSS London. For personal reasons he preferred to go to Switzerland where he had served at the end of World War I and where he could stay in touch with some German contacts associated with the legal firm of Sullivan and Cromwell, of which his brother John Foster Dulles was the senior partner. There was little love lost between Allen Dulles and Earl Brennan, and it was obvious that Dulles had found out that Brennan was planning to send MacAdoo to Switzerland. Since he wanted no competition on his turf, he contrived to delay Dale's departure.

Allen left for Switzerland in early November 1942, perhaps having foreknowledge of the impending Allied North African landings on November 8.[1] He got to the Franco-Swiss frontier on November 11, as the Germans were taking over the border control stations. He barely made it across the frontier into the safety of Switzerland. All Allied personnel in Switzerland were trapped in the country for the next two years.

With the Eighth Army moving west across the Libyan coastal escarpment and with the "Torch" operation underway in French North Africa, the planners of the operating branches in "Q" Building suddenly felt that events were threatening to overtake them. A crisis arose when the SO Branch attempted to take jurisdiction over some of the Italian SI personnel (including Corvo and Scamporino). At that time, SO was under the command of Colonel Preston Goodfellow and SI was still under the command of David Bruce, who then held the rank of major. A donnybrook ensued at the lower echelons of both branches, which were endeavoring to put together the organizations that would undertake the dangerous infiltrations into enemy territory necessary to provide information for successful diplomatic and military operations.

The infighting between intelligence and SO operations became intense and threatened to be disruptive. It was at this point that Goodfellow and Bruce agreed to put an end to the uncertainty by having the director chair a meeting in which both sides would be represented. The meeting was chaired by Colonel Ned Buxton, Donovan's close assistant director; among those present were Goodfellow, Bruce, Brennan, Corvo, and Scamporino. After discussing the grounds for the discord, Buxton cut the Gordian knot by leaving the decision up to the individuals who were in contention, with the understanding that no matter what branch they opted to join, there would be full cooperation in the future.

Scamporino and I decided to stay in the Italian SI Section under Earl Brennan and to Brennan's obvious pleasure, the episode was closed.

Both Bruce and Goodfellow, who respected each other, were spare with their words and by their rationally cool approach ended what, at a lower level, had been a heated battle.

Despite the Joint Chiefs of Staff's utmost priority to the cross-Channel invasion, at this point it was obvious that the Mediterranean campaign would not end in North Africa but would be logically pursued against Sicily and Italy. The OSS Planning Board was convened to put together the first composite OSS operational plan ever attempted. This plan was designated "Implementation Study for Special Military Plan for Psychological Warfare in Sicily.[2] The preliminary work on the plan was undertaken under my direction by Italian SI and included three phases of OSS work: Secret Intelligence, Special Operations, and Psychological Operations. A vast amount of preliminary intelligence, including safe contacts, safe houses, underground leaders, Masonic connections, public officials and religious leaders was collected for SI penetration purposes. For SO, military targets, vulnerable road and railroad bridges, power stations, transformers, harbor installations, beach erosion information, and technical data were collected. For Psychological Warfare (M.O.) a number of pamphlets and appeals were prepared, and a program for the distribution of literature and word-of-mouth propaganda was developed.

The implementation study was broken down into various phases: 1. the Preparatory Phase; 2. the Pre-Invasion Phase; 3. the Invasion Phase; and 4. the Post-Invasion Phase. The study was actually an expanded version of the original plan I had put together at Camp Lee. It had been enriched by a wealth of detailed information collected from a variety of sources and was calculated to assist the armed forces in all phases of operations. The only OSS branches that were assigned roles in the implementation of the study were SI, SO, MO, and in the Post-Invasion Phase, C.E. (Counter Espionage, later X-2). The Research and Analysis Branch was assigned no role in OSS operations in this first test of OSS operational capability.

The basic plan for Sicily had been devised in 1942 and early 1943. Yet the implementation study of the Sicilian plan was not submitted by Colonel A. H. Onthank, secretary of the Planning Board, to General Magruder, deputy for intelligence, until June 4, 1943. It was not finally adopted until June 10, when copies were distributed to the branch chiefs and the theater officer, Colonel Bill Eddy. *This was less than one month before the actual invasion of Sicily!*

I attended the early sessions of the Planning Board in civvies in order not to embarrass the generals, admirals, and the other brass who made up this prestigious group, with my lowly military rank of buck private. The sessions ran over a period of time during which I established a close rapport with Don Minniffie, a Board member, who had been the New York Herald Tribune's correspondent in Italy. The Board was aware that Italian SI was putting a crash program together for the inevitable invasion of Sicily, but at no time was Brennan made remotely aware of any timetable. In fact, there was much indecision in the highest military circles about the invasion of Sicily.

As the administrative work mounted, the staff of Italian SI was strengthened with additional key personnel whose experiences in prewar Fascist Italy or in a variety of administrative posts in the United States made them valuable contributors to the sustained support of the contemplated field intelligence operations.

Louis Fiorilla, a graduate of Wesleyan University who had attended school in Sicily and who spoke and wrote Italian fluently, was sent to Radio and Cryptographic School; Nato DeAngelis, who had studied painting in Rome and Catania before the war, volunteered as a penetration agent; Naval Lieutenant Pomp Orlando was transferred from the Navy to take on the post of administrative assistant to Earl Brennan; John Henderson, former Foreign Service officer who had served in Italy, took over briefing functions; Dr. Lester Houk, a pleasant, intelligent giant of a man who had studied in Italy, took over analytical and writing functions; Robert Marr was brought in from Cleveland to take over transportation and administrative functions; Major Theodore S. Cutting handled military liaison; and Phil Adams, an old State Department hand and great-great-grandson of John Quincy Adams, managed Albanian affairs.

In addition, Lieutenant Joseph Bonfiglio, a diminutive officer of Sicilian parentage, who turned in an outstanding performance, was put to work on special programs; Captain Alexander Cagiati, whose Italian background, knowledge, and linguistic ability proved to be of great value; Lieutenant Andre Pacatte, who came from Cleveland's Berlitz School, was taken on board for his knowledge of Corsica; Attorney Emilio Q. Daddario, football great of Wesleyan University, who was to distinguish himself in Italian operations, became my assistant operations officer; and Dick Mazzarini, an old friend of Brennan's from his Roman days, was sent to school and shipped as Italian SI liaison to London; and John Ricca, chief prosecutor of the Detroit Municipal Court, went on to develop a close friendship with Marshal Badoglio who succeeded Mussolini as Prime Minister.

Then there were Mike Chinigo, a reporter for International News Service (INS), who had returned to the states on one of the last ships from Italy and who would go back under newspaper cover to participate in the Sicilian campaign; Attorney James Montante, who became executive officer to Vincent Scamporino, SI Italy's field chief; Joseph Russo, outstanding feature writer for the *Bridgeport (Conn.) Herald*, who became station chief at Palermo after the Sicilian campaign; Attorney Joe Caputa, whom I recruited from Thomas E. Dewey's staff in New York and who became reports officer in Rome; Egidio Clemente, a Chicago printer and long-time collaborator of Girolamo Valenti; Lieutenant Frank Tarallo, a platoon commander with the First Infantry Division, who would lead surprise landings at Lipari and Ventotene; Umberto Galleani and a number of men who had served with the Spanish Loyalist forces in the Spanish Civil War; Sal Principato, a New Jersey labor leader; Tony Ribarich, an old active anti-Fascist; Joseph Salerno, a Lawrence, Massachusetts labor leader and anti-Fascist—these were among the first recruits whom we started pushing through the OSS training centers and intelligence school. Soon they were joined by well over a hundred other recruits who created logistic and security problems in a Washington that was security conscious and spy shy.

I recall one especially large group that was brought to Washington to start its training program. The members of this group, who had been cleared by Security, kept trickling in all day at Union Station, where they were picked up by our people and lodged in various Washington hotels. They were told to gather promptly at 8:00 P.M. the next day at a wing of Union Station where they were to be given further instructions. In the meantime, word got back to the office that the FBI had been alerted that a number of suspicious looking Italians seemed to be drifting into Washington. Afraid that some of our men might be picked up and questioned, we made a tremendous effort to contact them, which was not very easy because they were trying very hard to be invisible. We finally succeeded in finding them and putting them in Army trucks whereupon we rushed them to training school—without benefit of "secret instructions"—and not a moment too soon! While these groups were being trained, a constant liaison was being maintained with the New York anti-Fascist community and with Pacciardi in particular.

We believed that in late 1942 there might still be time to recruit a legion of volunteers among the Italian prisoners, both in East Africa and North Africa.[3] Augmented by anti-Fascist volunteers from South America and the United States, we thought they could be trained to spearhead an attack against Sicily. Such a unit, we felt, should be placed under the command of Pacciardi and assembled in North Africa for use when the Axis was driven completely from Libya and Tunisia. Brisk fighting was being waged in these areas while Axis forces in Tunisia were being reinforced, despite a partially effective blockade of the Sicilian Straits. Reference to the utilization of such a unit was incorporated in the OSS Special Plan for Sicily (page 34) as a responsibility of SI.

This Branch will also, on receiving approval of the Theater Commander, organize spearhead Sicilian speaking troops in Tunisia to accompany an invasion. Responsibility for equipment and training, etc. would rest with the Theater Commander, as would their transport to the scene of action.

As discussed with Colonel Pacciardi, the Italian volunteer legion was to establish beachheads in one of the following places: Licata, Gela, Scoglitti, Pozzallo, or the Cape Passero region. The unit was to storm the beach and expand the beachhead until U.S. troops took over the operation.

Pacciardi, through OSS sources, established contact with some of his old legionnaires who were in North Africa and provided the names of others. He discussed the matter at length with Vincent Scamporino, whose departure for Algiers was imminent, and he provided letters of introduction to some of his trusted friends at Oran and Casablanca.

While on the surface the problem of an Italian legion looked simple, time dragged on and either the White House or the State Department changed its mind—often under British pressure. So much time was lost that finally even Earl Brennan, who had been one of the legion's most enthusiastic supporters, was forced to throw up his hands. Scamp pursued the matter in Algiers and convinced Colonel Eddy, the OSS theater officer, to intervene in Pacciardi's behalf, with a request that he be commissioned as a U.S. Army officer and be immediately assigned to Algiers.[4] The matter was brought to the attention of General Marshall who, in a radiogram dated June 23 to General Dwight Eisenhower, indicated the State Department's "reluctance" to have Pacciardi commissioned and sent to North Africa. The reasons cited were his "factional" political involvement as well as their feeling that because he had fought on the Spanish Loyalist side, objections to him might be forthcoming from the Catholic Church and conservative elements. Marshall's radiogram to Eisenhower pointed out that Pacciardi could be highly useful to OSS in Italy for recruiting or other "matters." When Eisenhower and his staff, still under negative British influence, refused to authorize Pacciardi's commissioning or entry into the North African theater of operations, the project was pronounced totally dead. Brennan's and Italian SI contacts with Pacciardi continued until long after the end of the war.

Overlooking occasional distractions, the office staff was being strengthened, and a totally dedicated crew worked like beavers from early morning until late evening readying personnel and equipment for overseas. The theater office repeatedly requested that we start getting our personnel to the field and begin our operations. This priority became all the more important because the British were having a tough time in Sicily and had lost all their agents on the island. I discussed the matter with Brennan and suggested that I be sent to Lisbon immediately to see if I could set up some kind of courier intelligence system which would provide the much needed military information from Sicily. At first he agreed, and I went ahead with the processing of my passport and arranging transportation via the PanAm Clipper to Lisbon. After thinking it over, however, Brennan changed his mind and decided that I should stay stateside and complete the planning and recruitment program.

In order to comply with the requests from the North African theater of operations, arrangements were made for Scamporino to leave for

Algiers in January 1943. There he would join Colonel Eddy's staff and pave the way for the arrival of some of the trainees who were scheduled to participate in the SI operations in Italy. Scamp was designated by Brennan as his deputy in the field, given overall responsibility for Italian SI activities, whereas I would continue in Washington with my planning and recruiting endeavors until such time as I would fly out to the theater to direct the military side of the operations. Despite my desire to go to the field immediately, Brennan's decision made sense. I could see his reluctance to let me go as I was handling so many facets of our Washington operations that he would have had a hard time replacing me on short notice.

In the early 1940s Washington was like an overgrown small town. While it had indeed become the center of the democratic world, it had managed to retain a warm and friendly atmosphere. Although the war had created a sense of urgency in most of us, it had not allowed us to forget the human equation.

Watergate was many years away from the cynical connotations it has today. It included an inn by the Potomac that served good food and was famous for its corn popovers; the Occident served the best beef in town; O'Connell's had the best fish; and the little Trianon Restaurant on the corner of Pennsylvania Avenue and 22nd Street was a favorite lunch spot for many OSS and State Department people. The Trianon served many excellent French dishes, and our group frequently went there evenings after work. We became friendly with the owner, Luigi, a Sicilian from Palermo. He would occasionally ask us to come after closing hours, and he would prepare a delicious dish of spaghetti alla marinara, which we consumed with a great deal of gusto, particularly since in those days there were very few good Italian restaurants in town. Those were the days when Fortune Gallo used to bring his opera company to Washington during the summer. In the evening one could sit on the steps along the Potomac and watch a superb performance of a Lehar or Strauss operetta staged on a barge anchored on the shore. Unfortunately, the moments of relaxation were rare as our entire section was working at a feverish pace, trying to put together the highly classified program which was to be a pilot for future OSS operations in other parts of Europe and the world.

Not all of our concentration was directed to resolving our operational problems. OSS was no different from any other large organization where internal competition, jealousy and envy sap up much productive energy. Early on, the SO Branch had attempted to take over the operation from SI. When this effort failed, an attempt was made to ship me and Scamporino to Italian East Africa where the war was over with the surrender of Italian troops. We saw clearly through the SO ruse to sidetrack us into an unproductive sector. Earl Brennan thundered and threatened until the effort was aborted. This was only the first of many efforts to take over the section and its personnel.

Soon after Scamporino arrived in Algiers, we began final preparations for dispatching the first group of agents to the field. These were designated the Earl Groups and the personnel was made up of Sardinian- and Sicilian-speaking men. For security purposes, we found it expedient to induct them all into the Army, regardless of their age or their assignments. The only ones not inducted were Scamporino and Vacirca. One reason for the military induction was that transportation to the theater was at a premium because fighting troops and equipment had absolute priority to North Africa where, despite the early success of the Allied landings, the fighting was becoming heavy in Tunisia. At the same time, the British Eighth Army was regrouping after the race across the Libyan coastal escarpment, in preparation to crack the Mareth Line.

The first of the "Earl" groups was made up of nine men and two officers. After Bill Donovan personally signed their letter orders on March 13, 1943, they embarked on a troop ship headed for Casablanca.[5] From there they proceeded by rail across Morocco and Algeria to the outskirts of Algiers, where British SOE shared a holding and training area at what had been an exclusive beach community known as "Club des Pins."

At the "Club" the SOE people had training facilities which included a parachute jump school, telegraphy and communications training, some maritime training and cryptography. Scamp made arrangements for Captain Frank Tarallo, who commanded the group, and the men to be billeted at the seaside resort and to attend the "finishing schools."

The main OSS installations were located in Algiers itself and included a headquarters villa overlooking the city and a vast expanse of the Mediterranean, where Colonel Eddy and his staff lived and worked, and a second villa, where the services and supplies were located and run as a military unit. The entire operation had been placed under the direction of G-3, Allied Force Headquarters (AFHQ), and was designated Experimental Detachment, G-3, AFHQ. It was an outgrowth of Eddy's pre-"Torch" operation which had been based in Tangiers.

While the first group was being readied for overseas shipment, I was still flying about the country recruiting personnel for other regions of Italy. The Washington staff was occupied in processing applications, arranging for training and the myriad details that had to be taken care of in order to be ready for all the eventualities of the impending Italian campaign.

I continued attending meetings of the Planning Board to help finish the plans for the Sicilian campaign. As the work neared its end, we were satisfied that the method which had been adopted in developing the Sicilian plan, with few modifications, could be used on any other area of the world. Throughout this period I was still an Army private. When I deemed it convenient I would don my civvies, as was the case when I attended Planning Board meetings. Brennan had talked about obtaining a direct commission for me and had discussed the matter with the military people in the organization, but little action had been taken.[6] The problem had slowly become an embarrassing one, since some of the people on my staff were field officers and once my work was completed in Washington I was expected to go to the field and direct operations that were essentially of a military nature and would necessitate contacts at the highest military level.

Seeing that the military detachment people were taking their time about working on my commission, I finally showed up at one of the Planning Board sessions wearing my private's uniform. The board was made up of several generals, one admiral, and a number of colonels, and they had become accustomed to seeing me at meetings as a civilian. They were obviously comfortable working with civilians and became visibly uncomfortable working with an enlisted man who voiced his opinions as a peer. They were all good sports, and the meeting continued with the usual banter and exchange of ideas.

Not long after the meeting I was discharged from the Army as a private first class, for the convenience of the government Sec. X AR 615-360. On the same day, I was appointed a second lieutenant, Army of the United States (AUS), by order of the Secretary of War.[7] The commissioning process which had been bogged down in red tape for many months had been miraculously accelerated.

Chapter 6

On the Way . . .

By the end of April 1943, the time had come to get operations underway in Algiers. The radiograms coming from Colonel Eddy were insistent that OSS do something to justify its presence in the field and that Eisenhower's headquarters were sorely in need of intelligence from and about Italy.[1] Meanwhile, the second of the "Earl" groups had already arrived at Club des Pins and was undergoing additional training.

The military situation in Tunisia was continually deteriorating for the Axis as both Germans and Italians were being wedged in the northeast pocket with the Mediterranean at their backs. Brennan was still determined to keep me in Washington. However, as inquiries kept coming in from the field and as the new chief of Secret Intelligence, Whitney Shepardson, put pressure on Brennan to get moving, it became clear to him that if any military operations were going to be undertaken, I must get out to the field to direct them. With the granting of my commission as a second lieutenant, the stage was set for my departure.

Brennan arranged for a courtesy call on General Donovan. This was to be my first meeting with the man who as commander of the Fighting Sixty-Ninth in World War I had become a legend in military circles. Donovan was then 59, and although a quarter of a century had gone by since his battlefield exploits in France, he was still in top physical condition.

After Brennan introduced me to him, Donovan asked a question to the effect, "Is this the young man who was the cause of the turmoil between the SI and SO branches?" Brennan, playing innocent, asked, "What turmoil?" Donovan, fixing him with a piercing look said, "You know, Earl!" Then, turning to me, he wished me well and stressed the importance of my mission. He asked me a few elementary questions, and the interview was over. I got the feeling that he was either not overly impressed or had something more important to do. In parting, he suggested that it might be a good idea to cut my hair shorter before leaving for the war area. Brennan, who hated facing any superior, was visibly upset, but fortunately our visit was coming to an end, as Donovan shook hands with both of us and promised to see me in the field.

In the remaining days before my departure, the section worked feverishly to obtain the important documents and maps I would need in North Africa to plan the final phase of the operations. This work had to be put off because we had to talk to people in New York, Detroit, Boston, and Chicago about securing names and safe houses as well as political ties in Italy. Brennan and the staff made arrangements for my departure by air, and I was assigned a cover number which was to be substituted for my name on all communications relative to the trip.

As the time grew closer, I reviewed the progress the Italian SI Section had made since that hot August day when I reported for duty at "Q" Building. Working together, we had built up one of the most important sections in the OSS. At no time did the SI chief attempt to interfere with the work that was being done. It soon became clear that other sections in SI, as well as a number of individuals in the SO Branch were envious of our section. A major reason for this envy was that ours was the only section that had done any deep planning, recruiting, and training and was ready to take to the field in a timely fashion. The personnel of the section, having worked together for so many months, had developed an esprit de corps which some of the other people in the organization could not understand. Finding no other motivation, they attributed it to the fact that most of the recruits were of Italian origin and were not shy about standing up to be heard.

We all felt a sense of loyalty to Brennan who, as the section chief, had encouraged and participated in all of our efforts. Brennan was not an easy man to understand. Not only was he moody but he was not above throwing tantrums. He was also secretive, rarely saying anything about himself. Sometimes he would lock himself up in his office for hours, and then only his personal secretary, Olga Pavlova, could go in to see him. Pavlova, a recent addition to the staff, had met Brennan on his last Foreign Service assignment in Canada. She was a vivacious redhead who would have looked more at home on the stage than in our office. After her husband, a member of the Royal Canadian Air Force, was killed in action, she moved to Washington with their little boy. She had been cleared by security in order to be employed by OSS.

The time to leave Washington finally arrived when Brennan handed me a communication which stated cryptically:

This will be your authority to direct the above (383-A) to proceed to the Washington National Airport on Thursday, May 20, 1943, Hangar 6 at 9:00 A.M. with all luggage.

In order to get to this point, it had been necessary to get my War Department orders amended. The first set of orders were issued on May 17, 1943, and assigned me to "Permanent station outside of the U.S." On the same day, Brennan insisted on having the orders changed to read: "Directed to proceed on temporary duty . . . and . . . return to his proper station, Washington, D.C." He had insisted on this language change because in the event of an emergency stateside he would be able to recall me on short notice. As it happened, my "temporary" duty overseas lasted two full years, and I did not get back to Washington until late May 1945.

That day, May 20, 1943, I was up early with all my baggage, including my 100-pound barracks bag full of classified documents for which I had been designated as a courier. Transatlantic flying was still in its infancy, with the only regular commercial overseas routes being flown by the Pan Am Clippers. Our plane was a converted TWA airliner named "Comanchee." TWA owned only four of these four-motor transcontinental planes and they had been taken over by the Army and designated as C-75s. However, the Army retained their original Indian names as well as the pilots and part of the crew.

The flight took off from Washington promptly and was full of Air Force second lieutenants who had just received their wings and were being ferried over to North Africa for their first combat duty. Also on board was a sprinkling of other officers, including a brigadier general who was flying to Algiers; a couple of chaplains; a Captain Head, a tall, middle-aged heavyset man who was assigned to the Engineers; and a British captain who was returning to Africa from Hollywood where he had been technical adviser for the movie *Five Graves to Cairo*, starring Franchot Tone.

After a brief stop at Miami, we proceeded to Cuba and then to Georgetown, British Guiana, where we refueled and continued to Natal, Brazil. The interior of the huge plane had been modified so that it could carry more passengers; our fare was a box lunch, fresh fruit, and hot coffee from a thermos. The plane droned slowly over the Caribbean, flying over the historic islands which dotted the seascape; in the distance we could see the coastline of Venezuela. Soon we were flying over the verdant rainforest of Venezuela, past the wide delta of the Orinoco, and headed for the mouth of the Amazon in Brazil.

Just as we crossed the Guiana-Brazil border, we became aware of a problem with one of the engines. The motor began sputtering, and the Captain shut it down, feathering the prop in order to cut down the vibration. As a result, the plane lost both speed and altitude. Many of us who were seated at the tail end were asked to move up front, so that by shifting the weight we could help balance the airframe.

As I glanced over to my left, I noticed Captain Head tying and untying a piece of rope in his hands, seemingly reviewing every knot he had learned in the Boy Scout Manual.

The pilot announced that he was also having difficulties with one of the other engines and that he was turning back and heading for the nearest airport that could accommodate the plane. In the meantime, we could hear the second engine occasionally skipping and the lumbering plane was slowly losing altitude. Our situation was made all the more precarious by the fact that we were flying over a dense, unexplored jungle which had already claimed a number of American transport planes.

As it turned out, the nearest airport was at Paramaribo, Surinam (Dutch Guiana). As we approached the airport, we experienced yet more bad luck when the landing gear failed to function automatically and the crew had to lower the wheels manually. As if this were not enough, once the landing gear had been lowered, gasoline had to be dumped while we were in the air because the airport runway was too short for the plane and the pilot was concerned about braking the plane to a halt. The moment of truth finally arrived. The pilot gradually got the plane into position and made his pass at the landing field, setting his wheels to the ground so gently that most of us on board were hardly aware that we had landed. Then he got to the end of the runway and miraculously stopped the plane. Everyone sighed in relief, and as the captain emerged from his cabin, the grateful passengers burst into enthusiastic applause.

Paramaribo was not then, nor is it now, a favorite port of call, and in the war year 1943, it had even less to recommend it, even to the most dedicated tourist. A colony of the Netherlands, Surinam posed a dilemma to its Dutch authorities who were unsure to whom they owed their loyalty after the Nazis took over the Netherlands. Washington resolved the quandary by ordering the Caribbean command to occupy the country whose ample supplies of bauxite were in great demand by our war industry for the production of aluminum. The Army Air Force manned the field at Paramaribo and built a camp where our small force was stationed. The Dutch continued to govern the country, however, which, outside of the capital, was in an almost aboriginal state.

Discovering that the damage to the engine could not be repaired, the crew decided that a new engine should be flown in from the United States. The work would take almost a week, during which time we would be stuck in a malaria-infested area. I quickly sent a telegram to Earl Brennan, informing him of a week's delay in my arrival in Algiers so that he could pass on the news to Scamp who would be wondering what had happened to me. There was little for me to do at the base, and I was assigned the temporary duty of censoring the base mail. When I completed this chore, I was free to visit the countryside.

Paramaribo itself was an overgrown village with a government square as its centerpiece. Dominating the scene, in the middle of the square, was a statue of Queen Wilhelmina. The climate was hot and humid, an atmosphere made all the more oppressive by the pungent odor of rancid banana oil mixed with the aroma of Javanese cooking. On the outskirts of the capital were clustered homes resembling the architecture of Java and the East Indies. Many of the people had migrated under Dutch patronage and were engaged in farming and rice cultivation, using the same techniques as their Javanese and East Indian forebears, including the same type of water buffalo to till the fields. In the surrounding rainforest were villages of blacks who were the descendants of the slaves who had been brought to Surinam from Africa in the seventeenth century. Upon being freed, they had reverted to their original way of life, building thatched hut villages and wearing very little clothing.

The most interesting item I could find about Surinam was that it had one of the most costly roads in the world. It connected the town and the bauxite mines in the interior, and ran through soft marshy jungle land, following the path of a Toonerville-type, narrow-gauge railroad which had been used to transport bauxite to the port. The tracks were also used by a passenger train which was so crowded that passengers literally sat on the roof. It made so many stops that a person could jog almost as fast. The base of the road had been created by felling massive mahogany trees which were then surfaced with bauxite rock.

Four days after leaving Washington, I convinced the base adjutant, Captain Edward Hart, to allow me to make a telephone call to Brennan in Washington so that I could find out if he had received my telegram. Brennan informed me that he had and had also alerted Scamporino of my delay.

After about a week a C-47 picked us up and took us on the next leg of our flight to Natal, Brazil, which was the departure point for the transatlantic flight to Dakar, French West Africa. We were all relieved to be leaving Surinam with its giant mosquitoes and assorted insects, and we eagerly crowded into the plane. It taxied to the end of the runway where the pilot revved up the engines and made a quick takeoff. Following the French Guiana coastline to the almost never-ending estuary of the Amazon River, past Belem, Fortaleza, and finally, some five hours later, the pilot landed the lumbering craft at Natal Airport.

The transatlantic flight started early in the morning aboard a converted B-24 bomber which had been fitted out to carry passengers and cargo. The cast of passengers had not changed—the general, the chaplains and pilots were still part of the tour.

Natal had become the airport of the Ferry Command which had been busy delivering aircraft to the Royal Air Force (RAF) during the Battle of North Africa. The "Boston" medium bombers did not have enough autonomy to fly directly to Dakar and had to stop to refuel at Ascension Island, halfway across the Atlantic. Ascension was a speck of land in a vast, seemingly never-ending body of water. If the navigator missed plotting a course to the island, the plane was destined to wind up in the drink.

At the time of our takeoff, both the Ferry Command and Air Transport Command (ATC) of the Army Air Force were busy flying the South Atlantic to bring both men and machines to the fighting fronts.

After what seemed to be an interminably boring flight, we saw the African coastline and the port of Dakar fast approaching. Landing at dusk, we were taken by truck to the U.S. station at Rufisque, a few miles west of Dakar. The camp was used to temporarily feed and house transient Army personnel and was guarded by giant Senegalese French troops whose height was exaggerated by the fez they wore on the back of their heads.

In the morning they rushed me to the airport as a plane was leaving for Algiers. I was in luck. They had sent a plane to pick up the general, and there was room for a few more officers, including one of the chaplains and me. In my rush I forgot to pick up one of the bags with my personal belongings. They promised to send it on to Algiers, but it never did catch up with me. However, I did not neglect my barracks bag with all its classified papers.

The C-47 which had been sent down to pick up General Miller (the brigadier general referred to above) was a luxury aircraft fitted out as a flying command post with soft chairs and tables. We were making the trip in easy stages as we flew over Mauritania and over the western fringes of the Sahara Desert, finally landing at the remote Oasis of Atar, near the border of Spanish Sahara.

The oppressive heat felt like a blast furnace. We taxied up to the station which was manned by the French Air Force and got out of the plane for about an hour. Half a dozen ancient French biplanes were parked in the field; they had obviously been cannibalized for parts. We were happy when the pilot announced that we were ready to take off. We clambered aboard the plane and waited for it to gain altitude so that we could enjoy the coolness of the upper air.

As the plane flew high over the desert, we could see the desolate landscape that stretched out in all directions. After several hours, the peaks of the Atlas Mountains could be seen in the north, and gradually splashes of green became visible below. We flew right over the ridges of southern Morocco and landed at the airfield of historic Marrakech.

Perhaps because we were included in the general's party, we were picked up and lodged at the exclusive Hotel Mammunia which a few months before (January 14) had hosted some of the principals of the Casablanca Conference. This luxury hotel was of Moorish design and was surrounded by beautiful gardens with colorful bougainvillea, hibiscus, and flowering shrubs. This interval was too brief as we were told to be ready next morning to fly on to Algiers.

Four hours after leaving Marrakech, we buckled up to land at Maison Blanche Airport outside of Algiers. Below us was the city of Algiers whose colorful streets wound their way up from the Mediterranean to the mountains in the south. It was the early afternoon of May 28, exactly eight days after my departure from Washington and sixteen days after the Axis surrender in North Africa (May 23, 1943).

My instructions were to contact AFHQ at the Hotel St. George on Rue Michelet and to ask for Colonel Eddy at the Villa Magnol. Discovering that there was a regular service from Maison Blanche to AFHQ Headquarters, I grabbed my documents and bag and rode into town, up the serpentine Rue Michelet.

On arrival at the St. George, I asked to be placed in contact with Villa Magnol and spoke with someone who promised to send a Jeep to pick me up. Within half an hour we were riding to Magnol which was located high up on the mountain overlooking the magnificent panorama of the city of Algiers with its mysterious Casbah and the shimmering blue Mediterranean as the backdrop. As I looked north at the line where the ocean melded into the sky, I involuntarily took a deep breath at the beauty of the scene and thought about what lay in store for us beyond our line of vision. I could see the Port of Algiers full of ships with barrage balloons dotting the sky as protection against possible enemy dive bombers. Then we arrived at our destination.

I reported to Colonel Eddy whom I was meeting for the first time. After welcoming me and expressing his relief that nothing serious had happened to me, he told me that our men were quartered at Club des Pins and that later in the day, after talking to Scamp, I could take operational command of the unit.

"Scamp is upstairs," he said, "and he'll certainly be glad to see you."

So saying, he called Scamp who was upstairs in his room. (The Villa also served as living quarters for a number of the branch and desk chiefs.) Scamp immediately came downstairs and gave me a welcoming hug. We continued chatting with Colonel Eddy who emphasized, as he had in his many cables, that we must start operations against Sicily, Sardinia, and Italy.

Then Scamp and I went to his room and sat on the balcony that overlooked the port, where I filled him in on news from home and the office and he brought me up to date on events at AFHQ. He had established an excellent relationship with Colonel Eddy and the rest of the top staff; Colonel Arthur Roseborough, who headed the Western European Division; Henry Hyde, the chief of the French desk; Ted Ryan, head of the Reports Board; Rudy Winnacker, the Research and Analysis representative; and Jerry Van Arkel of the Labor desk. The men and officers were undergoing training at camp, and Scamp stressed that we had to start producing results at the earliest possible date. Eisenhower's staff was putting daily pressure on Colonel Eddy for OSS to deliver on its commitment to provide intelligence, as the British were up a blind alley in Sicily.

As it was getting late, Scamp called for a Jeep, and we drove out together along the shore road to the holding area. It was late afternoon by the time we arrived at the cluster of Mediterranean-type beach houses where our men were quartered. We had an excited reunion: they had been waiting over a month for my arrival and they had only limited contact with headquarters. Scamp had an appointment in Algiers, he left saying he would call me the following day.

Italian SI had been assigned two cottages, and I moved in with Captain Tarallo and Marine Lieutenant Sebastian Passanisi, both of whom had come over with the first Earl Group and were among the first men I had recruited. It was almost time for the evening meal, and we walked down the road to the cottage where the mess hall was located. Somewhat taken aback, we noticed that the appearance and cleanliness of the waiters and other personnel in the kitchen left much to be desired, and, not surprisingly, the food they served the men and officers was little more than slop. On our return to our cottage, I asked about the food and the general conditions under which our men were living. The answers I received were not very comforting. The men were continually being fed bad food; trench mouth was rampant among the cooks and dining room waiters; meat made only a rare appearance on the table.

I learned that the officer in charge of the American contingent was Marine Lieutenant "Pinkie" Harris. The installation was being run by the British SOE, which had a full complement with parachute and maritime training facilities. OSS was only a minority partner in the operation. I resolved to have a frank talk with "Pinkie" Harris as soon as possible.

While we were chatting night had fallen, and it was dark outside. All of a sudden all hell broke loose. The sirens started wailing, antiaircraft guns began popping, and we could hear an occasional thud and explosion. "Pep" Puleo, one of the men, ran into the room and shouted "Air Raid!" He beckoned me to follow him, and we ran into a thicket of pines, right across from the cottage. East of us, in the direction of Algiers, I could see hundreds of searchlights from the batteries on shore and on ships searching the sky for enemy planes. Occasionally, a plane would be caught in the web of triangulating searchlights, looking much like a silver moth caught in a spider web. We could hear the engines of the enemy bombers which must have come from Sardinia or Sicily and see the spectacular fireworks display as thousands of tracers raced skyward in search of a target. After fifteen minutes, the excitement was over as suddenly as it had begun. This was my first night in Algiers.

The next morning I had a long talk with the officers and men in order to find out what had happened since they had arrived in North Africa. Little had occurred and few OSS facilities were in place to further the specialized training needed to undertake the arduous work ahead of them. For example, although Tunis had been liberated fifteen days before my arrival, Scamp had been the only one to seek out some of the people we wanted to contact. He had met with some of Pacciardi's friends in Casablanca and Oran and some recruiting had been done, but operating alone in all of French North Africa was not easy. In Tunis he had been working with U.S. Vice Consul L. Pitman Springs, but besides the initial contacts there had not been enough time for a followup.

Scamp had also established a good rapport with the local French military authorities and through them had recruited a grandson of Alfred Dreyfus who had powerful connections in northern Italy. With the aid of the French desk's agent "Tommy" he had managed to infiltrate Dreyfus into southern France with the intention of gradually working his way into northern Italy. (He never got to northern Italy but went to Switzerland and was absorbed by the Dulles organization until the end of the war.) Scamp also kept in touch with the British Interservice Liaison Department (I.S.L.D.) people in AFHQ on Italian matters. Occasionally, he requested background intelligence on specific situations which they courteously supplied.

After reviewing the situation, it became obvious that something had to be done to get the operation started. Some of the men were assigned to the special parachute course, and others were assigned to maritime training. I talked to Commander Jerry Holdsworth of SOE about the special training available and participated in a couple of beach operations. To my amazement, the men were encumbered with heavy metal backpacks that, though waterproof, would have caused them to drown if they had fallen into the water.

At that time, OSS was entirely dependent on the British for clandestine maritime transportation and for air operations—a situation I found intolerable. To make matters worse, there was no document section that could provide our agents with the necessary identity documents, ration cards, military papers, and other paraphernalia which were so important for an agent to survive unobtrusively in a hostile police environment.

The first priority, however, was to improve the group's living conditions and morale. When Lieutenant Harris showed up, after preliminary niceties, we exchanged a few harsh words about the conditions at the mess hall and the quality of the rations. While "Pinkie" Harris towered over me in size, I was not intimidated for I felt I had right on my side. He promised to improve the conditions, and, indeed after several days, there was marked improvement in the quality of the food. Later, our relationship turned out to be both cordial and friendly.

Anxious to sort out the problems we faced and to find a solution to them, I drove to Algiers to meet with Scamp and discuss the entire situation with him and get a fix on the AFHQ operational priorities. If possible, I wanted to find out the approximate time of impending military operations. I planned to land a group of our agents, led by Anthony Camboni, in Sardinia. With the rest of the limited personnel, I planned to undertake the first SI operations against the southern coast of Sicily. In order to undertake these operations, the agents needed proper documents so that they could move around in comparative freedom. Among these documents were military discharge papers, driver's licenses, and identity cards issued by the cities of residence. Scamp started making phone calls and quickly came up with the answer: none of these documents was available nor were facilities to produce them available at AFHQ. Because the nearest British facilities were in Cairo, we decided to send Captain Tarallo to Egypt as soon as possible with photographs and personal data on the agents scheduled to go on mission.

Communications was the next problem on the agenda. Several of the men had been trained in the United States as radio telegraphers and cryptographers, but they needed equipment and further training to familiarize themselves with transmission procedures and the equipment. The problem was posed to Colonel Eddy who promised to get immediate action from the communication officer, Lieutenant Colonel John O. Weaver, to whom he sent the following memo:

1. It is my desire that all other business be set aside if necessary to complete immediately equipment of an intelligence team in the Earl Group, details of which can be explained to you by Mr. Scamporino.
2. This request has first priority, and will be a critical test with the Allied Force Headquarters of our ability to meet an urgent request for our service.

> W. A. Eddy
> Col. U.S. Marine Corps
> Commanding[2]

Operational transportation was next in the order of business. The French Section had occasionally been using a French Navy submarine for its penetration of Corsica and the southern French Coast. The chief of the section, Henry Hyde, lacking operational transportation, had run into a buzz saw when he attempted to take a couple of his agents to Britain in order to have them parachuted by SOE. Henry and his men, caught wearing British uniforms were detained in London and were sent back only after a good deal of fuss by British authorities who got their noses out of joint.

OSS also had available for its use fishing vessels which were both slow and highly risky. Dreyfus had been landed from one of these vessels. British subs were, of course, available, but they were carrying high-priority missions for SOE and SIS. I suggested to Colonel Eddy and Scamp that if we were to operate effectively from North Africa, OSS had to develop some autonomous operational transportation. Otherwise, our organization would become completely subservient to SOE. I asked why we had not been working with the U.S. Sixth Fleet to develop operational transportation. Since the United States had a squadron of PT boats operating in the Mediterranean, I urged Colonel Eddy to make the necessary contacts to work out an agreement to use them on some of our operations. Eddy, agreeing that it was a good idea, promised to give it his immediate attention. He pointed out that most of the Sixth Fleet was then stationed in Bizerte, but he would see the Navy people at AFHQ and would get back to me.

We still had no precise information about the invasion of Sicily or what role we would be allowed to play in it. We had sent Tarallo to Cairo to secure documentation from SOE for several operations, and it was apparent to me that this sort of thing could not continue. Nothing seemed more futile or ridiculous than having to send an officer thousands of miles to procure a few documents which should have been produced by our own OSS document section which, unfortunately, did not exist. The documents Tarallo had been sent to get were especially urgent for the Sardinian mission I was trying to launch. I dubbed the mission "Bathtub I," and the code name stuck. The men who were assigned to the mission were Tony Camboni, a Chicago scale salesman, and John DeMontis, a Detroit grocer. Both of these men were natives of Ozieri, a town in the north-central area of the island. It was planned to have them find operational cover with outlaws who operated in eastern Sardinia. Their task was twofold—to set up an intelligence operation and to build up an armed resistance group. Sardinia was one of the places in Italy that was truly suitable for such operations because it was sparsely populated and the people in the mountain wilderness were fiercely independent.

In the meantime, Scamp got in touch with ISLD-AFHQ to see what the British might have on Sardinia. On June 13, he received an official note warning that

1. A P.O.W. who was recently in Sardinia, stated that two British agents were recently caught there because they had betrayed themselves by approaching a shepherd whilst he was guarding his flock.
2. No native, according to the P.O.W., would dream of doing such a thing.
3. This may be a tip worth heeding.

On the same day, the same staff officer sent another note, No. 1045, in which he officially offered to show Scamp the names of "certain individuals" who could be counted on to give local assistance in the event of an invasion of Sardinia. He offered to share these contacts if Scamp would visit his office, providing there would be complete mutual understanding as to the "use which is to be made of such people." This was all that was available from "our cousins," as the British were referred to in U.S. circles in those days. Scamp retained his liaison with the ISLD because other important matters were pending. In the meantime, Colonel Eddy had been prodding communications to be ready for "Bathtub." He also spoke with Admiral Henry Kent Hewitt at AFHQ who arranged a meeting for me with Admiral R.L. Connolly at his headquarters at Bizerte to discuss operational transportation.

While we were working to sort out the problems which the OSS should have already resolved before any agents were sent to the field, the Sicilian team was being put through its paces. They, too, needed documents as well as transportation so that they could be landed in southern Sicily. During this same period, urgent messages were arriving from Washington requesting information about Admiral Massimo Girosi of the Italian Navy and specifically inquiring about his present assignment and whereabouts. Scamp turned to his friends at ISLD who, after addressing the inquiry to their London headquarters, came back with scant information about Girosi. Although the request was a bit strange considering that Girosi did not occupy a crucial place in the Italian Naval Command, we sent back whatever information we had gleaned from British and French intelligence sources.

On June 18, Colonel Eddy called to say that Admiral Hewitt had okayed my suggestion to use U.S. PT boats and had asked that I personally go to Bizerte to talk to Rear Admiral Connolly. Arrangements were made for me to fly to Tunis Airport on a priority basis, and AFHQ issued travel orders for the flight.[4] The orders authorized me to travel to "Bizerte, thence to Phillipville and such other places in the North Africa Theatre of Operations as may be necessary to carry out the instructions of the C-in-C." Eddy provided me with a letter of introduction to Admiral Connolly which stated: "In accordance with instructions received this morning from Vice Admiral Hewitt, 2nd Lt. B.M. Corvo is proceeding on or about Sunday, June 20th, to report to you and to Lt. Commander Barnes, to discuss a special operation prepared by the Office of Strategic Services." [4]

Armed with Colonel Eddy's letter and a musette bag with a few necessities, I went to the airport and waited around until a flight took off for Tunis. There were few passengers on board the plane, which was loaded with freight. After a two-hour flight, we landed at the airfield on the outskirts of the city. The destruction at the Tunis airport was total. The field was littered with skeletons of Italian fighter planes and German Junkers transport planes. Almost every hangar had been gutted by our bombing and strafing attacks, and the only thing that had been repaired was the runway. The steel structures in the hangars looked like the skeletons of prehistoric dinosaurs. Even the operations building was barely patched up, but it was functioning under the command of Lieutenant Earl Miller who had been sent to open up the airport for ATC. German prisoner work parties were busily engaged in removing rubble in various parts of the field under the watchful eye of GI guards who seemed to relish the task.

I walked from the plane to the Operations Building and asked the officer in charge if there was any transportation to Bizerte. He suggested that the only way was to stand at the airport gate and thumb a ride from a passing GI truck. It was noon by the time I picked up a lift from a quartermaster truck going to Navy headquarters in Bizerte. The driver was a sergeant from Brooklyn who had originally made the landing in Morocco. As the truck raced along the bumpy road to Bizerte, we passed a number of Arab villages which had been completely destroyed. People were walking among the rubble, and an occasional mangy dog could be seen sniffing among the rocks. Enemy POW work units were also at work here trying to tidy up the rubble as a first step toward normalcy. As we got closer to Bizerte, the damage was even more extensive, and the POW work parties were more numerous. Everywhere there was a film of white dust—dust raised by trucks and dust raised by the marching feet of the German POWs.

As the truck slowly made its way through the streets to get to the port area, you could look into the windowless, doorless, abandoned homes which were still standing among piles of rock that had once been homes. An occasional sign pointed the way to naval headquarters at "La Pecherie." At the port area, which was formerly the French Naval Command headquarters, there were a number of large old buildings, some of which had been converted into living quarters, mess halls, and offices. The men and officers who ran the U.S. Navy MTB Ron (the Motor Torpedo Boat Squadron attached to U.S. Mediterranean Fleet) lived and worked in this area and the Naval Command headquarters were nearby.

When I reported to the duty officer at headquarters, I explained that I was coming from Algiers and had a letter for Admiral Connolly. The admiral was at a staff meeting, however, and so the duty officer sent him a note. A few minutes later he came out of his meeting to see me, whereupon I handed him Colonel Eddy's letter. He nodded, saying that he was aware of my mission and that he had already received a signal from Admiral Hewitt. He thought it would be better for me to discuss the details of the operation with Lieutenant Commander S.L. Barnes who was the CO of MTB Ron 15, and he would send him right out to talk to me.

A few minutes later, Commander Barnes came out of the room and invited me to his office in one of the adjacent buildings. When we got there he introduced me to his executive officer, Lieutenant John Mutty, and said I would probably be working out the operation with him. Both Barnes and Mutty were professional Navy officers and were interested in participating in the top secret mission I outlined in the course of our discussion. Their PT boats had been operating off the coast of southern Sicily looking for shipping, but they rarely had the opportunity to engage in firefights with enemy surface craft and there were very few enemy ships at which they could aim their torpedoes.

Commander Barnes had to return to the staff meeting but before he left he promised that if OSS needed operational transportation we could definitely count on his outfit to provide it. As he left the room, he instructed Mutty to make arrangements for my overnight stay and to work out the operational details of "Bathtub" with me. John Mutty was a very intelligent man who did not need pictures drawn to understand a situation. He actually relished the idea of daring surreptitious forays in enemy waters, and the "Bathtub" operation offered a number of new challenges. He took out a bundle of naval charts to make a series of calculations of distances, depths, shoals, and any other possible factors to be considered in meticulously planning the operation. Then he asked me how many boats I thought we would need for the operation. I suggested we use three boats which, upon arrival at our destination, could split up in order to confuse the enemy, should our flotilla be spotted. The command boat would transport the agents and head directly for the landing point while the other two boats would head north and south so that in the event of an alert, the longest possible part of the coastline would be alerted while the command boat slipped in under its auxiliary power to land the mission, undetected.

Plotting the course from Bizerte to the northwestern corner of Sardinia, Lieutenant Mutty came to the conclusion that our landing point was out of range. Perhaps, he suggested, he would take his three boats and meet us at the Port of Bone, Algeria, some 100 miles west of Bizerte. That would place us in a navigating position 250 miles due north before turning east to approach our landfall pinpoint. He calculated that going and coming, the trip would be more than 600 miles. In order to go such a distance, the boats would have to be equipped with auxiliary tanks topside. This would pose extra danger if we were spotted, and fighter planes were sent to intercept us.

Mutty asked me how soon I could ready the mission, and considering a number of factors, including the return of Captain Tarallo with the documents from Cairo, we set June 28 as the target date. This meant that I would have to rush back to Algiers and complete the training of the men. It was agreed that we would meet at Bone on June 27 so that we could work out final details and conduct some landing exercises, as well as test the life belts. By this time it was suppertime and John invited me to the officers' mess. Walking over to the mess I had a chance to look around the base.

The port was still cluttered with sunken ships, and there were a number of ancient French hydroplanes whose fabric skin was tattered and flapping in the breeze, half submerged in the murky waters near the quays. They were relics of another period of history, having been superseded by the all-metal bombers of World War II. Finally, we arrived at the mess hall and I had a chance to meet some of the other PT boat captains. They were all enthusiastic young men who wanted to see action. The fact that an Army lieutenant was joining them for supper was an unusual occurrence and was the subject of some speculation. After supper, Lieutenant Mutty assigned me to one of the officers who found me overnight quarters and promised to see me off the next morning. I was hardly in bed when all the sirens in the port and on the ships in Lake Bizerte started wailing, and every gun available cut loose at enemy planes that were raiding the fleet. There was no point looking for shelter, inasmuch as the bombs were already coming down and you could hear the explosions above the din of the ack ack fire. The lake and port were full of ships, and anywhere the bombs fell they could do damage. The barrage of fire into the heavens kept the enemy aircraft high, and after about ten minutes, they abandoned the raid. I was told that German and Italian planes from Sicily and Sardinia took turns every night bombing Bizerte because the enemy could see the concentration of shipping gathering for the next phase of the Battle of the Mediterranean and hoped to delay the blow by these spoiling raids. They did not, of course, know where the next blow was going to fall, but both Sardinia and Sicily were prime candidates. When the raid was over, everyone hit the sack to get some sleep in the event the enemy should decide to put on a repeat performance.

The next morning after breakfast I stopped in and thanked Commander Barnes and Lieutenant Mutty for their important decision to help OSS and promised to meet the boats at Bone on June 27. They had assigned a Jeep and a driver to take me directly to Tunis where I went to visit Vice Consul Pittman Springs at his home. Then I spent the rest of the day meeting some of Scamp's contacts.

The city of Tunis had experienced some uncomfortable moments in the last five months. Avenue Jules Ferry was the main artery of the capital with trees lining both sides of the street. During the siege, part of the sidewalks had been dug out in order to create zig-zag trenches which the public could use during enemy air raids. Tunis reminded me a great deal of some Sicilian cities; indeed, Sicilian was spoken in certain quarters of the city where many immigrants lived. Surprisingly, even some of the Arabs spoke Sicilian.

I walked around the streets to familiarize myself with the place and people. Later, I stopped at the ATC terminal to make arrangements to catch a return flight to Algiers. All I could get was a flight to Telergma which was a stop-off point where thousands of prisoners were being collected for temporary detention, but the flight would not leave until noon the next day. They assigned me a room at the Transient Officers Hotel at Rue Ferry.

At noon the following day I took the courier bus to the airport and started my trip back to Algiers, hoping that I would not be held up too long at Telergma. Flying over the arid terrain around Telergma I could see the prisoner-of-war pens with thousands of the Afrika Korps and the Italian Army units which, until recently, had fought against the combined might of British and American forces. The plane banked around the airport and then lowered its landing gear. As the wheels hit the runway, we rolled halfway down the field when one of the tires suddenly blew and the plane started thumping its way and nearly turned over when the pilot skillfully brought it to a halt. We got off in the middle of the airfield and walked to the dispatch office where, fortunately, I was able to grab a plane to continue my trip and arrived at Algiers late that afternoon.

I immediately reported the results of my trip to Colonel Eddy and Scamp who were elated to know that the OSS transport problems had been solved and that we could count on the support of the U.S. Navy for the impending operations in Sicily and Sardinia. "Bathtub" was "Go," except for the fact that Captain Tarallo was experiencing delays in procuring documents and clothing in Cairo and we only had a few days to put the mission together. I decided that it was imperative that the mission go off on its scheduled date. Inasmuch as we were the only OSS division present that could operate in Italy, I suggested that the mission be augmented and be landed in uniform as a probe of the defenses of the area.

The men were briefed accordingly, told that they were the advance guard and that they should try to make contact with sympathetic elements in the interior. The mission was expanded to five men: Anthony Camboni, Leader, John DeMontis, Joseph Puleo, Vincent Pavia, and Lieutenant Charles Taquay as the radio communications officer. Lieutenant Taquay volunteered at the last minute when the designated wireless telegrapher (W/T) of the mission fell ill.

On June 26, I left Algiers for Bone with the members of the mission and a backup team. Also with the group was Marine Lieutenant Sebastian Passanisi who had worked with these teams ever since they left the United States. We traveled overland in a motor convoy and spent the night of June 26 encamped on the outskirts of an Arab village on the Plain of Setif—an expanse of flat land that extended south of the Mediterranean coastal escarpment and the western extremity of the Atlas Mountains. A guard was mounted to protect the equipment from possible pilferage and for security purposes. The Plain of Setif was a widely cultivated grain-growing region. During the night, the distant skyline reflected a number of grain field fires that had been set (we were told) by incendiaries dropped from either German or Italian planes.

In the morning we proceeded to our rendezvous with the PT boats which had arrived at the port of Bone the day before. After we set up camp on the outskirts of the city, I drove down to meet with Lieutenant Mutty, the executive officer of MTB Ron 15 who personally took command of the three-boat flotilla that was to participate in the operation. After pouring over the charts of the northwest coast of Sardinia, we picked a landing site near the town of Argentiera.

Camboni, who was leading the mission, spoke the dialect perfectly, even though he had been away from the island for many years. Both he and John DeMontis had friends and relatives in the interior and at Sassari, the second largest city in Sardinia. We knew that the British, through Emilio Lussu, the island's most famous and active expatriate, had talked of attempting to incite the Sardinians to revolt against

Mussolini. Lussu had made several trips to the United States to enlist anti-Fascist support for some of his projects. Major Adams of ISDL/AFHQ had offered to show Scamporino a list of contacts on the island, but most of them were in another part of the island.

It was calculated that the worst that could happen to the mission was that it would be captured and interrogated and that some attempt would be made to contact the base. In order to make certain that we would know whether the mission was reporting freely and not being used for enemy purposes, Lieutenant Taquay, the radio operator, was to provide a prearranged alert that would indicate he was operating under duress. The mission's capture in uniform would probably alarm both the Italian and German High Commands and would center attention on Sardinia and Corsica as possible sites of the coming Allied invasion of Europe. This might convince them to shift additional forces to defend the island and take attention away from Sicily, which was becoming the focus of Allied air bombardments. These bombardments had brought about the surrender of the small fortified island of Pantelleria on June 11, 1943. The following day the nearby island of Lampedusa capitulated.

Lieutenant Mutty suggested that the "Bathtub" personnel be brought on board to familiarize them with procedures and to carry out general practice landings along the African coast. We selected an almost deserted cove to carry out the landing exercises, which went off flawlessly and provided the men with some necessary experience in the operating of a PT boat simulating actual landing procedures.

When we were satisfied that the men had gained sufficient expertise, we returned to the docks at Bone and set our departure for early next morning.

Under cover of predawn darkness, the members of the mission, Lieutenant Passanisi, and I went aboard the command boat and Lieutenant Mutty gave orders to "Cast Off." The three boats slowly made their way out of the port. When they reached the open sea, they set a course directly northward for 250 miles deep into enemy waters. To our knowledge, no Allied surface craft had operated in these waters during World War II. To maintain security, Lieutenant Mutty ordered total radio silence, and all communications between the boats were conducted by wigwag code. In order to have operational autonomy, all three boats carried auxiliary plastic tanks topside so that the entire trip could be made without refueling. The speed was adjusted so that the minimum consumption of fuel would be achieved.

June 28 was a beautiful sunny day, and the blue waters of the Mediterranean were as flat as the top of a table. Both the radios and radar were being closely monitored. Time passed slowly and the sun was hot despite the movement of the boat. About noon we had a brief alert when a small blip was sighted ahead. Since it was first thought to be a floating mine, the speed of the boat was dramatically reduced. On closer examination, however, the blip turned out to be a huge sea turtle lazily swimming on the surface of the water.

The demeanor of the men who were about to be landed was somber. They sat on the deck reading or talking as the hours slipped by. Occasionally someone would go down to the galley for coffee and something to eat. I talked to Camboni and the others and told them they would be well advised to get some sleep while they had the chance because once they landed their endurance would undoubtedly be put to a severe test. Some of the men took my advice and stayed below deck.

At about 1600 hours the radar picked up a blip in the sky, and the flotilla was alerted. Suddenly, the atmosphere became charged; the constant beep of the claxon called the men to battle stations; the signal men were busy in each boat transmitting their flagborne messages. The three boats widened their distance from each other, while the guns in the turrets rotated to test the swivels. Despite the alert, we kept up the same speed. Soon the blip in the radar could be seen topside as a speck in the distance. It slowly got larger and larger, and then it could be seen to be an Italian hydroplane circling about like a huge bird of prey but cautiously keeping its distance. After fifteen or twenty minutes, which seemed like an eternity, apparently it decided that everything was all right and it gradually disappeared in the distance. The situation returned to normal.

At this time we were deep in enemy waters. Had the pilot of the hydroplane suspected that the boats he had spotted were enemy PT boats, the fighter planes based at Alghero would have made short work of us. Fortunately, he took it for granted that we were an Italian naval formation, and we continued on our way unmolested.

The sun gradually sank in the west, and the shadows of evening began to fall. We all welcomed the blanket of darkness which provided a natural cover for the surreptitious activities we were about to engage in. The night of June 28, 1943 was totally moonless. The date of the mission had been selected for this reason. When the darkness had totally enveloped us, we turned east to approach the coastline of Sardinia. The deck was alive with activity as the rubber boat was inflated in preparation for the landing. The speed of the boats was reduced, and the command boat with the mission components aboard headed toward land. The other boats, as prearranged, headed north and south for about ten miles to widen the probable alert zone if anyone on shore should suspect our activity.

Soon the land mass loomed ahead. All was in darkness. We were within several hundred yards of the shore. The rubber raft was lowered over the side. One by one the men stepped down onto the raft and disappeared into the darkness. The crew handed down various packages which were placed at the bottom of the raft. The entire operation was made more difficult because of the heavy groundswell that pitched the PT boat and rubber raft about.

The crew on the PT boat was tense, not only because of concern for the brave men who in a moment would be rowing toward the enemy shore, but also because they anticipated that at any moment searchlights would be turned on and a hail of enemy tracers would be fired at us. The gunners on the boat were at the ready in order to give covering fire should the raft be forced to return to the PT boat.

At last everything was ready and the raft started to pull away from us, but no matter how hard the men paddled they seemed to be making no headway. I took a look. Leaning over the side of our boat, I could see that a line had been attached to the raft. I took my commando knife and cut the line. The next time the men dipped their paddles in the water, the boat literally leaped toward shore and was enveloped in the murky darkness. All that was visible was a phosphorescent wake. Lieutenant Passanisi standing beside me whispered jokingly, "You finally put the commando knife to good use."

We waited some twenty minutes, scanning every point of the shore, to observe any sign of enemy activity. There was none. When we had waited sufficient time to give our men the opportunity to gain land and did not observe any enemy activity, Lieutenant Mutty asked me if we could get underway. Looking toward the shore and hearing and seeing nothing unusual, I answered that it was about time. It was important that we get underway under the cover of darkness so that the PT flotilla could be well out of enemy waters by dawn, thus lowering the risk of being discovered by enemy boats or aircraft.

We had been under way only a few moments when Lieutenant Passanisi and I saw a star shell being fired from the interior of the land mass. But we saw no other activity along the shore, and the PT boats kept their rendezvous and headed west for some miles before turning south toward our base at Bone. It was already June 29 and the OSS had conducted its first autonomous Special Operations against Fascist Italy with the aid of the U.S. Navy.

By the early hours of dawn, we were well out of enemy waters and were approaching the Algerian coast when one of the PT boats started running out of fuel. The water had become choppy and the boats were wallowing from side to side, but we managed to throw a line and at reduced speed made it to Bone. I thanked Lieutenant Mutty for the smooth, courageous handling of our first joint mission and promised to see him again within a few days to conduct an operation to infiltrate Sicily. We proceeded rapidly to break up camp and return to Algiers to report on the landing of the "Bathtub" mission and prepare for further landings.

On reporting to Magnol I was told that General Donovan was staying at headquarters and wanted a personal report on the mission.[6] He was alone in the room when I got there, and his first comment to me was, "I see that you haven't gotten your hair cut since you left Washington." He was smiling, and I knew he was just trying to make me feel at ease. I replied that, in truth, I had been so busy I had not had time to get a haircut.

"Sit down," he said, "and tell me about Sardinia. How did it go?"

I gave him a play-by-play account of what had happened and told him that the only sign of an alert was the firing of a star shell from the interior long after the landing had taken place. I observed that I was completely surprised that enemy aircraft had not been sent out to intercept us, especially after we had been spotted by the hydroplane. I attributed this to the fact that we were so far from our own base that the spotter must have surmised we were friendly boats. I told the general that if the coast was guarded in the same fashion on the rest of the island that a landing in force would be feasible and that once such a landing took place, the Sardinians might confirm Emilio Lussu's contention that the island would fall like a ripe plum. I also explained the reasons why the mission was infiltrated in uniform and that delay in delivering the mission would have meant it would have had to be scrubbed.

He concurred that there were a number of viable reasons for landing in uniform and that in the event the mission was captured it could still play a vital role in alerting the enemy in the wrong place and perhaps tie down troops that would be needed elsewhere. General Donovan was obviously very pleased with the report and asked me to amplify my verbal account in writing, pointing out any operational weaknesses that should be corrected. He said he would be around for a few days before going to the Far East, and he promised to see me before departing.

I returned to Club des Pins to spend some time with the men and officers. Tarallo had returned from Cairo with some Italian civilian clothes, but with no valid documents with which to undertake safe undercover operations in enemy territory. During my absence some British officers had been around to see me, but they had left no message and had promised to return as they had urgent and top secret business.

While I had been busy procuring transportation from the Navy and delivering the "Bathtub" mission, a good deal had been going on. On June 11, the island of Pantelleria in the Straits of Sicily had been bombed into submission and had surrendered to the British First Division. The island had been heavily bombed since the end of the Tunisian campaign, and Allied planes had dropped almost 7,000 tons of bombs during 5,200 sorties. With little hope for relief, the admiral commanding Pantelleria decided to surrender. It was the first time an island had been bombed into submission. The next day the nearby island of Lampedusa also surrendered to stop the avalanche of Allied bombs. To me, these events indicated that if we were to do any advance work in Sicily we should start moving immediately. I had hardly reached this conclusion when the phone rang. It was Scamporino who asked me to drive in to headquarters as he had some important matters to discuss with me. I couldn't imagine what it could be about since I had left him only a few hours before and we had exhausted almost all important topics. Nevertheless I met him at Magnol where he asked if I would like to go to Sicily.

I replied jokingly, "Isn't that why we're here?"

I could see that he was serious, and I thought that AFHQ wanted me to land in Sicily to perform some special mission. Scamp explained that "Operation Husky" was on and that Colonel Eddy wanted me to get the men in shape to participate in the Sicilian invasion. Since the time was limited, AFHQ had given orders not to land any mission in Sicily so as not to alert the enemy about the impending invasion. He told me that Eddy himself was to head the OSS contingent and that I would be second in command as chief of operations. Inasmuch as there were no other OSS personnel qualified to undertake operations in Sicily, SI would be constrained to undertake all OSS operational functions. He explained that I was to get the men combat ready with field radios and other special equipment to leave on short notice when Colonel Eddy was given the final orders.

I was saddened that lack of transport and operational support had deprived us of the opportunity to contribute our intelligence effort to ease the burden placed on the Allied invasion forces. On the other hand, I was happy to learn that the moment of liberation for Sicily had come and that many of the studies that the Italian Section of OSS had undertaken were being used in the "Husky" invasion plan.

When I asked Scamp if he had been given any inkling as to time, he replied that he had been told only as much as he had conveyed to me, namely, that Colonel Eddy and the OSS contingent were to report to General George S. Patton's headquarters at U.S. Seventh Army which was located in Bizerte. While conversing about Sicily, Scamp suddenly realized that Major Vladimir Peniakoff of British Special Forces had been looking for me to see if we could lend the Second SAS (Special Air Service) Regiment some men for special missions and to borrow some special maps of Sicily which I had brought from Washington. He thought that the major would be at the Club des Pins the next day and that I should try to accommodate him.

After our discussion ended, I saw Colonel Eddy and told him I was going back to camp and start getting ready. Fortunately, some of the men and officers whom I had recruited and trained in the United States had landed at Casablanca and others were already in the pipeline, because the invasion of Sicily and Italy would surely make great demands on OSS manpower.

Early the next morning Major Peniakoff was at the door asking for me. The major, a stocky middle-aged man, had fought in the North African desert with a special unit he commanded. This unit fought behind the Axis lines, often disrupting enemy traffic and blowing up fuel supplies and ammunition dumps. He was undertaking a special mission with the Second Regiment and was looking for personnel to guide this special RAF unit in both Sicilian and Sardinian missions. I turned over to Peniakoff a set of maps I had found in the Congressional Library. It pinpointed every cavern and cave in Sicily. The original map was from 1859 and had been printed in Great Britain. History was coming full circle. I also turned over to him old admiralty charts on which were drawn the profiles of both the Sicilian and Sardinian coastlines as they looked from out at sea. Peniakoff pressed for more. He wanted to borrow a couple of men, and I finally agreed to lend him Jasper Salerno and Primo

Timpanaro, both of whom spoke Italian as well as several dialects fluently. Timpanaro was a veteran of the Spanish Civil War in which he had used the nom de guerre "Louis Trunk," whereas Salerno had migrated to Detroit from Sicily only a few years before the war. At this early stage of Allied offensive operations, it was difficult to gather intelligence about Italy and Germany. Men risked their lives for mere bits of information. Submarines, motor torpedo boats, as well as airplanes with their respective crews, were placed in extreme jeopardy in order to obtain military, industrial and political intelligence. Peniakoff left my office in a happy frame of mind, carting off a bagful of maps and charts and assured of the loan of two key men. The two had to be convinced of the importance of the mission, as they did not relish being loaned to the British.

During the day we could see lumbering convoys of Liberty ships, LSTs, and warships, trailed by silvery barrage balloons, steaming eastward in the Mediterranean. It presented the rather incongruous image of an endless naval parade which I thought must arouse the interest of any spectator. I also thought the time for "Husky" must fast be approaching, and so I started packing and altering long-term plans in favor of improvisation. For the first time, OSS was being tested by being attached to an operating army.

Without doubt, General Eisenhower and General Mark Clark had a high opinion of the OSS, but the middle-level staffs of the Seventh Army had little faith in this new-fangled organization which threatened to disrupt operational normalcy in order to replace it with strange, unorthodox procedures.

On July 8, the SI Detachment that was to be attached to Seventh Army (Rear) left Algiers for Bizerte. The detachment consisted of enlisted men, Captain Frank Tarallo, and Second Lieutenant Corvo under the command of Colonel Eddy. The equipment included a small field radio station code named Garibaldi (in honor of the liberator of Sicily), three field SSTR-1s, and civilian clothes and documents. None of the personnel had been trained to do combat intelligence under battlefield conditions, and the detachment had not been assigned any particular mission, either by OSS or the Seventh Army headquarters. I had my own ideas as to what should be done once we landed in Sicily, but I kept my counsel and waited for events to develop.

Our convoy traveled along roads which by now had become familiar to me. I drove the lead jeep with Colonel Eddy sitting on my right. Eddy's right leg had been practically shot off in the Battle of Belleau Woods during World War I. He had a habit of dangling his leg outside the jeep, which made me a little nervous because I was afraid an accident might shear it off. As it was not my place to lecture him, I compromised by driving a little bit more carefully, which was difficult in view of the twists and turns of the Atlas Mountain roads. Bill Eddy was one of the outstanding American Arabists and had played a leading role in engineering the North African landing. He was assisted by a handful of capable men who operated under diplomatic cover. They had won the respect of General Clark, who had been secretly landed in North Africa from a submarine in order to make the final arrangements for the "Torch" landing.

As we drove to Bizerte, we occasionally stopped at villages along the highway. Eddy would get out of the jeep, walking around to exercise his leg and swapping stories with some elderly villager or talking to the children. At nightfall we pitched camp outside one of the villages and took turns securing the tents and vehicles from possible thievery by the natives who seemed to be ever ready to appropriate even the most worthless trinket. Their abject poverty was undoubtedly one of the main reasons for their rapacity but then they also had a centuries-old reputation as jackals of the battlefield, a reputation that had been upheld as recently as the U.S. retreat at Kasserine Pass.

Chapter 7

All Aboard for Sicily

Next morning (July 9) we got an early start in order to drive straight to Bizerte where the Seventh Army Headquarters was embarking for the invasion of Sicily. Other units were being loaded from other Algerian and Tunisian ports. We arrived in early afternoon and set up camp on a hill overlooking Lake Bizerte. Colonel Eddy and I reported to headquarters in order to be assigned shipboard transportation. We found that the first-wave troops had already embarked and were on their way and that we had been assigned for D plus 4 aboard an LST that would carry all vehicles and supplies. When I gave Colonel Eddy an incredulous look, he said he would talk to General Lyman Lemnitzer who was in charge of AFHQ (Rear).

Troops were bivouacked on all sides of the lake and it was difficult to find the way, but we finally found General Lemnitzer's headquarters. Since Colonel Eddy was an old friend, we were immediately ushered in to see the general. Unfortunately, the boarding assignments had already been made and it would be too difficult to make any changes at this stage of the game. The first troops were scheduled to hit the beaches in a few hours, and the boats would be coming back again to load up with supplies and reinforcements. We were tremendously disappointed because it meant that we would be delayed in getting OSS operations underway and we would have to adjust to the intelligence needs of the front-line units.

It was incomprehensible to me that the OSS should have been given such meager information about both the planning and execution of the invasion of Sicily. It was particularly difficult to understand in view of the fact that we had the only pool of manpower and expertise in the U.S.

Army which was familiar with both the language and terrain and that our planning was so advanced. There was little to be done except to make up for lost time once we landed in Sicily. We drove back to the temporary camp and spent the night half dozing through the repeated air alerts.

Lake Bizerte was filled with a variety of ships. Some were loaded and getting ready to leave, while others were waiting to be loaded from lighters at the first light of dawn on July 10. When the air raid alert sounded, all the ships on the lake created a babble of sounds with their steam whistles which seemed to harmonize in a strange, hair-raising dissonance when heard from a distance.

The next morning the news of the invasion quickly spread among the GIs who were getting ready to embark. The news was alternately reported as good and bad and rumors were circulating with the speed of lightning. There was word of a disaster to the Eighty-second Airborne, of strong enemy resistance against the First Infantry Division at Gela. As the day progressed and ships returned, we started to piece together the plight of the Eighty-second and its tragic story as many of the planes carrying paratroopers had been shot down by friendly anti-aircraft fire from the invasion armada and from the troops at the beachhead who mistook our planes for enemy aircraft.

We fretted with great impatience at being left behind, aware that we could be performing valuable services for the front-line troops on Sicily. Unable to stay still, later in the day I drove to AFHQ where I ran into Colonel David Bruce who had come down from London to see the show. However, he told me that he had been unable to get clearance to go to Sicily, and he indicated that Colonel Eddy was not keen about his visit. Bruce, commander of all OSS forces in the United Kingdom, wanted to get a feel of the amphibious and intelligence problems connected with the invasion in preparation for the eventual cross-Channel invasion of Europe.[1] He had been one of the staunchest supporters of Italian SI and had made it possible for me to do most of the groundwork in preparation for the Italian campaign. A man of high social position and influence, he was nevertheless quiet and unassuming—though firm in his principles and beliefs.

I told Bruce that once our unit had landed I would talk to Eddy and ask him to have Seventh Army headquarters authorize his visit to the beachhead. Several days later, the Seventh Army sent out a signal approving his visit and I saw him at First Division CP (Command Post) with General Terry Allen.

July 10 seemed interminably long as I returned to camp and joined Tarallo and the men. Colonel Eddy was still out visiting with some of his friends at Seventh Army headquarters. Everyone was anxious to get started regardless of the mixed news from Sicily and the reported attacks by enemy bombers in the Gulf of Gela. We estimated that we would not go on board until the next day and would probably land on July 12.

When the colonel returned, he confirmed the shooting down of a large number of our C-47s carrying the men of General Matthew Ridgeway's division.[2] He also reported that lively fighting was going on in the Plain of Gela where German and Italian troops were counterattacking.

Night fell on the huge encampment of U.S. troops that awaited transportation for the beaches of Sicily — time enough to experience the uncertainties which every soldier who faces the unknown feels in his innermost being.

For security reasons a complete blackout was imposed as though the light of a single match or cigarette would bring the wrath of the Luftwaffe on our heads or as though the enemy needed a light from us to find his way to the huge lake. The enemy did not keep us waiting long. At about midnight the sirens and ships' whistles wailed their strange penetrating wail as the first enemy plane dropped flares. This went on intermittently throughout the night, until at the first light of dawn, everything suddenly quieted down.

On the afternoon of July 13, our waiting period was over as we were alerted to embark an LST which had just returned from Sicily. Captain Tarallo had taken our vehicles to be especially greased for the landing and to have a rubber tube attached to the exhaust pipe. Every vehicle had to be waterproofed and then lined up to be embarked.

It was late afternoon of July 13 when Colonel Eddy and I finally went on board. Our vehicles were placed on deck, and the officers were assigned bunks in a small cabin. The heat and humidity had become oppressive. There was little or nothing to do. Then the LST backed its way from the shore and found its place in a line of ships which was forming to join a convoy gathering outside of the port. We started moving forward, and the pennants that were flying on the mast started to flap smartly in the wind created by the ship's speed. We sailed through the ship's channel that led from the lake to the open Mediterranean, and then we could see the large convoy shaping up with its tiny escorts, destroyers, Liberty ships, and, in the distance, the hulking grey shadows of several cruisers.

In contrast to the placid waters of the lake, the Mediterranean was choppy and the almost flat-bottomed LST yawed generously, much to the dismay of many of the men. We were amply supplied with rations, but the Navy crews provided us with hot coffee which everyone welcomed. Soon darkness enveloped the slow-moving armada which was following what seemed to us an erratic course. Colonel Eddy spent a good part of the time sitting with us on the jeep. The next vehicle to us contained part of a PWB team that included Colonel John Wittaker and Lieutenant Archimedes Patti, two of our OSS people who were working with the Psychological Warfare Branch. John, the *New York Times* correspondent to Rome prior to the war, knew and appreciated the Italian situation. Patti spoke Italian and Sicilian well, having come from a family that was deeply rooted in Sicily.

The ships in the convoy plowed through the dark waters, hugging the Tunisian coastline. Occasionally, the semaphores communicated in Morse code and shattered the blackness of the night. In the distance we could see the red and green lights on the ships ahead of us and behind the wake of our ship. The phosphorescence of the water was alarming and left a trail which the enemy could easily follow if he was conducting a recce mission. The line of ships then merged with one of the other convoys and struck out for the open sea in an easterly direction toward Malta and then, after some hours, turned northward toward the coastline of southern Sicily.

The sea was choppy, and a good stiff breeze was blowing through the Sicilian channel. Most of the men were so tired that despite their excitement they were falling asleep in their vehicles. Knowing that enemy airfields were only a stone's throw from us, I expected that at any moment dive bombers would plummet down on us to at least break up the continuity of the convoy that was bringing reinforcements to take over the island. As the hours passed, I began to believe they were waiting for sunlight. When dawn broke in the east, I looked out over the expanse of water and the convoy as it edged closer to Sicily. The water was turbulent yellowish-green. Then, in the distance, the coastline of Sicily became visible; the gun turrets on the LST immediately went on alert; the line of ships divided as if by magic into three single files. Shadows of warships patrolled the area and protectively herded the transports toward land.

The approach to the beach was slow as one by one the ships disgorged their human and mechanical cargoes on the beach where the beachmasters worked hard at their orderly dispersion. Now we were close enough to see the activity taking place along the beach. Immediately beyond the beach ran the railway line, and the Army Engineers had pressed into service a steam engine that was pulling a few flat cars back and forth. Lines of vehicles were coming and going to the beach, picking up supplies to deliver inland to the troops trying to expand the perimeter of penetration only a few miles down the road.

Lines of infantrymen were moving inland from the beach and disappearing over the ridge. As they moved forward in single file, they resembled columns of warrior ants on the march. The engineers had lashed pontoons to which the ships edged up to unload their cargo. Some LSTs snuggled right up to the beach where they lowered their ramps and the vehicles were driven directly on shore. In the background loomed the foothills of formidable mountains that had been fortified with gun emplacements. A series of fortifications had been built on the beaches and along the coastal highway.

Our landing area was west of Gela which had been assigned to the "Dime Task Force" under the command of Admiral Hall. It was in this area that the First Infantry Division and Darby's First and Fourth Ranger Battalions had landed; the front was only a few miles up the road. Some of the men in our unit who had fled Italy after the advent of Fascist oppression displayed understandable emotion when they again set foot on liberated Italian soil. They broke forth in popular political songs of the early 1920s.

By the time we got to land, it was already noon. We were directed to a bivouac area just beyond the beach and told that we would spend the night there. The beachmaster did not know exactly where the Seventh Army headquarters was located. He thought they might be located somewhere around Licata, an ancient town a few miles to the west. He explained that the military situation was rather fluid and that at one point panzers of the Herman Goering Division and Italian tanks had attempted to take the initiative, but artillery fire from the ships and field artillery recently landed had stopped them just short of the beachhead.

During the entire morning there was no sign of enemy air activity, and the ships continued to unload men and cargo on the beach in a leisurely fashion. The day was blistering hot and the vehicles, as they moved along the roads, kicked up columns of fine powdery white dust which permeated everything. Long columns of German and Italian prisoners were being marched down to the beach and loaded on empty vessels returning to Tunisian and Algerian ports. There was no room yet to set up any large prisoner-of-war camp in Sicily. It was easier to transship them in the empty ships so that they would not constitute a logistics problem for the Army. This part of Sicily seemed to be an extension of North Africa because the climate, terrain, and vegetation were almost the same and there were no real metropolitan centers.

Colonel Eddy suggested that we pick out a spot to bed down while it was still light. In the morning we could report to G-2 at Patton's headquarters to pick up our assignment and find a place to set up our headquarters.

We moved up forward and found a hillock that was not occupied, parked the vehicles, and ate some C rations. By now it was getting dark, and the men talked about the work that needed to be done. Colonel Eddy set his bedroll nearby from which he extracted a bottle of whiskey he had brought along. He offered me and Tarallo a drink but we both declined; during the next few hours he managed to put a sizable dent in it.

Darkness fell over the area, and the silence was interrupted only by the intermittent sound of counter battery fire and the roseate flashes as the firing increased in intensity. We knew that the German and Italian troops had given a good account of themselves in Gela on D-Day, launching a tank attack that for a while seemed to be endangering the beachhead. We also knew that the U.S. Third Division under General Lucian T. Truscott had landed on the beaches east and west of Licata and were reported making good progress toward Palma.

The night of July 14 seemed interminably long. In the early hours the sounds of artillery fire died down, and the encampment came alive with the sound of the GIs who were facing up to their first day on the firing line. It was still early when our convoy picked its way to the highway and headed west toward Licata and Patton's headquarters. On the road I saw in the distance what appeared to be an oasis of green pine and palm trees dominated by the battlements of the ancient Falconara Castle. The Bordonaro family of Palermo owned the castle and maintained it as an historic showpiece. When we drove into the courtyard of the castle, the caretaker came running out to find out what was happening. I asked him the whereabouts of Baron Bordonaro. He was so surprised that I should know the name of the owner and that I was speaking to him in Sicilian that he feared something unpleasant was about to happen. I calmed him down by assuring him we were really Americans, and he took me on a tour of the castle.

From the battlements of the castle one could see the Sicilian coastline for miles in either direction. The castle jutted out into the water on a little peninsula. The small cove to the east had been a defense point with several machine gun emplacements surrounded by barbed wire. Nearby were some buildings in which the Italian troops that were part of a coastal division had been quartered. In their precipitous haste to get away, the men had left their few miserable possessions behind, including uniforms and helmets. The moment I looked at the helmets and clothing I knew that the campaign in Sicily would be of short duration. The helmets were relics from World War I, and the clothing was of almost the same vintage.

The caretaker explained that the troops were quartered in these buildings and did not have any disinfectants. The officer in command of the company had been quartered in the castle, and after a few moments of resistance, some of the men had fled and some had been taken prisoner.

From the caretaker I determined that the unit was part of the 207th Coastal Division which was supposed to defend this sector of the Sicilian coastline. The men and officers of this division were members of older military classes which had been pressed into service, and they were mostly from Sicily.

The caretaker, a man in his late forties, had worked for the Bordonaro family for many years. In their absence he was the undisputed master of the place and of the staff of five or six men and women who lived in the servants quarters in nearby buildings. I decided to requisition the castle and set up the first OSS headquarters in Italy. I told the caretaker to lock up anything of value because we would be moving in immediately.

Leaving Captain Tarallo in charge, Colonel Eddy and I drove off to report to General Patton's headquarters to see about our assignments as well as any incoming messages from OSS headquarters in Washington or Algiers. I reminded Colonel Eddy to clear passage for David Bruce who was waiting at Bizerte and to inquire as to Donovan's whereabouts. We already knew that he had boarded the command ship just before the invasion.

The road to Licata ran alongside the shoreline almost directly west, and part of the city jutted out into the sea. It was in these waters that in 249 B.C. the Roman fleet under Attilus Regulus defeated the Carthaginian fleet in one of the classic battles of the ancient world and opened the way for the Roman domination of the Mediterranean. As we approached the city, which had been taken only several days earlier by troops of the Third U.S. Infantry Division and U.S. Rangers, we noted that the people were attempting to return to some semblance of normalcy.

Everything looked dusty and neglected. The port was used to ship out Sicily's sulphur production and there were a number of refineries that produced large, rectangular blocks of bright yellow sulphur transported in the familiar horse-drawn, two-wheeled Sicilian carts. The city was also a terminus for mule trains coming from the interior bearing wheat and other goods, and its affinity to some large North African towns could not be debated. Dust seemed to settle everywhere as mules, horses, and military vehicles pulverized the poor roads and broke up the sunbaked topsoil of the fields.

In the square I noted that a barber had opened his doors for business. Several doors away AMGOT (the Allied Military Government) had put its sign up and was ready for customers. I walked over and introduced myself to the officer-in-charge, a major in his early forties. He was a doctor and was busily medicating several children whose legs were full of sores. He looked up, said hello, and went about his business. When he had finished bandaging a little girl's legs, he introduced himself as Dr. Bizzozzero from Waterbury, Connecticut. He was in charge of Colonel Charles Poletti's advance party. Their function was to set up civil affairs for the transitional military government which was to rule all captured territory until a long-term political solution could be worked out.

When I told him I was from Middletown, Connecticut, a bond of friendship immediately developed between us. From his sympathetic treatment of the children, I could see that he had a deep humanitarian commitment to the work he was doing. We promised to keep in touch with one another and to collaborate in the programs to better the lot of the people of Sicily who were lacking almost every necessity of life.

As I passed a barber shop, I was reminded of General Donovan's recommendation to get my hair cut and decided to get it done before going to Patton's headquarters. When I spoke to the barber in Sicilian, he was pleasantly surprised and set to work with gusto. In a few minutes his scissors had done as much work as one of our electric clippers. I paid him five lire with a crisp new AMGOT note. These notes had been printed as occupation currency and were the same size as U.S. paper dollars. The established value was based on 100 lire to the dollar.

After that chore was completed, I met Colonel Eddy and the driver, and we found our way to Army headquarters, where we met with Colonel Oscar Kotch, who was G-2 of the Seventh Army, and some of his staff. When Eddy asked what services were needed the answer given was tactical and strategic intelligence from behind enemy lines. He was informed that this activity should be coordinated with each divisional intelligence unit that would know the immediate situation and needs better than Army headquarters. I made the point that this type of intelligence work required the use of native elements. Accordingly, I suggested that I go to the east coast of Sicily where we could establish contact with a number of my father's friends who could undertake the dangerous missions. Both Colonels Kotch and Eddy agreed, after which Colonel R. E. Cummings, Deputy Chief of Staff, Seventh Army, gave me a letter of presentation to General Bernard Montgomery, Commanding General of the British Eighth Army, asking that in view of my mission I should be allowed maximum freedom of movement in Eighth Army territory.[3]

We asked for news about General Donovan and were told that he was at the First Division area and that they would get word to him that we had set up OSS headquarters at Falconara Castle. In the meanwhile, it was agreed that before I left for the east coast I would visit the front and talk to the intelligence officers of several U.S. divisions on the firing line in order to find out their intelligence needs and see how we could be of help.

I left with Tarallo for the First Division command post, north of Gela on the road to the little village of San Cono. The CP was set up in a little empty country school. When we got there, Tarallo, who had served with the First Division at Fort Devens, Massachusetts, discovered that he already knew many of the officers.

After discussing their intelligence needs, we concluded that there was only a limited field for tactical intelligence. In order to be of assistance, it would be necessary to effect deep penetrations well ahead of the troops whose rapid, forward momentum threatened to overrun the penetration teams, thus pointlessly exposing the men to extreme risk without achieving any of our intelligence goals. We needed to recruit native personnel in order to successfully undertake tactical intelligence missions. Such missions could not be encumbered with radio-transmitting equipment, which would result in quick detection and execution under the rules of war. The information would have to be delivered by courier to the army units that needed it.

Obviously, these operational details should have been worked out weeks in advance. If they had, the OSS unit would have participated in the planning phase of "Husky." The AFHQ's lack of confidence in the OSS was regrettable inasmuch as we had gathered together qualified personnel and detailed information which could have made a tremendous contribution to the military campaign. Through our help, we felt that the errors and pitfalls in the various phases of the "Husky" plan could have been avoided.

One of the primary reasons why the OSS was sidelined may have been the British. Even though "Husky" was an Anglo-American operation, the British dominated the planning staffs and Whitehall wanted to direct and channel the various phases of the first assault on Europe, especially in an area that was considered one of primary British political and economic interest. On the U.S. side, the traditional intelligence services such as G-2, CIC, and the Office of Naval Intelligence (ONI) often displayed open hostility toward the OSS because they did not understand its work and its objectives. Another factor was that, while it was ostensibly under the aegis of the Joint Chiefs of Staff, it was also subservient to the operating theater command or operating army, and ultimately its role depended on the whim and perspicacity of the Army commander and his immediate staff.

The first experience in integrating the work of OSS with an operating army was in the Sicilian campaign, although Professor Carleton Coon had made some efforts in Tunisia with the U.S. Second Corps at the time of the German breakthrough at Kasserine Pass.[4] Carleton and his small group attempted some demolition work and were experimenting with plastic explosives shaped in the form of camel dung. Obviously, no samples of these charges were left in the OSS inventory by the time of the invasion of Sicily, as no one tried to palm off on us this "potent" secret weapon.

We returned to Falconara Castle to review the situation and to see what could be done with the personnel at hand to penetrate the lines ahead of the First U.S. Division. Colonel Eddy was sanguine about Special Operations—commando style—but the SI men had been trained for deep penetration and undercover work. It was obvious that since OSS had been caught short and no SO teams were available to perform in the field, SI would have to improvise. Thus, it became most urgent that I travel to the east coast to recruit personnel with whom I was familiar to undertake this tough job. I decided I would leave the next morning (July 16) and would take a driver and radio man with me.

A little later in the day General Donovan, together with a number of OSS officers who were on their way with him to the Far East, stopped by at Falconara and spent several hours reviewing theater plans with Colonel Eddy and Italian operations with me. The general had visited front-line units and was convinced that, if the Army continued its rapid advance, line infiltration by our agents could not possibly be of much value. He felt that we should nonetheless make every effort to help the Army intelligence people. He also suggested that we keep our eyes open for opportunities to obtain intelligence on Italy and Sardinia for future military operations. We discussed the problems the OSS faced in the field in view of the reluctance of higher headquarters to take advantage of our expertise, and he asked a number of probing questions about possible developments in Italy.

Next, I brought up my plan to recruit native personnel to infiltrate the lines. I advised him that I was going over to the British sector on the east coast where I would contact some of my father's friends who would provide volunteers for the work. Since Colonel Eddy would soon be going back to Algiers, General Donovan suggested that for a while I should work under a senior officer of sufficiently high rank who would handle liaison with higher headquarters while I handled the intelligence operations. When he returned to Algiers, Donovan immediately sent a message to Washington OSS headquarters asking that I be promoted from second lieutenant to captain.

After the general left, Tarallo and I met with Colonel Eddy to plan operations to be undertaken during my brief trip to the Eighth Army zone. I arranged to set up temporary radio communications between Falconara and my vehicle so that we could be in touch with developments. I chose Private Carl Bonmarito, whom I had recruited in Detroit as my driver, and Private Serafin Buta, a radio operator and code clerk, to handle the SSTR-1 agent set which would keep us in touch with Falconara. The signal plans and operating procedures were worked out with Ralph DeHaro, a Navy chief petty officer, who had been placed on temporary duty with Colonel Eddy from Tangiers, and with Charles Groff, an outstanding wireless operator and radio technician.

Early on the morning of July 16 we headed for the east coast on coastal road 115 to Vittoria where we started climbing the hairpin turns of the Hyblean Mountains, the barren, rocky outcrop that dominates southeastern Sicily. As we climbed higher and higher, we looked down on the Gulf of Gela which was teeming with hundreds of ships. What an awesome sight this must have been for the peasants and enemy troops on the morning of the invasion. From this distance the ships resembled toy models. The armada spread out as far as the eye could see.

We kept climbing until we came to a rocky plateau along a road lined with carefully stacked fieldstone fences that could have been put to use by determined defenders. The stone walls served both as pens for a locally famous breed of cattle and as protection against the fierce winds that often swept across the desolate plateau. From time to time in the distance, we could see small groups of men who would scamper as we approached. These were obviously soldiers from the coastal divisions who had made their way to the sanctuary of these mountains to avoid prison camps.

During our drive through this area, we found no evidence of an Allied presence until we finally came to the ancient city of Ragusa, the capital of the province. As we drove through the winding streets the people waved. The British were clearly in control, and we finally stopped at a refueling point for gasoline and water. We inquired if all were quiet in the zone and were told that night skirmishes had been reported along the road that crossed the plateau. It was evident that the small groups that had scattered on our approach could have been enemy troops cut off from their main body during their retreat north.

We talked to a number of *Ragusani* who had congregated in front of the Church of San Giovanni, the cathedral of the city, and they expressed joy at being liberated. We took the time to inquire about the Lupis family, as Joe Lupis, editor of *Il Mondo*, an anti-Fascist magazine published in New York, was a native of the city. We finally found his younger brother Giovanni, to whom I delivered a letter of introduction. After a lengthy talk, we agreed that he could help us by recruiting several middle-aged anti-Fascists who would report for duty at Falconara Castle.

It was already afternoon when we made our way down the winding road that led to Modica, a city dominated by its outstanding baroque architecture and its unique position on a steep Hyblean hillside, at the crest of which was the Cathedral of St. George. From Modica, the road started winding down to the Ionian shore of Sicily to ancient Ispica, from which the sea and luxuriant orange and lemon groves of the coast could be seen. In the distance were Rosolini, Noto and Avola, all cities that had fallen to the Eighth Army in the first few days of the invasion. When we arrived at Avola, we saw British troops camped under some olive groves and stopped to talk to them. The sergeant suggested that we camp nearby for the night and proceed to Syracuse the next morning because many vehicles were attacked by snipers at night and it was still dangerous to travel without a motor convoy in the dark. We took his advice and hunkered down in the jeep in the olive grove surrounded by British infantrymen. Several times shots were exchanged that night, but nobody was disconcerted because they sounded far off.

With the first faint light of dawn, we managed to get a canteen full of warm tea and we hit the road to Syracuse. A couple of miles down the road the sharp volley of rifle fire broke the silence, and we were stopped by an MP, who waved us to the side of the road. Some snipers were at work, and a patrol had been sent out to hunt them down. He cautioned us not to proceed until the skirmish was over. Within half an hour the firing had died down, and we continued on our way to Syracuse.

As we drove toward the city, the terrain flattened out and the military traffic became intensified. The headquarters of the Eighth Army was established in a stylish villa by the sea, but I decided to make a dash for Melilli and Augusta where I knew I could make immediate contact with a number of people who could help out. With each mile we traveled along the coastal road the density of the British forces increased.

The front was only about 30 kilometers to the north, near the town of Lentini. The Germans were reported to have organized a strong line of defense below Lentini in the Plain of Catania, utilizing the ditches and streams that flowed to the Ionian Sea through the flatlands. The British had tried to capture the Primo Sole bridge across the Simeto River through a *coup de main* operation. Although they had attained their objective by surprise, the Eighth Army was held up and failed to reach the beleaguered handful of troops that had taken the bridge.

When we arrived at the town of Priolo, it was still early in the morning. I remembered the area well from my childhood. We started climbing the Hyblean hills towards Melilli, a hill town of some 11,000 people, many of whose relatives had settled in Middletown, Connecticut. As we drove into town, past St. Sebastian's Church, I could see that considerable damage had been done and that a number of buildings had been demolished. There were not too many people walking around so I decided to stop at the most popular bar in the town which was run by Roberto Scamporino, a relative of "Scamp," our Italian SI theater chief. I walked in and called him by his first name, which utterly amazed and alarmed him. When I identified myself, he broke into a happy smile and immediately asked about my father. He could not believe that the little nine-year-old boy who had left Melilli fourteen years before had come back as an American officer. I could hardly restrain him from telling everyone in the bar about it. Finally, I calmed him down and asked him where I could find Reverend Salvatore Fiorilla, the rector of St. Sebastian Cathedral. He pointed to a nearby street and house.

After asking Sam (Serafin Buta) and Carl Bonmarito to wait at the bar, I walked up the steeply inclined steps which followed the upward contour of the hillside. When I got to the house, I knocked on the door and a corpulent woman's face appeared in an upstairs window to see what was happening. I recognized the rector's sister and told her to call her brother. She disappeared and, after a few moments, a head with a crop of short, white hair appeared. I instantly recognized Father Salvatore Fiorilla, an old friend of the family who had maintained such a fierce independence during the two decades of Fascist domination in the country. He looked quizzically at me, not quite comprehending why an enemy soldier speaking Sicilian wanted to see him.

When I finally told him who I was, his head disappeared from view and I could hear him running down the stone steps to open the door. He threw his arms around me in an emotional huge of welcome. He invited me in, and we went into his study while his sister prepared a cup of ersatz coffee which was made of roasted barley and other herbs. He apologized for the poor quality of the coffee, explaining that real coffee had vanished from the market a long time before. The people had learned to do without even the bare necessities of life like soap, sugar, salt, and pepper.

To my inquiries about my father's friends, he provided a complete rundown of their whereabouts. When he expressed surprise at my presence in Melilli, I simply said I was on special assignment to British headquarters, that I would be staying several days, and then would return to Gela and the American sector.

As we talked, he decried the fact that they were under British Army administration. Most of the damage in the town had been inflicted as a result of retreating German tanks. The Colonel Schmaltz group had decided to counterattack on the high ground of Melilli, and the British had called for naval fire support from ships in the Gulf of Augusta, which fired a number of salvos at the town.

Father Fiorilla told me that most of the townspeople left the city at night seeking safety in the open country and in caves. They returned to their homes during the day. He then offered me the use of the parish guest house where traveling preachers were usually housed. I readily accepted because it was one of the few places with modern sanitary facilities.

Having only limited time available, I excused myself and promised to see him later. As I walked back to the cafe, I was met by a large group of acquaintances who had been waiting for me to ask about their relatives in America. They had had no word from them since December 1941 when Mussolini declared war on the United States.

The Town Hall had temporarily been converted into a hospital and I was invited to visit some of the wounded. The conditions I found there were shocking. There were no medicines, and little medical care was offered because the nearest hospital was at Syracuse. The doctor in charge was even out of gauze bandages. Since I had brought a number of emergency medical packages with me, I turned over some of them to the grateful doctor and I promised to speak to the British authorities.

Walking around town, I ran into Sebastian Bongiovanni, a former resident of Hartford who had run a weekly bilingual newspaper there. He had been deported in 1938, having stepped on the toes of the local political boss who dredged up a twenty-year-old charge as a pretext and the Justice Department deported him as a bigamist. Bongiovanni, unable to charm the Italian consular official in Connecticut, was met by the political police upon repatriation in Naples and was quickly pressed into army service in Libya. He had written repeatedly to Senator Danaher asking him to look into his case because his wife and two children still lived in Hartford. I had known Bongiovanni well and was familiar with his case. In fact, his paper was printed in my father's printing plant and he had written several times from Libya asking my help. He had recently been discharged from the army and had returned to Melilli. When the British captured the town, he presented himself to the major in charge who needed an interpreter and was very happy to find someone with such a fluent command of English.

I had no idea he was in Melilli until, to my surprise, I heard him shout my name several times. I turned and quickly recognized the balding, middle-aged Hartford editor. I invited him to join me and promised to do what I could to reunite him and his family once the war was over. Although he wanted to join me, he said, he wanted to stay around Melilli to punish some of the Fascist officials who had mercilessly persecuted him. He provided me with several candidates and promised to meet me in a few days. I left instructions as to my whereabouts should he decide to come.

I spent a good part of the day talking to various contacts, and I selected three persons of the right age and background to take back with me. Sam Buta, our radio operator, had been busy contacting our "Garibaldi" base station at Falconara in order to keep in touch with events. We learned that Tarallo had tried to infiltrate a team but had been thwarted by an enemy barrage. Just before sunset we observed the streets becoming deserted as the people returned to the open country and caves.

We spent the night in the priest's guest room. With no electricity in the room, we ate our "C" rations by candlelight. The men spread their bed rolls on the floor while I took the only bed in the room. Suddenly, at about 12:30 A.M., the British antiaircraft battery located near the church opened fire, and we could hear the motors of enemy aircraft overhead. As I readily surmised, the Germans and Italians were dive bombing the port of Augusta located some 10 kilometers away. They were starting their diving run at the ships in the port at a point directly over our heads. All the ack-ack fire from the ships and batteries was directed at the skies over Melilli, and the lead and shrapnel were coming down like rainfall.

As the enemy bombs fell on Augusta, you could hear the deep sound of the explosions. There were so many ships in the harbor that it was relatively easy to hit a target. Overhead the black night sky was illuminated by the eerie light of slowly descending parachute flares which gave so much light one felt naked. The enemy attack went on as relays of bombers coming from the German airfields near Catania took turns for about two hours. Suddenly, it was all over. The only comfort we could take was that they were not aiming their bombs at us; they were merely using Melilli as the key point to start their dive on Augusta, almost 1,500 feet below us.

In the morning I said goodby to Father Fiorilla and my other friends and started down the mountain road to Augusta. About halfway down I looked up and saw a German fighter plane getting ready to attack us. We stopped the jeep and took cover on the side of the road. But the pilot, perhaps spotting more important quarry, kept right on going. As we drove by the huge dirigible hangar which had become a landmark in the area, we could see that the landscape was pockmarked with bomb craters. The hangar, now empty, had been built during World War I out of cement, and near it had been the headquarters for the hydroplane base. The British had taken over the base and barracks. The entrance to the city, which was across two small bridges and through an ancient 500-year-old Spanish gate, was practically sealed. The damage to the city was widespread as the Germans continued their raids intermittently. The population had been evacuated to a nearby basalt mountain which was full of natural caves and quarry holes. We drove around inquiring about my mother's family, and we finally ran into someone who knew where we could find them.

Finally, we came to a small farmhouse and as our jeep approached, children surrounded us. When I called out my grandmother's name, the children pointed to the house, one of them running ahead to alert the residents. All of them were visibly alarmed at the approach of uniformed strangers, for they imagined the worst: they thought we had come to take away their men, just as the British had done in the first few days of the invasion.

An old white-haired woman with weatherbeaten skin came toward us as though to plead her cause. Although I immediately recognized her, I did not make myself known. She had no idea that I was the grandson who had left for America. As the other people in the farmhouse gradually made their way to the jeep, I recognized my uncle and several cousins, though again I did not hint at my identity. I spoke to them in Sicilian, producing a great deal of relief that someone could understand them. When I asked if they had relatives in the United States, their faces brightened. Even when they mentioned Brooklyn where my aunt lived, I did not tell them who I was. When I finally told them, they were overwhelmed, making the reunion one of the memorable events of my life. We relived that meeting in great detail almost every time we met thereafter.

My cousin "Pep" Catalano immediately set to work to find me a half dozen trusted middle-aged men who could leave right away to join our group. One of the men I chose was a mule driver because I planned to use mules for penetration and movement behind the German lines. One of these groups was to leave immediately from the east coast, work its way through the interior to the Sortino-Vizzini road, then to Caltagirone, and through the First Division lines in the central Gela front. The other three men would leave with me on the morning of July 19 when I expected to get back to the Falconara headquarters.

Sam Buta set up the radio in the jeep to signal the success of our mission and to inform the base of our return, but we failed to establish contact.

During the afternoon, I visited Brucoli and the Costa Saracena where the British had established their front lines near Agnone, below Lentini, and where the Schmaltz Group had recently carried out a brief, if unsuccessful, counterattack. From the heights above Agnone, we could see the Plain of Catania shimmering in the July heat. The movement of trucks and mechanized equipment could only be discerned by rising clouds of dust.

That night we camped outside the farmhouse in Augusta, but hardly had we settled down when the sound of ships' whistles and sirens sounded their alert. All the guns in the area started firing toward the heavens. The people in the farmhouse ran for the trenches which served as shelters. The din of guns and the screeching of bombs as they came hurtling earthward caused the adrenalin to surge. With nowhere to go, Sam, Carl, and I squatted under the imaginary protection of a tree. The attack continued for almost three hours when the pilots must have gotten tired of the marathon; of taking off in relays from airports located only 30 kilometers up the line, loading bombs, and returning to Augusta to dump them. Occasionally, one of the bombers was hit and would come down in a ball of flames on the port of Augusta. These raids had been going on since the British had taken Augusta without the fight they had anticipated.

The "Gela exit group" took off on the morning of July 18 on three mules bearing sacks of grain which, ostensibly, was to be sold to "clients." Their destination was Sortino and Vizzini — slow travel on mules. They were to move back of the German lines, take mental note of strong positions and military conditions along the mountainous terrain to Caltagirone, turn southward, and make their way to Seventh Army headquarters and ask for Lieutenant Corvo.

After they left, we made our way back to Melilli where I met with Bongiovanni. Again I tried to persuade him to come with me. He promised he would join me in a couple of days and he would bring several men with him. I left him some money for expenses and a note identifying him as a civilian attached to our unit. Also at Melilli I learned that Colonel Vittorino Cannata, who had been a close anti-Fascist friend of my father, had been called into active service and was stationed in Palermo. I had a talk with the acting mayor and promised him I would seek funds for Melilli to repair the damage the town had suffered during the naval bombardment.

We returned to Augusta to pick up our three agents and to say goodbye to my grandmother and relatives before returning to the American zone of operations.

On the morning of July 19, we were back at Falconara and after briefing Colonel Eddy, I left for the Forty-fifth Division sector just south at Caltanissetta. I arrived just as the city, which had been seriously bombed from the air, was captured by fast-moving infantry. I immediately headed for the Prefettura building where I seized the files and arrested the agents. After interrogating the men, I turned them over to the military as POWs. Among the documents I picked up were enemy codes and information which would be useful for the penetration of continental Italy.

As I went through the deserted streets of the mountaintop city, I could hear the moans of victims trapped in the ruins. The people and officials, panicked by the bombing, had left in such a hurry that no rescue squads had been organized. Swarms of black flies had infested some of the ruins where bodies were putrefying under the scorching summer sun. The infantry did not have time to help these unlucky souls trapped beneath the ruins. I asked a nearby POW camp for help; meanwhile, some of the returning townspeople and relatives feverishly went to work removing the rubble. The first rescue efforts were at last underway.

As we left with a jeep full of vital records, we ran into a group of senior Italian officers who wanted to surrender. The ranking officer was an ancient Reserve Colonel Pagano from Syracuse who was in charge of the area's food stores. The group was waving a dirty white pillowcase tied to the end of a stick. Looking over the group, I suggested they open the storehouse and make the food available to the people who looked emaciated from their long period of privation. I also informed Pagano that after he opened the storehouse I did not want to know what happened to him and his staff. We took their weapons, and they opened the storehouse, which soon became a hive of activity as the hungry people shouldered sacks of flour, salt, sugar, and other foods they hadn't been able to buy since the beginning of the war.

On this same day (July 19) our base radio station ("Garibaldi") started its regular contacts with OSS headquarters ("Yankee"). From that point on, Ralph DeHaro, our expert cryptographer, kept a record of the most important communications. The first series of messages sent to Scamp (whose code name was Maxim) outlined our situation:

Rapidity of Sicilian campaign has nulled the value of infiltration and makes it almost impossible. One team has been sent out. Imperative you send eight teams as soon as possible. "LaPaz" radio transmitter must stay at Bone. Have met with lawyers whose names have been on our list a long time.

Delivery by PT boat to western sector is no longer necessary as teams are urgently needed here. It is possible for us to deliver a letter to Rome. Have made contact with underground groups here and they are mostly professionals who have been meeting in Palermo. Among them are a few well known friends.

Due to speed of the campaign here our operations are limited in scope and General Donovan wants us to prepare a full-scale operation against continental Italy. I personally arrested Prefect and Questore of Caltanissetta Province; also seventy agents who are undergoing interrogation. Have valuable intelligence that should facilitate our operations in Italy. Vital you come at once to take charge as I'll be busy with operations.[5]

On the following day, July 20, the first message was received from "Yankee." The message was from Arthur Roseborough to David Bruce: "Donovan here but leaving 22nd. Suggest you return here immediately."

Eddy answered: "Re yr No. 1. Arthur from Eddy. Bruce left today by plane for Algiers."

The early day-to-day communications log between the Army detachment and OSS Algiers reveals the direction in which Donovan tried to propel the organization's theater command. He wanted to expand the scope of OSS field operations to include as many branches as possible. It was obvious that Donovan did not realize how far the other branches lagged behind Italian SI in state of preparation. We were the only ones with a pool of manpower and a set of plans on the U.S. side of AFHQ. We had lent the British SAS men, charts, and maps. Despite our strict intelligence training, we were now being asked to do special operations work because Colonel Eddy was gung ho and was anxious to perform a service for the Seventh Army.

Until its final phase in northeastern Sicily, the campaign had moved too swiftly for us to mount an effective tactical intelligence operation on foot or on mule. Donovan appreciated the military situation, and his parting words to me were to plan for the invasion of Italy while attempting to assist the Seventh Army with its intelligence problems.

On July 21 he directed Rudy Winnacker, the R & A AFHQ representative, and Lieutenant Colonel Guido Pantaleoni, an outstanding New York lawyer, together with four teams of men and communications equipment, to proceed to Sicily. Eddy accordingly asked for Seventh Army permission. Donovan also directed the X-2 representative, Captain Holcomb, to proceed to Sicily once Patton's headquarters granted permission to operate within its jurisdiction.

Captain Holcomb, a Marine who had been wounded in the Pacific and whose father was commandant of the Marine Corps, arrived accompanied by Angelo Lanza, a professor at Connecticut College for Women. He was related to the Trabias of Palermo, an old noble family which owned many of Sicily's mineral rights. Lanza's wife, Frances, worked for the Justice Department in Washington; I had met her through Dale MacAdoo during a luncheon break at the Trianon.

At this time, the western flank of the Seventh Army had greatly expanded its bulge into Sicily, with General Lucian Truscott's men capturing Agrigento. The citadel of Enna, the highest point in central Sicily, was enveloped by U.S. and Canadian forces. It became evident that the efforts of our "Gela exit group" must have failed because of the rapidity of the Allied advances. (This fact was later confirmed when the leader of the team reported to our Palermo headquarters.)

We moved OSS headquarters to a villa in Agrigento which was located on the crown of a hill. From Agrigento we prepared several teams that attempted to penetrate the lines with horsedrawn carts. The infiltration usually took place at night. By morning, the Germans had pulled out of their forward positions, and our infantry would overrun our missions.

Being shorthanded and working with CIC, AMGOT, and the front-line intelligence units took its toll on the personnel. I was stricken with an unusually high temperature and they rushed me to an evacuation hospital where I refused to be evacuated. I lay on a stretcher for several days in the oppressively hot hospital tent. Wounded men from the front were brought in, patched up, and evacuated to more comfortable and better equipped facilities in North Africa. Some of the wounded were in such pitiful condition that the medics could do little for them. After several days my driver stopped by, and I managed to talk my way out of being evacuated. While I was in the field hospital, Palermo fell and our headquarters were set up in Villa Maggiore, a two-story structure surrounded by a high wall and located in a very poor section of the city. Scamp and Rudy Winnacker had finally arrived, and twelve men and officers were on their way to join us. The PT base was making plans to transfer its activities from North Africa to the port of Palermo. It finally appeared that we were putting the show together.

After Colonel Eddy returned to his command post in Algiers, the section started to perform some of the functions that had been neglected by chasing after the needs of front-line units. OSS intelligence was not supposed to perform shock troop or engineering functions; rather, its mission was to collect secret intelligence in an intelligent manner.

Rudy Winnacker was assigned two of our men to help with his R & A work.[6] Attorney Nick Olds, one of the men I had recruited in Detroit, became his assistant. Private Charles Moia helped Rudy communicate with contacts at the University of Palermo to translate many of the documents that had fallen into our hands.

Meetings were held daily with the Seventh Army, G-2, and CIC, and a liaison was established with Colonel Poletti and Major Bizzozzero at AMGOT. Training exercises were started with Barnes' PT squadron, and operational plans were made to land agents on the Italian coast.

Then it happened. On July 25, the people of Palermo turned out en masse to celebrate the fall of Benito Mussolini who had been arrested and replaced by Marshal Pietro Badoglio. The bells of the city pealed as they did during the historical "Vespers," and the people joyously danced in the streets, believing the war was coming to an end. But we knew differently.

Chapter 8

The Palermo Station

For a number of days we had been receiving messages regarding a special mission which General Donovan and Secretary of the Navy Knox had sanctioned. This mission had been the subject of Scamporino's circumspect inquiry of Major Adams, British SIS, about a certain Admiral Girosi. Although we had received only sketchy background information on the admiral from "Broadway," we were still pursuing the subject. A number of radio messages had come in to secure Seventh Army approval for transportation to Sicily for John Shaheen, Mike Burke, and Captain Hayes of the U.S. Navy in order to undertake this mission.

These messages had become more urgent and stressed the importance of the operation codenamed "McGreggor," the principal aim of which was to take Italy out of the war through Admiral Massimo Girosi, who was, as yet, unaware of the effort. "McGreggor" was the brainchild of the admiral's brother, Marcello Girosi, who lived in New York and was now in North Africa with John Shaheen, head of the mission. Their immediate problem was how to contact the Admiral and deliver a letter to him.

Attempts at contact were made through two other channels: through Allen Dulles in Switzerland and through an official of the Ankara Italian Diplomatic Mission.[1] Neither effort was successful, and it was apparent that delivery could only be made by landing an agent along the coast. At the same time, pressure was increasing for us to carry out a commando-type operation to cut the northern coast road at the rear of the retreating German troops. This request had originally been made to Colonel Eddy, who, on July 22, had radioed Scamp and Colonel David King in Algiers to see whether they could put such a team together. Lieutenant Colonel

Guido Pantaleoni, the recently arrived SO representative awaiting authorization to proceed to Palermo, indicated that he would like to lead the mission with a team consisting of SI people and rangers, but he needed Army permission to come to Sicily.

Within a few days, the Seventh Army finally provided the authority for Pantaleoni and other OSS personnel waiting at Bone and Bizerte to proceed to Sicily. These men had been waiting to move forward, but since procedures were so complicated, it took ten days or longer to obtain the necessary orders. Meanwhile, personnel needed for vital operations requested through Patton's headquarters remained blocked at various ports in Algeria and Tunisia by red tape created by the same headquarters that was requesting the service.

As the month of July was ending, all of the OSS's attention was riveted on the events taking place in Palermo where the organization was undergoing the first practical test to try its theories about intelligence and unorthodox warfare. These efforts would be hampered by the rigid discipline imposed by the command of the Seventh Army.

The arrival of Guido Pantaleoni, John Shaheen, Mike Burke, Henry Ringling North (who was designated as our finance officer), several officers, and a group of specialized enlisted men augmented not only our strength, but also our problems. Scamp's presence allowed me to spend some time at the front lines where I could examine the problems of combat intelligence at first hand and where I could establish a personal rapport with the divisional intelligence officers. Throughout this period I was suffering recurrent bouts of high temperatures which the medics failed to diagnose and which on several occasions forced my hospitalization. These bouts with fever also brought on excruciating stomach pains. My health deteriorated so greatly that they recommended I be sent back to the United States where facilities existed for diagnosis. But I refused to be sent home.

The Navy PT squadron command was established in the building of the Capitaneria di Porto of Palermo at the exit of the quaint horseshoe-shaped Cala. The development of an excellent relationship with the men and officers of the squadron gave OSS its first true operational independence and allowed us to roam the lower Tyrrhenian Sea almost at will.

Villa Maggiore became a beehive of activity. Communications were placed in the capable hands of Sergeant Charles Groff, who worked tirelessly around the clock, training personnel and keeping us in touch with Algiers which relayed radio traffic from Washington, London, Berne, and Cairo. This radio traffic included administrative messages as well as operational transmissions. All the traffic had to be coded and decoded by Navy Chief Rafael DeHaro, who, prior to the war, had served in the secretariat of Vice President Henry Wallace.

Rudy Winnacker and the R & A Washington staff saw the possibilities of an expanded role for their objectives. The presence of the X-2 field team in Palermo caused the first full-blown confrontation between OSS and CIC, which claimed sole jurisdiction in the field of counterespionage. Only the fact that SI was providing a good deal of assistance to CIC saved the day and made possible the adoption of a procedural relationship. Even ISLD (British SIS) got into the act by requesting our assistance for one of its missions, "Operation Sunshine," to be landed along the coast of Calabria. This help was delivered in due course, courtesy of Barnes' PT boats.

During this period we began to transmit battle order information covering all Italian forces in Italy, Sardinia, Corsica, southern France, and the Balkans. We produced highly valued intelligence about the Italian generals in command of divisions, army corps and geographic sectors; their morale; their political loyalty to king or Fascism; and the general condition of their armaments. The information was documented from the dossiers provided by an anti-Fascist Lieutenant Colonel who commanded the 103rd Coastal Battalion at Cefalu and whom I had brought back as a prisoner of war from one of my trips to the front. The colonel also saved an eight-page intelligence bulletin and an analysis of the impending Allied invasion of Sicily. Predicting the date of the landings and the participating units, the Servizio Informazioni Militare report, circulated among the ranking officers, was so accurate that it amazed AFHQ; it clearly indicated the broad extent of the Italian intelligence-gathering capability in North Africa even after the collapse of Axis resistance.

July 31 brought two new developments when Eddy advised Scamp that he was assigning part of our personnel to the OSS Fifth Army unit, which was being organized under the direction of Donald Downes.[2] Donald was one of the early COI/OSS operators in Washington who was later involved in operations against Franco Spain. These operations, carried out from North Africa, made use of former Spanish Republic soldiers whom he much admired. When this operation was discovered, it ended disastrously for the OSS "Banana" team.[3] (Many of the men were killed in a firefight with Franco's police.) The result was a donnybrook between OSS and the State Department.

During the same day the first message from "Bathtub" was received by Algiers and relayed to Garibaldi. Though no "alert signal" was transmitted, we correctly speculated that "Chock" Taquay was transmitting under duress. We therefore decided to "play the game" as long as possible in order to save the members of the mission. We began transmitting a series of queries about battle orders of Axis troops, fortifications, air strength, troop morale, and the possible organization of D-Day reception committees on Sardinia. We urged them to pledge money in the name of the U.S. government in order to insure the continuity of contacts, and we finally advised caution, adding that we could safely get to them if necessary.

That same day, Donovan, in answer to a radio message from Shaheen, pointed out that even though Mussolini had been overthrown, the "McGreggor" plan scenario need not change. The main objective still remained to get Italy out of the war, and this objective was to be pursued. Accordingly, we would have to make an effort to land an agent who could make his way to Rome, deliver the letter to Admiral Girosi, and wait to be exfiltrated by sea to a rendezvous at a prearranged date and time.

In the meantime, a measure of coordination with OSS Switzerland was necessary, and instructions were sent for the agents to meet at the Hotel Reale on Via XX Settembre to coordinate their efforts. Our agent was to wait every morning at 10:00 until August 20. If no contact had been made by that date, arrangements for the exfiltration along the coast would get underway. A number of landing exercises were staged at the Gulf of Castellamare, west of Palermo, in which Johnny Shaheen and his group participated. Included in the group was Joe Savoldi, Notre Dame football great, Mike Burke, and Marcello Girosi.

The operation of the PT squadron was under the control of Commander-in-Chief—Mediterranean (CINCMED), and in early August, Admiral Sir Andrew Brown Cunningham determined that no PT operations were to penetrate waters north of 38° 40'.[4] This was operationally restrictive and hampered any effort to land our agent on the coastline near Rome. It was therefore decided to land the agent, a youthful former Italian soldier named Domenico, along the Calabrian coast near Cape Vaticano. Preparations went ahead for the mission.

In early August, as the German and Italian forces shortened their combat lines in northeastern Sicily in an effort to prepare for the evacuation of the island, I decided to spend some time reconnoitering the front lines around Capizzi, Cerami, and Troina, where the U.S. First Infantry was finding the going hard because of the easily defensible mountain terrain. All plans had been abandoned to put an augmented mission ashore to cut the coast road (No. 113) behind the German lines, and we were examining the feasibility of infiltrating a team over land to secure information about enemy fortifications and strong points.

On my return to Palermo, Guido Panteleoni pleaded for the chance to head the team inasmuch as he expected to lead the French show and he needed experience. I acquiesced, spending a number of hours briefing him and going over the maps of the terrain. Then I assigned four enlisted men and two civilians to him, cautioning him, under no circumstances, to operate in civilian clothes.

On August 3, the penetration team left Palermo and spent the night in the town of Petralia Sottana.[5] The next day the group moved to Nicosia, where they bought two mules and were given two more by the U.S. commander in the town. From this point they proceeded to the mountain town of Capizzi, which is high in the Nebrodi Mountains. From there they made their way to the command post of the First Division which was attacking the German stronghold that was fiercely defending the area to cover the German withdrawal from Sicily.

Private Anthony Ribarich, who played one of the leading roles in the operation, traced the progress of the mission in his report when he finally got back to headquarters, after escaping from the Germans:

On Friday, August 6th, we made our way to Mt. Battaglia and without incident proceeded to Mt. Finocchio, where we spent the night. On Saturday morning, after having asked several local peasants who knew the area to guide us, we put on civilian clothes over our uniforms.[6]

We started crossing enemy lines at Acquarossa (Passo dei Tre) and in order not to be too conspicuous to the enemy patrols, we decided to split into three sections. The first group, which included Treglia, DeAngelis and one guide with a mule carrying a part of the radio, preceded the second group by forty-five minutes; the second group with Pantaleoni, Buta and Ribarich and a mule carrying the radio was led by guide; the third group which included two civilians and two mules remained at Acquarossa to wait for the return of the first guide who was to pick them up.

After a half hour of walking on the trail we came upon an Italian army sergeant who was going in our direction. He asked me if I would allow him to place his pack and rifle on the mule and I told him yes. As we walked, I realized the great danger that lay ahead of us if we continued in the company of the sergeant and was able to get the Colonel and Buta to slow down and put some distance between us. Gradually they got the mule, sergeant and guide some three hundred yards ahead of us and at a bend in the road we lost sight of them. The Colonel asked me to go and look for them as I was the only one in the group who could speak Italian. A hundred yards ahead I accidentally stepped on a mine which exploded and I was wounded on the back of my neck. This was about ten a.m. and I returned to the colonel and Buta who gave me first aid.

We continued to move ahead until we decided to hide in a gully and wait for the third segment of the mission that we had left behind at Acquarossa.

After almost two hours I saw a German patrol guided by a civilian (which was also seen by the third segment of the mission). I hardly had time to alert my teammates before the enemy saw us, shouted orders to surrender and then began firing at us. Considering our situation, we decided to get rid of our civilian clothing which we had put on over our uniforms. I unloaded my pistol at the civilian whom I am certain I hit. The exchange of fire lasted about twenty minutes. We were only armed with 45's while the enemy was using hand grenades, rifles and machine guns. Buta was wounded in the spinal area and the colonel, I believe, was wounded on one leg. When it became obvious that any further resistance would be useless, the colonel decided to surrender.

Disobeying the order, though wounded in several places, I rolled down the hillside chewing part of the communications code that I was carrying. While running away I exploded another land mine. I heard for the last time the colonel's voice as he was saying to the enemy that his group included Sergeant Buta and Sergeant Ribarich, thus promoting me under battle conditions. I had barely time to hide our civilian clothing and money. After about an hour, surrounded by enemy troops, and without possibility of escape, I gave myself up.

They took me to the Acquarossa farm where I found Buta on a stretcher. I did not see the colonel whom I believe they had immediately taken away after his capture. The two owners of the farm who had befriended us were also taken prisoner. They were summarily executed.

The two civilians and I were escorted to the headquarters of the 7th Company, 15th Panzer Regiment whose C.P. was located at Passo dei Tre. Interrogated by the C.O. of the 7th Company and by an Italian officer, I made out that I did not understand either German or Italian and spoke only English. They took all my personal belongings including my "dog tags," but neglected to take my pen knife. They had found the transmitting key and the ear pieces of the radio in the gully.

At approximately 9 p.m., Buta was brought in on a stretcher and the entire regiment began to retreat toward Randazzo. I heard the order to leave Buta on the road so that he could be found by our troops. They ordered me to get into the car with the German Lieutenant. As they retreated, the Germans were mining the road and the trees on the side of the road. We alternately retreated and stopped during the rest of Saturday and Sunday. Finally about 10 p.m. Sunday, the lieutenant, who was somnolent, sent the driver to find out if he should go ahead with me. The lieutenant was not a member of the 7th Company and I believe he belonged to the Abwehr.

When the driver had disappeared and the only thing I could hear was the slight snoring of the lieutenant, I slowly felt for my knife, and when I was certain, with a rapid movement, I pressed the spring that released the blade and in a moment sliced his throat.

I jumped out of the car and fled as fast as my legs could carry me, despite the pain from my wounds, as I knew what it would mean if they recaptured me.

Towards dawn I approached a farmhouse and after several hours of observation, I was convinced that it was safe to make my approach. Inside I found some kindhearted peasants who gave me some civilian clothing, some food and pointed the way toward our own lines. I followed their directions and I saw artillery fire and our planes bombing the enemy positions in the distance.

I walked all day and night, stopping with shepherds and peasants who were helpful in every manner. Tuesday morning, August 10, I found cover in a wooded thicket a few kilometers from the town of Tortorici, and in that neighborhood I saw a number of tanks, artillery pieces and almost four hundred Germans who were seizing all draft animals who happened to be going into the town.

I moved along and took the road to the town of Cesaro where there was an American headquarters. I arrived at 4 p.m. and was stopped by an M.P. who was on duty at the Town Hall. From there I was taken to a United States Captain who commanded a battery and to whom I reported all points of enemy activity. Then an intelligence officer was called and I repeated my information. I could not provide any identification documents as I had only a piece of paper that the Germans had given me when I was captured. I was immediately sent to the Divisional G-2 to whom I pointed out the enemy positions and areas that were not defended.

At 2 a.m. of Wednesday the 11th I was taken to the 11th Evacuation Hospital where they patched up my wounds and took me to the 228th Evac Hospital in Cefalu' and the following day I reported back to my headquarters in Palermo.

While the Pantaleoni mission was undergoing its baptism of fire and tragedy, the pressure was on to get "McGreggor" under way. The communications between Washington, Algiers, Berne and Palermo were pressing and our problems were compounded by the continued CINCMED prohibition to limit our operations south of 38 degrees 40".

Regardless of the high priority assigned to "McGreggor" and the importance of the sponsors of the operation, there was no way in which Admirals Hewitt and Davidson could prevail on the British to clear the mission.

In a radio signal on August 8 from Shaheen to Donovan, it became apparent that someone was blocking the operation and Shaheen inquired: "Could it be that other negotiations have progressed to a point that higher echelons don't want 'McGreggor' carried out?"

(As it later turned out, the Italians made the first approach for an armistice to the British on August 2 and this was followed by a meeting in Madrid on August 15, during which Badoglio's emissary, General Castellano, offered to make Italy a co-belligerent on the Allied side.)[7]

Finally, in sheer desperation to get something done, on the night of August 12, our PT boats landed "Domenico" near Cape Vaticano in Calabria and from there he was to make the difficult trip to Rome on foot or on some train going north. At the same time, we helped the British ISLD team "Sunshine" to land in the same area. Eventually, Domenico made his way to Rome and delivered his letter, but the Italian government, which was already conducting high echelon negotiations with the British and AFHQ, put him on reserve in case other channels of communications were needed. During this period the personnel at the Palermo base were working around the clock.

On August 8, Nate DeAngelis and Benny Treglia came back from the front with the first accurate report of what had happened to the Pantaleoni mission. In view of the fluid situation at the front, we decided to examine the possibility of mounting an operation to rescue Colonel Pantaleoni. I sent DeAngelis and Treglia back to the front to see if Passo dei Tre had been overrun and if the people in the area knew anything about the incident.

On August 11, the medics brought Buta to Palermo, and some information became available so that we could put the pieces together. The final details did not fall into place until August 12 when Ribarich reported back to headquarters from the evacuation hospital. DeAngelis and Treglia went back to San Stefano from which the Germans had already pulled out, but they could find no trace of information about Pantaleoni. Successive efforts were fruitless nor did the Red Cross inquiries turn up any information about the colonel. Unquestionably this courageous man would have been of great value in the command post he was scheduled to fill.

Early in August, Dick Mazzarini, Italian SI's man in London, informed us that Major Robertson, until then head of SIS's Italian Section in London, was coming to Sicily to head the mission for the infiltration of Continental Italy and that he was being replaced in London by Majors Alexander and Wallenstein. This information dovetailed with a later radio message from Eddy informing us that a "hostile campaign in certain quarters threatens our position with army. Charges we have become largely merely another C.E. agency, instead of producing results in espionage in enemy territory. Important you push infiltration of intelligence teams to Italy. S.I.S. is promising army several teams northern Italy next moon."

We needed no nudging from Algiers to realize how vital it was that OSS produce tangible results in the intelligence-gathering field, but in order to produce those results the organization had to create an infrastructure and support system that would guarantee the agents a minimum chance of success, and not simply embark on thoughtless squandering of our valuable human resources.

Although SI Italy had been ready to take to the field, having had the foresight to plan ahead, it had been hampered in carrying out intelligence operations because the theater headquarters could not provide transportation and cover documents. What was worse, we had been deprived of participating in "Husky" planning and had been given only the most meager details about the invasion at the eleventh hour. As late as mid-August 1943, only a trickle of other OSS personnel was being rushed to the theater.

On August 7, Scamp, in compliance with an operational request from Patton's headquarters, inquired whether any of the Operational Groups had as yet arrived in Algiers. Eddy replied that only Colonel Russ Livermore and Lieutenant James Russo as well as five GIs had arrived, and these would prepare in Algiers for the "next operation." As a result of this shortage of qualified manpower, SI personnel was assigned to the OSS Fifth Army unit. Instead of consolidating operations, another command structure was being created for the invasion of continental Italy.

As yet, attention was still concentrated on the Sicilian operation which was reaching its peak phase. The Germans and Italians were shortening and strengthening their battle lines and stiffening up their resistance in order to gain time to extricate themselves from Sicily and take up the fight on the mainland.

The Seventh Army's repeated requests for special operations to cut the coastal highway to Messina, which variously ranged from small teams to 50-man units, while not intelligence work, came within the province of the OSS mandate. Without specially trained personnel, however, it was impossible to comply with the Army's request. Finally, in an attempt to cut off the German retreat, the Second Battalion of the Thirtieth Regiment was landed at San Agata Militello under cover of a naval bombardment by the U.S. Navy units of Admiral Davidson's Task Force 88. The landing was successful, but the enemy escaped. On August 10, a unit was landed at Brolo, but owing to lack of coordination and loss of communications, the American unit lost ninety-nine dead and seventy-five wounded. The enemy, while suffering casualties, again escaped the trap.[9] How a few OSS men could have been expected to undertake such an impossible task defies reason. All our unit would have been able to accomplish was to blow up a bridge or a tunnel, which, in the absence of a followup by a substantial force, the German pioneers would have quickly repaired. The Army had never contemplated any such followup.

The arrival of Holcomb and Lanza, who comprised the first X-2 field mission, caused a direct confrontation with the Seventh Army CIC whose CO, Colonel Young, pointed out that our status had not been regularized with the Fifteenth Army Group. He therefore proceeded to stake out CIC's claim to head counterintelligence work in Sicily. As we pointed out, we had been working with CIC from the beginning and had been instrumental in providing expertise in various facets of its work. The matter was finally straightened out during a meeting at Army headquarters where it was explained that we were working under the authority of the Joint Chiefs of Staff and would retain our status as an independent agency. Colonel Koch, Patton's G-2, participated in the meeting and approved the agreement. After reporting to our Palermo headquarters at Via Danesini, Holcomb and Lanza went about their business. We rarely saw them during their stay in Palermo.

Rudy Winnacker organized the work of the first field office of R & A with the assistance of personnel we lent him. His backup man in Algiers was Peter Karlow, a young naval ensign and a recent arrival. Together, they kept our radio center hopping with messages to Langer in Washington, Sherman Kent, Stewart Hughes, and Don McKay, all requesting Italian-speaking personnel to expand and process the material we were turning over to them. In his first report to Colonel Eddy and to R & A Branch Chief Langer, Winnacker concluded:

Needless to say, this work has to be carried on with innumerable problems of liaison with G-2 and other American organizations in this field, with extreme caution and tact in the handling of the local personnel, and with patience which is getting near the breaking point. I believe, however, that this work will prove to be valuable to the local consumer and OSS in general. Moreover, the experience gathered here should prove valuable in the organization of similar and more valuable institutions on the continent, where a higher type of personnel could be recruited. However, assistance is badly needed. As far as I know at the present time, Ensign Karlow is still the only R & A man in this theater. Nothing has been heard as yet of either Lt. Burke or Frederick Fales, who, as agreed with General Donovan, will not work for Mr. Oechsner, but for R & A. Additional men can be usefully employed here, and also to be trained for future work in other places. All the personnel requested should be sent over as quickly as possible. So far the work has been carried on by myself and Pvt. Moia, lent to me by the Italian Section. During the last two days I have had the help of Pvt. Olds (Italian S.I.) who is supervising some of the processing work. These men, however, are not trained for this type of work, and though helpful are not an adequate substitute for R & A personnel. (Nick Olds had been a practicing attorney in Detroit when I recruited him and he went on to become a key member of the attorney general's office in Michigan. Charles Moia was a student who knew Italian and acted as Winnacker's interpreter as Winnacker did not speak Italian. This report was dated August 25, 1943.)

Rudy lived at Villa Maggiore which served as headquarters billet and offices in Palermo. Our working relationship and coordination were always excellent.

As the Sicilian campaign was drawing to a close, with the British Eighth Army slugging its way northward to Catania and Messina and our own Seventh Army under the dynamic Patton, leapfrogging eastward along the northern coastal highway, our thoughts ran to the impending Italian campaign. It was envisaged as a long and arduous one, even if Badoglio opted to get out of the war. As early as August 9, we advised Colonel Eddy to get ready for followup operations against the Italian mainland. We repeatedly sought to get the 38° 40" operational ban lifted so that we could land our agents along the coast, close to Rome.

The PTs, with some of our people on board, even violated the ban on one occasion and approached the Gulf of Gaeta. The approach was made in the nighttime and we found that German F lighters and MAS boats were patrolling the area. Our boats backed off rather than precipitate a firefight and alert the coast. With the advantage of on-board radar, the enemy did not even know we were in the area.

On August 14, a radio signal alerted us to prepare a number of special teams that would be picked up at Palermo by a task force commanded by U.S. Navy Captain C. L. Andrews, Jr. The teams were to be landed on the mainland. Eddy's signal did not specify further and seemed to be a chance opportunity to land a couple of teams for the Rome area under the auspices of our Navy.

On August 15, at a staff meeting of G-2 of the Seventh Army, I proposed that our detachment be authorized to carry out a special operation to capture the Aeolian Islands (Lipari, Vulcano, and neighboring islands) some 75 miles northeast of Palermo. These islands were garrisoned by Army and Navy units and had served for many years as penal colonies. During the Fascist period, they were used as detention areas for political opponents of the regime. Their "guests" included many prominent leaders who were now attempting to return from exile under British, American, or Communist sponsorship. After a consultation with G-3, the operation was approved, providing it could be carried out by using exclusively OSS assets.

On the way back to our headquarters I stopped off at Commander Barnes' headquarters and explained the details of the operation. He agreed to assign three PT boats under the command of Lieutenant DuBoise, and we set August 17 as the date when we would launch the operation.

Since we had only limited manpower, I decided that if we were to take the islands we should try a stratagem in order to avoid shooting and possible casualties. We knew beforehand the location of the defensive positions and their armament and that only through a daring daylight operation could we hope to shake up the defenders into surrendering without a fight.

I assigned seven men and one officer to do the job. At the last moment, however, Lieutenant Henry Ringling North, our finance officer, who was hankering for a more active role, joined the small unit which was to be assisted in its task by a landing party from the PT boats. The SI men who were assigned to the mission were: Captain Frank Tarallo, Lieutenant Henry Ringling North, and Privates Louis Fiorilla, Benny Treglia, Peter Durante, Egidio Clemente, John Ballato, Carl Bommarito, Nate DeAngelis, and Barney Tumbiolo. Captain Tarallo was placed in command of the mission, which also included Captain Camby, an AMGOT officer, who was to reestablish civil government.

The official report gives a good account of what happened after the flotilla left Palermo harbor:

Lt. DuBoise, USNR in command of the PT boats, lay a straight course for the island group. . . . S.I. personnel were equally distributed among the three PT boats. The group was escorted by an American destroyer which screened the approach by keeping about five miles distant, ready to support if any Axis ships intervened. This formation continued without incident.

At 12 noon of the same day, this force approached the outer zone of the islands. Lt. DuBoise lowered the speed of the boats and held a conference with Tarallo in the Chart Room. Plans were made for a surprise landing and the details were communicated to the members of the team. The Axis shore defenses were immediately sighted along the commanding ridge overlooking the harbor and port. These defenses consisted chiefly of machine gun emplacements and of howitzer type shore batteries for the inner defense of the island of Lipari.

Deliberating a plan for approaching the harbor, Captain Tarallo and Lt. DuBoise finally decided to approach at a quarter speed, maintaining constant vigil on the shore defenses, and signalled the destroyer to stand by for action and cover the withdrawal force from the harbor zone in the event that the shore defenses opened fire, forcing the PTs to sheer off and delay the landing. The Three PT boats rounded the western end of the island and the port lay in full view, with the harbor itself two hundred yards away. Captain Tarallo and Lt. DuBoise, after scanning the harbor, finally decided to proceed with their plan by running one boat up to the dock with the other two boats standing by ready to cover any action. The destroyer remained at a distance, constantly in radio contact, manning battle stations. Tarallo and two men jumped off the boat onto the dock, at which time the enemy naval commander of the archipelago, a lieutenant, appeared coming out of his port office, carrying his sabre in his right hand and a white flag in his left hand. Immediately negotiations for the surrender of the islands got under way. After the acceptance of the unconditional surrender terms by the enemy, Tarallo established his headquarters in the naval port office.

Small groups of men, previously designated to perform specific duties, were immediately dispatched to the various parts of the island and patrols were sent out to capture the semaphore station and return with all the documents and codes and with military prisoners.

Another patrol was sent out to seize all arms and ammunitions that were stored on the island, while another was sent to round up all military personnel and bring them all to the port office for interrogation. Tarallo and two S.I. men interrogated 45 prisoners, and two anti-Fascist prisoners who had been held in the local prison for two years were freed.

Groups were sent to surrounding islands to contact the mayors and orient them on the unconditional surrender. All boats belonging to the military were examined and disarmed.

When these missions were completed, all U.S. personnel was assembled at the port office. All documents and equipment captured were stored on board one of the boats. A proclamation was ready and posted liberating the islands and placing them under the authority of AMGOT whose representative was a member of the mission, and temporarily, Italian civil officials were appointed to help the AMGOT captain to govern the islands. Secret warehouses which had been kept under lock and key by the Fascist officials were opened and food was distributed to the public which had long been kept on minimum rations. [10]

During the interrogation, the enemy commander revealed that he was ready to engage our force and that only the brazen manner in which the lead boat approached the port made him hesitate. This, plus the destroyer circling in the background, and the fact that a number of other U.S. vessels were also operating nearby, convinced him. He pointed out that when he saw the U.S. personnel immediately go about their assigned tasks and heard Tarallo talking to him in Italian, he made up his mind not to put up any resistance. Privates Durante and DeAngelis assisted Captain Tarallo in obtaining the surrender.

Lieutenant North was assisted by Privates Louis Fiorilla and Ben Treglia in capturing the radio station and code books and operators. The code books were salvaged, although an effort was made to burn them. Captain Camby and Privates Ballato, Clemente, and Tumbiolo searched for important documents and intelligence. Upon completion of the mission, the islands and their 8,000 inhabitants were left under the jurisdiction of the Allied Military Government.

Before sunset on the evening of August 17, the PT flotilla returned to Palermo with 45 prisoners whose continued interrogation was considered to be worthwhile, and with documents, record and code books, and radio equipment. The men were slowly marched up Corso Vittorio Emanuele to the inquisitive stares of the people lining the sidewalks. They were delivered to the Seventh Army Prisoner-of-War Compound, whereas the documents and equipment were brought to OSS headquarters at Villa Maggiore.

The Lipari operation brought the OSS participation in the Sicilian campaign to an end on the same day as U.S. and British troops victoriously entered Messina. The first person to enter that city was "Sorel," (Michael Chinigo), an Italian SI agent operating under media cover.

In a brief period of thirty-five days, the small SI detachment had been transformed and bloodied in the collection of combat intelligence and had carried out operations ranging from assistance to CIC in counterespionage, collection of political intelligence, assistance to AMGOT, intensive prisoner-of-war interrogation, and landing of agents for "McGreggor" and ISLD along the Calabrian coast; had loaned British SAS both personnel for operations and documents and charts; and had carried out a commando strike to capture the Lipari archipelago. In addition, Italian SI had collected and transmitted to AFHQ vital strategic intelligence on Italian Army battle orders in Italy, the Balkans, and the Aegean Islands, and had trained a number of civilians for future OSS operations in continental Italy and the Balkans.

In the course of doing its own work, Italian SI made it possible for the R & A Branch to set up its first field office by providing Rudy Winnacker with the interpreters and translators to establish the branch office in Palermo as well as the contacts to undertake its work. Many of the key documents were turned over to R & A for processing.

The early criticism which Eddy voiced in a radio message to Roseborough on July 22, which said in part: "tell Scamp to send me men, not mice . . .," was to turn a full 180 degrees with the expression of admiration and praise on August 10 in the following message: "sorry to hear about casualties Orlando teams.[11] Admire their bravery," and on August 5, "hearty congratulations for Ribarich . . . we are proud of you." Finally, on August 5 from Donald Downes to Scamp "You and your people are doing miracles for us."

As for General Donovan, he would always have a soft spot in his heart for the handful of men who made up the OSS Seventh Army Detachment in Sicily. At an early date, he foresaw the difficulties of collecting combat intelligence in the rapidly moving military action of the Seventh Army's campaign. He rightly viewed the invasion of Sicily as a prelude to the much more important and complicated Italian campaign. His early advice at Falconara Castle had been to prepare to carry out long-range infiltration and intelligence operations against the Italian mainland. On the basis of our "Bathtub" mission and other intelligence gathered during the Sicilian campaign, he correctly forecast that Sardinia could easily be liberated through a special OSS effort. He so advised President Roosevelt at the "Quadrant" conference held in Quebec in mid-August 1943.

Chapter 9

The Creation of a Hydra

The end of the Sicilian campaign heralded a period of organizational turmoil. Already on August 5, Eddy had advised us that plans were being developed to create a new OSS unit that would be attached to Fifth Army G-2 for the invasion of the Italian mainland. General Donovan finalized the arrangements during a visit to Mark Clark's headquarters, and Donald Downes, who had worked with the Fifth Army's CIC, was named to head the unit. Since most of the personnel available for Italian operations then present in the theater had been recruited, trained, and shipped overseas by Italian SI, the cadre of the Fifth Army unit was made up of our people. Included in the transfer were Captain Alexander Cagiati, Lieutenant Andre Pacatte, and a large contingent of our enlisted men.

Background information and intelligence were made available to Donald Downes. Scamp met with him in Algiers to brief him on a number of situations and turned over a list of contacts in Rome and Milan for possible use by the Fifth Army's agents, once they hit the mainland. The plan to create the mainland group was ostensibly temporary, as both the Seventh Army unit and the Fifth Army unit were to be combined once Naples was occupied by our forces. On the same day (August 5), Eddy, in answer to a query from Scamp, had designated Colonel Pantaleoni as CO of the advanced OSS base at Palermo, in charge of personnel discipline and as official liaison to the Seventh Army.[1] Pantaleoni had already left on his tragic mission to San Fratello, however, and never was aware of his designation.

After the capture of Lipari we urged that our personnel, then arriving from the states in greater numbers, should be shipped to Palermo to receive further training so that it could participate in future operations, but constant delays occurred owing to red tape and transportation priorities. At this time, the "McGreggor" project was still hanging fire as John Shaheen awaited word from Allen Dulles in Berne and "Domenico" in Rome about the outcome of the contact with Admiral Girosi. The "McGreggor" personnel made repeated trips in PT boats to the prearranged rendezvous off the coast of Gaeta, but the courier did not show up. Shaheen made a final try on August 30 without any apparent result. The reasons for the "no-show" were becoming clearer as preparations for the participation in the projected Fifth Army invasion at Salerno went ahead.

On August 2, the Italian ambassador in Lisbon had opened secret negotiations for peace with the Allies. On August 10, Italian General Giuseppe Castellano met with Allied representatives in Madrid. The Badoglio government offered to become a co-belligerent with the Allies after renouncing its alliance with Hitler. The Allied representatives insisted on a formula of unconditional surrender, and arrangements were discussed for joint operations in the Rome area.

On August 31, the people of Sicily were surprised to see an Italian transport plane come winging in without a single AA gun trying to shoot it down. It was General Castellano who had come to meet with Allied officials to inform them that Marshal Badoglio wanted troop-strength guarantees before agreeing to the surrender terms, as German reprisals against the Italian forces had started in the Aegean area and in Slovenia.

While the OSS Fifth Army was being constituted in Morocco, AFHQ also intended to utilize OSS assets in Palermo by assigning to our detachment a difficult commando operation on D-3 of "Avalanche." The OSS operation would be carried out in conjunction with Commander Barnes' PT boats, which would become part of a special U.S. Navy Task Force commanded by Captain G.L. Andrews.[2]

At the same time, it became obvious that we were in a position to do something about Sardinia. We had a number of Sardinian recruits from the States available, and others were already in Palermo. Feeling that OSS could do the job, I sent the following message to Eddy:

Please find out whether the Fifth Army is going to tackle "Bathtub." If not, it becomes OSS-PT job . . . we must seek permission from Hewitt to assign six PT boats to us for an indefinite period. Eddy from Marat [Marat = Corvo]. I am confident that job can be done by us . . . large scale plans and preparations underway. Job should be carried out from Bone, Bizerte with trips to Palermo to pick up manpower. Have discussed this at length with Barnes. He may be able to give you more information. These operations will give us the opportunity to bring into play the full force of OG and SO Groups.

In looking around to see how our position in Sicily could be exploited to the utmost in favor of the Allied cause, we were in touch with the leadership of a large number of Yugoslav irregulars who had been brought to Sicily and interned. Some of them had fought in the ranks of General Draza Mihailovich's Yugoslav Chetniks. I signalled Eddy that about 45 of those whom I had interviewed were willing to work with OSS and go back to Yugoslavia. Their leader was Lieutenant Budimir Veljko. At the same time we contacted a number of Albanians who had also been interned in Sicily. Some of these men knew Phil Adams, who headed the Albania desk under Brennan. The men were anxious to be infiltrated back into their country.

The fragility of our organization in the field was demonstrated by the fact that no replacements were immediately available for any of us. "Chuck" Groff, our radio expert, and Ralph DeHaro were working around the clock without any relief. In mid-August "Chuck" came down with malaria, but he kept working anyway. As noted earlier, I myself had been sick on and off most of the time during the Sicilian campaign. Several times Rudy Winnacker had sent messages to Algiers asking for an assistant operations officer, but I managed to hang on as no substitute was available. In the meanwhile, preparations were being made for our participation in the invasion of Italy, but details given by Algiers were very sketchy. It was therefore decided to recruit and train civilians to undertake the penetration of the mainland and later work out the details of each mission based on directions from AFHQ.

Toward the end of August, the Fifteenth Army Group (AG) headquarters almost put our radio communications out of business when it issued orders to the Seventh Army that all communications of our unit and other units such as CIC and PWB who were attached to G-2 must channel their communications through the Army. We countered that this was impossible because we needed direct contact with our agents and had to maintain a schedule with headquarters in Algiers and other OSS stations.

The chief of staff, Seventh Army, was most helpful in that he required only a radio signal from AFHQ to authorize us to continue. Eddy had the message sent out over Eisenhower's signature to both the Fifteenth AG and the Seventh Army outlining the importance of our mission and authorizing continued operation of "Garibaldi."

Armed with the knowledge that the Fifth Army would make its landing south of Naples in the Bay of Salerno, we were on the lookout to question many of the refugees and deserters who were trickling back to Sicily from the mainland. One of these, an officer who had been in that zone only a few days earlier and who was familiar with the defenses, was found on August 29 through one of our contacts. We were able to transmit to Algiers, for action by the Fifth Army, the accurate disposition of some of the units that were located at the various strong points along the coastline from Capua to Salerno. All indications were that a landing in the Salerno area was expected and that, since the fall of Mussolini, the Germans had started to move increasing number of troops into Italy. Certainly, the Germans were aware that some negotiations were going on with the Allies. The daylight flight into Bocca di Falco airport of the Italian plane carrying General Castellano could not have gone undetected by German intelligence which had left behind agents in Sicily during their retreat.

As we saw the role of the Palermo OSS base at the end of August 1943, we believed that we were in a position to conduct both tactical and strategic operations against the mainland and to mount a modest effort to take over Sardinia. At the same time, the availability of Yugoslav and Albanian personnel in Sicily opened the doors for operations in the Balkans.

The creation of the Fifth Army OSS unit in Morocco made a great deal of sense from an administrative point of view, but it unwittingly created a competitive unit within the Italian theater of operations. The truth was that since the AFHQ/OSS command was the only theater that was in a military offensive mode, it was attracting many ambitious men who were influential in OSS/Washington but needed to see action to advance their careers.

Both the expanded scope of OSS operations and the rapid expansion of personnel became difficult problems for Eddy to cope with as his small staff could not handle the logistics. Colonel Eddy was accustomed to running a small, tightly knit operation in which he knew all of the people working with him. While valiantly trying to cope with the infinity of new problems, he also had to deal with requests from Washington by people who could not visualize the actual difficulties in the field. General Donovan's frequent presence in the field did not simplify Eddy's problems because Donovan often made decisions on the spot. Such decisions were based on the reality of existing conditions. Eddy did not challenge them; rather, he ratified them.

Donald Downes, who was assigned the command of the Fifth Army unit, which was staffed by our people, had worked with the Spanish side of the show in Morocco and did not claim to know much about Italy. He leaned heavily on help from Scamporino and our Palermo unit, but he was not taking into consideration the changes which field conditions often inflict on the best laid plans. In the meanwhile, we at Palermo were busy preparing a series of operations which headquarters in Algiers had assigned in connection with the landings on the Salerno beaches. The most important of these assignments was the capture of Ventotene Island, a stony crag rising out of the sea some 50 miles south of the port of Gaeta. Ventotene was one of the harsh penal colonies which had forcefully hosted some of Fascism's key opponents, as was the smaller nearby island of San Stefano. Although AFHQ wanted the island captured, it could not afford to assign troops to the operation. They turned to Colonel Eddy who, as a man of action, could never conceive of turning down the proposal.

When Eddy first asked us to take on the operation, I could not readily fathom why AFHQ was even remotely interested in this godforsaken island. I was certain that it had nothing to do with rescuing the debilitated anti-Fascists who had languished for years in the prison—and I was right.

The only troops AFHQ could commit to the operations was a platoon of parachutists from the 509 Scout Company, Eighty-second AA division. Their job was to erect a directional beacon on the island to point the way to Rome for the U.S. Eighty-second Airborne Division. According to the early game plan, this division was to be dropped on the outskirts of Rome and was to link up with the Italian Mobile Armored Group, commanded by General Giacomo Carbone.[3] The island was to be captured on September 8, twenty-four hours before any Fifth Army troops hit the beaches at Salerno.

Upon receiving the assignment, I immediately met with Commander Barnes and Lieutenant Mutty who had already been alerted to the formation of a "80.4 Andrews Task Force," which would help us carry out the operation. I looked about for a map of the island but could not find anything larger than a 1:100,000 which I gradually enlarged. With the fortuitous help of a man who had been on the island four months earlier, I was able to reconstruct the roads, main geographic features, gun emplacements, and the location of the prison and command posts. Captain Frank Tarallo and some of the SI men who had participated in the Lipari operation were assigned to the project. Lieutenant North, having tasted excitement and the surge of adrenalin of Special Operations, gave up his post of finance officer and was placed as second in command of the operation.

We selected some of the best of our local civilian recruits and immediately started training exercises. At the same time, we began training a special group which was designated as "Detachment 7." Its objective was to land at Salerno and to assist the G-2, Fifth Army, with combat intelligence. Sixteen civilians, who had been split up into three combat intelligence teams, were placed under the command of Nate DeAngelis, who had gained considerable experience in line penetration work as a member of Colonel Pantaleoni's San Fratello mission and subsequent thereto. Assigned to the mission as wireless operator was Private Henry Calore of Meriden, Connecticut. A third mission, codenamed "Greenbrier" was also to be dispatched to the Salerno area. It was made up of the "McGreggor" personnel under the command of John Shaheen, and it was provided with a radio operator who would keep in touch with our Palermo headquarters through the use of one of our agent SSTR-1 sets. This W/T was Peter Tompkins who had transferred over to SI from PWB. Having lived in Italy before the war, Peter Tompkins spoke Italian fluently.

By this time negotiations for the Italian Armistice were an open secret, but Shaheen pursued his goal until the last minute, trying to contact Admiral Girosi to get Italy out of the war. The final approval for our three-pronged operation was given by AFHQ on August 29 and relayed to us by Eddy in a radio signal: "Three operations, first 21 men for mainland; second eight men for Ventotene; third 'Bathtub' on D+ _____ ."

As we were at the terminal point of frenzied operations for "Avalanche," a signal arrived informing us that OSS Washington was taking over the "Bathtub" operation and that the coordination would be entrusted to Sherman Kent, one of the key R & A people in the area. The signal explained:

Colonel Buxton wires the following regarding project recently assigned by G-3, Sherman Kent, civilian in charge. Bonfiglio and Montante, S.I.; Major McCallen, S.O.; Squadra, civilian, M.O.; Major Deane, Services. Also to participate Minnifie, Mathieu and Winnacker. For agents, some of Brennan's men now in route, are natives of the target area and Buxton hopes some of Scamp's men who are natives can also be assigned. Kent expected to coordinate all aspects of this job, responsible to Eddy and his executive officer. Buxton hopes that in spite of mainland projects Scamp will have time to take this project under wing and give guidance and assistance that would be invaluable. Though Lussu seems unavailable at this time, Brennan is trying to gain his support either personally or through delegates named by Lussu.

We had no doubt that these were General Donovan's instructions and that the selection of Sherman Kent had been agreed on in talks with Dr. William Langer, head of R & A. Brennan had been dragged into the planning both to provide personnel and to establish contact with Lussu, the outstanding Sardinian anti-Fascist exile. Lussu was also tied in closely with British SOE through his wife Joyce and his brother-in-law, British Major Max Salvadori, an outstanding anti-Fascist in his own right who was in service in the theater.

It was also obvious that Washington's planning did not take into account the actual operating conditions in the field and the developments that could take place once the general passed through Algiers to participate in the Salerno landings.

In preparation for "Operation Avalanche" General Castellano made another "secret" journey to Sicily and met with Allied officials on September 3. This time the meeting was held at Cassibile, near Syracuse. There he signed the so-called short armistice which was kept secret until the night of September 8 for fear that the Germans would take over Italy and pour massive reinforcements down the Brenner Pass. The short armistice did not mention unconditional surrender, but a full document signed on September 8 spelled out the unconditional capitulation of the Italian government.

The Salerno landings opened the second phase of OSS operations in Italy, with one unit attached to the Fifth Army and others operating under the control of the OSS base in Palermo and AFHQ.

Early in September, Task Force 80.4 under the command of Captain C. L. Andrews put into Palermo.[4] The task force included the destroyer

Knight and a number of small British and American craft, including crash boats which through recording devices could simulate the sounds of invasion landing craft.

On September 4 an intensive briefing with all of the key personnel attending was held at OSS headquarters in Villa Maggiore. Present were Captain Andrews, part of his staff, Lieutenant Douglas Fairbanks, Jr., Captain Tarallo, Lieutenant Henry North, and several other officers who were assigned roles in the Ventotene operation. Also present was John Steinbeck, who was accompanying the operation as a war correspondent and who wanted to get to know the mood of the men. I went over the operational plan in detail and based on the intelligence available, pointed out how important it was for the deception to be carried out during the hours of darkness. There was an Italian garrison on the island, and a number of strong points were manned. I also suspected that a few German specialists might be stationed there. I could not guess just how strong the German garrison was or what its primary functions were, except that the island was being used as an outpost to signal the probable invasion which everyone anticipated.

The official mission report filed by Captain Tarallo tells the full story:

. . . on the afternoon of September 8 the task force departed from Palermo harbor and set course NE to Ventotene Island. At 5 p.m. we sighted the main Allied invasion fleet sailing slowly towards the coast of Italy. Our small diversionary fleet sailed around the invasion fleet, then proceeded under full power for Ventotene.

The Italian S.I. personnel were billeted on board the U.S.S. Knight and final preparations for the assault were discussed in the officer's wardroom where Tarallo coordinated his assignment with the Naval Intelligence officers. The men were given their assignments.

Shortly after midnight the task force reached the rendezvous area, several miles off the island. All hands stood by for action prior to boarding the crash boats that were to take them to shore.

The crash boats were going through their routine in the darkness making noises associated with the landing of large shore parties. The night was exceedingly dark and finally the landing party made up of Captain Tarallo, three S.I. men and a small naval landing party boarded the dinghy and headed towards shore.

The actual port entrance was not visible as a thick haze hung low over the water. The island's dark volcanic soil blended in with the darkness of the night. Some three hundred yards from the port the dinghy struck the rocky shore. Tarallo and Pvt. Peter Durante jumped out of the boat to get their bearings. Durante moved quickly and captured the first German prisoner of war who was trying to blow up a supply boat with a stick of grenades. Tarallo shouted instructions to the men in the dinghy who soon found the harbor entrance.

The Germans, realizing what was happening and not trusting the Italian military which was already parlaying with us, decided to sabotage everything they could lay their hands on and were retreating up the steep hillside where they established a defense line to resist the "massive" attack they thought was coming. The German sergeant as well as twenty-five Italian miltary were rounded up and taken to the local caserma.

Captain Andrews, C.O. of the Task Force, Captain Tarallo of S.I., and Captain Howland, C.O. of the 509 Para Scout Detachment met and decided to postpone the attack against the German positions until daylight. Only a small detachment under Tarallo and Howland was left on the island. The naval task force moved on to carry out diversionary attacks against the mainland.

Upon interrogation of the prisoners it turned out that the German Detachment was composed of three officers and eighty-five men who included radar specialists and they had set up the advance German radar station that had the capability to monitor a long stretch of the Tyrrhenian coast. Taking over the caserma building, Tarallo established his headquarters there and mounted machine guns on the roof to ward off any surprise attack by the enemy.

While plans were being discussed for the early morning attack, a series of rocket attacks were carried out against the island from some of our own PT boats whose initial shots fell on the southern end of the island without injuring any of our personnel. The PT's then lifted their fire to the German positions, fired several salvoes and left.

About 5 a.m. of September 9th, Captains Tarallo and Howland began to carry out their plan of attack. Tarallo led the way to the semaphore station, accompanied by Pvts. Bommarito of Detroit and Benny Treglia of New York and preceded by two Italian soldiers who had joined our unit. One of these men led the way with a flag of truce and the other, who spoke German, was to act as interpreter.

If at all possible, it was decided to negotiate before fighting.

While this was going on, Captain Howland with forty-five of his paratroopers were standing by to go into action if there should be need. Communications were maintained by the use of walkie-talkie radios.

Lt. North remained in charge of headquarters at the caserma with Privates Egidio Clemente, Peter Durante and radio man Louis Fiorilla.

The climb up the steep stone-walled road was arduous because the Germans were said to have booby-trapped parts of it and abandoned machine gun posts and ammo boxes could be seen on both sides of the road.

Arriving near the crest, the flag bearer and the interpreter, who had been instructed, went forward to the German position. Tarallo and the two enlisted men took up positions and waited. Finally, after almost one-half hour, they came back and reported that the German C.O. was ready to negotiate.

Tarallo and his party went up forward to talk to the German officer who was told that he must surrender unconditionally. He hesitated until one of our Italian soldiers in an aside to his comrade mentioned the "fact" that a force of five hundred men were waiting to attack the German positions and that a fleet was standing by to land more men.

Hearing this distressing news, the German commander decided to surrender.

Tarallo notified Captain Howland to bring up his men and place them at intervals on both sides of the road down which the German prisoners were to be marched into captivity. As there were not enough men to cover the entire route of march, it was decided to allow the column of prisoners to march by and then the parachutists who had been passed would double down and get at the front end of the line—sort of the endless belt effect—until the prisoners had been confined for safekeeping in the caserma.

When this was over, Captain Howland set up his directional beacon pointing the way to Rome for the Eighty-second Division, but the jump had been canceled on the advice of the Badoglio government because General Carbone's mobile armored force was surrounded by German divisions. Lieutenant Eingler, the German CO on Ventotene, signed the surrender papers, but when he became aware of the ruse he had fallen for, he was infuriated. The next morning, September 10, the German prisoners were picked up by the destroyer *Knight* and taken to Palermo—the first prisoners bagged in "Avalanche." Thus, without firing a shot, the German advance radar station was eliminated by a handful of men who had been trained to do intelligence work but who were pressed into undertaking a commando operation on short notice. From AFHQ John Steinbeck wrote a series of articles about the exploit. The work of this SI detachment did not end with the capture of the island of Ventotene.

On September 10, Captain Tarallo and Private Carl Bommarito rowed to the island of San Stefano where another political prison was located and freed some 400 prisoners, including Yugoslav and Czechoslovak nationals and Italian anti-Fascists. The prison superintendent was ordered to produce all prison records, and many of the prisoners were interrogated. Private Bommarito was left on the island to represent the Allies, while the prisoners and documents were transferred to Ventotene and from there to our Palermo headquarters.

The OSS group restored normalcy by reopening the local hospital and closing all the caves where the civilian population had taken refuge. The medic of the parachute Scout Unit asked the population to return to their homes. The school was reopened, and 100 children returned to their studies.

Meanwhile, the island was kept under observation by the Luftwaffe which believed it was still under German control. Tarallo, however, had the Stars and Stripes flown from the semaphore station so that Allied ships that were prowling these waters in order to protect the landings further south would know it was under U.S. control. The Germans then became aware that the Allies had taken over the island. German planes carried out a number of strafing attacks, fortunately without any serious consequences.

Tarallo dispatched Lieutenant North and three enlisted men to Ponza to take over the island. Two days later North returned with assurances of collaboration from the mayor of Ponza, as well as with 25 prisoners. It was on the island of Ponza that Mussolini had been held after his over-throw by the king and Marshal Badoglio. At that time we had repeatedly asked permission from AFHQ to raid the island and capture Il Duce. Owing to the 38°40′ prohibition, however, we lost the opportunity, and he was transferred to the naval base at La Maddalena in the Straits of Boniface between Corsica and Sardinia.

The Ventotene unit maintained contact with our radio station in Palermo through the use of our agent sets operated by Louis Fiorilla. As a result, operational orders could be transmitted every day. The group also received the surrender of three Italian naval units which had escaped German seizure in Naples. The flotilla, under the command of Italian Lieutenant Nortarbartolo, included Corvette C-18 and MAS boats MS64 and MAS 35. When they saw the American flag, the units took refuge at Ventotene. Lieutenant North took temporary command and finally arranged for an American destroyer to escort them to the port of Palermo.

Orders were issued for the OSS to move out of Ventotene which was turned over to the command of Captain Howland and an Air Corps liaison lieutenant who had set up a directional beacon at the semaphore station. Following orders, Tarallo dispatched a small group of his men, together with liberated anti-Fascists, to Ischia to observe enemy activity along the coast and to report to naval headquarters which had been set up on the island of Capri.[5] Tarallo himself led a contingent of OSS men and former political prisoners to the island of Procida and, together with a naval contingent from MTB Ron 15, forced the military and the mayor to relinquish control. As the island was located close to the mainland, the German command at Pozzuoli kept it under constant observation. In an effort to procure vital intelligence, the detachment started dispatching native agents to the mainland who came back with accurate intelligence of high military value. Telephones to Italy continued to function through a German snafu and were also used as a source of valuable information until the Germans caught on and shut off communications. The German command at Pozzuoli even sent a message to Tarallo ordering him to evacuate the island and threatening that if he did not do so, they would send over troops. The enemy was already sending German troops in civilian clothes to hunt down Tarallo, and so, for security reasons, he and his men donned civvies in order to confound the hunters.

Intelligence gathered included harbor installations and German shore batteries; mine fields from the Gulf of Gaeta to the Gulf of Naples; 88 mm shore batteries at Pozzuoli heights; information on the booby trapping of public buildings, including the main post office in Naples (which later blew up); information about the location of 100 Allied war prisoners and the liberation of Italian Admiral Minissini who was turned over the Lieutenant Shaheen in Capri for debriefing and processing.

Tarallo and Privates Bommarito, Fiorilla, and Treglia remained in Procida for six days. At midnight of the seventh day, after having eluded a German patrol for twenty-four hours, the four men were evacuated on a PT boat from the north side of the island. On September 19, Tarallo returned to Palermo with the SI complement and 25 political prisoners. Other political prisoners found their way to the mainland where they joined the underground movements which were springing up in almost all areas of Italy.

On the evening of September 8, as the seemingly interminable convoys transporting the Fifth Army to its designated land areas in the

Bay of Salerno were nearing their objective, news of the Italian surrender spread like wildfire among the thousands of British and American soldiers on board the ships. On one of those ships was the OSS detachment which had been placed in charge of Donald Downes. A former teacher, Downes had a varied intelligence career, having worked, by his own account, for the Navy, then the British, and thereafter transferring to COI, the new U.S. intelligence organization formed by Donovan. Downes worked in Washington for a while, where he concentrated on obtaining secret codes from a number of neutral, Axis-leaning nations. One of these operations was blown when the FBI interceded and arrested the men who were taking part in the embassy burglary, causing a tremendous flap. Downes was involved in a number of other minor incidents, but in a new organization that was struggling to find a place in wartime Washington, a number of mistakes were tolerated, especially since he was on a first-name basis with David Bruce, Allen Dulles, and some of Donovan's early recruits who would occupy prominent places in the Pantheon of OSS.

After the invasion of North Africa, Downes was sent to Morocco, where he worked with Fifth Army CIC and with AFHQ. There he worked to turn up intelligence that would give early warning of possible Spanish armed intervention in North Africa which might constitute a danger to Mark Clark's Fifth Army from the direction of Spanish Morocco. Here, too, he became involved in an undercover operation against Spain by infiltrating a number of former Spanish Republican veterans into Malaga. Transportation was provided by a British-controlled fishing boat. The operation, codenamed "Banana," wound up a tragic failure when the British canceled further transportation to the Spanish mainland and the entire "Banana" fell into a trap set by the Spanish counterintelligence. All the participants were captured or killed in a shootout with the Spanish Guardia Civile.

Although the incident created great embarrassment for Donovan in Washington, he stood by Downes, who continued to work with the Fifth Army CIC. In this work as well as in "Banana," Downes had been assisted by Captain Andre Bourgoin, an old Deuxieme Bureau hand who resided in Casablanca for many years and had worked both sides of the Spanish Civil War, selling gasoline to both the Franco forces and the Loyalists. His single published work, *The Scarlet Thread*, a short volume of his experiences, reveals that he did not like Colonel Eddy, his chief in North Africa; that his political sympathies tended to be left of center; and that he had deeply admired the Spanish Loyalist veterans. His dislike for Eddy was not so overt, however, that it prevented the colonel from designating him as head of the Fifth Army detachment for the Salerno invasion.

In the early hours of September 9, 1943, Downes was struggling over the side of the SS *Duchess of Bedford*, an invasion ship, on his way to "Red Beach" which was near the famous ancient Greek temples at Paestum. His peregrinations from the beach to one hillock after another, under constant artillery fire from the Germans, as well as his efforts to bury his ample body in the sand, are described in detail in the opening pages of his book. His task was to find a suitable location for Fifth Army headquarters, a job he had been given because he had once visited the temples and had spent some time around Amalfi.

After several days of digging holes in the beach and gazing at death's many faces and modes, Downes was ordered to the command ship *Ancon* where Major General Alfred Gruenther assigned him to assist Colonel Darby's Rangers who had landed at Maiori and were hampered by logistical problems. Reporting at Maiori, he ordered OSS to organize worker brigades to carry supplies from the beach to the mountaintop; to provide interpreters for Darby; and to do some CIC work in helping ferret out enemy agents who were reporting Darby's positions to the Germans. But in his book he seldom mentions the work of the unit that he was heading or any of the individuals who made up his group.

As was already clear in the first few days of the invasion, Donovan was thinking in terms of consolidating the OSS Fifth Army show under the command of Lieutenant Colonel Ellery Huntington, SO chief in Washington, who was visiting the theater and was on his way to Salerno to visit the beachhead. The Downes detachment included two base radio stations named "Concord," an assortment of jeeps and trucks, some twenty men, and two officers. The lone report that was made covering OSS activities from this group was sent to Scamp by Lieutenant Andre Pacatte, one of the SI officers who had been assigned from our section to the Fifth Army unit. The report covered the period from September 9 to September 26.

Dated September 26, 1943, OSS Advance Operations, Colonel Ellery Huntington, AUS, CO (Donald Downes had obviously been superseded), it reported:

Landed at Paestum September 9th on D-Day at 10:00, cooperated with 6th Corps C.I.C. on checking local people. We supplied C.I.C. with Italian-speaking personnel as they did not have any. U.S. forces took over Paestum and Capaccio. On September 11th, Lt. Hoagland, Lt. Judson, Captain Cowles and I entered Agropoli, being the first Americans to do so. We immediately established our authority by interrogating the Podesta (Mayor), Carabinieri, etc. Capt. Cowles of the C.I.C. did not choose to remain with us in Agropoli having some understandable trepidation regarding the possible return of the enemy . . . after two days of orientation in Paestum, I began the infiltration of agents for the gathering of military information . . . Lt. Hoagland cooperated with me splendidly on several behind the lines missions . . . all the information was forwarded to 6th Corps G-2 and 36th Division G-2. With very limited personnel, only 3 Italians that I had recruited in Tunis, we proved ourselves the most important source of information . . . then we moved to Salerno to infiltrate agents either north or south. However, Donald Downes ordered me to Ischia to organize surrounding island territory (Ischia and the surrounding islands had already been captured by Captain Tarallo who headed the Ventotene group). In two days we sent five teams to Naples . . . three were successful, providing highly valuable information, while two failed due to fire from the German shore patrols which are daily becoming more numerous . . . on the 25th I moved my operation to Capri where PT boats are based and I was advised by Lt. North that Capri was becoming the center of political and intelligence activity, as well as a refuge for increasing numbers of evacuees from the mainland, the latter, of course, splendid subjects for interrogation. From here I hope to dispatch agents in the immediate future to the mainland . . . Lt. Hoagland is still at Salerno as far as I know. I wish to recommend him for promotion for excellent work under constantly dangerous conditions . . . we have contacted several important politicos and found them eager to cooperate. For example, General Pavone . . . today (26th) I met here in Capri with Major Stacy Lloyd, now an S.I. officer in this area under Col. Huntington. He informed me that it was Huntington's desire that for the moment I remain in Capri as operations officer responsible to Lt. North, acting coordinator for O.S.S. on the island area.[6]

Meanwhile, we at Palermo had not been idle. Besides the highly successful Ventotene mission, on the previous day we had attempted to land the first OSS teams in the area. A brief summary of the operational report sent to Eddy and Donovan stated:

On September 7th at 1420 hours, a special detachment from this organization made up of ten especially recruited individuals cleared the harbor of Palermo aboard two MTB's. Their destination was the Italian mainland in the region just east of Terracina. This detachment had been speedily trained with the large type of rubber raft which is most convenient in these waters. All practice runs were held under actual landing conditions, including the lowering of the boats about three hundred yards from the shore from American PT's. These exercises were held for five consecutive days in all types of weather and on stretches of the Sicilian coast ranging from perpendicular cliffs to sandy beaches. None of the individuals who participated knew how to swim and no life belts were issued to them.

Upon arrival off the coast of Terracina, the crews of the MTB's prepared to lower the boats. However, just as they were in the process of doing so, a German ship quietly slipped in between the two MTB's. The enemy ship, believing the two boats to be friendly, commenced to signal them. For ten minutes, one of the boats was able to simulate answers, then seeing that further signaling would lead to complications, the leading boat maneuvered into position and shot a torpedo at the German boat. The enemy craft immediately blew up, proving by the sequence of explosions to be an ammunition ship. This unexpected action forced our boats to call off the landing party. German shore batteries immediately commenced firing and the boats had to move out.

Two days later, having changed the landing point, arrangements were completed for transportation of the unit, and

Late on the evening of September 14th, HMS destroyer "Hoffa," cleared the harbor of Palermo with the O.S.S. mission on board. The mission was in charge of Acting Sergeant Nate DeAngelis and Acting Sergeant Henry Calore, with a complement of sixteen Italian civilians. Their destination was "Red Beach" in the Salerno sector. Aboard the same destroyer were General Mark Clark and General Harold Alexander and their staffs. The Generals questioned De Angelis about his strange group and he gave them a brief account of their purposes.[7]

At 5:00 A.M. the next morning, the group landed in the midst of heavy shelling and bombing by the Germans. Sergeant De Angelis talked to the beach commander and obtained transportation for his group. The driver and truck were temporarily assigned to the unit. De Angelis and his group immediately reported to Fifth Army headquarters where they met Colonel Wells of the G-2 section who took them to Lieutenant Colonel Kenneth Mann and Lieutenant Andre Pacatte of OSS Fifth Army detachment. Mann introduced Sergeant De Angelis to Colonel Edwin B. Howard, chief of G-2. Howard, after having discussed several phases of operations which had been planned at Palermo, told Nate to wait for further instructions while he coordinated the entire program. The group then headed for Salerno, but in view of the heavy shelling they were forced to turn south to Agropoli. When he arrived at Agropoli, Colonel Howard and Colonel Mann sent word that they wanted to see him immediately. All of the original missions planned in Palermo were approved. Two other missions were discussed by Sergeant De Angelis and Colonel Howard, and orders were issued to carry them out. The Fifth Army was in need of accurate intelligence, and we agreed to provide it.

The group then worked its way to Salerno under heavy enemy shelling and set up its headquarters there. Within hours the "Lauria" mission was briefed on its objectives. It was assigned the task of infiltrating the lines in a southerly direction and of reaching Sapri, Lagonegro, and finally Lauria. Immediately after departing, they reported that the bridge at Rutino was mined. At this point the two-man mission hitched a ride to Perito where they encountered German tanks going in an easterly direction toward Potenza. This meant that the Germans were retreating from the coast to take up positions in the mountainous interior. Several miles south of Sapri, they met the advanced elements of the British Eighth Army, becoming the first Allied group to make contact. This task had been assigned by Colonel Howard, but in order to obtain further confirmation they continued on to Lauria and confirmed the British occupation of the entire area. The team completed its mission and returned to Salerno on September 19; it was highly commended for its work.

The second mission requested by Colonel Howard was the "Potenza" mission which departed for its destination on the morning of September 16. The task of this mission was to estimate German strength in the area. The group proceeded to Giungano and thence to Monforte without observing any enemy activity. They decided to continue to Magliano without incurring any hostile activity. Finally, at Piaggine, they encountered fourteen German tanks headed for Sala Consilina, where the enemy was consolidating its position. They identified the tanks as belonging to the Herman Goering Panzer Division. Upon questioning local civilians, they found that at Paola, an estimated 10,000 Germans were awaiting the withdrawal of other units. This was a clear indication that the enemy was retreating from Potenza. Their mission completed, the group backtracked to Salerno and reported to Colonel Mann. As a result of this information, elements of the Fifth Army extended their control over the southeastern part of the Salerno beachhead.

The "Napoli" and "Avellino" missions, made up of twelve agents, were dispatched the same evening of their arrival at the beachhead (September 15). The missions were approved by Colonel Howard and moved out to their respective jumpoff places as per plan. The "Napoli" mission struck out through the lines in a northwesterly direction and headed toward the town of Cava. En route the group was machine-gunned, and after some observations, they decided to turn south. Splitting up, they decided to reunite at Amalfi, which, though under Allied control, was actually no-man's land. From there they proceeded toward Positano, where they found no enemy activity. They therefore continued toward Sorrento where they observed German armor evacuating the town on their way to Castellamare di Stabia. The Germans were shooting down the crews of the local radio station and had killed a number of civilians.

Upon arrival at Sorrento, a runner was sent to Salerno with the information that had been gathered. This man turned over valuable information and reported strong German artillery positions at Montepeltuse and Monte San Angelo. Heavy armor concentrations were reported near Pagani, and heavy vehicular movement of every description was observed at Cammerini, a few miles before Nocera at the intersection of Castel San Giorgio and Mercato. This further report was made on September 20, at which time the Naples team was making its way into Castellamare di Stabia and to Naples. The runner departed to join his mission the very same day.

The "Avellino" mission ran into heavy enemy fire, and two of the group returned to Salerno. Later in the day, as the other four members of the mission were returning to Salerno to change their routing, they were caught in a heavy barrage. All four were hit. One died instantly and another was seriously wounded and died in the hospital shortly thereafter. The mission leader was wounded seriously in the spinal column and, after much suffering, died. The fourth member was wounded in the legs. There being no U.S. Army hospital nearby, DeAngelis prevailed on a British hospital unit to take the men. The British later turned them over to an Italian hospital whose medical facilities and available medical personnel were extremely limited.

The cooperation of Lieutenant Colonel Lane and Major MacDonald of AMGOT, who made a building available for headquarters, as well as rations and supplies, was helpful in getting the unit settled. Lieutenant Colonel Mann designated Lieutenant Hoagland as liaison officer between OSS/Fifth Army and the group.

Direct radio communications were established with Palermo headquarters and the first transmission took place on September 17. This was accomplished through the use of an SSTR-1 set codenamed "Kate Smith." Two contacts a day were also arranged between the detachment and G-2 headquarters. On September 20, Colonel Mann and Colonel Huntington paid a visit to the Seventh detachment and attempted to take the radio operator with them. However, DeAngelis protested so vehemently that they abandoned the attempt.

DeAngelis returned by air to Palermo for a conference on September 23 during which several operations were planned to survey damage to the harbor of Naples. He was supplied with a jeep and other equipment, and Private Benny Treglia, who had participated in the Sicilian and Ventotene operations, was sent to Salerno to help him with operations.

While these operations were developing, a collateral operation was taking place in the Salerno area. This operation, whose radio code name was "Greenbrier,"[7] involved the personnel of the "McGreggor" mission led by Johnny Shaheen. It included Marcello Girosi, Joe Savoldi, Mike Burke, and Peter Tompkins as radio operator. The Greenbrier radio came on the air on September 11 when Shaheen reported that his party was located at Vino, three miles north of Salerno, with Darby's Rangers and a group of British commandoes. At this time the area was under violent German artillery fire. "Greenbrier" transmitted the intelligence it received from refugees who were sifting through the battle lines. This information, which was turned over to G-2 for action, reported the disintegration of the Italian Army forces and the battle taking place between the German and Italian forces south of Rome. (The Italian division, though surrounded, fought gallantly; it was under the command of General Raffaele Cadorna, later military commander of CLN (Committee of National Liberation) forces in northern Italy.)

On September 14, shelling at Salerno had become so furious that this mission went on board a British rescue tug and it joined Commander Barnes and the U.S. PT squadron at Capri. The mission, alerted that Colonel Huntington was on his way to Salerno, was asked to look for him and try to arrange accommodations for him.

While the "McGreggor" objective remained the same, a new dimension was added on September 19 when the Luftwaffe first started to use its radio-guided bombs against the Allied fleet in Salerno Bay with telling accuracy, inflicting losses on the British and American naval units supporting the invasion. British and U.S. naval brass immediately put a top priority on intelligence regarding the threatening new weapons. This gave John Shaheen the opportunity to expand the goals of his mission by encompassing the search for technical Italian Navy personnel who could shed light on the guidance mechanism. Shaheen found two Italian admirals who had reached safety in Capri. One of them was the chief of Naval Ordinance Production, and both knew Admiral Girosi well. They willingly cooperated. Their knowledge about the radio bomb and the magnetic torpedo was communicated to Admiral Hewitt and Captain Gerauld C. Wright in the name of General Donovan, and they urged that the contacts be developed, and if necessary, permission should be sought from Marshal Badoglio to assign them for service with the secretary of the Navy.

On September 22, Mike Burke flew to Palermo to brief us, but while he was there, a radio came from "Greenbrier" that Donovan had arrived in Capri and that Burke should join Shaheen to work on the expanded "McGreggor" project. From September 24 to September 30 when "Greenbrier" stopped its transmissions, the station transmitted military intelligence gathered from refugees by Peter Tompkins. Donovan's presence on Capri and at Salerno was a harbinger of deep changes whose repercussions were to be felt in Italy for the rest of the Italian campaign.

Lieutenant North attempted to get Scamp to go to Capri where he cabled in French text that it would be to our advantage to be present as Donovan was making key decisions relative to the Italian campaign. On September 26, Eddy recalled North to Palermo ordering him to bring all documents and information collected, but on September 27 North replied from Capri that he had received orders from Donovan to remain on the island and coordinate OSS activities and to continue his duties as PT liaison officer. Donovan further ordered that all of the important Italian personages were to stay on Capri and not be sent to Palermo.

On September 29 North signalled that he would be coming to Palermo to pick up his personal gear and to bring the documents that had been collected in the various island raids and by the Seventh Detachment. He asked that we carefully check the radio equipment captured on Ventotene for spare parts and German tubes because the Navy was interested in examining them. Then, on September 30, he announced that the reports were being sent via one of the PT boat captains. This was the last message transmitted by "Greenbrier."

Palermo continued to transmit to "Greenbrier" until October 2, 1943, informing North that

September 30th Order from Eddy for you to remain in Capri. Marat to North. Your immediate commanding officer is Huntington and all 5th Army operations are under his command. Continue contacts with this base.

Oct. 1 Cianca and Tarchiani have reportedly arrived from the States in your area.[9] They are working for Cousins and their movements should be watched closely and reported to us.

October 2. Take Mariani away from San Stefano as he is urgently needed here for special operations.

October 3. Final transmission. Can you arrange PT transport from Capri to North of Civitavecchia for two special missions now ready. Transport from here to Capri can be handled this end.

There was no reply to the last four messages from Palermo, signalling a rupture of communications between the two OSS units. It also heralded a period of serious and needless bickering between OSS theater headquarters in Algiers and Fifth Army OSS Detachment under Huntington and succeeding COs.

Chapter 10

The End of "Bathtub"

The expanded "Bathtub" operation was suggested to Eddy in one of my signals on August 19. I had pointed out that a number of Barnes' PT boats should be assigned to service the OSS mission to take over Sardinia and that the mission should include SO and Operational Groups (OG) personnel.

Washington had other ideas and made plans to turn over the project direction to Sherman Kent, one of the senior men in the R & A Branch. Instructions were given to Colonel Eddy that he would have overall responsibility for the operation, and Washington hoped that Scamp and Italian SI would give Kent a hand.

On September 9, following the surrender of the Badoglio government, we sent a special signal to "Bathtub 1" in Sardinia informing the mission leader that Italy had surrendered but that the Germans continued to fight and that the Italian military and civilians were to sabotage German supply lines. The mission leader (Tony Camboni) was asked to pledge aid and credit if it were necessary. The message was deciphered by Italian intelligence which had been in control of the mission since two days after landing in Sardinia.

The mission had actually been captured on June 31 in a series of tragicomic incidents after landing and encountering an Italian patrol with which it exchanged friendly greetings in Italian. The Italian Army patrol had failed to identify the U.S. uniforms, for the nearest Allied troops were in North Africa. However, after a while, realizing something was not right, they sent out a patrol to track the OSS mission.

As our mission had been briefed not to engage in a firefight, it was taken prisoner after a comic negotiation and the almost apologetic noncom of the Italian patrol which alerted headquarters. A major with 100 men armed to the teeth was sent to pick them up, and they were taken to nearby Porto Torres to be interrogated. When a general came to interrogate them, they "confessed" that they were an advance party of a U.S. invasion force. They were threatened with execution as spies, and their interrogation was eventually turned over to an SIM officer, Major Faccio. They were finally transferred to Sassari, where they were placed in single cells. Later, the four enlisted men were put into a single cell and had an opportunity to exchange information. On July 31, Lieutenant Taquay came on the air. The message was relayed to us in Sicily and we started to "play the game" with the Italian counterespionage people.

The members of the mission were never turned over to the Germans and, as a result of the Italian Armistice (September 9, 1943), they were freed just moments before they were to be flown to the mainland. They were told to put on civvies so that they could not be recognized by the Germans who were still in Sassari, and they were given a police escort to protect them. They were eventually taken to Macomer under protective escort. There they met Lieutenant Colonel Serge Obolensky of OSS, who, at the behest of AFHQ and General Donovan, had been parachuted into Sardinia to establish contact with the Italian military command in Cagliari.

The German troops were ordered to evacuate Sardinia. With few exceptions, they managed to extricate themselves without having to fight the Italian forces that were nudging them to get out.

General Theodore Roosevelt, who had been sent on mission to the island, personally thanked the members of "Bathtub" for having volunteered to be infiltrated in Sardinia under such difficult conditions. The Obolensky mission to Sardinia brought a quick end to the proposed expanded "Bathtub" operations. The organization now turned its attention to the mainland where the Fifth Army was bogged down in the Salerno beachhead. The military situation had become so critical in the early phase of the invasion that Mark Clark had given serious consideration to a possible withdrawal of the U.S. Sixth Corps.

With Italy the focus of attention, there was no dearth of ambitious personalities who yearned to take over command of the OSS station in Naples. The first of these personalities was Lieutenant Colonel Ellery Huntington who had visited MEDTO (Mediterranean Theater of Operations) several times as the divisional chief of Special Operations. He had visited the Tunisian front in early 1943, and now he was back in Algiers with Donovan on the "Grant" mission. Huntington had stopped off in Palermo before proceeding to the Salerno invasion beaches. He reviewed several situations with Scamp, including the problem of a number of Yugoslavs and Albanians whom we had recruited at Lipari and Ventotene and were holding pending a decision as to where to take them for training and infiltration. On September 13, while in Palermo,

Huntington, in a signal to Donovan and Eddy in Algiers, urged that something be done "with the excellent group of Jugoslavs in Palermo and that Obolensky with two O.S.S. officers be sent to train the men." He also urged sending supplies. At the same time, he suggested that Donovan, McKay, Hughes, and Barnes proceed to Palermo via Tunis and that transport be arranged by OSS Palermo.

With pressure building up at AFHQ to do something about Sardinia, both Donovan and Eddy urged Scamp to join them in Algiers. That same day Scamp replied that he was sending Corvo "who knows all to discuss Bathtub operations." By the time I arrived in Algiers on September 14, Colonel Obolensky had been sent on his singular mission to Sardinia. Serge was not convinced that he should make the jump into Sardinia. A person who was present while the general was trying to convince him to undertake the mission reported that "Oboe," as he called him, kept saying: "But, General, I don't speak Italian. I know France and speak French fluently. . . ." The General in a very convincing voice would reply: "I know you can do it, Oboe—I have confidence in you and I know you will do it." Finally, Serge succumbed to Donovan's siren song and decided he would make the jump. His pride apparently overcame his qualms. Because of his age, the paratroop boys had to tape up his ankles for support. They also assigned a British wireless operator to him, there being no OSS personnel immediately available for the task. As a result, on September 19, word went out officially canceling the "Bathtub" operation.

In the interim, Huntington was on his way to the hectic beaches at Salerno, and for several days we lost track of him. Donovan was anxious that we contact him and relay a message indicative of things to come. Donovan inquired if Huntington had the means to execute a plan that was being prepared to demolish communications and transportation routes in central Italy. Soon thereafter, Donovan went to Salerno and met with Donald Downes at the OSS headquarters which had been set up at the Hotel Luna at Amalfi.[1] While on his way to Capri on board a PT boat, the general gave Downes the bad news that he was removing him from command and that Colonel Huntington was replacing him. Downes was at first given the choice of remaining in Italy as counter-intelligence chief of the OSS unit. Even this possibility was rescinded, however, as the general realized that Downes was suffering from physical fatigue. Thus, he was immediately sent back to the States for convalescence with orders that he be assigned anywhere except Italy.

By September 18, the situation in OSS had become tense as Colonel Eddy attempted to ward off a challenge to his authority by a combination of forces that wanted total responsibility for Italian operations taken away from him and AFHQ. That same day we received a radio signal from Eddy that "new O.S.S. directive" demanded that all OSS resources should be concentrated on disrupting German communications in central and northern Italy. He cautioned, "do not use good men with 5th Army which has already a large number of OSS men." The internal battle intensified as the mobile radio unit under Captain Smith, which had been temporarily assigned to Palermo, was ordered to proceed to Salerno and join Fifth Army OSS.

The dramatic moment was soon to arrive when Donovan decided that all OSS assets in the Salerno area were to be placed under the command of Colonel Huntington. Donovan's message to Eddy on September 25 fully spelled it out:

Huntington has been directed by the 5th Army to prepare plans setting up network to and including Rome and beyond to Leghorn for the time being. This embraces their present tactical situation. Also Huntington has been instructed to organize and train at once small groups of native Italians for guerilla action. Six of sixteen men of Scamporino are out of action, 2 killed, 2 badly wounded, 2 nervous invalids. An 88 hit their midst. DeAngelis has been working with others but in no sense doing a strategic job and it is not possible to handle this from Palermo. He is right in the middle of this operation that can't be done because it is ridiculous. DeAngelis station will be taken over here by reason of a particular operation. You can't have one man in a theatre responsible only to another. You and I don't like that ourselves. Please tell Scamp. Scamp could give valuable aid here. Expect McKay in Tunis. I am leaving today.[2]

On the same day headquarters Seventh Army, Fifth Army and Fifteenth Army Group received a radio message from Eisenhower that all OSS personnel in Palermo would be moved and would operate only under direct orders from AFHQ. The radio message from Eddy to Corvo concluded: "You are not to take orders from Huntington."

This message was followed by one from Eddy to Huntington:

Scamporino's men, who are now on tactical operations in your area may report to you. You are forbidden to touch personnel in Palermo area which only operate at AFHQ direction. See telegram from Eisenhower No. 8866 of September 24th to 15th Army Group for info to 5th Army and 7th Army.

Later in the same day Eddy followed up with another message on the same subject:

Eddy to Corvo: General Donovan has agreed that 5th Army should take over all OSS personnel now in Naples area. Consequently your team including DeAngelis should now report to Colonel Huntington. However, in order to avoid further drain on your personnel, send no more men to Fifth Army without instructions from AFHQ.

While this battle was shaping up, Scamporino had to leave on mission to establish contact with the Badoglio government which was being reorganized at Brindisi. There the Allied Control Commission, on which

General Maxwell Taylor was the U.S. representative, had set up shop to supervise Italian government operations.

The Italian General Staff was being reconstituted under General Ambrosio and Marshal Messe who had been liberated from captivity and returned to Italy. Scamp had already established a friendly relationship with General Castellano and the staff of the Italian Military Mission to AFHQ, Algiers. Among the staff officers were Major Marchesi, Captain Vito Guarrasi, and Lieutenant Galvano Lanza di Trabia, the last two being from Palermo. They suggested that when Scamp got to Brindisi he should contact Colonel Pompeo Agrifoglio, the head of Italian military intelligence. Agrifoglio had gone underground in North Africa after the surrender of the Axis forces and for some time operated in Allied-occupied Tunisia, sending meticulous reports to Italy. He finally turned himself in as a POW to an American unit and was sent to a camp in the United States. After the armistice, he was released at the request of General Castellano and returned to Italy to head military intelligence. Colonel Agrifoglio was a professional officer who had served the Italian Army since World War I. His loyalty to the Crown was unquestioned, although he was of democratic bent in his views. He had never been a Fascist and was a scrupulously honest individual who commanded respect and placed great weight on keeping his word.

Scamp was accompanied to the Italian Court by Paolino Gerli, an outstanding Italo-American industrialist. Gerli was the world's most important silk importer and had important contacts among the leading industrialists and financiers in both Italy and the United States. The contacts with Agrifoglio and other members of the Italian government led to the establishment of a high degree of collaboration and paved the way for future OSS operations in northern Italy.

Arrangements were also made to establish a permanent liaison with the Italian government and with the Allied Control Commission. Soon after Scamp had returned to Palermo, one of my recruits from Detroit, Major John Ricca, whose parents had come from Piedmont to the United States, was sent to Brindisi. There he became a personal friend of the marshal, who also came from Piedmont. John, who was chief prosecutor in Detroit, spoke the Piedmontese dialect perfectly, just as his parents had spoken it half a century before. This fact helped to establish a bond of friendship between the elderly marshal and the then middle-aged Detroit attorney. The contact proved useful for OSS sometimes serving as a pipeline to get personal messages to the White House.

Chapter 11

Implementing the Hydra Complex

General Donovan's decision to leave tactical operations to the Fifth Army unit and allow the OSS theater officer at AFHQ to retain the strategic aspects of intelligence gathering and unorthodox warfare operations deprived us of jurisdiction over many of our own people. The result was a spirit of tense competition which produced endless confrontations. It became necessary to redefine our operations in compliance with theater restrictions. Strategic operations in northern Italy on the Tyrrhenian Sea, for example, could only be conducted by OSS/AFHQ from bases north of the convoy routes going to Naples.[1]

After a flurry of naval activity in connection with the Salerno landings, Commander Barnes informed me that PTB Ron 15 was planning to move its operational base to Sardinia. Colonel Eddy therefore approved my request to set up an operations base at the naval port of La Maddalena, a fortified island at the eastern approaches of the Straits of Boniface, between Corsica and Sardinia.

Eddy and AFHQ also approved our recommendation to create the principal strategic infiltration base at Brindisi. At this point, I commenced preparation of nine missions which were to cover northern Italy from the Apennines to the Alps.

A third SI base was to be set up at Pozzuoli to help gather political intelligence and to continue the liaison with the Badoglio government which was transferring its headquarters to the Naples area.

The Palermo base was to be retained for some time to cover both political and economic intelligence. The station was placed under the command of Joe Russo, a crackerjack newsman who had left the *Bridgeport Herald* in order to join the Italian SI Section.

The establishment of the OSS Maddalena command was given imme-diate priority.[2] I organized a group of 30 agents, including several radio operators, a number of Sardinians, and some of the personnel I had re-cruited in the United States. As assistant operations officer, I chose Captain Tarallo, who had led our incursions on Lipari and Ventotene.

While waiting for our moving orders from AFHQ, we sought a means of operational transportation which we ourselves could control. Our experience had taught us that, despite the good-will of the U.S. Navy and the PT officers, we were operationally controlled by CINCMED. There was no way to circumvent some of the ironclad edicts it issued, even when we had the full support of Admiral Hewitt. Operational transpor-tation was one of the key roadblocks to OSS clandestine operations. Before my arrival in Algiers, the organization had been totally dependent on British transportation and some French naval lift. My visit to Admiral Connolly's headquarters and the agreement worked out with PTB Ron 15, permitting the use of the U.S. Navy boats, had been our first real breakthrough.

Now we attempted to have AFHQ assign some other mode of trans-portation. On September 28, after consultation with the local Navy authorities, I made the following proposal:

Navy have recommended you inform AFHQ to request CINCMED that Hewitt place at our disposal one corvette and two MAS boats for operations in the Mediterranean and one corvette and two MAS boats for operations in the Adriatic. Also that AFHQ request that Hewitt give us all assistance, mainte-nance and fuel and American personnel. Italian crews will remain. Captain Andrews, Lt. Fairbanks, Commander Kremer and Captain Olds all enthusiastic re our work and promise full cooperation.

On September 30 Eddy informed me that an official request had been made for the assignment of the Italian naval units through G-3, but that he would only approach Hewitt on specific operations to be conducted from Palermo. Nothing came of the request. Desperate for a means of operational transportation, we finally spotted a beached 15-knot merchantman at Scylla in Calabria. The SS *Luigi Rizzo* seemed ideal for a floating OSS base; it was equipped with a modern radio transmitter which could have been used as our base radio station.

On October 2 I asked Eddy's permission to requisition the *Rizzo*. On the following day he replied that we were forbidden to acquire a base ship and that after a long discussion we were authorized to acquire and operate several small fishing boats in Bastia, Corsica. Eddy concluded: "Garibaldi must use naval craft not privately owned craft." That reply closed all doors to solution to the problem. The movement to La Maddalena now became crucial if we were to operate along Italy's west coast and the Ligurian Riviera.

In mid-October CINCMED issued orders to the commanding general of the Seventh Army in Sicily authorizing the movement with the following signal:

Ship to Maddalena O.S.S. personnel designated by Italian Section G-2, Commander NOB Palermo has been notified for action and personnel is to be ferried to Maddalena to carry out certain special operations for O.S.S. These operations will be carried out in conjunction with PTB Ron 15.

Signed COMNAVNAW

On the morning of October 25 a British-manned LST sailed into Palermo harbor to pick up the OSS unit, supplies, and equipment needed to set up the base. The LST also took on a U.S. antiaircraft unit which was needed to defend the naval base against anticipated German air raids. Among the old SI hands who embarked with me were Carl Bommarito, Louis Fiorilla, Joe Ferrara, "Pep" Puleo, Vincent Pavia, Peter Durante, John Ballato, and 27 Italian civilians, U.S. civilian Tom Stoneborough, and Captain Tarallo.

The LST left in the late afternoon without any escorting vessel. Lack of an escort seemed strange inasmuch as we were sailing into enemy-infested waters: we were skirting the east coast of Sardinia and were within easy range of the German fighters based on mainland airdromes. Fortunately, we sailed unmolested all night. In the early morning daylight, we were within sight of the island of Caprera, where Italy's great liberator, Garibaldi, had spent his final years and was buried. The LST headed for the Gulf of Arzachena when suddenly the pounding of the ship's engines stopped. The LST kept moving forward by inertia. We were wondering what had happened when the loudspeaker blared out that we had accidentally run into an unmarked minefield. Slowly, the lumbering ship backed away from the area, and on instructions from the shore station, extricated itself from the heavy minefield.

Needless to say, everyone on board stopped breathing while the LST slowly worked its way out of the predicament. After that harrowing experience, we all wanted to feel land under our feet. It did not take long to empty out the ship once we were in port.

The town of La Maddalena was essentially a naval station which, during the war, was populated by thousands of sailors from the Italian fleet. There were still some civilians left on the island, which had been under constant German attack since the Armistice, but most of them had been evacuated to Sardinia. Once on the island, we quickly requisitioned the small hotel on the main square and started settling in before contacting Admiral Aristotle Bona, who was the Italian CO, and a British naval captain, who was the Allied officer-in-charge. We never got the opportunity to relax because the Germans, aware of the Allied buildup, were on top of us dropping bombs and strafing the island.

I was at the window looking out onto the square when I saw a mass of sailors running to take cover in the shelters. After the wave of blue uniforms had subsided, it was followed by a wave of civilians, and then the tail end was brought up by a handful of women who nonchalantly walked to the shelters, arm in arm with young sailors. The Luftwaffe was caught by surprise because the newly arrived U.S. antiaircraft unit had found time to set up its guns. Before the Germans knew what was happening, three or four of their planes had been shot down by our radar-directed artillery and the fire from the ships in the port. Soon the all clear was sounded, and the human wave from the shelters disgorged itself on the square on its way back home. In my curiosity to see what was going on, I had failed to notice that most of my men had also disappeared and that I was practically alone in the office. Soon, one by one, they also started finding their way back to headquarters.

Hardly an hour had gone by that the sound of gunfire and the siren's wailings warned that the enemy was back. Confirmation of their return was the sound of the deep thumpings of bombs exploding in the distance. Again, the blue tidal wave of sailors swept into the square scurrying for cover, followed by the few civilians and then the ladies, walking arm in arm with their escorts. This time the sailors seemed to be different. Another twenty minutes passed and the all clear sounded, with the tide reversing itself on and off the square, on their way to wherever they had come from. Another hour passed before the process repeated itself— with the ladies always accompanied by new escorts. Finally, came the dawn.

The Germans seemed determined to inflict a lot of punishment on the base for some reason we could not fathom. In the process they were taking a terrible shellacking as the American ack-ack was taking a heavy toll—and in between raids the ladies were in business as usual.

The following day Louis Fiorilla, who was operating our agent set codenamed "Messina," called Palermo and made his first contact with "Garibaldi." We informed Scamp that we had met with Commander Barnes who had arrived some time before us and that operations would be underway in about ten days. However, the operations would have to be coordinated with the regular squadron sweeps, and as the weather was starting to foul up, operations would be restricted.

Before embarking for La Maddalena, I knew that once I had set up the unit I would have to immediately return to Palermo in order to go to Brindisi and meet with the Italian officials who would be working with us. The nearest Allied airfield to Maddalena was at Cagliari in the southern part of the island. On the morning of October 28, I drove the jeep onto the ancient ferryboat (which almost tipped over under the weight), and landed at the town of Palau on the northern tip of Sardinia.

I took the road to Sassari, where I stopped briefly to get a shave at a local barber shop. A lot of Italian paratroopers were casually strolling around the square and in front of the barber shop, and some of them did not look very friendly. One or two occasionally fingered their long daggers as they walked back and forth in front of the barber shop I had just entered. I called Carl Bommarito, my driver, and planted him in front of the door with a Thompson slung over his shoulder as a cautionary move. Nothing happened outside, but inside the old barber became so nervous that his shaky hands nicked my face in two or three places. All my assurances notwithstanding he could not stop his hands from shaking.

Leaving the barber shop, we immediately headed south for the long drive to Cagliari. As we drove through a number of villages, the people cheered and clapped, shouting what to our ears sounded like "Miicani." They were obviously happy that, at least for them, the war and its privations were over and that there were no Germans around. By late afternoon, we had reached the airport at Cagliari, and since there was no flight to Tunis until the next morning, we bedded down in nearby barracks. The airport was under British control, and the morning flight was an RAF C-47. I instructed Carl to stay in Cagliari and await my return as I expected to be back in a few days. There was no direct transportation to La Maddalena, except by water.

When the flight to Tunis took off, I was the only American passenger on board. The others were a few Allied administrative officers on the island which had been nominally left under Italian administration, supervised by the Allied Control Commission (ACC). Once at Tunis, I had to wait until Sunday for a flight to Palermo, where I arrived on November 1. Scamp was away, and I prepared to leave for Brindisi in order to establish contact with the Italian intelligence officials with whom we would be working to undertake the infiltration of our agents into northern Italy and to examine operational and transportation facilities in the area.

We were aware that an agreement had been worked out between the British and Italian intelligence services for maximum cooperation; that SOE had set up schools in the Brindisi-Bari area; and that the British controlled most of the sea transportation in the Adriatic, including the movements of the Royal Italian Navy.

On November 3, I started to drive overland to Brindisi with Sergeant Tony Ribarich. The trip was a long one, made more difficult because many of the bridges and tunnels on the coastal highway to Messina had been blown up during the Sicilian campaign and had not yet been repaired. With the roads from Reggio Calabria to the Gulf of Taranto, where the Germans had retreated across Calabria, no better, we did not arrive in Brindisi until November 6.

As part of my objectives to set up a radio link between our Italian office in Brindisi and our Palermo station, I took a reliable Italian navy W/T operator, Salvatore Amodio, with a radio and cipher code worked out by

Chuck Groff and Ralph DeHaro. The plan had been codenamed "Brooklyn." The first contact with Palermo was made on November 7, and the station remained active until December 26. We were able to transmit both intelligence and administrative messages, which were relayed to Algiers, Naples, and Washington via Palermo. The "Brindisi" mission was headed by Major John Ricca who had been in touch with both Allied and Italian elements ever since Scamporino and Gerli had set up the station.

Almost from the first meeting, Colonel Agrifoglio, head of SIM, and I struck up a warm friendship. A World War I veteran and then in his mid-fifties, the colonel had just returned from a U.S. prisoner-of-war camp. He told me he had been well treated there and had pleasant recollections of that period. A true Sicilian, he preferred to speak the dialect when speaking to Sicilians. His piercing black eyes when fixed on someone, would cause the greatest discomfort, giving one the distinct feeling that he could read one's inner thoughts. Of all the officers in Badoglio's government, Agrifoglio commanded the respect not only of the men who served under him, but also that of the British, French, and Americans, of whom he had been a recent enemy. His task of rebuilding Italy's military intelligence service from the chaos caused by the disastrously implemented Armistice was not a simple one.

Cut off from SIM's headquarters in Rome, with few of the necessary key intelligence files available to him and desperately short of experienced manpower and equipment, Agrifoglio dedicated himself to reconstituting the staff. Gradually in late September and October, loyal General Staff officers filtered through the lines and made their way south to Brindisi to rejoin their organization. Not all of them made it. Some remained in the north to reorganize the intelligence organization of the newly formed puppet government of Mussolini's Social Republic.

Brindisi, while an important naval port, was hardly Rome, and so the Italian government and armed services found themselves short of even the most elementary necessities. The arrival of Scamporino and my followup visit were welcomed by the SIM people who, until then, had by necessity been tied in closely with SOE for even their minimal needs.

Whereas relations with the British were based on mutual professional respect and both sides harbored suspicious motivations, the relationship with the Italian Section of OSS was open and friendly and involved mutual trust. That is not to say that SIM's cooperation with the British was not loyal, it was simple an arms-length relationship.

At our meeting, we reached a number of agreements:

1. OSS/SIM would combine a certain number of missions.
2. SIM would provide a number of W/Ts who could be trained at our communications center.
3. SIM would provide a number of northern Italian key agents who would be culled from the Italian armed forces.

4. SIM would appoint a permanent liaison officer to our Brindisi headquarters.
5. SIM would make available its documents centers.
6. OSS would control all communications with northern Italy.
7. OSS would finance, equip, and deliver teams by air and arrange for surface and underwater transportation.
8. OSS would provide financing for all teams going into the field and would take care of all resupply operations.
9. OSS would collaborate in reestablishing SIM/CE operations in Sicily, which was still under AMGOT and was soon to pass to ACC control.

This verbal agreement was to form the basis of a long-term accord, which, in combination with other Italian SI assets, was to produce outstanding results not only in the intelligence-gathering field, but also in the buildup and supply of the guerrilla movement throughout northern Italy.

One of the Italian officers who participated in the SIM conferences was Lieutenant Colonel Giuseppe Massaioli, who had been placed in charge of offensive intelligence operations by Agrifoglio. An outstanding officer who had won a number of battlefield promotions and awards on the Russian front, Massaioli was a professional soldier who had very clear ideas about ethical comportment. He was highly intelligent and inherently honest, and he worked loyally with his British SOE counterparts throughout the war. Massaioli and I struck up what was to be a lifetime friendship. Even though we never worked together in any of his operations, we met quite frequently to discuss operating problems and the military situation of the northern Italian patriot movement. As Agrifoglio's operations officer, he had a panoramic view of what was going on behind the German lines.

During my travels, a very important change had been effected in Algiers: Colonel Eddy was replaced as CO of the OSS/AFHQ unit by Colonel Edward F. Glavin, a West Pointer, who had studied at Oxford. Glavin began his new job by visiting the stations under his command and reviewing the work of the various desks operating out of his headquarters. He brought in a small staff, which immediately started sorting things out under the leadership of his deputy, Major Norman Newhouse, a newspaper executive from Staten Island. During part of the tour of the Italian stations, Glavin was accompanied by Scamp. As a consequence, Scamp could not participate in the meetings I was holding with Agrifoglio in Brindisi and later in Palermo.

The replacement of Colonel Eddy had been a foregone conclusion once the OSS expanded its operations. OSS needed restructuring if it were to function efficiently and produce the intelligence needed to help the Fifteenth Army Group fight its way to northern Italy and to plan for the invasion of southern France.

Returning to Palermo in a convoy with Colonel Agrifoglio and his chief of CE Major Giuspino Dotti, we continued to discuss operational plans for northern Italy and details of his effort to reorganize SIM's counterespionage service in Sicily by reactivating their stations in Palermo, Messina, Catania, and Trapani. This could only be done with the permission of AMGOT, ACC, and CIC, who on our advice concurred with the plan. In the meantime, the Maddalena Command, which had been awaiting my return, was experiencing assorted difficulties from bad weather, German air raids, and lack of direction. My trip to Brindisi and the delay in my return to Sardinia had caused indecision. Finally, on November 2, a two-man mission requested by Commander Barnes was landed on the island of Giglio. Wayne Nelson, conducting officer of the mission, described its objective:

to put two men with radio on the island of Giglio, located nine miles off the Italian coast and approximately 30 miles north of Civitavecchia, for the purpose of gathering and transmitting intelligence to our Maddalena base, with particular reference to German shipping and convoy movements along the Italian coast. [3]

The two men selected for the job were U.S. Army Private Joe Ferrara, W/T, and an aging Franco-Italian recruit from Casablanca, Emilio Vierin. The PT boat conducting the operation was under the command of Lieutenant Sinclair. Signor Scotto, the captain of a fishing boat which had recently arrived with the American airmen he had rescued from Giglio, provided information as to where clandestine landings could be made. He also provided the names of islanders whom our people could safely contact.

The landing proceeded with a slight delay owing to squalls encountered by the PT boats. After landing, the men gave the Morse signal "A" that everything was OK on shore, the rubber boat was hauled, and the PTs returned to their base. Unfortunately, because of radio failure, the "Paternoster" mission could not communicate with its home base at Maddalena, and Palermo was advised to try to pick up their signal, but the station never came on the air. A number of days passed and several attempts were made to rescue the mission, but foul weather thwarted all efforts.

Finally, on the night of November 21, Wayne Nelson and Italo Vierin, son of Emilio Vierin, managed to land in the dead of night. Seeing a dim light half way up the cliff facing the beach, they found the elder Vierin and Joe Ferrara, who had escaped a Fascist police attack only a few hours before, thanks to a timely warning from friendly islanders. The weather was so bad at this time of the year that it was practically impossible to carry out many operations. The U.S. Navy planned to move the PT base to Bastia, Corsica.

The weather, combined with the remoteness of La Maddalena from any real civic center, and with the difficulty of obtaining transportation to our base in Palermo, once the PTs had moved to Bastia, completely disheartened Tarallo who had proved himself capable of carrying out complicated orders in prior dangerous operations. He was not up to improvising and planning special operations. My delay in returning to Maddalena and his physical illness added to his command problems.

On November 26 Tarallo sent Wayne Nelson and Tom Stoneborough to Lieutenant Colonel Russ Livermore, CO of the Operational Group detachment in Ile Rousse, Corsica, in order to discuss a working arrangement for joint operations. Russ liked the idea. Inasmuch as PTB Ron 15 was going to be based in Bastia, the decision was made to continue SI operations in conjunction with Commander Barnes' squadron.

On November 28, the Italian civilians were returned to Palermo on board an Italian corvette doing courier service to La Maddalena. Many of them were afflicted with gonorrhea, having kept company with those same women I had seen escorted to the air raid shelters the first day we were on the island. It was little wonder: there were some 5,000 sailors and only about a dozen women on the island.

On November 29 I left for La Maddalena on board the Italian destroyer *Oriani* to make a determination about conditions at the base. After reviewing all of the evidence and the fact that the PT squadron was moving out, the decision was made to close down the base. However, I authorized the continuation of some infiltration efforts along the Ligurian coast from Bastia, where we planned to create an SI unit. Tom Stoneborough and Wayne Nelson, who were already in Bastia, were advised to stay there. The next evening the *Oriani* picked up the remaining personnel, including Major Tarallo, en route to Palermo, where we arrived the following morning.

In answer to a request from Russ Livermore, on December 3, Scamp informed Colonel Glavin that Italian SI was prepared to ship Captain Joseph Bonfiglio and eight men to Bastia to bolster the seven men already there. Glavin immediately ignalled:

Have authorized Livermore to keep Nelson and Stoneborough and any other Maddalena personnel at Bastia. Please inform Captain Corvo that all personnel at Bastia should stay there until ordered by Livermore or myself to move.

In keeping with Glavin's newly instituted procedures, Scamp returned to Algiers on December 5 with my plans for nine missions to be infiltrated into northern Italy from the base to be set up in Brindisi.

On December 8, a committee representing the various branches and services of OSS met in Algiers under Glavin's chairmanship to review the operations I had prepared and set up a timetable and the material requirements for the missions. Members of the panel were Glavin, Lieutenant Colonel Obolensky, Lieutenant Commander Warwick Potter, Major Peter Mero, Captain Gerry de Piolenc, Captain Jim Lawrence, and Scamporino.[4] The CIA did not declassify the notes of that meeting until mid-1984:

1. Major Mero will arrange signal plans for all parties and will establish a base station in the Naples-Caserta region, with preferably two alternate pick-up stations.
2. Mr. Scamporino will provide the staff at Naples for sifting and relaying information to 15th Army Group and AFHQ. Colonel Obolensky and Capt. dePiolenc will furnish Mr. Scamporino with information pertaining to arrangements with resistance groups for reception committees, location of dropping points for personnel and supplies.
3. Captain Corvo, Operations Officer, who will be at Bari, will arrange for sea transportation.
4. Col. Obolensky and Captain de Piolenc will furnish information as to what we are prepared to deliver to resistance groups in the way of money, food, clothing, arms, demolitions, radio equipment.
5. Two radio operators, under command of Captain Corvo, on arriving at Bari, report to Squadron Leader Denis, "A" Force.

Team #3
6. Team No. 3, in addition to mission specified, obtain information on labor situation in the Venice-Padua-Treviso area.
7. In addition to the three men already designated for this party, there will be two radio operators provided by Mr. Scamporino whose primary duty will be to work with "A" Force. "A" Force, in return, will pass on to us any intelligence or information on SO possibilities and resistance groups as they may obtain through their prisoner of war chain.

Team #4
8. Team No. 4 will be informed of Team No. 3's coordination with "A" Force.

Team #6
9. The party consisting of 3 men assigned to Team No. 6 will be brought to Algiers.
10. As we have four operations scheduled for the 5th Army and as weather during December is normally unfavorable, it is doubtful whether this operation will be dispatched during the December moon, unless it is given priority over some of the 5th Army operations. This will be decided as soon as we know more about the 5th Army requirements.

Team #7
11. Team No. 7 will be sent to Bari for training subject to Col. Dodds-Parker's approval.[5]
12. It probably will be desirable to dispatch this team from Algiers rather than Bari. This team is scheduled for the January moon.

Team #8
13. Mr. Scamporino stated that he preferred to move his team by surface craft. It was therefore decided to send this team to Bastia for dispatching.

Team #9
Team #9 will be sent to Bari for training, subject to Col. Dodds-Parker's approval and will be dispatched from here. This team is scheduled for the January moon.
Copies all officers present; ISSU-6; ISLD; A Force.

The following day Scamp instructed Lieutenant Joseph Caputa to handcarry a letter outlining the modifications that had been made to my original operations. These modifications reflected an unrealistic timetable for the execution of the missions. Furthermore, as outlined, I knew from past experience that the commitments which the representatives of the various services made at the meeting would never be fulfilled because the necessary OSS facilities did not exist in the field. Having visited the OSS base in Bari, I knew that the personnel there were having difficulties taking care of their own affairs. Considering the way the staging of the operations was devised, they would have had to assign a private plane to me so that I could comply with their schedules. Finally, from the distribution of copies listed at the foot of the memo, British intelligence and SOE were fully informed and were in control of what we proposed to do.

According to the instructions, we were to depend on the radio communications that had been set up at Bari, and our base was to be located at Brindisi, 100 kilometers to the south. That would mean that, in order to send an administrative message, we would have to send a messenger and our agents in the field would have to be serviced in the same manner. Some teams were to be trained in Brindisi and then flown to Algiers, from where they could be flown to their drop zones in northern Italy. Others were to be infiltrated through the lines in conjunction with "A" Force, a British prisoner-of-war escape operation; still others were to be taken to Bastia for infiltration by the U.S. PT boats. Lastly, Lieutenant Caputa had brought a set of travel orders for the overland movement of the unit which was headed for the Naples area under Captain Seb Passanisi and for the unit under the command of Lieutenant Samuel Fraulino to Brindisi. These travel orders issued by 2677 Headquarters Company Experimental were insufficient.

In order to straighten out the matter, I sent Scamp a message on November 14:

Even though ready for movement, orders brought by Caputa insufficient. All of our movement is controlled by AFHQ and a cable must be sent to G-2, 7th Army immediately for movement to be carried out. Clarify my position and have orders drawn up properly.

Because the Committee memorandum had failed to answer many questions, I urged Scamp to come to Palermo so that we could straighten out the most important ones. Later that same day, I offered to fly to Algiers and then, unable to get a flight out of Palermo, I sent the following wire:

Please answer the following questions today, urgent:

(1) Am I authorized to move "Garibaldi" and personnel?
(2) Can signal plans made here be used for NE groups?
(3) Do missions NE have to contact Bari?
(4) Is Brindisi station out?
(5) Is "Garibaldi" to be set up at Pozzuoli or does it go out of existence?

Answers must be known if our operations are to run smoothly and more important, successfully.[6]

As Scamp was nowhere to be found at the moment, Major Mero answered my signal:

In Scamp's absence Mero is answering. We shall get Scamp who cannot be found and give him message first thing in the morning. Re your message: para 2 Groff, all matters regarding communications are to be answered by me. (This was an admonition to Sergeant Groff that he was not to supply communications advice and constituted another reason why I was wary of the committee instructions.)

Sergeant Groff and Chief DeHaro had been working with me since July without stop and without much help from the communications people in Algiers for most of that time. In addition, Chuck Groff and Ralph DeHaro had trained most of the W/T operators, and together they had devised the system of communications and ciphers that had kept us in touch with all of the missions. Their work had been selfless and grueling, and their dedication exemplary.

A few days before this radio message arrived, Mero had sent a signal to Groff. The tenor of that message had created some suspicion in my mind that Mero had requested an accounting of the radio equipment on hand and admonished that "the accuracy of the information requested is your responsibility." Not long afterward, on January 7, Sergeant Groff summarized the chronological history of his service to his superior in a memo entitled "Communications Report."

From July 10th at Mateur to July 25th at Palermo, while in route to Sicily, three days after the invasion, using portable equipment, maintained contact with Algiers and Bone and contacted one field mission and attempted another. During this time 19 messages were received and thirty messages were sent.

From July 25th, using the same equipment, augmented by one Italian transmitter and one communications receiver for use as standby equipment when repairs were necessary to the original sets (handicapped by lack of local electricity for two months) until December 26th, nine missions were prepared and given additional training to insure successful work. All were successful completely except two which did not endanger our security and with no loss of life. Messages handled from these missions total 124 (5,762 groups) received, and 88 sent (4,623 groups).

Also regular contact with Algiers and Bone (which later moved to Tunis) was kept, directly accountable for intelligence reports, operational and supply requests, 251 messages totalling 12,097 5-letter groups were received and 281 messages with 21,183 groups sent.

This totals 793 messages for 45,374 groups handled. 875 contacts were made, averaging 5.2 contacts per day during five-month period.

All this was done without help with the exception of three weeks of assistance by Sgt. O'Brien. No provisions were made for sickness or accident. Installation and maintenance equipment for the station with all the responsibility, servicing field sets, cutting antennas, charging batteries, and, in addition, training four civilians for radio work in the field. Help has been asked repeatedly, which has been promised, but none has been received. Chief Petty Officer DeHaro has done all of the cryptography work unaided also, except for a period of one month when he was assisted by second class yeoman, Peters. All of the above details are vouched for by all connected with this detachment and material is available for proof.

While the situation in Algiers was undergoing numerous changes and while personnel from the States were beginning to arrive in greater numbers, the situation of the Fifth Army unit was also in a state of flux. Unlike the Seventh Army detachment which had to gradually overcome most obstacles and win the confidence of the Army staff people to gain acceptance as part of the G-2 structure, the OSS Fifth Army detachment did not have to prove itself with Colonel Howard or General Clark. Both of them had worked with OSS in Morocco, and Clark himself had secretly landed in North Africa, where Colonel Eddy and his OSS team had helped pave the way for the North African landings. True, the predicament of the Fifth Army during the early days of the Salerno landings was precarious, but AFHQ and the Fifth Army had been provided ample intelligence on German Order of Battle by OSS Palermo. This intelligence had been confirmed by the Italian Armistice emissary General Castellano to General Strong, the chief intelligence officer at AFHQ.[7] The lack of perspicacious planning in conjunction with the Salerno landings had been appalling, and the bungling of the liaison and coordination with the Badoglio government was inexcusable.

The reasons why OSS had been kept in the dark about the negotiations and why it was not called to play a role in the negotiations with Castellano or the Badoglio government are inexplicable inasmuch as OSS controlled an impressive pool of Italian-speaking specialists in the Theater of Operations. Instead, Major Roseberry of SOE was called in and provided the radio to establish communications links between Rome and AFHQ. To operate the radio, Roseberry asked Castellano to free an SOE officer who had been recently captured on a secret mission to Italy.

There were three basic differences between the situation of the Fifth Army and the Seventh Army OSS detachments.

1. After the Gela landing, the Seventh Army moved swiftly and its need for tactical intelligence was not acute. The Fifth Army was in dire need of intelligence because for many days the success of its beachhead was in doubt and its landings were carried out in a restricted area where the enemy could rush forces to contain the beachhead.

2. The Seventh Army OSS detachment was at first led by Colonel Eddy himself, and there was no dissent or competition on the operations staff.

3. The Fifth Army detachment suffered from too many prima donnas who were driven by ambition without the sterner stuff which is a prerequisite for success. Unfortunately, this lack of discipline quickly brought about rapid changes in the detachment command. Within three weeks after the landing, Donald Downes was succeeded by Colonel Ellery Huntington; Huntington was succeeded by Colonel John Haskell; who, in turn, was succeeded by Colonel John Reutershan, who was replaced by Colonel Carter.

There was constant turmoil in the lower ranks as each individual aspiring to be the "best" operations officer sought to outdo the other.

The competition was keenest among Andre Pacatte, Andre Bourgoin, and Peter Tompkins. Pacatte, a French teacher from the Cleveland Berlitz School had become a member of Italian SI, solely on the basis of his experience over a couple of summers as a Boy Scout in Corsica, and he was supposed to infiltrate that island. (He did not speak Italian, and much less did he understand the Italian temperament). Captain Bourgoin, who had for many years been an officer in the Deuxieme Bureau, was a long-time resident of Morocco, a friend of Downes, and a participant in the tragic "Banana" project with him. Peter Tompkins, a bright young journalist who spoke fluent Italian (his family spent a good deal of time in Italy and he had attended school there) was serving with the Psychological Warfare Board. Tompkins' transfer to SI was requested by Scamp who thought he could make a valuable contribution to the work that lay ahead. All three burned out early in the game as they lacked strong direction and control from the top.

The man who should have headed the operations for the Fifth Army was Captain Alex Cagiati of Boston, who had been born in Italy, spoke fluent Italian, and understood the Italian mentality. But he was not aggressive, and so for the duration of the Italian campaign, he was satisfied to play a background role, counseling whoever was in charge of the Fifth Army detachment.

With the Huntington takeover of all OSS personnel operating in the Fifth Army area at the end of September, Andre Pacatte assumed the duties of operations officer at Capri. By October 15, Huntington had entrusted him with the task of finding operational transportation by water or air to northern Italy. Pacatte described his efforts colorfully in a memo covering the period from October 15 to December 7, recounting his meetings with various British naval officers at Taranto-Bari and numerous other places along the Adriatic coast. Finally, he described a trip on board the Italian submarine *Aksum* which he loaded with fifteen agents who, against all prudent security practices, were landed by Pacatte and the Italian submarine commander, Captain Sorrentino, near Castel di Mezzo.[8]

Pacatte's report bristled with criticism of the British naval staff's control over Adriatic operations. When he finally got the fifteen agents in the sub, he took his "Italian" assistant with him, "so as to protect the security of my agents, preventing them from talking too much to the crew of the submarine and to be certain that our former enemies would not pull a fast one." It is difficult to understand why Pacatte, with his expressed lack of confidence in the Italian crew and officers, should have entrusted his own fate and that of the agents to them.

A few weeks after the voyage of the *Aksum*, the log which the submarine's commander, Captain Sorrentino, kept was delivered to me at my Brindisi office.[9] It covered the precise time and place, as well as conditions under which the landing of the fifteen agents had taken place. The location was quite a distance from where Pacatte had reported the landing.

Salerno, and later Naples, became priority areas for OSS operations, but the detachment lacked a steady hand at the helm and became engaged in a series of quasi-political undertakings that diluted its potential accomplishments. Soon after the landing at Salerno, the detachment came face to face with competition from the British SOE unit which was in charge of Major Malcolm Munthe and Captain Max Salvadori, Emilio Lussu's brother-in-law.[10] The British were old hands at Italian politics and had a number of anti-Fascist leaders in tow. Among them were Alberto Cianca and Alberto Tarchiani who had left their New York hustings to get back to Italy under SOE patronage. In addition, SOE had Leo Valiani and Dino Gentili. Early on, they managed to rescue Benedetto Croce, Italy's venerated philosopher, from Sorrento and established a contact with his son-in-law Raimondo Craveri, who had already met Donald Downes and Peter Tompkins after he crossed the lines at Maiori. Through them Craveri met Donovan, who had come on an inspection of the Fifth Army detachment. Donovan was taken to visit Croce, and an idea that had germinated in the group found ready acceptance by Donovan. This was Craveri's idea of establishing an Italian Volunteer Corps (Gruppi Combattenti Italiani) to be commanded by a retired elderly Italian general, Giuseppe Pavone, who, in his day, had assisted Gabriele D'Annunzio in the capture of the city of Fiume.

Although Donovan had espoused the proposal enthusiastically and the project had won Major Munthe's support, when Craveri and Tarchiani were sent to Brindisi to secure Marshal Badoglio's support, they were turned down flatly.[11]

In anticipation of the approval, recruiting had been going on in the Naples area. When Craveri came back with the news that Badoglio had rejected the proposal, it became necessary to disband the yet unorganized unit. Craveri, who had developed a genuine friendship with Tompkins, instead of giving up hope, decided to see if some of the key people who had been recruited could be used in intelligence operations.

In the interim, relations between British intelligence and the Fifth Army unit had become strained.[12] Much of this tension arose from the anti-British attitude of Captain Bourgoin and Andre Pacatte whose recruitment of personnel from the disintegrated Italian armed forces units should have been duly reported to the military district control office which was supervised by the British. Some of the resentment also originated from British sympathies for the monarchy, whereas Tompkins and Craveri were militantly antimonarchist.

Upon assuming command, Ellery Huntington found himself caught in the crossfire. Moreover, the production of tactical intelligence was totally inadequate to the needs of the undermanned Fifth Army, and the insistence that tactical teams carry radios was a passport to certain detection and death for the agents. In the early days, the need for tactical intelligence was so acute that Huntington even suggested to Johnny Shaheen, who was in the invasion area with one of our missions, that he and Mike Burke should undertake some of the work.

In a note to Burke, Shaheen wrote from on board the USS *Biscayne,*
Admiral Hewitt's flagship:

Had a talk with Admiral Hewitt and he said by all means our work on the radio
bomb should be pursued. Plenty of hot dope!

Saw Huntington who wants us to join him immediately after McGreggor and
bomb job done, to help infiltrate agents through lines???? Our Navy orders send
us back to Washington But!!!! Joe (Savoldi) is to join Commander Breed. That's an
order from Huntington, but say nothing to Joe now!

I sent to Lt. Rand of Remington Rand to aid on radio bomb, at Huntington's
order, and I will be on board the flagship Biscayne with Admiral Hewitt. If you
have to reach me, do so through Barnes. Tell him about working directly through
Admiral Hewitt. Have Peter (Tompkins) continue with Minissini, but my *orders*
are he is to be inconspicuous (and verbally) and not to bother Minissini himself
unless necessary. Tell Little Mike to sit tight until I return with details about
Taranto.   John   13

Needless to say, when the "McGreggor" mission was over, Shaheen
and part of his mission went back to Washington where he was assigned
by General Donovan to head a special projects mission.

In order to avoid dangerous line-crossing operations, sea
transportation was needed, and this, except for Barnes' PT Command,
which at this time was moved from La Maddalena to Bastia, was under
British navy operational control. Special air transportation and packing
station facilities in Allied-occupied Italy were mostly British or under
British control. Bourgoin had temporarily moved his headquarters to
Bastia so that they could use the U.S. Navy boats and Italian MAS boats.

On November 17, Colonel Huntington wrote a personal report on the
situation to General Donovan and sent it to him marked "personal and
confidential" via pouch.[14] He also sent Donovan notes of a discussion
with General Alfred Gruenther and Colonel Howard and other
members of the G-2 staff. The text of these communications was
declassified in 1984 without any deletions. The Huntington charges are a
summation of the various incidents that impeded and hamstrung
independent OSS operations of the Fifth Army detachment. They
constitute a documented litany of grievances against British
obstructionism and interference starting in September until early
November.

Unknown to Colonel Huntington, Peter Tompkins and some of the
other elements under his command were playing a brand of politics that
did not please either the British or some of the professional Italian
officers who were in contact with the OSS detachment. These officers
resented the heavy criticism leveled at the Badoglio government and the
constant questioning of the loyalty and competency of the men assigned
to carry out intelligence functions. At the end of November, as
Huntington left the Fifth Army detachment, OSS had little to show for
its efforts.

The schism that had developed as a result of the de facto establishment of the separate command at Salerno would not be easily healed. It would ultimately result in a change of command in Algiers, with Colonel Eddy assigned to the State Department as ambassador to Yemen and Colonel Edward F. Glavin appointed to the OSS AFHQ post. For the Fifth Army detachment, it meant the trauma of a series of frequent changes by a succession of colonels until August 1944, when the Italian theater operations were consolidated with the establishment of Company D, 2677 Regiment AFHQ. The command went to Captain William Suhling, a Fredricksburg, Virginia, tobacco grower, who had just been transferred from a medical administration unit.

Chapter 12

The Establishment of the Brindisi Base

After a number of delays created by administrative snafus, on December 17, Palermo SI was able to start moving out with two convoys. The first convoy, under the command of Captain Sebastian Passanisi, set out for Naples where it was to set up an SI headquarters in the vicinity of Pozzuoli. Arrangements for its quarters were being made by Major John Roller. The second convoy, commanded by Lieutenant Samuel Fraulino, was headed for our Brindisi base, where Major Ricca was awaiting its arrival before moving his liaison office to the new provisional headquarters of the Italian government on the outskirts of Naples. The third, which was to include the radio equipment, was to move out under my command as soon as Scamporino arrived at the Palermo base with clarification of the technical problems I had posed in my repeated radio messages to Algiers.

As Scamporino was delayed in Algiers, I flew there on December 23 in an attempt to get an answer to the operational questions. As a result of meetings in Algiers, it was decided that I should take the base radio station with me to Brindisi in the event that Bari could not handle our radio traffic. Operations at "Garibaldi" (Palermo) would be continued through the use of an agent set and would keep its contacts with Algiers until the final decision to transfer the communications responsibility to Special Bari Section was made.

On Christmas Day, 1943, I left Maison Blanche for my return to Palermo. I arrived late in the afternoon and gave orders to start packing for the move to Brindisi.

Early on December 29, the convoy moved out of Palermo, and by driving at a steady pace through the mountainous terrain of Sicily and

Calabria, we finally arrived on the Ionian side of the Calabrian coast. The flat shore road along the Ionian led to the instep of the geographical boot which Italy resembles. By steady driving, we finally got to Brindisi in the wee hours of December 30.

Fortunately, the move to Brindisi coincided with the arrival of Lieutenant Emilio Q. Daddario (Mim) whom I had recruited back in the States, where he had recently started to practice law. He got to Palermo just in time to join the convoy. The staff was also bolstered by the addition of Captain Marcel Clemente, a New York bank official who spoke impeccable Italian and who was a native of Trieste. "Mim" Daddario was designated assistant operations officer and Captain Clemente was placed in charge of the translation and distribution of field intelligence. Also on the staff was Captain Edward Baransky, whose transfer I had obtained while we were still in Palermo. Baransky was made CO of the newly created training station at Fasano (Puglia) whereas Lieutenant Fraulino was placed in charge of our training station at Ostuni.

The operational headquarters were set up in the center of the city of Brindisi. Nearby, a few streets away, were the SIM headquarters which were commanded by Colonel Pompeo Agrifoglio, with Lieutenant Colonel Giuseppe Massaioli, as his deputy. The staff included some outstanding members of the General Staff who had come south with Badoglio. Thus, the first day of 1944 saw Italian SI operations set up at its new location, ready to go to work and finally undertake the strategic infiltration of northern Italy by utilizing our own manpower, as well as Italian armed forces personnel.

The Palermo SI station remained open under the command of Joe Russo. The station was to retain its radio communications to Algiers for some time and relay messages from Brindisi. Its functions were to cover economic and political intelligence; help CIC with its counterespionage mission; and assist AMG, which had recently become part of the Allied Control Commission. In cooperation with Livermore's Operation Groups, an SI detachment was set up at Bastia, Corsica, to operate in the islands off the coast of the Tuscan Maremma and the Ligurian coast.[1] This detachment was commanded by Captain Joseph Bonfiglio, with Wayne Nelson as operations officer.

At Pozzuoli, Captain Passanisi had set up the SI base on December 20 and had been joined by Lieutenant Joseph Caputa as SI reports officer. The SI command post was located in an apartment in the Vomero, overlooking Naples and the Bay. The Naples base was to be used principally for political and economic intelligence-gathering operations under Scamp. Eventually, Naples would have served as the consolidated base for OSS Italian operations. The eventual fall of Rome and the move by AFHQ to Caserta from North Africa changed all this.

The move to Brindisi was partly undertaken on the basis that the Italian intelligence chief, Colonel Agrifoglio, had decided to remain in that city, despite the fact that the Badoglio government had moved to Cava dei Tirreni near Naples, in anticipation of the fall of Rome. Agrifoglio had made available a detachment of some 50 men and officers to the Fifth Army G-2. As the situation developed in northern Italy and SIM managed to establish contact with the resistance groups, he felt that it was necessary to be close to the available naval and air transportation and the Puglia region was the center of those activities. Nearby, British SOE had set up both training facilities and a packing station.

The first problem which confronted SI was to set up adequate communications with the field agents and the OSS base stations in Algiers and Caserta. On my Christmas trip to Algiers, I had made it plain that Bari was not equipped to service the anticipated Italian SI radio traffic. The value of strategic and tactical intelligence collected by our agents would be considerably diminished if we could not relay it almost immediately to AFHQ, Fifteenth AG, and Fifth Army, which needed it to make vital battlefield decisions. I had been assured that Bari could handle the flow. In order to confirm its capability, Master Sergeant Buta, who represented communications, and I drove to Bari on January 2, where we met Lieutenant Brodie, the communications officer of SBS.

The trip was disappointing, to say the least, as Brodie stated that he was in no position to handle a single one of our contacts and that, as a matter of fact, he had received no advance communications on the matter. Had it not been for my insistence during the Christmas trip to Algiers, the Brindisi base would have been cut off without any communications. At the same time, a stringent timetable, which I had been commited to without final consultation, could have had disastrous consequences for the secret intelligence agents in the field. As previously agreed with Major Mero on December 24, the results of our trip to Bari were relayed to him through our triangular "music box" communications whose emergency use he had approved.

I became so provoked over the communications debacle that on February 6 I compiled a sizzling memorandum of fact to Colonel Glavin, with copies to Colonel Gamble, Scamporino, and Mero.

The memo summarized the events in chronological order:

1. I have found it necessary to submit this memo to highlight the situations which this desk has had to face during the last two months. I do so because as operations officer for this section, I am responsible for the life of every agent sent to the field from here and because it has always been my object to do good and thorough work which will place our organization in the front ranks of all intelligence units in this Theatre. We, as an organization (O.S.S.) have undertaken the task of providing the armed forces in the Theatre with vital and timely intelligence, and since this is our goal, I propose that it be done with the cooperation of all concerned.

2. On December 6th nine operations in northern Italy, prepared by this desk were presented by Colonel Glavin and approved by AFHQ. On December 8th these operations were still being discussed, and from the minutes of a meeting held on that date, the following commitments were made:

A. Communications
  a. Major Mero will arrange signal plans for all parties and will establish a base radio station in the Naples Caserta region, with preferably two alternate pick-up stations. (Memo of Dec. 8, 1943)
  b. The signal plans for the operations did not arrive at this headquarters until December 21, though commitments had been made that the first operations would be run off in the middle of December. Even so, only five signal plans were brought by M/Sgt. Buta. The Sgt. also gave us the news that the contacts would be handled through Bari and not as originally planned, Naples-Caserta.
  c. On December 23 I made a special flight to Algiers to straighten out the communications angle of the operations. I held several discussions with Major Mero in the presence of Captain Clemente and Mr. Scamporino. The major assured me that Bari would be in a position to take care of all our communications needs and he had already notified that station. At my insistence we also discussed the possibilities that Bari might fail to supply our needs and he agreed that his special representative and I should go and size up the situation. Major Mero also verbally approved "triangular music box" communications between Naples, Brindisi and Palermo. We also discussed at length the future needs of this section. (See memo from Mero to Communications Officers on Itops.)
  On January 2, 1944, I went to Bari to discuss our problems with Lt. Brodie, Communications Officer of S.B.S. He definitely stated that he was in no position to handle a single one of our contacts and that, further, he had received no communications on the matter. All of this took place in the presence of M/Sgt. Buta who is Major Mero's special representative. In accordance with my talks with Major Mero on December 24th, the following cable was relayed to him through his verbally approved triangular "music box" communications:
  Jan. 4, 1944. From Marat and Buta to Mero and 622: Talks held by Corvo and Buta who said that under existing conditions Bari station cannot accommodate Marat requests. Obvious reasons given in Bari report Jan. 2nd to Algiers Hq. Location of Bari station found unsuitable for future operations, due to mechanical and atmospheric difficulties. In accordance with your suggestions regarding finding Bari set-up satisfactory we proceed to establish base unit with Groff and DeHaro at once. Bari conditions not found same as those expected your headquarters. Seems to be confusion and lack of organization.
  Transmitters and receivers operating in same room thus blocking reception. If corrective steps not taken at once, probably will be breakdown in communications services to field units.
  d. On January 8, 1944, I relayed the following to Scamporino: ". . . Speeding all missions but working out certain problems a bit slow. Everyone ready. Documentation ready several days. Radio matter must be straightened out for security of operations. Three NE Groups may be parachuted. One sub leaving latter part of the month."

Thus, at an early date we had already arranged to ship some seven missions by air and sea with no communications station to contact.

e. On January 15, Lt. Brown, another of Major Mero's special representatives, came to Brindisi to size up the situation. At this late date—for the same night—our first air ops were scheduled, there had not yet been definite arrangements on the part of the Major to stabilize the communications situation. The base station at Brindisi had as yet no direct contact with Algiers, but operated through a relay system with Palermo; yet as a matter of emergency we were prepared to undertake the pick-up of agent traffic with the equipment on hand. Lt. Brown seemed to have experienced some difficulties in sending his messages out of Bari and he asked if he could use our relay system to get a message through to Mero. On January 18th, the following message was relayed to the Major through Palermo: To Mero from Brown and Buta (describing the Bari set-up): Arriving here I found all hostile to me and thus info on set-up was hard to get. Could not even send messages. Found message center left open, safes unlocked, etc. After much talking, I had Costello made message center chief. Brodie has things in such a mess that no one will use his facilities even if he had some to offer. Am doing best to do something. I sent several messages regarding Corvo and Smith set-up. Garcia should be sent here soon as possible to help Groff. Peter coming to help DeHaro and I am giving them 177. Am leaving here tomorrow if possible.

On January 28 Major Mero finally decided that the Brindisi station should have some contact with Algiers. Thus, after a month of deliberation, with three missions already en route, the Brindisi station was authorized.

This, then, has been one of the distinct setbacks of this operations desk. The question arises as to whether communications is operations or should merely service the operations of any section. Given definite areas of operation, approximate distances and some intelligence on the method of operation of the various agents should be considered sufficient information for any communications officer to lay his plans properly. I feel that we have done this thoroughly. I feel that before any vital decision is made on field communications, it is necessary for the individual making the decision to investigate personally what those conditions will be. Major Mero has never visited any spot where communications for the Italian section were contemplated . . . I have not quoted many other commitments made by Major Mero, including the oft repeated promise, never carried out, that radio sets for agents would be made available at Naples, and then Bari.

With the communications problem now in the hands of Sam Buta, Chuck Groff, and Ray DeHaro, the following day I drove to British headquarters at the Taranto naval base. Before going, I checked with SIM headquarters which informed me that several Italian subs were available for special operations. These subs, while manned by Italian crews and officers, operated under the British Special Operations officer, SOSO(A)FOTALI, Lieutenant Ben Levy. When I arrived at the British naval headquarters in Taranto, I had no trouble finding and talking to Lieutenant Levy.

Ben Levy resembled and talked like a bearded salt tar, but in civilian life he had been a film script writer and was married to a prominent

American film star. He was typically British in mannerisms. We immediately struck up a friendship, and he displayed a keen interest in what we were trying to accomplish. With a minimum of red tape, we laid on a special operation to be carried out by the Italian submarine *Platino* for the night of January 21, when we planned to land three missions (composed of seven men) at two separate landing points. This date was later moved to January 25 and then January 26.

Our arrival in Brindisi had almost coincided with the arrival of the representative of the OSS Para-Group Lieutenant Robert Cordell. Bobby Cordell was a young paratrooper who belonged to the unit commanded by Colonel Lucius Rucker, a tough, no-nonsense officer who was one of the original Fort Benning instructors and who, despite his toughness, was a very down-to-earth individual liked by his men. Cordell was a hard-working, motivated officer who never looked at the clock. He was very happy to see us set up shop in Brindisi, which was a totally British enclave. He had been sent to coordinate operational air transportation and training. The fact that we had brought along our own communications, which were made available to him, was most welcome and made his job easier. He made immediate arrangements to deliver three air missions for us through the Sixty-eighth Reconnaissance Unit which was stationed in nearby Manduria and was under the control of U.S. Colonel Smith.

The first of these missions, "Grape," flew over its operational area on January 15 but, owing to bad weather, was forced to return to the base. This team—made up of one Italian officer (Paratrooper Lieutenant Emanuele Carioni), an Italian para sergeant (Briacca), and a U.S. corporal (Louis Biagioni)—was the first joint OSS/SIM effort.

Early in January, at Colonel Glavin's insistence, Scamporino created the rear echelon of the Italian SI and was persuaded to spend more time in Algiers headquarters. This was in keeping with Glavin's desire to set up staff procedures that would allow the coordination of the organization's work. Lieutenant James Montante was recalled to Algiers from Palermo to become Scamp's assistant.

During a trip to Naples, early in December, Scamp, at Donovan's behest, met with Raimondo Craveri who had recently organized ORI (the Organization for Italian Resistance), utilizing some of the men who had volunteered for General Pavone's aborted Italian Volunteer Corps. Craveri had been working with Peter Tompkins, who was picked by Donovan to be infiltrated into Rome to coordinate the work of the CLN and the OSS. As a result of this meeting, Scamp and Craveri signed a preliminary agreement that ORI would work exclusively with SI in developing contacts in northern Italy and in establishing close ties with the CLN in Milan.

On January 4, I received a radio message from Scamp inquiring as to the status of the missions and advising me that "Mondo" (the code name for Craveri) "had approved and consented that we take care of all of his mission personnel. Seven teams can start soon. Two of them could be sent this month already. He will get in touch with you. However, don't mention to him that we are in touch with SIM." Some ten days later, Craveri showed up at headquarters in Brindisi. We had a long discussion about the basic motives of ORI and I understood quickly that we were dealing with an organization of relatively youthful people, many of whom were students motivated by democratic ideals. I also realized that in the beginning it would be necessary to keep them apart from many of the other agents who were being trained. After several other lengthy discussions with Craveri, we reached full accord on the type of operations that needed to be undertaken. We also worked out a priority timetable for the transfer of the men from Naples to Brindisi. In fact, within days, the first candidates started to arrive for training under the leadership of Dr. Enzo Boeri, a biophysics professor and submarine medical officer who came from a Milanese family noted for its democratic sympathies.

To take care of the increasing number of agents in our training programs, we opened up the full facilities of our substation at Ostuni and the holding area at Fasano. We turned to Colonel Agrifoglio and the SIM for help in clearing up several problems that had long hampered our clandestine operations. The colonel had placed at our disposal the services of the documents reproduction section of SIM and he had assigned one of his staff officers to recruit a number of radio telegraphists from the Italian armed forces. These were experienced operators who could easily be retrained in the use of our equipment and system with just a few refresher sessions. In addition, he appointed Lieutenant Signorile as a liaison officer to our headquarters. Through the Italian army chief of staff, we were assigned permanent guard units to look after the external security of all our installations. These guard units were a welcome addition to our internal U.S. security guards and were intended not only to keep out the curious, but also to defend all buildings and areas from possible attack by enemy commando units. The Italian troops were temporarily placed under our command and received the same rations as our own troops.

Several of the missions that were to operate in the Trieste area and in the Fiume region were among the first scheduled for delivery. According to the original instructions, arrangements were to be made with Marshal Tito's representatives in Bari to infiltrate these teams through Yugoslav Partisan territory. I discussed the possibilities with Lieutenant George Vujnovich who spoke with Major Koch, the SBS officer in charge in Bari, and with Bob Joyce, the SBS intelligence officer, who was an old Foreign Service hand. Bob invited me to meet him so that he could introduce me to the "proper partisan authorities" who would handle our request.

The meeting took place at Bari in mid-January, but although our discussion was congenial, the arrangements to send the northeast teams through Yugoslavia could not be worked out. As a consequence, the Trieste teams, which were codenamed "Fig" and "Plum," were rescheduled for delivery by submarine.

During mid-January, the "Grape 1" mission was flown a number of times over northern Italy, but because of inclement weather, enemy activity, and engine trouble, it had to return to home base. Two other teams that were ready to be dropped over northern Italy suffered the same type of operational delays. The Brindisi command continued to be plagued by communications problems. Lack of agent radios necessitated the frequent reallocation of sets from one team to another, and communications with Algiers headquarters could be maintained only by "music box" relay through Palermo. Strong protests were forwarded to OSS/Algiers almost every day, but the problem did not diminish.

The air transportation situation improved considerably when G-3 AFHQ issued orders that OSS could utilize the 334 Wing (RAF) to drop both agents and supplies over northern Italy. Through Lieutenant Vujnovich and Bob Cordell, we established a good working relationship with the RAF wing. Within days they had started flying our "Grape" and "Date" teams a number of times without any more luck than on the previous occasions.

Recruits from Craveri's ORI groups started to come in good numbers, and training programs were set up to condition them for field intelligence missions. Some of these programs, such as parachute training courses, were handled by British instructors at a British training school at San Vito dei Normanni, whereas most of the other training was handled by our own Italian SI.

One of our other major problems was resolved towards the end of January when Major Wooler of Advanced Force 133, the British Packing Station, offered to pack all of our equipment and material needed for OSS operations in Italy. He also offered to service all of our field operations to the extent of fifteen to twenty sorties a month. In order to officially undertake this work, Wooler asked that we secure authorization from G-3 AFHQ and that such authorization be addressed to Major Flinn, Advance Force 133, Bari, Italy. Without wasting time, Scamp, who happened to be visiting our Brindisi base, shot off a message to Colonel Glavin who, in turn, went to work and secured the vital authorization.

For our part we prepared the groundwork for a lengthy military campaign in Italy, with long-range plans to produce strategic intelligence and to effect Allied military control over paramilitary operations of the various guerrilla bands scattered throughout northern Italy. Meanwhile, the people in Algiers and Naples, who were waging an almost impossible military campaign along the Rapido River and in front of Cassino, became almost euphoric when, on January 22, British and American forces landed at Anzio, catching the enemy by surprise. So sanguine were AFHQ's hope that Scamp sent out a memo three days before the Anzio landing, giving instructions for the setting up of a central SI headquarters in Rome. Even before embarking on "Operation Shingle," AFHQ was certain that the Germans would withdraw from the Cassino front, once their flank was threatened. They had not taken two factors into consideration:

1. The brilliant defensive measures of Albert Kesselring.
2. The timidity of General J.P. Lucas, American CO of the Anzio landing force.

We would have to wait a number of months before Rome would fall.

With little help from the communications section and with the impending departure of a number of missions, Ralph DeHaro, our cipher expert, suggested that we modify the system we had been using for many months in our field communications. He felt that this change was vital for the security of the operations. He proposed the elimination of key groups at the beginning and at the end of the messages, employing two five-group numbers for designation of keys. In place of the key groups (or any other place in the message that would make it less confusing), he proposed introducing four dummy groups in each message. He believed that in short field messages, such as our agents would send, the four dummy groups would prove to be very effective and act as an additional security safeguard.

On January 26, three of our key missions to northeast Italy were ready to leave for their operational zones. The Italian submarine *Platino*, under the command of a bright young skipper, Commander Vittorio Campagnano, was to make the voyage to the upper Adriatic to drop off the missions at two separate landing points. Both points had been carefully selected with the help of the mission leaders who were familiar with the terrain and the coastline. The first landing would be made south of Chioggia, near the mouth of the Adige River.[2] This was a two-man mission which was to operate in the Venice area; the leader of the mission was an Italian Air Force captain, Bruno Rossoni of Padova. A man with excellent contacts and an enormous amount of courage, he had volunteered for the task and was sent to us by SIM. His W/T was an Italian Air Force petty officer, Gaetano Neglia, of Palermo, whom I had recruited in Palermo in September 1943.

The second landing was scheduled near Parenzo in Istria. There, two missions were to be landed. These missions were codenamed "Fig" and "Plum" and were originally to have been delivered through Yugoslavia with Tito's approval. The leader of "Plum" was Italian Army Lieutenant Egon De Basseggio, who was from Trieste. He was assisted by an Italian Navy petty officer from Palermo, Sicily, who had joined us after the surrender of Lipari, where he was a member of the communications staff. "Fig" was headed by Italian Captain Christoforo De Hartungen from Bolzano and his W/T was an Italian Navy seaman, Salvatore

Amodio of Palermo, who had also volunteered for the arduous task. These missions were successfully delivered by the *Platino* which landed the men at their pinpoint and stood by for a half hour to cover the landing party.

On February 2, the submarine was back in Brindisi, having successfully completed its first mission for SI/OSS. (An earlier mission had been landed from the submarine *Aksum* for OSS/Naples at the end of December 1943.) The SI "escort officer" sent on this mission was Corporal Peter Durante, who had already distinguished himself in the Lipari and Ventotene Island operations. Pete Durante was still an Italian citizen, despite the fact that he had lived in the United States a number of years and had volunteered for military service. We later helped him obtain U.S. citizenship. Durante was a professional seaman who spoke half a dozen languages fluently and had knocked around Europe doing odd chores to pay his way. His only fault was that he would periodically go on a monumental binge and destroy the barroom in the process. He was absolutely fearless under pressure and totally in control.

As it became obvious that the missions were going to be fielded with timetable precision, the communications problem became more acute. On January 30, we decided that in order to break the deadlock, it would be necessary to take some decisive action. Discussing the situation with "Mim" Daddario, we decided that someone would be sent to Algiers to alert Glavin and Mero to the critical situation and the perils which our agents behind the lines would be facing. As there was no scheduled air transportation from Brindisi, arrangements were made to have Mim fly on one of the Sixty-eight's B-25s to Algiers.

On arrival there, Daddario was greeted coldly and found an almost hostile ambiance. After much tugging and pulling, Glavin and Mero finally agreed to direct radio contact between our Brindisi base and headquarters in Algiers. Several days after Mim was in Algiers, the first of our clandestine stations, "Pear", came on the air from Venice with some very important intelligence which we immediately relayed to Algiers. Daddario later described the changed attitude at headquarters as miraculous. Everyone became solicitous, and the key problem of securing a number of agent sets and other equipment was quickly resolved. He was given four sets to bring back with him; orders went out for additional sets and personnel to help De Haro and Groff; and the radio station in Brindisi was authorized.

During this period, the Brindisi command was working night and day to prepare field missions. Administrative personnel that were scattered at various stations in the theater were regrouped, and the work of the Italian SI was divided into two principal phases. The collection of political and economic intelligence was taken over as Scamp's principal function and centered in the Naples area, whereas the military side of the show was based at Brindisi under my command.

At the end of January 1944, the section personnel were assigned to the following posts:[3] Naples: 4 officers, 2 civilians, 28 enlisted men; Brindisi: 6 officers, 1 civilian, 29 enlisted men, 40 civilian agents; Bastia: 1 officer, 2 civilians, 5 enlisted men; Sardinia: 10 enlisted men; Palermo: 1 officer, 5 civilians, 42 enlisted men (many of the enlisted men were awaiting reassignment); Naples: 1 officer, 2 enlisted men assigned to the ACC; on loan to the OSS Fifth Army detachment: 3 officers, 1 civilian, 19 enlisted men, and 10 civilians recruited in North Africa.

The use of U.S. personnel for intelligence work in enemy-occupied territory had become extremely risky and posed many drawbacks. It soon became advisable to use available Italian volunteers who knew the terrain, had personal contacts, and were patriotically motivated to do the dangerous job. SIM assured our sources of manpower, and by the end of January, we were able to draw a blueprint of our future plans and eventual goals.

Despite the fact that we had enjoyed the utmost cooperation from the British services in the area and that our common goal was to end the war as quickly as possible, maintaining the independence of U.S. intelligence functions was uppermost in our minds. The British policy was to treat Italy as a private preserve. Their field officers expected Italy to become a zone of exclusive British influence once the war came to an end. But SI Italy had other ideas. We wanted the Italians to make up their own minds about the future. We envisioned a postwar Italy that would stand side by side with the United States in the international alignment which would undoubtedly take place after the war. We were not interested in having OSS play a subservient role to British intelligence because we felt we were equally qualified. We possessed excellent expertise in Italian affairs, and we were equipped to play a primary role in the development of intelligence, paramilitary policies and strategy. The problem of coordinating intelligence and special operations was not neglected at the AFHQ level, which placed those operations under the supervision of a special unit designated as G-3 Special Operations.

While at first we felt that we were being hobbled with red tape, gradually we came to realize that the increasing complexity of the problem and logistics required that a central clearinghouse be set up to control and maintain overall knowledge of operations, due to the fact that the Allies were never able to muster the optimum manpower ratio required by armies conducting orthodox offensive operations, especially in the type of mountainous terrain that characterizes central Italy.

On January 22, the British-American forces, in order to break the stalemate on the Cassino front, landed at Anzio in an effort to turn the flank of General Heinrich von Vietinghoff's Tenth Army. But despite the fact that they caught the Germans by surprise, General Lucas, CO of the Allied landing force, failed to take advantage of the situation and decided to hunker down and set up defensive perimeters. The Fifth Army's frontal drive at Cassino was bogged down. Instead of catching the Germans in a nutcracker, the Anzio beachhead became a liability to AFHQ and the Fifth Army.

A unit of the OSS Fifth Army detachment had landed with the U.S. troops.[4] This unit was equipped with a radio that was to be used to intercept messages from the 504th Parachute Regiment of the Eighty-second Airborne, which was to have been dropped before the naval landings. This air drop was canceled at the last moment and the 504th went in by sea.

The Anzio OSS unit had no prearranged operational plan. Consequently, it was not ready to infiltrate personnel through the almost nonexistent German defense lines. Lack of coordination with OSS Rome operators deprived U.S. forces of counterinfiltration of intelligence operators from Rome. (At the time of the landings, an American correspondent drove his jeep to the outskirts of Rome without any challenges from the Germans, whose organic units were still in transit to the front.)

The radio-equipped jeep of the OSS Anzio unit was put to good use to intercept the intelligence from the "Vittorio" mission which had been landed by Andre Pacatte from the submarine *Aksum* in late 1943. These messages provided valuable intelligence for the beleaguered Allied forces in Anzio, until the "Vittorio" station was captured by the Germans on March 17, 1944.

It was not until D+5 that a small group of agents, whom Bourgoin had recruited for long-range work in Naples, were landed at Anzio and went to work under the direction of Captain Jones, Lieutenant Thiele, and Sergeants Michelino and Aliano, who had landed with the U.S. Rangers. John Croze, a French lieutenant who had been recruited by Bourgoin in North Africa, also landed in Anzio and controlled the radio jeep which was in contact with Caserta and "Vittorio."

The Anzio detachment infiltrated a number of combat intelligence missions, but such work was of limited tactical value. The opportunity to take advantage of the nonexistent German defenses to infiltrate teams with the minimum amount of risk of detection was therefore lost. Also lost was the opportunity of the Roman underground to muster a mass uprising to create chaos for the Germans.

Because of its remote distance from both immediate political and military pressures, the Brindisi base was ideally located for the training and delivery of our strategic intelligence missions. The pressure which proximity to the battlefront often generates did not exist. Pressure came only through radio messages and courier pouches. In this superficially relaxed atmosphere, it was possible to hold conferences with important members of the Italian General Staff, representatives and friends of ORI, and people whose business was pressing enough to travel several hundred kilometers away from wherever the center of activity happened to be.

Gradually, as the OSS paratroop detachment began to function fully, OSS Brindisi became a hub of activity. Our SI command became a focal center as it controlled radio communications with Algiers, Naples, and Palermo. It also became a departure point for a number of operations to the Balkans and Central Europe. Naples Fifth Army OSS Group was also forced to use Brindisi as its staging area for air personnel and supply drops, as were Colonel Livermore's Operational Groups which were stepping up their operations in northern Italy with SI assistance.

With the arrival of some outstanding members of Craveri's ORI group, it became possible to do some long-range planning and to attempt to shape future political and military developments. Together with Craveri and Dr. Enzo Boeri, we made a considerable effort to examine the creation of an intelligence network that would cover every region of German-occupied Italy and that would establish close contacts with the leadership of the Committee of National Liberation in Milan, in order to place them in direct contact with AFHQ through OSS. This planning examined the probability of extending our control over the principal guerrilla bands and providing a radio communications link between such bands, AFHQ, and CLNAI in order to exercise operational military control over their activities. Gradually, it became possible to discuss some of these plans jointly with ORI and SIM because they wanted Italian participation in Allied planning. This desire was so overwhelming that political philosophies were set aside until the end of the war.

On January 22, after a series of lengthy conferences with Lieutenant Colonel Massaioli, SIM's director of operations, I submitted a plan to AFHQ for a series of extensive operations to bring the guerrilla movement under military supervision in order to supply operations, communications, and military activity.[5] This plan envisaged the delivery of liaison officers to all major guerrilla formations behind German lines. These would be provided with radio communications under the control of OSS. Specifically, the plan proposed to deliver some twenty of these liaison missions during the month of February by air and by water and asked for operational control of three B-25s and two B-17s. It further proposed to create landing fields for the B-25s and DC-3s behind enemy lines so that guerrilla groups could be directly resupplied.

Ultimately, the plan proposed to create a joint OSS/SIM command behind enemy lines which was to be in direct contact with the Fifteenth Army Group command and could give military direction to the partisan effort in conjunction with Allied military plans. Unfortunately, Eisenhower had already left AFHQ theater command to take up his post as supreme commander of Supreme Headquarters Allied Expeditionary Forces (SHAEF), and the new commander of AFHQ was British General Maitland Wilson. The CG, Fifteenth Army Group, General Harold Alexander, was also British, and so the plan got nowhere because SOE probably voiced opposition to it. Nonetheless, we persevered in another direction by pushing the same plan with ORI civilian personnel without ever enunciating the ultimate objectives or extent of the intelligence web which Craveri's organization and OSS/Brindisi were spinning.

One of Donovan's basic tenets was that OSS should never involve itself with indigenous politics, but the very nature of our business made this principle almost impossible to honor. Clandestine movements are spawned by political and philosophical unrest and motivation. German-controlled Europe had become a hotbed of political intrigue which manifested itself in paramilitary expressions through the organization of urban counterterror undergrounds and the formation of guerrilla bands in the countryside. Craveri's ORI was the ideal vehicle to achieve ultimate military control over Italy's growing underground movement and to exploit the deep-seated hate which the majority of Italians had built up against Nazi-Fascist abuses, torture, and mayhem.

In order to bolster his tenet against political involvement, Donovan had made it clear that the OSS mission was military. As such, we were not to discriminate against any guerrilla band because of its political affiliation. The policy was to arm any band that fought the Germans and the Fascist forces, and thus helped the Allied effort to bring the war to a successful conclusion.

ORI/OSS's prime mission in Brindisi was to weld a powerful force that could help the Allies liberate Italy and restore the country's self-respect after so many years of Fascist abuses and blunders. This was also the principal goal of most of the officers on Agrifoglio's SIM staff. It would take many months of arduous work and the lives of countless devoted men and women to achieve these goals, but the men of the Brindisi OSS base dedicated themselves to this task.

By February 1944, OSS headquarters in Algiers was beginning to expand and adopt bureaucratic practices as more and more activities were being encompassed. Its jurisdiction expanded over a greater geographic area, including the Balkans base at Bari and Central Europe. Colonel Joseph Rodrigo, whom I had first met at the War Department during my visit to G-2 in Washington in 1942, was brought in as the OSS theater intelligence officer. A well-prepared officer, who spoke fluent Portuguese and Spanish, Rodrigo had been an officer of Giannini's Bank of America before the war. As intelligence officer, he toured all stations in his jurisdiction in order to acquaint himself with the situation and needs of the branches under his command, and then he set to work helping the operations sections in the field. Miss Catherine DuBois who had been my assistant in Washington now served as Rodrigo's executive assistant.

A number of other appointments were made: Colonel Thomas Early, a pleasant, outgoing Air Force officer who knew his way around top official circles in Washington, was brought in as deputy to Colonel Glavin. A dynamic newspaperman, Captain Norman Newhouse, was named as Glavin's executive officer. Norman followed day-to-day progress at headquarters and made sure that the staff functions and decisions were speedily carried out. Operations officer for the theater was Lieutenant Colonel Edward Gamble, Jr., and his field representative was Lieutenant Colonel Serge Obolensky, who had previously been parachuted into Sardinia. Colonel Gamble was a softspoken but firm individual who never came to conclusions hastily. His assistant, Obolensky, was a flamboyant Russian nobleman who had hobnobbed with the upper strata of New York and European society for many years.

The military impasse at both Anzio and Cassino, as well as the British Eighth Army front, did not augur well for an early end to the Italian campaign. The fact that the Fifth Army had never reached the manpower ratio necessary to undertake the all-out offensive operations against the well-entrenched enemy made the rapid fall of Rome and the conquest of the Po Valley unlikely. This shortfall of the entire Fifteenth Army Group made the work of the OSS and SOE extremely important to the development of future military plans. Unorthodox warfare was coming into its own and would become a necessary ancillary in the G-3 arsenal.

The theater policies were now set by the British general officers who were influenced by their traditional Foreign Office policies. As members of the U.S. armed forces, however, we paid little heed to British long-term interests and were preoccupied with the problem of doing the best possible job in helping the Allied armies in Italy by creating havoc at the enemy's rear and securing information that would assist Allied military planning. Our persistence in establishing the strategic intelligence base at Brindisi, despite the uninformed opposition of the communications branch and the misguided attempts by some people at headquarters to derail many of our proposals, was starting to pay off. The excellent working relationships that were forged with the British and U.S. field organizations at the working level had indeed proven beneficial.

In the months of January, February, and March, an increasing number of Italian volunteers from Craveri's ORI and Agrifoglio's SIM arrived at our base to be trained for dangerous missions behind enemy lines. The importance of our base finally became obvious to both the Fifth Army/OSS and OSS/Algiers. The radio communications that had been forged at our insistence gave OSS the opportunity to transmit orders and intelligence with the least amount of delay. Thus, on February 16, we prepared the first of our weekly summaries of activities which were incorporated as part of Scamp's overall reports and which, in turn, were included as part of the 2677th Regiment's reports, most of which the CIA declassified in 1984 and are available at the National Archives.

The reports not only reflected the problems of the Brindisi base but also outlined achievements and covered operational activities in the planning stage.

A. Summary of operational activities
  1. The meteorological conditions during this lunar period limited all

operations into northern Italy. Although seven missions, fully trained and packed, were ready to be dropped in their various operational zones, we were only able to drop one mission. The missions prepared to drop were: Grape, Date, Peach, Apricot, Citron, and Guava. The approval for the last three mentioned came at such a late date that it was impossible to get them off because the moonless period had been reached. The number of men involved in these operations was 18, including seven radio operators. The mission which finally did get off was Date, which was dropped in the Carnic Alps region.

Some of these missions made as many as four flights this month but found conditions at the given pinpoints so bad that they had to return to their base. One of these missions was forced to drop all of its equipment, including the radio set, when one of the motors of the aircraft in which they were flying developed mechanical trouble. Another mission, after having circled over the Udine area for 20 minutes, had to return because ack-ack batteries in the area opened up on the plane flying the mission, scoring hits.

2. Special rubber boat training was held for missions scheduled to land in northern Italy. The Italian Navy command lent its aid by assigning a MAS boat to this section so that landing operations could be carried out along the Adriatic coast.

On the afternoon of February 16th, the missions Lemon, Banana and Raisin cleared the port of Brindisi on board the submarine "Platino" to be landed in two special places in the Gulf of Venice and in the Valle di Comacchio. Escort officer for these groups was Sgt. Peter Durante, whose report on the previous cruise you already have on hand. Further maritime training for teams to be landed along the coast will be held this coming week.

3. One of the real impediments to the successful prosecution of operations has been the lack of radio equipment. The equipment on hand had to be shuttled in such a manner so that those teams which we were able to get out during the month were taken care of first. The return of the various teams from the operational zones because of unsuccessful flight caused a great deal of inconvenience, inasmuch as the radio equipment allotted to them had later to be assigned to those teams leaving by sea. Of the 4 already in their respective operational zones, one has been heard of, one is scheduled to go on the air after a few days, and others have not yet been heard from. But this is in line with instructions given radio operators before leaving—that they are not to go on the air until such time as they believe that everything is well from a security point of view. They have been instructed that if necessary, they are not to go on the air for a month or a month and a half.

The three groups which departed on the 16th will not be heard from for at least another 15 days, and they have the same instructions as previous teams.

B. Sectional Activities

1. We have had requests from other sections of OSS for civilian clothing and other operational equipment. We have provided some civilian clothing for the German section and have also provided civilian clothing and other items on very short notice for the OSS Fifth Army. We have been asked by the Operations Officer for SBS whether it would be possible to furnish some of

the personnel with civilian clothing. The answer has been yes.

2. We have furnished communications to all OSS groups in this area. These groups include the Para Detachment and the OGs. This has been done despite the fact that we are short of radio division personnel and vital base station equipment. The cipher men and radio operators attached to this section have worked many hours in order to accomplish this vital task.

3. Our personnel has been taxed with the burden of acting as supply and maintenance while it is yet operational. We have lent aid in various forms to those OSS elements which are operating at this area and will continue to do so in the future. Our transport is in such shape that something must immediately be done to bolster it. Many of our vehicles, which are rather old, are being fixed at the local Ordinance fifty percent of the time.

C. Future Operational Activities

1. For the month of March the following missions are scheduled for operations:

By air: Apricot, Citron, Guava and Orange, Grape, Peach

By water: Prune and Apple

The last two will have to be delivered from our base at Bastia. The others will leave from Brindisi, and transportation has been applied for. Many of these missions have been given topmost priority because of the many trips they have made into their zone of operation. Time and information schedule of these missions is herewith enclosed.

2. It is essential that Grape, Prune, Citron, Guava, Orange and Apple be furnished radio equipment for their operations. Peach and Apricot already have theirs packed and only awaiting the March moon. In view of past experience, it is believed advisable that one or two extra radio sets be kept on hand for emergencies which may arise, such as in operations similar to the Grape incident. We also believe it advisable that if this station is to continue as the focal point for all OSS strategic infiltration, that facilities to accommodate any arising exigencies be made available at once. These facilities are few and simple, having to do only with transport problems and materials for the utmost comfort of the agents while they remain here. These include field ranges and other Quartermaster equipment.

During the early part of February, Serge Obolensky came to Brindisi to make arrangements for the OG operation "Dallas" which was to be dropped in the vicinity of Porretta Terme in the Apennines. The object was to interdict rail traffic through the important Bologna-Florence rail line and block German supplies and reinforcements to Cassino and Anzio ("Operation Strangle"). While in Brindisi, Obolensky spent some time reviewing our coordination problems with OSS Caserta and with the Allied Central Mediterranean Force (ACMF) and attempting to establish lines of communication to secure the rapid approval of our operations.

Once again, it became obvious that there would be a struggle for control of operations in Italy between OSS/AFHQ and the Fifth Army OSS Command under Colonel Reutershan. A number of attempts were made to head off such needless waste of time, and Colonels Glavin and Rodrigo visited Caserta.

In discussions with Obolensky, it was decided that he would personally deliver a list of our operations, with complete details for approval of G-3 at Caserta. On February 11, he flew from Brindisi to Naples to meet with Reutershan and the people in G-3 ACMF.

That same day I sent Colonel Gamble a memorandum updating him on the situation and spelling out the procedures that had been worked out with Obolensky to avoid the confusion and another internal struggle within OSS.

1. Last night I talked to Colonel Obolensky about the approval of the operations which Lt. Daddario presented to you on his recent trip to Algiers. The Colonel had received your letter of February 7 and requested that I answer those paragraphs concerning Italian SI operations. He will shortly leave this station and go to Caserta to obtain the approval of the G-3, A.C.M.F.

2. During our discussion it was thought that in the future it would be convenient to prepare two copies of all proposed operations. One would be submitted to you and Col. Glavin and the other to Lt. Col. Obolensky. As soon as your approval of the operations would come through all that would be needed by Col. Obolensky would be a cable with the nominatives approved. A map showing the various areas of operation would also be submitted.

3. Capt. Harris left this station several days ago. He did not have the necessary information on Italian operations to present to A.C.M.F. He did have some information on operations already approved. These were: Orange, Apple and Berry. To the best of my knowledge, I do not believe that he intended to present them, as the information he had was meager.

4. As we here see the chain of command, all operations would have to follow a definite pattern of approval:
   a. A copy to be submitted to Col. Glavin and you.
   b. Upon your approval copies would be pouched to Col. Obolensky.
   c. Upon approval of A.C.M.F. these copies would be returned to you for presentation to A.F.H.Q.
   d. Upon approval of A.F.H.Q. the missions would go into effect and transport for them would have to be arranged and air transport, we suppose, would have to be arranged through Col. Obolensky.

5. Since our arrival here on January 1, this operations desk has worked incessantly preparing special groups for northern Italy. In no case has a group been prepared to operate any further south than Bologna. Due to weather conditions and other difficulties, it has been impossible to deliver any groups by air. We have had several missions alerted every day this moon period, but have found it impossible to deliver them.

6. We have prepared four special Alpine teams to cover the entire area of the French and Swiss Alps. These teams are equipped with snowshoes and skis and in each one there is at least one Alpine guide who knows the area of operation well. Some of these have been submitted and are waiting for approval and equipment (radio).

7. In order to appreciate the amount of work done by this section in the last forty days, it is really necessary to visit this base. I hope that in the very near future you will have the opportunity to do so.

Despite these efforts to avoid another contest for the control of Italian operations, the OSS Caserta group brought matters to a head. On his return from meetings at Caserta, Obolensky sent a message to Gamble advising him that the "control over all operations and W/T contact in Italy through Reutershan is insisted by ACMF." There was no reason why Washington should not have settled an internal OSS jurisdictional dispute, inasmuch as it involved a chain of command decision in which the authority of Algiers should have been automatically upheld. Disregarding these apparent differences, we in Brindisi kept servicing the Caserta operations. Daily we transmitted to Reutershan all intelligence arriving from our field agents, much of which was vital to assessing the enemy's order of battle at the Cassino and Anzio fronts.

For the Brindisi operations base whose links with the outside world and our field agents was the vital radio station, the time to produce outstanding results was of the essence. The daily radio contacts with Algiers had been authorized by Glavin and Mero only until February 15 (message from Glavin to 622, January 28, 1944). Later, operation of the radio station was authorized until May 25, by which time the Bari communications center was to have worked out many of its technical bugs and was to be ready to service Italian SI operations.

On February 14, the "Date" team, made up of two Italian-speaking GIs and an Italian soldier, was finally parachuted near Caporetto (the site of the disastrous Italian retreat in World War I) in the picturesque Carnic Alps region.

On February 17, after many attempts, the key intelligence teams "Apricot," "Guava," and "Orange" were dropped into their operational zones in Piedmont and Lombardy.

Meanwhile, since early February, when Captain Rossoni of the "Pear" mission made his first contact, a daily flow of vital military, industrial, and political intelligence from northern Italy was established as each new mission came on the air. The amount of information transmitted to AFHQ and Caserta became impressive.

On February 16, the submarine *Platino* made its second voyage to the northern Adriatic to land the Italian SI teams at Comacchio and Capo Salvore, Istria. [6] This time the teams were made up of ORI personnel and Italian officers from SIM who were landed on separate missions. Supervision was in the expert hands of Peter Durante. The submarine returned on February 23, having completed its hazardous mission. The teams landed were codenamed "Banana," "Raisin," and "Lemon."

On the evening of February 15, Lieutenant Bob Cordell, whose air operations office was beginning to function methodically, assigned the "Goat" mission to Reutershan's Caserta headquarters. Another of Caserta's missions had been so poorly prepared that Cordell felt constrained to admonish the Caserta command that "CAT arrived poorly equipped. Have barely enough information to fly the operation. Air transport forms must, repeat, must accompany operations." That same evening Italian SI "Operation Grape" was flown for the fifth time. and had to return to the base.

Corporal Louis Biagioni, W/T of the mission, wrote the following report upon his return:

They took off at 20:40 with the same plane which had returned the night before on account of engine trouble. The weather conditions were not very good all along the way, but they had no trouble with the plane until 24:30.

A half hour before reaching the target there seemed to be something wrong with the motor, therefore, the pilot decided to turn back. On their way back, the motor failed completely and we started to lose altitude. They flew over the sea and dropped everything overboard in order to make the plane lighter. After dropping all available material, we were called to emergency stations to hook up and be ready to jump. In the meantime, they were flying towards land over enemy territory.

The pilot had originally planned to land at Foggia, but when reaching Foggia decided to keep on going. Meanwhile, we were at the emergency stations ready to jump at a moment's notice.

The balance of the trip was uneventful and they finally reached Brindisi at 3:15.

The attempts to get the mission behind enemy lines proceeded at full speed, with allowances for the foul winter weather, meanwhile, we kept preparing missions to cover all parts of German-occupied Italy. By February 18, a number of these missions were fully trained but could not be sent into the field because they lacked radio communications equipment. Again I brought this situation to the attention of the Operations Division in the following message that was transmitted on February 18:

The following teams are prepared and need "music boxes": Grape, Citron, Guava, Apple, Orange, Berry and Prune. Have also requested that two sets be sent here in case of emergency such as Grape's recent one. Last night Apricot departed by air but was forced to come back after 9½ hours flight. I am pouching full report, including the situation of agent's "music boxes."

Sergeant Groff had already prepared an accounting of all agents' radios that we had received since the start of the Sicilian campaign (July 9, 1943), and the report clearly indicated a precarious communications problem. Out of sixteen sets, three had been lost in operations, six were in the field operating; two were unusable because they had old type receivers; two were being used in Palermo as station communications transmitters; and three were packed for impending operations. During the same period, our Brindisi base station had experienced a blackout, and I was forced to send Sgt. Groff to the Air Force quartermaster to beg and borrow needed communications equipment and a reliable emergency generator.

Finally, on February 19, I sent Scamp and Colonel Glavin another seething document, which said in part:

I would like to bring to your attention certain factors regarding our communications which do not make for ideal operational conditions. On February 18th, our local electric power was suddenly cut off, due to some break in the lines some distance from town. A contact with Algiers was at the time being carried on and was interrupted.

To my knowledge this station has been operating with a German power unit which was captured during one of our September sorties. This power unit is quite old and is not in condition to give dependable service when required. We have called the attention of Major Mero at various times to the existing conditions and have requested an American power unit. As yet, nothing has been done about this.

It is important that if prompt and efficient communications are to be had with Algiers and with our agents in the field that something be done immediately to rectify the situation. Under the present conditions we cannot continue to give proper and efficient service to anyone, much less our agents in the field risking their lives so that our organization may profit from the information they gather.

Even the base station equipment which we have on hand and the personnel which is operating it must quickly be bolstered for the sake of the service. Approximately 50% of the equipment which we have was also captured in one of our September sorties and redesigned for use by M/Sgt. Groff. Miracles cannot be performed with old and inadequate equipment continuously.

The OG mission "Dallas" continued its attempts to drop at the Porretta Terme pinpoint, but the weather made it impossible. Scamp and Colonel Gamble asked that I assist with a ground reception. Major Al Cox of the Bastia station was sent to Brindisi to coordinate and get the mission off. Once Cox had arrived in Brindisi, we offered to provide guides for every OG team that was to drop with "Dallas" and some of the other OG missions. Finally, on March 17, "Dallas" was definitely canceled, and on March 24, Mero and Gamble told Cox to "turn the radio equipment over to Corvo." On March 20, Gamble had already sent an encouraging message that he expected some music boxes any day and that "he would forward them upon receipt." The situation became so acute that Scamp ordered Sergeant Jim D'Amico and the two music boxes that were still in Palermo to be sent to Brindisi because field missions were being held up for lack of equipment.

On March 27, Major Mero decided to ship a power unit from Naples to Brindisi via air and to send several men to help Groff and DeHaro who were overwhelmed by the amount of work they were forced to handle. On March 29, Mero went to work, based on Sam Buta's recommendations, and promised to have two receivers made available through the Signal Corps unit in Bari. He asked that we provide the number and name of the communications unit so that he could have AFHQ issue the necessary orders.

The internal wrangle was coming to another boiling point in Caserta. Near the end of February, I received a radio message from Scamp to go to

Naples for a conference with Reutershan and bring with me all the papers and plans for pending operations. Taking turns with my driver, Sergeant Charlie Gattuso, we drove all night and arrived at Scamp's apartment in Naples on March 27. Scamp explained that the Caserta group had demanded that all operations in Italy be placed under Reutershan's command and that our Italian SI operations be absorbed by the Caserta headquarters. I told him that from what I had seen of the Caserta operations we should have no part of such a merger. If such a merger were ordered by either Algiers or Washington, I emphasized that we should object strenuously to losing our identity in a command whose right hand did not know what its left was doing. He agreed and pointed out that Colonel Glavin, Colonel Rodrigo, and Colonel Gamble shared the same opinion.

From what I had been able to observe, the Reutershan command was in shambles. A number of operations were being conducted by various officers, including Captain Bourgoin and Lieutenant Croze, who were French Intelligence officers, without any real control being exercised over them. As a matter of fact, there seemed to be a race among them as to who could send the greatest number of missions behind the German lines, regardless of the casualties. Young men were being sent on tactical and strategic missions with little or no training, and many agents were motivated solely by materialistic objectives.

In truth, quantity sometimes produces an occasional qualitative surprise. One of these was the setting up of the "Vittorio" radio in German-occupied Rome which transmitted valuable military intelligence to the Anzio beachhead until its personnel were captured by the S.D.

As a result of the conference which was held at San Leucio, the OSS headquarters near the Royal Palace at Caserta, it was agreed that SI Brindisi would transmit all intelligence from the field to Colonel Reutershan's headquarters (which we had been regularly doing) and that he would make it available to the various commands at Allied Armies in Italy (AAI) and Fifteenth Army Group. As part of the agreement, SI would help to dispatch Caserta's teams in the field and would assist SO and OG with receptions at drop zones in northern Italy. Caserta, which was in touch with A.A.I. on a daily basis, would help obtain approval of operations proposed by SI Italy. It would also help to obtain allocation of arms and supplies for the northern Italian partisan groups who were in touch with SI field agents. The basic agreement was the result of the first meeting which we had with Reutershan, Pacatte, John Roller, Cagiati and MacAdoo.

As a result of the agreement arrived at in Naples, the situation was defused and SI Italy was given a free hand in implementing its intelligence plans. We fully disclosed the outcome of the meeting to Lieutenant (Navy) Tom Beale, an old friend from Washington, and SI Chief Whitney Shepardson's assistant. When he returned to

Washington, Beale informed both Shepardson and Earl Brennan of what was happening in the theater.

On March 19, the *Platino* made its third trip to the enemy-infested waters of the upper Adriatic. This time the components of three SI teams—"Apple," "Grape 1," and "Prune"—were landed. We also landed two of Colonel Reutershan's teams which were part of the groups that were trained and operated by Lieutenant Irving Goff. A veteran of the Lincoln Brigade in the Spanish Civil War, Goff worked closely with the Italian Communists—with the full knowledge of his superior officers, including General Donovan. Three days prior to the departure of the *Platino*, the SI teams "Guava," "Orange," and "Apricot," were parachuted into their operational zones in Piedmont and Lombardy. Orange and Apricot were to become two of the most important missions operating behind enemy lines in Italy.

It was becoming increasingly obvious that the submarine operations along the Adriatic coast were too risky for the submarine and its crew. They were most dangerous to the agents who were being landed and had to make their way to the interior to take up their duty stations.

Alerting the operational desk of OSS to the dangers connected with maritime landings on both enemy-held coasts (Adriatic and Tyrrhenian), we suggested that except for extraordinary reasons, such operations be curtailed for several months. We would therefore have to step up our air operations if we wanted to deliver more teams to the field.

The radio traffic from behind enemy lines increased daily as did the volume of intelligence being transmitted about enemy movements, military production, and other invaluable data which AFHQ and the operating armies needed to asssess enemy strength and intentions. As this intelligence came in, it was translated and checked in our files by Captain Marcel Clemente and Captain Bruno Uberti, who immediately prepared relays to Algiers and Caserta.

On March 20, a second conference was held at Caserta at the request of Colonel Reutershan. On arrival there I sensed an atmosphere heavy with tension. It was clear that even though we had lived up to our agreement, the colonel and his staff were determined to take over SI and its operations. There was no doubt in my mind that Reutershan was being egged on by several former members of Italian SI who might have felt threatened by the successful operations we had conducted in the brief period of a few months.

Reutershan's background had not prepared him for intelligence work. He knew little or nothing about Italy, and he had tolerated a state of operational anarchy among the competing factions under his command. Algiers OSS was too far away to exert any influence on his command. As a result, the situation was gradually heading towards a showdown.

After several days of confrontations, I decided to return to my base in Brindisi, where we were continuing to train the ORI group and other handpicked SIM officers. I made this decision on the basis that nothing would be accomplished by further bickering. Part of the difficulties could be attributed to the fact that, once in the field, some of our teams established contacts with guerrilla bands and started requesting supply drops in various parts of Italy. These requests accounted for a high percentage of the sorties allocated to OSS. In addition, Caserta was saddled with the procurement of tactical intelligence along the Cassino front and at the Anzio beachhead. This phase of the work was not going too well and, as a consequence, agents and teams were being sent to do strategic intelligence work in violation of the limitations that AFHQ had placed on Caserta.

No sooner had I returned to Brindisi than the rumble started up again. On March 23, I received an information copy of an order that had been issued by Colonel Gamble to Reutershan. It read:

Captain Corvo is ordered to temporary duty to proceed to Caserta to head all Secret Intelligence operations of the Office of Strategic Services, Allied Armies in Italy. In this position he will be present at Special Conferences concerning operations. We understand that this will in no way interfere with the Brindisi operations.[7]

On the same day, Colonel Rodrigo, the OSS Theater Intelligence officer, sent a message to me through Reutershan. Its language was unequivocal. It stated:

You will adhere to the following policy in reference to message 745 to Reutershan from Gamble, and please confirm your comprehension of the subsequent:[8]

Merely the general data in which our agents and resistance groups are situated may be disclosed. In no repeat no case are you allowed to discuss the identity of the resistance groups, their leaders, or our agents' names, or pinpoints of their location.
The above is in accord with the fundamentals of the cable AGWAR from JCS to Royce and Devers, the same cable discussed with you by Rodrigo.

Although I had just returned to Brindisi from Caserta, after reading the message, I sent confirmation to Algiers that I would leave the same night.

I turned over temporary command of the Brindisi base to Mim Daddario who had constantly worked with me since his arrival in the theater at the end of 1943. I left to join the fray in Caserta. When I arrived at Reutershan's headquarters, the reception I got would have made the Sahara feel like the South Pole. They refused to recognize my appointment by Algiers. However, I managed to get word to Daddario and asked him to communicate my predicament to Rodrigo and Gamble which he did on March 26.

Since Caserta continued to stonewall my Algiers appointment, Daddario sent a second message on March 30. It read:

Caserta had been untruthworthy concerning the orders you cabled to Captain Corvo in your message 93, kindly send a clarifying cable, explaining just what his position is.

I stayed on, commuting between SI headquarters in Naples to Caserta, and continued to have often heated discussions with the operations people. I insisted on my right to attend AAI meetings. I could discern that Reutershan and his people would lose their struggle against the Algiers command structure.

Then, early in April, the command structure at Caserta changed. Colonel Reutershan was replaced by Colonel Clifton C. Carter, a professional Army officer. The operations post was turned over to Major Koch, who until then had been in command of the OSS Balkan base in Bari, handling Yugoslav and Albanian operations. Reutershan left the theater without ceremony.

Before I returned to Brindisi, I had a meeting with Colonels Head and Brown of the G-3, AAI during which they approved ten SI missions to various parts of northern Italy: Strawberry, Trentino; Pricklypear, Florence; Pear 2, Verona; Pomegranate, Aosta Valley; Berry, Alessandria; Medlar, Parma-Piacenza; Prune 2, Massa; Pineapple, Milan; Orange 2, Pinerolo; and Guava 2, Brescia. Personnel for these missions were already being trained, while other agents were being recruited. During this same conference, it was agreed that SI would provide the mass of tactical ground intelligence for use of the Twelfth Air Force, which was executing a special plan to cut off all railroad traffic leading south of the Apennines. The two-pronged objective of the plan was: (1) to stop all manpower reinforcements to front-line units, and (2) to stop the flow of munitions and supplies from the north.

On April 10 I was called to conference at Algiers to meet a new officer who had joined Rodrigo's intelligence staff and to see Scamp, Glavin, and Gamble, who wanted to discuss future plans for Italy. On my way to the conference, I stopped off at Palermo to be briefed on the situation in Sicily and to give instructions on the disposition of SI personnel, some of whom were to be sent back to the United States.

Arriving in Algiers on April 12, we started a series of round robin meetings during which I learned that AFHQ was planning to move its headquarters to the Royal Palace at Caserta and that Glavin's headquarters would take over the San Leucio installation. Glavin and his staff planned to restructure the Italian show along military lines, giving responsibility and authority to Colonel Carter for all administrative and operational decisions, including control of all movement of personnel in Italy.

Promoted to the position of intelligence officer on Carter's staff was Major Andrew Torrielli from Boston, an older man who had been brought into OSS by Rodrigo who had known him in the War Department in Washington. After the conference, Rodrigo urged that I work closely with Torrielli and that I accompany him on a visit to Caserta, where he could become acquainted with the Italian operations. On April 15, Torrielli and I flew to Naples for his first visit to the AAI. I took the time to brief him on the background of OSS Italian operations and on the struggles for control that had taken place from the time of the Salerno landings. The power structure at AAI/OSS was now in the hands of Carter as CO, Koch as chief of operations, and Torrielli as intelligence officer. Obviously, the Algiers headquarters had agreed to this transfer of authority to Caserta in an effort to put an end to the constant jurisdictional friction.

Carter, who was a West Pointer and came from a military family, began to issue numbered general orders. One of these was General Order No. 2 prohibiting travel by all OSS personnel within the theater without his permission. This included the personnel of SBS, Bari.

The joint Algiers/Caserta planning had also contemplated establishing the OSS communications center in Naples. This move had been made without consultation with Italian SI whose operations were the most numerous and active in the theater. I found out about this plan when a radio message from Major Mero informed his assistant, Captain Atlas, who was visiting Brindisi, that "the problem of frequencies at 'Concord' was more serious than we had imagined. The movement of 622's circuits to Concord (Naples) is out of the question. Therefore, it would be better to arrange a movement to Houston's place (Bari)." There was no question in our minds that the Caserta people would make an all-out effort to eliminate SI's independent status, and thus, finally, take over control of personnel, missions in the field, and, finally, future operations.

While this situation was festering in the background, we were busy infiltrating more missions from our stations in Brindisi and Bastia. The Bastia SI operation was run by Captain Joseph Bonfiglio. Its transportation included the U.S. PT boats and Italian MAS boats which were stationed there. It had landed a mission along the Ligurian coast and several others on the islands off the coast of Italy. Although the Bastia base was essentially run by Livermore's OGs, Bonfiglio often teamed up with them and with the Fifth Army Detachment in the infiltration of some of the operations.

As Livermore's OGs became involved in the Italian campaign, where they were parachuted to help partisan bands, their participation in operations to the various islands off the Tuscan coast was turned over to SI. The order to do so was signed by Brigadier General B. F. Caffey who had discussed the change with Russ Livermore.[9] The order was contained in a radiogram to the OG chief, which stated:

Action will be taken immediately by you to replace OGs, which are being withdrawn from the islands of Capraia and Gorgone, with small SI teams, with radio for each island.

Their roles will be:

a) To give early warning of attack on Corsica; b) To observe and report enemy shipping and aircraft; c) To give weather reports; d)To assist Allied PWs; e) To obtain intelligence information from refugees.

Meanwhile, at Brindisi, the third operational voyage of the *Platino* on March 19-24 was followed by almost three months of naval inactivity. We had issued a warning to all OSS stations that infiltration by water had become dangerous and that it would be prudent to cancel such operations for the next several months. Unfortunately, our warning came too late. On March 21, the OG mission "Ginny" was landed on the coast near La Spezia to blow up a railroad tunnel (in furtherance of "Operation Strangle") and interdict railroad traffic at Stazione Framura.[10] After landing the OG party, which included two officers and thirteen enlisted men, the PTs picked up enemy boats on their radar screens. The operations had obviously been detected by German E boats which fired some flares. Searchlights went on and off along the shore, and the PT boats withdrew to their base in Bastia. The entire "Ginny" mission was captured, tortured, and executed on March 26 by order of General Anton Dostler, CO of the German Seventy-fifth Corps in compliance with Hitler's Commando Order decreeing execution for enemy-uniformed sabotage troops. (After the war, General Dostler was tried and found guilty of violating the rules of war. He was executed by a U.S. Army firing squad at Aversa.)

Our own "Prune" and "Grape 1" missions, which had been landed on March 19 on the upper Adriatic littoral, also ran into extremely bad luck and were captured a few hours after landing. The leader of "Grape 1," Italian Army Captain Fiorentini and his radio operator were executed on the spot without benefit of even a summary trial. The mission leader of "Prune," who was a talented painter, was taken prisoner and interrogated personally by SS Chief General Wolff.

To counterbalance this bad news, on March 26, our team "Apricot" came on the air from Milan, and the "Orange" mission started its transmission from Turin. These teams, which were well connected and led by extraordinarily intelligent men, immediately started sending vital intelligence. This stream of information, added to what was already being transmitted by "Pear," "Date," and "Raisin," gave us a pretty comprehensive picture of the German and Fascist military situation; provided bombing targets; and placed us in touch with the various guerrilla formations and with the General Command of the patriot forces in Milan.

Already at Rossoni's ("Pear") request, the first shipment of arms had been parachuted to the Monte Grappa formations and to the patriots operating in the Apennines who were in touch with "Raisin." The dropping of these supplies had been arranged through the British, and with the limited supplies available to them, we had to guarantee their replacement. The cooperation of Major Wooler and his staff was excellent.

On the night of April 2, the "Grape II" mission was finally parachuted after repeated efforts by this three-man group (approximately 80 hours of flying time) over enemy territory. Unfortunately, the team lost its radio, which was reported to have been found by the Germans. However, the leader of the mission contacted the base through another of our missions which reported his predicament and asked for another radio. In the interim, "Franco," one of the leaders of the Italian resistance, contacted us through Dr. Boeri, chief of our Milan mission, "Apricot," and asked OSS for the sum of 20 million lire for the Committee of National Liberation to "enlarge and implement patriot resistance." This clearly indicated that the central command was beginning to function and that direct contact had been established between OSS and the Committee of National Liberation Upper Italy (CLNAI).

Several days later, "Franco" sent a second message through "Apricot" inquiring as to the possibility of arranging a meeting between one of the leaders of the CLN and General Maitland-Wilson of AFHQ. Such a meeting might be arranged, they suggested, by exfiltration via Argo Giordani, a seaborne escape route being established by SI and Captain Rossoni of "Pear." This escape route proposed the use of fishing boats operating from the delta of the Adige River and surface craft coming from the south. The first of these operations had already been planned to exfiltrate leaders of the Venetian underground. The transfer was to take place some ten to fifteen miles at sea after prearranged Morse signals.

While the base in Brindisi concentrated on strategic intelligence penetration, our Palermo station, under Joe Russo, was busy working with the Navy, State Department, and CIC. It had also been occupied with a special project that had been organized under the code name, "Cavaliers of Liberty." This was a group that had been recruited by Air Force Captain Aurelio Di Bella, one of the heroes of the Italian Air Force Torpedo Squadron, who had been awarded the highest military decorations for his exploits by the Italian government.[11] When the armistice was announced, Di Bella managed to escape from a hospital in northern Italy in a bomber which he stole. He flew to Allied-occupied Sicily, where he reported for duty with the Allies in obedience to the orders broadcast by Marshal Badoglio on September 9.

Di Bella was a fearless aviator who had accounted for some of the serious losses inflicted on the British fleet by the Italian torpedo squadrons. With his black Balbo-style beard and moustache, piercing black eyes, and broad athletic frame, he cut an impressive figure. He was anxious to get back into the fray, but since the Italian Air Force was practically out of business, he had been put in contact with Italian SI to see how he could be of service.

One of Di Bella's first ideas was to organize a volunteer fighting force of Sicilians, who could be trained, armed, and deployed in front-line military operations. He set to work with great gusto, unleashing a recruitment plan before proper permission could be obtained from both AFHQ and the Seventh Army, which, upon hearing of the proposal, quickly turned it down. Undaunted, Di Bella continued his recruitment program and enlisted the support of Colonel Umberto Paroli, an anti-Fascist Italian officer whom I had captured during the Sicilian campaign and who was assigned to my headquarters by orders of the provost marshal, Seventh Army. Not the kind of fellow to be discouraged by a setback, Di Bella flew immediately to Brindisi to talk with Colonel Agrifoglio of SIM and with Marshal Badoglio. When he was finished talking to them he came to see me.

It seemed a pity that all the effort to recruit and train the "Cavaliers" had gone for naught. I was certain that the men could have been used at Anzio, but inasmuch as the AFHQ decision involved its approval of the reorganization of the Italian Army with British equipment, under British hegemony, I could readily see why the proposal had been turned down. Accordingly, I set to work to try to find a way around the roadblocks. I proposed to Di Bella and Agrifoglio that the men be organized in teams of five and that each team be led by an officer from the Italian Army to be selected by SIM. I further suggested that each team include a W/T operator and that the groups be given intensified training in demolitions before being parachuted to assist guerrilla units behind enemy lines. Algiers received this suggestion and authorized the issuance of 100 uniforms and equipment from Insular Base Section (IBS) stores in Palermo.

At this point, it appeared that the project had the green light. Di Bella, Paroli, and the men were enthusiastic. However, several days later a radio message from Glavin canceled the entire operation, and the uniforms and equipment had to be returned to IBS. No one ever fully explained this change of orders. Di Bella's theory was that the British had pressured Badoglio to have the operation rescinded. Fortunately, impending SI operations were not affected by the cancellation of the orders and inasmuch as the operation really fell in the area of SO jurisdiction, we could not protest the order. But the disappointment of the men and their leaders was enormous and became quite vocal when they lined up in formation and were passed in review for the last time in one of Palermo's principal squares.

At the end of April, Scamporino received a message from Algiers advising him that "weather permitting, on or about May 4th Board from Washington headed by Col. Goodfellow will arrive your headquarters Palermo to investigate fitness of all personnel there. Arrange program so that all your personnel will be interviewed and given physical examinations. The party consists of five officers and one civilian woman." One of the officers was Goodfellow's assistant, Captain Frank

Ball, who had interviewed me in Brennan's office on my first trip to Washington. The secretary of the board was Miss Catherine DuBois, who had been my assistant in Washington and who had now come overseas as Colonel Rodrigo's assistant.

In reviewing the SI personnel records, on January 31, 1944, the dispersal of our people, as dictated by the needs of the OSS theater command, was as follows:

Naples station: 4 officers, 27 enlisted men, 2 civilians. Four of the enlisted men were assigned to the Rome S-Force.

Brindisi: 6 officers, 29 enlisted men who were engaged in communications and operations, and others who were earmarked for behind-the-lines operations, 38 Italian civilians who were being trained for intelligence penetration work behind enemy lines.

Corsica: 1 officer, 2 U.S. civilians, and 5 enlisted men.

Sardinia: 10 enlisted men assigned to Allied Military Government administration.

Palermo: 1 officer, 5 U.S. civilians, and 42 enlisted men, most of the enlisted men awaiting reassignment or orders to return to the United States.

Naples: 2 enlisted men assigned to the Allied Control Commission.

Foggia: 3 enlisted men and 1 civilian on temporary assignment to Colonel Robineau, A-2, U.S. Fifteenth Air Force.

U.S. Fifth Army detachment: 3 officers, 1 U.S. civilian, 19 enlisted men, 10 Italian civilians recruited in North Africa, one of these on loan to X-2.

MO: 3 enlisted men and 1 civilian on loan.

All told, there were a total of 167 American officers, enlisted men and civilians in Italian SI, North African theater of operations at this time. They participated in every facet of OSS work from intelligence to Morale Operations (MO), as they were helping all other branches of OSS, as well as such U.S. organizations as G-2, A-2, AMGOT, ACC, and ONI.

A number of those stationed in Palermo were earmarked for return to the United States and separation from the service, but arrangements for transportation were the responsibility of theater headquarters at Algiers. Only seaborne transportation was available, and passage back to the United States was scarce. Many of the individuals who were serving in uniform were beyond the military draft age and had been inducted into the service for the convenience of the OSS in order to facilitate their movements and provide superficial cover.

Italian SI had provided the manpower for OSS detachments operating in Italy which were spread out all the way from North Africa to Palermo, La Maddalena, Salerno, Bastia, and Brindisi, as well as points in between. This had been made possible because the recruitment program of Italian SI was so well advanced by the time of the Salerno landings that we controlled the only manpower pool with expertise and language qualifications in NATO. We loaned personnel to Rudy Winnacker to set up the first R & A field operation in Palermo; to the British Second SAS Regiment for Sicilian and Sardinian operations; and to the Fifth Army detachment where our officers and enlisted men made up the bulk of the forty-man unit under the command of Donald Downes.

The Goodfellow Board visited all OSS bases in NATO and the Middle East to evaluate and attempt to eliminate excess personnel.[12] The Goodfellow Board also visited Naples, Brindisi, Bari, and other stations to talk to the personnel. Many of the men it interviewed had been recruited for Sicilian and Sardinian operations. Since that phase of the Italian campaign was already behind us, they had been scheduled for return to the States. The Goodfellow Board simply accelerated the process, and by August 6, our rosters showed that transportation for fifty-five of these men had already been worked out. (The visit of this board resulted in no other action as has been erroneously intimated in Kim Roosevelt's *OSS War Report* and other books based on that report.)

During part of the month of April and throughout May of 1944, AFHQ imposed a total ban on the delivery of personnel missions behind enemy lines, but we managed to carry out a limited number of supply missions to our agents and the underground forces. Since we had planned to deliver a number of missions each month, the ban caused a backup in our training areas and delayed the scheduling of training classes for new agents.

This operational dearth was compensated for by the intelligence actively generated by teams already in the field whose information covered the broadest span. This information provided such a composite picture of German military activity that AFHQ and AAI could reconstruct a mosaic of what Kesselring and his generals were doing as well as the economic conditions prevailing in German-occupied Italy and the repression being exercised by Mussolini's Black Brigades against not only the guerrilla bands, but also anyone who aided them. Not only was the intelligence produced by our field missions followed closely in the theater, but Washington also scrutinized every item that was transmitted. On May 15, Dr. Lester Hauck, who handled the distribution of incoming intelligence at OSS headquarters in Washington, sent a letter of commendation to me through Colonel Glavin. The letter stated:

> The summary of intelligence from teams in the field had been received here with very high interest by the OB people. All of the items are of importance and those on troop movements are of greatest value. They have had favorable comment everywhere in Washington. A memorandum has been sent to General Donovan describing this type of information and itemizing in detail its evaluation and importance.
>
> Mr. Shepardson has asked that you be written commending you in the highest terms for the results of your difficult undertaking and urging that everything be done to expedite the dispatching of these reports.

Attached to the letter were a number of reports which I traced to information that had been received from our teams "Raisin," "Pear," "Orange," and "Apricot."

As part of our intelligence coverage of northern Italy, after our arrival in Brindisi, we had started to compile a monthly report and detailed maps showing the dislocation of patriot guerrilla formations throughout German-occupied Italy. This report was originally compiled by Agrifoglio's deputy for irregular warfare and updated as staff officers from disbanded army units filtered back to High Command headquarters. Gradually, as our intelligence teams established themselves with the guerrilla units, the reports were expanded to include details about officers, armaments, and other information which helped to assess the local, regional, and overall strength of these irregular forces.

Washington received these reports and whenever they arrived late, because of our lack of stenographic personnel, inquiries invariably started coming in. One such radio inquiry arrived in early June, stating:

The source of the following request is a high political echelon of our government. You must furnish us all available information on Italian guerrilla activities. This should be along the lines of previous reports which have proved themselves to be valuable. Since operations and policy may be determined by the information you send us, this request should be given great care in handling.

The "source," as I later learned, was the White House with which Earl Brennan was in contact through Jonathan Daniels.

Our liaison with SIM was growing daily in importance as our rapport with Agrifoglio and Massaioli was reinforced by mutual trust. SIM's close collaboration with SOE (Special Force No. 1) was a fact of life and came about as a result of British intelligence's monopoly in the conduct of the Armistice negotiations.

Most SIM/SOE missions operating behind enemy lines were made up of regular British and Italian Army officers of monarchist/nationalistic leanings. These officers had command experience and, together with former Army comrades, quickly organized resistance groups. Their communication lines were controlled by the British, but a copy of SIM's daily intelligence was delivered to me religiously. This information proved to be useful, not only to cover possible intelligence gaps, but also to doublecheck on our own intelligence reports. Annotated copies of these daily SIM reports were forwarded to Washington regularly. As time went by and our own agents assumed key positions in almost every region of northern Italy, the details regarding each group became more precise.

The arrival of the month of May generated optimism at both the Anzio and Cassino fronts, where preparations were being made to go on the offensive to shatter German defenses. All headquarters were making preparations for the fall of Rome as though that event would bring the war to an end. Many considered the fall of the city a milestone in the European campaign. General Clark was in a hurry lest the fall of the "Eternal City" be overshadowed by the cross-Channel landings in Normandy.

OSS and other intelligence organizations were again alerted to participate in the special task force that was being assembled under Colonel George "Budge" Smith. This task force was made up of intelligence specialists who had already preselected their targets in the various government offices and foreign embassies.

By May 15, the French colonial troops under General Alphonse Pierre Juin had penetrated the defenses of the Gustav Line. As a result, the Germans in the area began to retreat, endangering the positions of other German forces and causing a general withdrawal. When both the Fifth and Eighth Armies started moving, the Germans retreated to prepared positions in the Alban Hills, under constant hammering by Allied armor, infantry, and air forces. Rome fell on June 4, spared the destruction that had befallen most other Italian cities. As the last German troops were crossing the Ponte Milvio, retreating north to Tuscany, the remnants of a decimated underground could breathe freely again with the infamous torturer Pietro Koch and the Gestapo leading the enemy exodus.

Peter Tompkins, who had been sent to Rome by Donovan as the OSS emissary to the underground in January, had become ensnared in the web of the internal intrigues of the CLN.[13] His mandate to head OSS operations in Rome had been disputed by other OSS/Caserta operators who had staked claims to the same title in the Roman underground. Tompkins was at long last able to emerge in the daylight and breathe in the free Roman air, having thrown away his PAI (Italian colonial police) uniform and witnessed the tumultuous welcome which the Roman public gave the Fifth Army as it marched through the city and took up the pursuit of the retreating German Army along the Via Cassia and the Aurelia.

Among the intelligence organizations that were part of Colonel Smith's S-Force was a contingent from SIM which was eager to recover the old SIM archives that had been left in Rome at the time of Italy's surrender and the hasty escape of the royal family and Badoglio. The OSS took over several buildings in downtown Rome as well as Villa Camilluccia at Monte Mario, where it established a communications center and eventually Rome headquarters.

Scamp headed the SI contingent and set up his own headquarters in a modest ground floor apartment near the Parioli. The apartment had been used by a member of the underground, and there were still a number of hiding places in back of the walls. The OSS Rome office was in Via Regina Margherita and Major Andrew Torrielli, Colonel Carter's intelligence officer, ostentatiously took over the Croatian Embassy as his headquarters. (He was apparently certain that the puppet state of Croatia, which had been created with Hitler's consent, would not ever be able to make a claim to the building.)

The Italian SI Reports Board in Naples, with Captain Joseph Caputa in charge, was moved to Rome, and Scamp immediately set up the full coverage activities in the Rome area and Vatican City. He brought to bear all of the friendships we had established in Italy since the Sicilian campaign in order to set up a powerful intelligence network that could be of service to the United States' formulation of future policies. There was a wealth of intelligence material in Rome, and Scamp set to work mining the information.

Obviously, Scamp and Torrielli did not hit it off too well. When I arrived several days later, I could feel Torrielli's enmity as I met with him at his headquarters. The Italian SI Section had sustained a number of internal power struggles to fight takeover efforts by a number of individuals, but our internal esprit de corps and loyalty had managed to weld us together as a hard-working organization. Our working relationship was excellent. Good work was rewarded and we did not tolerate a lackadaisical attitude. Because of this policy we were able to compile a list of accomplishments which created envy in many places within the OSS organization. All of these resentments seemed to come to a boil once again during June 1944 when orders from Washington recalled Scamp to the States, giving no reason for his recall.[14] After discussing the matter with him, we came to the conclusion that some of our "friends" had managed to convince General Donovan to break up the Italian Section and that getting Scamp recalled to Washington was just the first step in the process. I told him not to worry about any operations in Italy. I emphasized that I would commute between Brindisi and Rome in order to keep my eye on things, and that the section would work effectively to seek his return to Italy. Nonetheless, Scamp made preparations to leave Italy permanently, convinced he would not be allowed to come back. However, a number of officials who had worked with him and Italian SI were determined that he should return. Accordingly, they wrote directly to Donovan and Whitney Shepardson, praising the quality of the intelligence we had produced and lauding Scamp's personal assistance.

Colonel Charles Poletti, chief of AMGOT, wrote to General Donovan on July 16 regarding Scamp's leaving Italy:

On the occasion of his leaving the Theatre I wish to write you that in my opinion Vincent Scamporino has done a particularly fine job. He has been very helpful to me on many occasions as have been his associates. Scamporino has intelligence, energy and has unusual balanced judgment. I am sure you know all of these things, but I just wanted the pleasure of writing it to you.

With warm personal regards

Sincerely, (s) Charles

I gave instructions to all SI stations that they were to continue to address their communications to Scamp as though he were away on temporary duty. All papers emanating out of AFHQ/OSS were sent out over Scamp's name by Captain James Montante, who had charge of the rear echelon in Algeria and then Caserta. In addition, SI military intelligence radio bulletins going to AFHQ and AAI were sent to the attention of Scamp, and the chain of command was maintained as though he were present in Italy. As for my own effort to have him sent back to the theater, I planned to make a personal appeal to Donovan who would be coming back to Italy prior to the invasion of southern France. In the interim, the entire Italian Section was told to work with renewed vigor to produce top-rate intelligence.

Colonel Glavin had forwarded a first-class, unsolicited encomium to Donovan in Washington on June 17. It was a copy of a memo Colonel Head of AAIG-3 sent to Colonel Carter. A copy was sent by the Director's office to Whitney Shepardson to be placed on record in the SI files. It read: "G.S.I. have asked me to tell you that a considerable amount of S.I. intelligence that you have been sending them recently has been most valuable. Congratulations to you and those responsible. Yours sincerely, Col. Head."[15]

At the end of May, the Brindisi radio station was officially closed down and all communications were moved to Bari. I assigned Captain Marcel Clemente and Captain Bruno Uberti to handle the traffic at Bari, and a courier service for the relay of operational messages was set up. The military operational training facilities remained at Brindisi, Ostuni, and Fasano.

On June 15, I received a message that had been transmitted by telephone from Major Torrielli in Caserta. The message which was received at Bari at 2125 hours read: "Captain Corvo is to proceed to Caserta with all of his papers and is to stay there until Major Torrielli has seen him." This, I mused, was the awaited second step in the process of destroying the structure of Italian SI, but I was confident that on my arrival at Caserta things would change substantially.

As there was no direct Air Force service between Brindisi and Naples, I drove to Caserta early the next day and arrived in the late afternoon. I took only my briefcase with a few papers that I felt I might need to discuss basic operational questions. Torrielli had been in the theater only a few months. I had accompanied him on his first trip to Caserta on April 15, during which I had provided him with background material on operations and our relationship with SIM, the British, and OSS/AFHQ (Caserta). When I arrived at San Leucio, contrary to the terseness of his message, he was almost cordial and he ascribed the entire matter to a misunderstanding. Then he got down to business, pointing out that as Carter's intelligence officer he had jurisdiction over our operations and that he intended to exercise this authority. Briefly put, he wanted me to organize tactical intelligence operations in all the forward areas and to give up my command as chief of SI operations in Italy. He also wanted all my files to be brought to Caserta.

Although I agreed to assume responsibility for tactical intelligence in the forward echelons, I pointed out that a decision on my status as chief of Italian SI operations was not within his command jurisdiction. The only person who could alter my command status, I stated, was Colonel

Glavin or the SI Division in Washington. Though Torrielli did not challenge my assertion, I could see he was not very happy with the outcome of our meeting. I told him that I would drive up to AAI headquarters at Lake Bolsena in the morning and talk to the intelligence people about their requirements for tactical intelligence, and that on the basis of that discussion I would make appropriate plans and select a staff for the forward echelons.

On the way to the front, I stopped off at Rome and had a long chat with Major Jack Ricca, bringing him up to date on what had transpired with Torrielli. He agreed that the best policy was to assume the additional responsibility for tactical intelligence and wait for events to unfold.

When I arrived at Lake Bolsena, I talked to several G-2 officers and saw no reason, on the basis of the optimistic outlook of the progress being made by the Fifth and Eighth armies to rush headlong to set up tactical headquarters. In order not to create additional discord, however, I drove back to Caserta to report that I would take on the assignment. Our work in Brindisi would continue under the direction of my assistant operations officer Mim Daddario who knew the background of the mission and the agents involved. Mim, who had been an outstanding football player at Wesleyan University in Middletown, could work around the clock and then start all over again. We had worked in this fashion from the beginning of January without any letup. Since circumstances had forced me to move around to fight for our survival, he had redoubled his efforts, as had the rest of the officers and men of the base. We kept in touch by telephone every day, and we developed a code that worked very well when we needed to use it to communicate any delicate information. Obviously, we had not been provided with any scramblers.

The swift forward movement of the Allied armies indicated that the need for tactical intelligence was not urgent as long as the Germans kept hastily retreating to their next defensive line under the withering attack of our Air Force. This much was evident from the great number of burned out vehicles that lined the Via Cassia, the Aurelia and the highway to Perugia. Beyond Bologna and the Apennines, some of our intelligence teams were already supplying a great deal of tactical information and were working with guerrilla groups to impede enemy reinforcements and supplies from arriving at the front.

On June 24, the final SI submarine mission carried out by the *Platino* returned from the Po Delta. The mission had left Brindisi on June 21 to rendezvous with a fishing boat which would meet it at sea, transfer supplies and personnel, and embark three members of the underground who were carrying plans of the fortifications and the defense lines being built by the Todt Organization to stop the Allied advance. (The Todt organization was named after Armaments Minister Fritz Todt and built fortifications and roads for the Wehrmacht.) We had already transmitted a detailed description of all the defenses along the shrinking Adriatic coast, where submarine operations had become almost a suicide mission. Disregarding repeated warnings from SI, AAI had made direct arrangements to land agents from an Italian submarine.

With the departure of Scamporino, Torrielli's plans to personally take over our intelligence operations moved a step ahead. On June 25, I received two written orders from him.[16] The first was issued to Chief Italian SI (who happened to be absent) and it was entitled "S.I. Forward Echelons." The order followed:

1. Forward echelons will be immediately established by S.I. with the following units: 5th Army, 8th Army, 7th Army, VI Corps and Polish Corps.
2. All intelligence functions now being carried out by Forward Echelons will be taken over by S.I. Division of functions will be decided in consultation with operations personnel.
3. All intelligence personnel now with Forward Echelons will remain and be absorbed by S.I. Forward Echelons. Chief S.I. will immediately assign personnel to staff Forward Echelons.
4. Communications with Forward Echelons will be arranged in consultation between the Intelligence Officer (Torrielli) and the Communications Branch (Mero).
5. Lt. Zacharias will represent the Intelligence Officer (Torrielli) in his capacity as Ground Intelligence Officer on all matters dealing with Forward Echelons.

(s) Andrew Torrielli Lt. Col. F.A.
Int. Off. OSS AAI

The second order was sent to me on the same date, June 25:

Subject: Forward Echelons, S.I.

    To: Captain Biagio M. Corvo, AUS

You have been designated by the Intelligence Officer and Chief S.I. to organize and direct Forward Echelons, S.I.

You will report to OSS AAI with full field equipment. Plans for staffing and conduct of forward echelons will be made in conjunction with the Intelligence Officer, the ground intelligence officer and operations personnel at HQ, OSS AAI (San Leucio).

All records of Italian S.I. will be delivered immediately to the same Headquarters and left with the Deputy Chief S.I.

(s) Andrew Torrielli, Lt. Col. F.A.
Int. Off. OSS AAI

On June 28, I drove to Rome by way of Caserta in order to discuss details of the operation and to work out a strategy to derail Torrielli's incessant new effort to destroy and take over the section. I also wanted to visit the front lines in order to determine where the headquarters for forward echelons would be set up. On this trip I met Lieutenant Zacharias whom I had known only casually. Although he was a nice guy, I doubted that he could fit the role that Torrielli was trying to cut out for him—or that he really wanted to.

Before leaving Rome, I was introduced to Moe Berg, who was on special mission to get information and secure copies of secret items being produced by the Galileo Labs in Florence. Knowing that I was going up to the front, he asked if he could join my party. We drove up the old route from Rome to Viterbo, past Montefiascone to Bolsena, and stopped at the Hotel Milano at Aquapendente. The hotel had been partly damaged in the savage fighting that had been waged in the area and the town was half destroyed. The hotel dining room and several bedrooms, however, were open. The menu offered only two items: barley soup and fried eggs. It did not take long to make up our minds. Gulping down the soup and eggs, we hit the road again and started climbing the barren hills of Radicofani.

The Germans had been hit hard during their retreat. The evidence of burned out vehicles attested to the deadly accuracy of Allied bomber and fighter fire. Here and there a burned out Tiger tank provided proof of how little protection armor plate afforded when attacked from overhead. Soon we started running into French colonial troops who were spearheading the drive to capture Siena. Mule-mounted Algerian and Goumier troops in colorful uniforms were pointed to drive the Germans out of the historic Tuscan city. Siena, said to be Hitler's favorite city, had been evacuated in order not to destroy its famous art treasures and landmarks.

The Sienese people, trekking back to their abandoned medieval town, made their way through the narrow winding streets to the Piazza del Palio, where several Algerian units in their native uniforms, their military band playing, were celebrating the official fall of the city. There, in the quaint Piazza, which has retained its full medieval splendor, on a clear July 3, 1944, history was being written by troops from far away Algeria, their colorful uniforms matching the setting of the square with its towering Palazzo Publico. It was a stirring sight, but Siena was simply another city in the seemingly endless itinerary of the Fifteenth Army Group.

The Via Cassia led northward from Siena to Florence, but the French troops could press the attack no further as they were about to be pulled out of the line and reorganized to participate in the attack on southern France ("Operation Anvil"). They were replaced by troops from the New Zealand Corps. The Germans, in the meanwhile, slowed down their retreat and took up positions around Poggibonsi in the heart of Chianti country.

We immediately returned to Rome and Caserta where our orders were issued to go back to Siena where OSS had already taken over Villa Poggio in Pini, a beautiful country villa on the outskirts of the city. Colonel Glavin and Tom Early were already there. The villa belonged to a Sienese nobleman, Count De Vecchi, (not related to the Mussolini crony De Vecchi of Valcismon, one of the Quadrumvirs of the March on Rome). Its location and spacious grounds made it an ideal place to set up headquarters for OSS/Italy, which was to move northward, while OSS/AFHQ would move from Algiers and take over the quarters at Caserta.

After we arrived in Siena, we scouted around and located the villa which occupied the crest of a hill; access was gained via a winding road flanked by stately cypress trees. A square in front of the villa housed a private chapel which had been used to celebrate private Masses attended by the DeVecchi family. It was late afternoon when we arrived. We decided to spend the night there so that I would have ample time to talk with Colonel Glavin and Colonel Early about the situation Torrielli was creating. Both of them counseled that I keep my cool and go ahead with the creation of the forward echelons. They promised that before long there would be significant changes in OSS/AAI.

We sat in the garden in back of the villa, under an enormous flowering magnolia tree. There, in one of the flower beds, the retreating Germans had buried one of their noncoms—a sergeant— and had placed a huge wooden Iron Cross at his head, bearing the dead soldier's name, rank and serial number, and the service to which he belonged. Occasionally, the thundering of the cannons, several miles up the line, could be heard as battery and counterbattery fire was exchanged north of us. Red flashes lit up the night sky as darkness fell. The presence of the German sergeant buried in the flower bed cast a pall over our small group as we talked for several hours before retiring for the night.

My room overlooked the garden, and I could see the cross on which the brilliant moonlight cast its yellow shards of light. The window was open and the night air wafted the powerful fragrance of jasmine from the huge plant which clung to the wall of the building below my window. As I write now, I can still vividly recall the scene and through some sixth sense recapture every essence in the air.

The next day we agreed that the new headquarters for OSS/Italy was to be set up in the DeVecchi villa which was officially requisitioned through the British town major's office in Siena. Glavin instructed me to go back to Rome and then Brindisi in order to prepare for the creation of the forward echelons. When I arrived at Caserta, the adjutant wrote the necessary orders for the movement and the requisition forms for the equipment that would be needed.

I met briefly with Torrielli with whom, by this time, I was barely on speaking terms. I told him that I did not intend to transfer the master files from Brindisi headquarters and that the base would continue to stage our operations until such time as SI headquarters would be moved up forward according to plans already outlined. The next day I departed overland for Brindisi to organize the move to the front. After scrounging around several Air Force supply depots, we drew enough tents, cots, and other supplies to get under way.

Daddario had been proceeding with the various operations which we had planned and the supply drops that had already been laid on for the partisan forces and our own missions. On July 7 and 9, successful supply drops were made to both "Pear" and "Raisin." Not long afterward these were followed by more drops to "Raisin" and "Orange" for a total of 55,000 pounds of arms, food, and medical supplies. "Drupe II," a highly complicated maritime operation to transfer men and equipment at sea off the coast of Porto Garibaldi, was laid on and cleared with the assistance of Lieutenant Ben Levy. This operation utilized an Italian MAS boat.

In order to cope with the additional burdens placed on our section and the moves that were scheduled, I assigned Major Tarallo and Lieutenant Icardi to the tactical headquarters in Siena; Captain Clemente and Captain Uberti were assigned to the Rome area to handle clandestine radio traffic; Captain Passanisi and his unit in Naples were moved to Brindisi; and the SI Bastia base was scheduled to be phased out. Captain Bonfiglio was sent to Sardinia to recruit W/T operators from the Italian armed forces. These men were to be sent to Brindisi to familiarize themselves with our equipment and procedures and to attend parachute school.

On July 12, the truck convoy with the tactical personnel, including a number of agents, moved north. We stopped off overnight at San Leucio where the OSS/AFHQ staff had already started moving in, and I had the opportunity to swap information with our rear echelon officer, Captain James Montante. Jim was in touch with the full situation and was responsible for preparing the SI semimonthly report in which he pulled in information from all our SI stations to keep Washington fully informed of our activities. Jim told me that substantial changes would be taking place and that Colonel Carter and Major Koch were being sent back to the States. Torrielli, who had been promoted to Lieutenant Colonel, was being transferred to the G-2 section of the Sixth Army Group which was being assembled for the invasion of southern France.

The next morning we made our way to Rome and set up our camp on the outskirts of the city. Meanwhile, I went to visit OSS headquarters to talk to Jack Ricca, who was handling the liaison with the Italian government. While looking for Ricca, I ran into Colonel Carter and informed him that I was headed north to set up tactical infiltrations and that I planned to return in a few days to discuss SI plans with him. It was clear to me that Carter had not yet been informed that he was being sent back to the States. Torrielli was nowhere to be found.

One of the last official meetings which Carter attended as CO was on July 3 when the Allied Control Commission, under the chairmanship of Brigadier M. S. Lush, met in Rome with the representatives of SOE, OSS, PWB, and AMG to discuss the administration of patriots' affairs in occupied Italy. [17] Representing OSS were Colonel Carter and Major Koch; representing No. 1 Special Force (SOE) were Major Tenent and Lieutenant Harris; participating at the meeting were Colonel Bernabo, Italian General Staff, and Riccardo Bauer of the Committee of National Liberation; representing the political interests of Great Britain was Harold Caccia, while Sam Reber represented the U.S. Department of State. The main topic of the lengthy meeting was the treatment and disarming of the guerrilla forces that were being overrun by orthodox military operations.

Since Allied government administrators were in charge of the newly liberated areas and would be busy with pressing economic problems, it was requested that OSS and SOE provide officers to identify guerrilla forces, disarm them in a decorous manner, and provide acknowledgment for their services. Both OSS and SOE declined to undertake the job as they did not have the personnel to manage this massive task. However, they volunteered to send information to identify legitimate patriot groups and their leaders. Representatives of the CLN would be designated patriot representatives and would act as advisers to AMG officers on patriot band matters. The meeting also worked out procedures to stack the arms of the patriot units; award certificates and provide employment in reconstruction projects, specifically rebuilding of roads and public buildings. The principal reason for the meeting was to avoid an explosion of armed political strife in the event of a massive pullout of German forces. Since such a pullout did not materialize until ten months later, AAI developed another plan which was codenamed "Rankin Plan B."

On July 15, the convoy finally made it to Siena where we established our permanent camp several miles north of the city.

While Icardi and the men were busy setting up the camp, I drove to Villa DeVecchi where the advance OSS/AAI party had set up its mobile radio station. In order to facilitate the administration of the 2677th Regiment, Glavin had decided to establish four subheadquarters to handle specific phases of OSS work.[18] Designated as Company A were the Operational Groups under Colonel Livermore; Company B was assigned to French operations; Company C was headquartered in Bari and handled Balkan operations; and Company D, whose headquarters were being set up in Siena, had the responsibility of coordinating Italian operations.

Returning to Rome from Siena around July 18, I stopped off to see Colonel Carter. I found him quite glum and disturbed as he had been told to pack up and return to the States. Major Koch, his operations officer, had also been ordered to return to Washington. Both of them were busy packing their bags. No successors had been designated to take their place. Carter was worried about the effect that his relief from the mission would have on his mother. He came from a family with a long military background.

The next day I continued to Caserta where Glavin's headquarters were settling down at San Leucio and where Captain Montante was holding forth in Scamp's absence. During the meeting with Colonel Rodrigo and Colonel Early, I outlined plans for our Company D and Brindisi activities. I also pointed out the communications bottleneck that was being created, where we were forced many times to use telephones to update operational details and where dissemination of vital intelligence was sometimes delayed several days by the transmission chain.

Daddario, who was running the Brindisi station at this time, complained in a letter to Montante on July 23 that

the wires from the field are received at Bari, and then piped out, as received, to

Clemente, where they are deciphered and processed. I therefore am a great distance from the final breaking of the wires and depend on teletype with Rome and on Air Pouch, for my information. That is the mechanics.

On the same day Daddario wrote to me to bring me up to date on what was happening in Brindisi. He advised me that many changes were taking place and that "Mike Jiminez had come lock, stock and barrel and will face the very pleasant task of being able to lay on transport for his own missions." Jiminez had served in the Abraham Lincoln Brigade in the Spanish Civil War and was part of an old Fifth Army Group that had worked with Donald Downes in Morocco and later at Salerno and Anzio.

The operations people at AAI were still racing each other to get off missions into German-occupied Italy. Daddario reported that since the AAI operation boys had

taken over across the street they are sending a lot of boys in, twelve men, for example, went out the last two nights and returned unsuccessfully, but they are going out. It is nothing to worry about as we know the quality of our men and know the job is a top flight one.

This air of administrative and operational confusion was about to come to an end with the consolidation of all the OSS Italian campaign elements under the proposed mantle of Company D, which would temporarily operate out of Villa DeVecchi in Siena. Rodrigo suggested that plans be made to provide the intelligence staff for Company D. He asked me to assume the task temporarily until communications could be consolidated and we could determine the success of the Fifteenth Army Group's efforts to cross the Apennines and break into the Po Valley.

Before returning to Siena, I stopped off at Rome and visited OSS at Viale Regina Margherita. There were few people in the office, and I was told that the new commanding officer of Company D was in the office. It was the first time I had met Bill Suhling, who was a captain in the Medical Administration Corps. A stocky, middle-aged man who had obviously volunteered for service, Suhling had a very pleasant manner complemented by his southern drawl. He was a gentleman farmer from the area around the city of Frederick, Virginia, who was totally unprepared to deal with the Italian situation. Although he had no intelligence background he possessed a good deal of horse sense and business experience.

When I walked in and introduced myself, Suhling was sitting alone in the big room behind a large plain antique desk, puffing away at a cigarette. We exchanged a few pleasantries, and after sparring around a bit, we seemed to hit it off, found common ground, and started to talk shop. I told him that I was heading toward Siena and that I would probably be spending time at his headquarters, organizing the intelligence side of the operations. I then outlined some of the difficulties that confronted us.

A frank person, Suhling readily admitted that he did not know a great deal about his assignment but was willing to listen and learn. Somehow I got the impression that James Rand, Jr. had recommended him to Donovan. At the conclusion of our meeting, I promised my full cooperation in pulling the Italian OSS show together and making a maximum contribution to the military campaign as it neared its climax. This unity was vital to our agents in the field and the operating Allied forces in Italy. It can best be illustrated by the constant complaint about the slowness of communications and the lack of central coordination of operations by higher headquarters. Suhling promised to make the correction of these shortcomings one of his first priorities and said that he intended to move to Siena in several days.

1. Augusta, Sicily. July 13, 1943. Part of the Allied invasion fleet in the Bay of Augusta, as seen from the heights of Melilli.

2. Four key men of the Palermo Station. C.P.O. Rafael de Haro, cypher expert; Sgt. Charles Groff, radio and communications expert; Serafin Buta, radio operator of the San Fratello Mission; and Sgt. Anthony Ribarich, also a member of the same mission. Both Buta and Ribarich were wounded on the mission.

3. Author discusses cypher problems with C.P.O. Rafael de Haro.

4. Palermo. Task Force 80.4 meets at OSS Headquarters. Top row (l. to r.): Commander Kremer, Capt. Olds, U.S.N., Captain Frank Tarallo, Ensign Mike Burke. Front row: Commander Dufek, Lt. Doug Fairbanks, Jr., Rudy Winnacker, R & A, and Major Steve Martin, A.M.G.O.T., and the author.

5. Friendly liaison session with AMGOT. Meeting at S.I. headquarters in Palermo. (l. to r.) : The author, Capt. Tarallo, Major Orfeo Bizzozerro, Col. Charles Poletti, Military Governor of Sicily, Vincent Scamporino, ISI Division chief, and OSS Major James H. Angleton, Sr. Standing are Tom Stoneborough and Vincenzo Vacirca.

6. Italian Military Mission to AFHQ (l. to r.) in civilian clothes, Italian diplomat and official interpreter Frank Montanari, Capt. Vito Guarrasi. Rear right, Major Galani and, at front right, General Giuseppe Castellano, who headed the Mission. Two unidentified U.S. liaison officers. (Photo courtesy of Avv. Vito Guarrasi, Palermo.)

7. British Naval Lieutenant Ben Levy and Peter Durante. Levy cooperated with OSS Brindisi station to provide transportation while Durante was SI escort officer for all submarine and maritime missions. He had previously distinguished himself at Lipari and Ventotene operations.

8. Members of a Secret Intelligence mission confer on the deck of the submarine *Platino* minutes prior to departure on a dangerous espionage mission in enemy terrain.

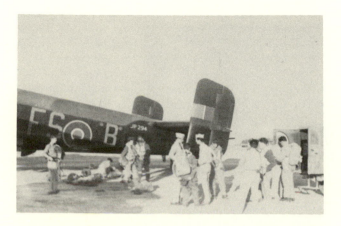

9. OSS/SI mission "suits-up" before departing on board an R.A.F. aircraft for a jump into enemy terrain to carry out a strategic intelligence mission.

10. Decoration ceremony. Col. Edward Glavin, C.O. 2766 Regiment, Capt. Donato Petruccelli and the author at the decoration ceremony of Sgt. Albino Perna, Pvt. Valeriano Melchiorre and Corp. Carl Bove, members of the SI section who bravely operated behind enemy lines.

11. Rome. A few days after the fall of the city, work parties unearthed the gruesome execution location of the 335 victims who were slaughtered in cold blood by the SS in reprisal for a partisan attack on a German military unit on Via Rasella. The Ardeatine Caves, where the Nazi atrocity took place, are now a revered national monument. This photo was taken during excavation.

12. Moe Berg, sent by Donovan on a special scientific mission, standing at Piazza del Palio in Siena on the day the city fell to Algerian Goumiers, June 3, 1944.

13. General Raffaele Cadorna (right), Commanding General of Italian patriot forces behind German lines, with Walter Audisio, the man who carried out the execution of Mussolini and Claretta Petacci. (Photo courtesy of LaPietra, Milan.)

14. A highly charged moment in Milan's uprising. The bodies of Mussolini, Claretta Petacci and other Fascist officials executed at Dongo are brought to Piazzale Loreto.

15. Chance meeting. Dr. Enzo Boeri (right), leader of the S.I. mission "Apricot" and Intelligence Chief of CLNAI and partisan leader "Bandiera" meet at Po River crossing near Reggio Emilia in early May. U.S. troop convoy in background.

16. Colonel Pompeo Agrifoglio, Chief of Italian Military Intelligence (S.I.M.), who commanded the respect of Allied military colleagues in the difficult times after Italian surrender.

17. General Giuseppe Massaioli, Chairman of the Italian Joint Chiefs of Staff, who as a Lieutenant Colonel in 1943-45 served as Agrifoglio's director of S.I.M. offensive operations.

18. Milan. General Willis Crittenberger reviews Italian patriot forces who liberated the city. With him are (l. to r.) General Umberto Utile, C.G. Italian Legnano Division; British Brigadier Harold Mathews, C.G. 59th Area; General Cadorna; General Crittenberger; and General Charles Bolte, U.S. 36th Infantry Division (Texas Longhorns). OWI Photo.

19. Communist partisan leader Cino Moscatelli whose well-equipped forces from the Valdossola area swept into Milan with other patriot forces and overwhelmed German resistance. Standing at his right is Father Russo, Military Chaplain of the Communist Brigades.

20. Bologna. Dr. Enzo Boeri, CLNAI Intelligence Chief, and Raimondo Craveri, leader of ORI, stop at a cafe soon after the liberation of the city.

21. The Rising. Patriots and people take over the textile center of Busto Arsizio, forcing the German garrison to surrender on April 26th, six days before "secret surrender" was signed.

22. Luigi Longo, Communist leader of the Garibaldi Brigades, was a lifetime anti-Fascist who had fought in Spain as Inspector General of the International Brigades. He is shown here with General Cadorna welcoming U.S. General Gruenther, extreme left. Longo, together with Parri, welded the underground fighters into a disciplined fighting force.

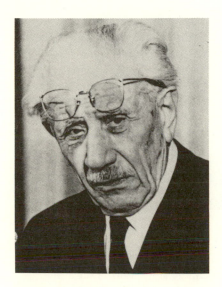

23. Ferruccio Parri, whose vision and devotion to freedom was an inspiration to the Italian underground, was a moving force behind the unity of the CLNAI and the principles of the Partito D'Azione. (Courtesy of LaPietra, Milan.)

24. Gian Carlo Pajetta, one of the top Communist underground leaders, was a member of the CLNAI Mission that negotiated an agreement with AFHQ and the Italian government. (Courtesy of LaPietra, Milan.)

25. Don Luigi Sturzo, father of the Christian Democratic movement, who opposed Fascism from the beginning and who inspired the world-wide anti-Fascist movement with his books and articles from London and New York. (Courtesy of LaPietra, Milan.)

26. Giuseppe Romita (left) and Giuseppe Lupis were in the forefront of the Socialist movement that fought Fascism from the beginning.

27. Milan. May 2, 1945. At OSS headquarters in the Hotel Milan, a young Russian named Timoshenko who had fought with the Italian underground is interrogated by Vincent Scamporino, while Martin Carney and "Mim" Daddario look over the *Stars and Stripes* which announces the surrender of German forces in Italy somewhat belatedly.

28. In Memoriam. In 1959 this marble plaque was erected to honor the work of the OSS/SI Mission "Raisin" in Romagna. The text reads: "This small church was built upon the ruins of the church which served as the operational base of the O.R.I. radio Zella which was in contact with the Office of Strategic Services for the coordination of resistance operations behind the Gothic Line. The original church was destroyed when the Canadian troops of the British 8th Army engaged the enemy on the spot. In memory of the fallen and as a remembrance of the horrors of war and as an invocation for peace."

29. Back Home. Some of the top Italian S.I. staff members back in Washington in late May 1945. Back row (l. to r.): Major Frank Tarallo, Attorney Nicholas Olds, Lt. Bruno Bisceglia. Middle row: Lt. Col. John Ricca, Maj. Joseph Bonfiglio, Joe D'Amato, Maj. Felix Pasqualino, Sgt. Mike Contrastino, Front row: Vincent Scamporino, Earl Brennan, and the author.

30. Retrospective. Reunion in Middletown. On the occasion of a testimonial to the author in February 1949. General Donovan was the key speaker and members of the Italian SI in the area held a get-together. Left to right: Louis Fiorilla, the author, General Donovan, "Mim" Daddario, and Dr. Stirling Callisen. In front: Vincent Scamporino.

Chapter 13

Friendly Inter-Allied Competition

In the months since early January, the rapport between Craveri and our unit had become very close, permitting long-range intelligence planning, which also laid the groundwork for a fruitful postwar relationship between the United States and Italy.

The men who had organized the Action party (Partito d'Azione) were among the outstanding political personalities of Italy, and we were certain they would play a key role in the life of the nation once peace had returned to Italy. The only disturbing factor was that a number of leaders like Riccardo Bauer and Leo Valeani had a closer relationship with the British than with us. Through Craveri, however, we managed to establish control over the activist wing that was participating in the guerrilla war behind the German lines and that was exercising command functions at CLNAI general headquarters in Milan, where Ferruccio Parri was one of the moving forces behind the Resistance. The other co-equal leader was Luigi Longo, head of the Communist forces in northern Italy.

SI Italy had trained and parachuted the intelligence staff of CLNAI. The staff was headed by Dr. Enzo Boeri, leader of the "Apricot" mission who was later joined by Tullio Lussi ("Landi") who became intelligence deputy of CLNAI. Early in June, Parri had asked that the Italian Section of OSS act as the sole distributor of the official war bulletins issued by the CLNAI and transmitted daily through our clandestine radios from Milan.[1] These bulletins were passed to AFHQ and all subordinate headquarters in the theater and were relayed to Italian Radio, the BBC, Armed Forces Radio, and other world news organizations. The increased influence of OSS in the theater was the subject of conferences in British intelligence circles. These conferences and the decisions arising from

them never interfered with the collaboration of British services in any of
our clandestine operations.

The first report that SOE was casting about to recoup its domination
of Special Operations in Italy came to me early in June. The plan had
obviously been the fruit of discussions between Commander Jerry
Holdsworth, SOE chief in Bari, and John McCaffrey in the British
Legation in Berne, Switzerland. It had been discussed with Marshal
Giovanni Messe who headed the Italian armed forces.

General Raffaele Cadorna, son of the military leader who led Italy's
armed forces at the beginning of World War I, was approached about
becoming commander of all guerrilla forces in northern Italy to help
Parri and Longo with the purely military phases of the CLN work.[2] At
the time the first report was relayed to me, I scribbled the following note
to myself:

General Cadorna is leaving for northern Italy with two radios and a British
officer and a large reception committee will await him in Lombardy. British
legation in Berne wants to recognize the Committee. Cadorna will leave as
delegate for all the political parties. People who know, Holdsworth, Bauer,
Casati, Bonomi, Marshal Messe, General Staff and SIM, are to say that Cadorna
will go on a foreign mission. From the Italian government 'will spring' a
commissariato for Resistance Groups. Bauer and Mondo both refused. Three
undersecretaries will make up the unit: War, Palermo; Pres. of Council,
Finoaltea; one other party. Bauer is empowered to act for the Rome Military
Junta of six parties. Bauer will handle all British contacts and Mondo all American
contacts.

There was no question that sending a military man to direct military
operations made a great deal of sense. The selection of General Cadorna
was fortuitous for all the political leaders respected his personal courage.
His acceptance of the arduous mission and his willingness to parachute
without training at age 55 attested to his personal high spirit and
patriotic dedication. Forewarned of the British plan, I had a long
discussion with Colonel Agrifoglio who confirmed all of the details I
already knew. The colonel concurred with my analysis that the British
Foreign Office wanted to be in a dominant position at the National
Committee of Liberation; otherwise, a proposal would have been made
to OSS to send a combined mission. Such a proposal was never advanced,
nor were there ever any consultations at any level on the subject. I
decided to keep fully informed as to the progress of the Cadorna mission
and relied on our field intelligence services to keep us informed once the
mission was parachuted. On July 15, 1944, General Cadorna,
accompanied by Riccardo Bauer, arrived at Jerry Holdsworth's
headquarters where he was also met by Max Salvadori. They discussed
broad plans to take over the Ossola Valley or the Aosta Valley and to
create a resistance enclave. Then Cadorna met with Major DeHan. Their
discussions revealed that the British did not wish to promote an
insurrection and were interested primarily in effecting sabotage

operations. Major DeHan handled the training program. When the general was ready, Jerry Holdsworth took him to a meeting at headquarters at Lake Bolsena, where he met Colonel John Riepe, G-3 Operations. On August 12, General Cadorna was parachuted into Val Cavallina to a prearranged reception committee of the Fiamme Verde group.

Training for across-the-line infiltration had been underway at our forward echelons camp, north of Siena, under the direction of Major Tarallo and Lieutenant Icardi. The agent personnel that had been selected were familiar with the Apennines terrain and the Po Valley, but on my arrival at Company D headquarters, I told Tarallo to ease up until the new CO arrived, so that we could get our long-term bearings adjusted. Together with Icardi, we decided to personally examine the opportunities of penetration which the German defensive positions would allow us.

Fighting and skirmishing were ongoing south of the town of Poggibonsi in the hilly Chianti country south of Florence. The Allied offensive in this area was in the hands of New Zealand troops under the command of General Bernard Fryberg, whose World War I exploit in swimming the Hellespont, during the Gallipoli expedition, was part of history. The fighting in this hill country was tough as the heaps of rubble of one village after another attested. Progress was slow, and fighting was intense for one rubble heap after another. After inspecting and testing the front and talking with several British intelligence officers, I decided that the central, less active Apennine front might be easier to penetrate. We therefore returned to Siena, from where I sent Daddario a message that more enlisted men were needed both at the forward camp and at Siena. I had to send the message via teletype to Bari, and from there it was delivered to Brindisi by courier.

On July 25, the Italian SI station in Bastia, which had been under the command of Captain Bonfiglio, sent out its last maritime mission under La Spezia. The "Kingston" mission was attacked by enemy surface craft while landing operations were under way and was never heard from again. [3] Thereafter, personnel were transferred to Brindisi, and Bonfiglio undertook a recruiting trip for wireless operators. He reported for duty at Brindisi at the end of July, bringing with him a number of operators from the Italian Army.

Chapter 14

August Reorganization

With the beginning of August, OSS planning activity seemed to take on new life under Donovan's constant prodding. He had come to Italy to rejuvenate the planning and coordination of U.S. intelligence and special operations activities. His presence was timely because a number of decisions had to be made that would influence the future course of OSS operations.

Four situations facing the Italian theater were reviewed, and their effect on Italian operations was considered. These were:

1. The U.S. Seventh Army under the command of General Alexander Patch was getting ready to invade southern France, and OSS had been assigned an important role in the unfolding invasion plans.

2. With the approach of the Russian armies to Warsaw, "General Bor," who commanded the Polish underground army in Warsaw, ordered the military uprising of the underground forces in the Polish capital. The Russians delayed their offensive and "Bor" found himself attacked on all sides by German forces without much needed vital supplies of food, ammunition, and medicines.

   In order to help the Polish underground, the RAF 334 Wing which had been assigned the air resupply job in Italy and the Balkans was diverted to supply the beleaguered Warsaw underground, flying all the way from Brindisi to Warsaw to carry out the suicidal low-level drops.

   Within a few weeks, the entire 334 Wing was almost put out of action by the heavy casualties it suffered over Poland, thus creating a crisis in the resupply of Italian and Yugoslav guerrilla forces.

3. The reorganization of OSS activities in Italy under the administrative control of Company D and its new CO Bill Suhling needed an input from the general.

4. OSS relations with Marshal Tito and his Partisan forces needed to be reviewed and a military mission to Vis, headed by Colonel Ellery Huntington, was appointed.

A series of high-level meetings were scheduled at Caserta and Capri from August 1 to August 15, at which General Donovan, Marshal Tito, Admiral Stanley (President Roosevelt's representative), former U.S. Ambassador Hugh Wilson, General Patch, Ambassador Robert Murphy, Colonels Rodrigo, Early, Gamble, and Huntington, and Marine General Miller participated as guests of Colonel Edward Glavin, OSS MEDTO chief. These meetings would assess the organization's role in the unfolding military and political strategy in southern Europe, North Africa, and Central Europe and would help chart the course of U.S. policy in the area. As these high-level meetings went on in the first two weeks of August, we attempted to organize Company D in Siena and to set the machinery in motion to make it function.

As soon as communications facilities were set up, I moved Captain Clemente and Uberti to Siena to service field traffic, while SO and Captain Andre Bourgoin also moved up and requisitioned a villa on the other side of town. The villa had a colorful name, "Serraglio," which in English translates to "Harem."

Not long afterward, Suhling's new executive officer arrived and the headquarters started to acquire the look of a military outfit. The executive officer was Captain William Hollohan, a Securities and Exchange Commission lawyer who came from Seventh Cavalry, a National Guard unit in New York. A middle-aged bachelor, Bill Hollohan was a tall, muscular man with hair cropped in a short military style and a sharp Indian-like profile. He was not a talkative man and seemed to prefer to listen in order to learn the business. He seldom spoke about himself.

In late afternoons Suhling and some of the other officers would customarily sit under the huge flowering magnolia tree in the garden at the rear of the villa, to have a drink or two, discuss the events of the day, and make small talk. The magnolia tree was near the flower bed where the German sergeant had been buried when I first arrived at the villa. Both the sergeant's body and the Knight's Cross grave marker with his name, rank, and serial number were now gone, having been removed to a more permanent resting place among his equally unfortunate comrades who had fallen in the German retreat from Siena.

Several days after my arrival, a message arrived from Glavin that a group headed by Marine General Miller, who was head of all SO operations, wanted to visit the front-line units. Included in the group were Tom Early, Joe Rodrigo, General Miller, and various staff officers. Bill Suhling joined the party, and we headed for the front, which at the time was north of Poggibonsi at the village of San Casciano.

Before going to the front lines, we found our way to General Fryberg's CP, which was located in an olive grove at the center of a New Zealand armored squadron. The day was stifling hot, and the tank men sat nonchalantly atop their tanks wearing felt hats to protect their heads from the hot sun. Nearby the men had dug slit trenches to jump into in case of enemy air raid. After driving around for a while, we finally came upon a large trailer which served as General Fryberg's command post. Close by was a rather large slit trench which had been lined with fresh straw. This was for the general's use in the event "Jerry" should decide to lob over a few shells or drop a couple of bombs. With Fryberg's aide leading the way, we finally gained admission to the trailer.

Fryberg was a broad-shouldered, heavy-set man with a very gentle voice. He took us to the situation map which showed the location of the enemy units and his own New Zealand troops. When General Miller had finished asking him questions, he thanked him, and we gradually made our way to the crown of a high crest which dominated a valley in which a series of skirmishes were taking place. We crawled to the edge of the crest on which was perched a picturesque Tuscan cemetery. From our vantage point we could see small infantry units skirmishing along the Via Cassia. We could hear the crackle of rifle fire and the sound of artillery. The patrols looked inconsequential against the massive backdrop of hills and deep valleys.

The air was suddenly shattered by the shrill sound of American fighter planes diving to strafe and bomb enemy positions, and the sky was filled with black puffs from German flak units. The planes completed their strafing runs and hurriedly maneuvered out of the line of fire. Now came the shattering noise of incoming artillery shells. We hit the dirt and hugged the landscape as shells landed at the edge of the cemetery, unceremoniously disinterring the occupants of several graves. Within ten minutes the artillery fire had subsided, and we found our way back to our jeeps to visit other sectors of the front.

Our convoy continued its eastward trek across the lower Apennines most of the day, stopping now and then along the battle line's forward positions until we hit the Adriatic coast at Ancona. This trip gave most of the officers a feel for the problems confronted by the Fifteenth Army Group, as it slugged its way north from one crest to another. While it was still summer, AFHQ and AAI were hoping to drive into the Po Valley and, with a little bit of luck, bring an end to the Italian campaign.

This sanguine outlook was not universally shared by some of us who knew the defensibility of the terrain and the wiliness of Kesselring and some of his general officers in improvising the defense of the mountainous terrain. What is more, the Allied forces in Italy were losing seven divisions which had been pulled out of the line in order to prepare for "Anvil," the invasion of southern France. These forces were undergoing reorganization and retraining for the amphibious landings on the French Riviera.

The next day we returned to Siena where we held long discussions on the continuation of the Italian campaign; the need to bolster the guerrilla movement and unify its command structure under the Committee of National Liberation; and the coordination of its paramilitary operations with AAI and AFHQ. I undertook to study the situation and to come up with a plan that would coordinate the operations of the "irregular forces" with AAI and would set up a communications channel with AFHQ.

Italian SI had already received a number of requests from Ferruccio Parri to send a liaison mission to the Mottarone area. This area was quite near Milan and was loosely controlled by Enzo Boeri's brother, who was a leader of a guerrilla band. At the same time, it became necessary to examine the duplication of effort that was taking place through the lack of coordination with the Swiss OSS effort. Because of Switzerland's geographic location, its declared neutrality, and its long-term lack of physical contact with the outside world, the OSS mission in Switzerland had been given discretionary operational autonomy.

Because Allen Dulles had the full confidence of Donovan and most of the key people in Washington, he was given free reign in the development of his three-pronged operations in France, Italy and Germany. However, once the "Anvil" and "Overlord" forces took over the Franco-Swiss border, his isolation would end and the independence which the Swiss desk had enjoyed would be subject to greater military and political control by SHAEF and AFHQ. Late in 1943, the Italian underground movement in Milan had established some contacts with both Dulles and SOE in Berne, but with the arrival of OSS missions from the south and their direct links with our base in liberated Italy, the Swiss desk at Lugano and Berne played a diminished role in influencing events in the underground. When our missions were forced to flee and seek refuge because the Germans or Fascist counterespionage people were on their trail, they found it prudent to seek asylum in Switzerland, where, by agreement with the local Swiss Service de Renseignments (SR), which was commanded by Captain Bustelli, they were put in contact with Donald Jones. Jones was officially posted as vice consul in Lugano, but was really Dulles' man for Italian affairs. The intelligence which these missions from OSS/Italy provided for Dulles was given OSS/Switzerland designations and was transmitted to Washington. This system caused a duplication which was confusing and led to the blurring of command channels, not to mention financial muddles.

Recognizing what was happening, in late spring 1944, Washington sent B. Homer Hall to set up a Swiss desk at AFHQ in order to unravel the lines of communication and to act as liaison between the OSS branches. At this time, Scamporino was still in Washington and while Italian SI in the field worked with Hall to recommend working arrangements with Dulles, Scamp and Earl Brennan participated in meetings to draft a working plan for the correlation of Swiss-Italian operations.

On August 3 a cable went out from Reginald C. Foster in Washington to Homer Hall in Algiers outlining the proposed working agreement.[2] The cable was followed by a memo and a letter providing complete details of the plan. The agreement was worked out in consultation with the SO Branch and was to be implemented by Italian SI in the field. The letter which accompanied the memo explained that the suggested S.I. plan was accepted in principle . . . and it seemed to me the ideal solution to the financial difficulties to have 110 (Dulles) after consultation with S.I. Italy, meet the financial needs of the various groups.

The author continued

I cannot tell you what satisfaction it is to all of us for you to take hold of the confused Swiss-Italian picture and make this valiant attempt to make order out of chaos. We all of us feel—and 'we' includes 109, with whom we have gone over this entire plan—that this Swiss-Italian relationship is the priority of the moment, and that other things should be considered until the Italian campaign is successfully concluded.

Briefly, the plan worked out by Washington suggested that Italian SI agent Cassini (Team "Guava") be set up as the representative of SI under the supervision of Allen Dulles but under the operating orders of Italian SI.
In this position Cassini would:

A. Receive instructions from SI Italy as to the location of W/T teams required by military needs;
B. This is necessary as no teams from Italy can be dispatched without approval of AAI;
C. Cassini will provide pinpoints and reception committees in the designated areas;
D. W/T operators will be provided by SI Italy;
E. 110 in consultation with SI Italy will arrange through Cassini to provide financing for these groups.
3 (a) It is recommended that Cassini establish a clandestine radio station on the Swiss/Italian frontier (Swiss side); (b) Equipment and W/T personnel to be dropped by S.I. Italy; (c) That this station to maintain a daily contact with OSS Italy; (d) That communications make available a radio station to SI Italy for the exclusive handling of radio traffic; (e) that Italian S.I. make the facilities available to S.O. and
4 (a) The work and needs of the CLN should be checked carefully by 110 and SI Italy and the amount of assistance, financial and operational, to be rendered would be decided jointly, based upon the reliability of the information on hand.

While Homer Hall had made many of the suggestions that were the fruit of his inquiry in Italy, the recommendations were tilted toward giving Allen Dulles or his representative (in this case Donald Jones) undue control. It was equally obvious that with the appointment of Captain Suhling as CO of Company D, and SI's agreement to take over the intelligence functions of the company, an era of operational coordination was being initiated in Siena.

As soon as communications permitted and we were working in Siena, I suggested that we undertake a number of projects. The first of these projects was the issuance of a daily intelligence bulletin which contained the pertinent intelligence data transmitted by our tactical and strategic missions behind enemy lines. By this time, Italian SI itself had enough active radio circuits going to publish a three- or four-page daily bulletin of military, political, and industrial intelligence. In addition, intelligence from the daily CLN Bulletin, for which we were the exclusive distributors, was included in the bulletin. The sources of information in the bulletin were identified through the assignment of code names, but we did not attempt to evaluate the information. The credibility of the sources was established by AFHQ, AAI, the Air Force, the Fifth Army, and the other services which received the bulletin daily. Gradually, the information from other OSS branches was added to the bulletin, as a result of which the task became so time consuming that it was turned over to Lieutenant Barnes of the Reports Board and became the Company D Bulletin.

During early August, the front line was less than an hour north of Siena, and the New Zealand troops were on the south bank of the Arno River. With the fall of Florence imminent, it was decided to organize an Allied intelligence task force to quickly go into the city and hit the designated intelligence targets before the documents were destroyed by the Abwehr or the SD. Florence was the first major Italian city in which the guerrilla forces were actively coordinating their military activities with the Allied forces. Because it was a primary intelligence target, I made arrangements with Colonel George S. Smith of AAI to join the Intelligence Collection Unit (ICU) Task Force. Colonel Smith, whom I had originally met in Washington, was a friend of Colonel Rodrigo. He hastily scribbled a note addressed to the Thirteenth Corps TCP (British) which was in command of the sector at that time. The note said:

The following personnel are proceeding to Hq ICU Florence on a necessary intelligence mission. Permission should be granted for this travel.

Mr. Morris Berg   (s) George S. Smith
Capt. B. M. Corvo   Col., G.S.C.
Lt. Aldo Icardi
Lt. Bruno Bisceglia

The New Zealand forces which had fought their way up from Poggibonsi to San Casciano and to the southern approaches to Florence, not wishing to inflict any damage on the cultural and historical center, had waited for the Germans to withdraw. A good deal of the fighting in the city had been done by the Garibaldi Brigade and other guerrilla formations. The Germans had blown every bridge across the Arno River except the historic Ponte Vecchio. The engineers had managed to put up a Bailey bridge despite the intermittent fire from the German 88s which were located in the heights at Fiesole.

We got across the Arno River, which the summer drought had reduced to a mere trickle and headed for the Excelsior Hotel which had become a sort of headquarters for the ICU Task Force. As we went down the streets, there was the crackle of sporadic rifle fire between partisan forces and Fascist sharpshooters who had purposely been left behind by the Germans to delay the advance of the Thirteenth Corps. Amidst the occasional hail of bullets and much shouting, we finally arrived at the Excelsior. Despite all the havoc, this famous hotel still served afternoon tea and kept its string quartet playing in its main salon, the music often punctuated by the staccato sounds of warfare, or a shell screaming its way toward the New Zealand troops across the river.

When I thought of it later, I realized that the entering ICU intelligence force had been a sitting duck for a German raid. We were all in one basket, protected by an occasional New Zealand or partisan patrol and by our sidearms. We immediately went to work. Icardi went in search of the Galileo Laboratories to pick up information for Moe Berg, while Lieutenant Bruno Bisceglia, who had recently arrived from Washington, came with me to the American Girls School.

While we were driving up the road, the German 88s, following the cloud of dust raised by our speeding jeep, opened up on us. We abruptly stopped and dove into a culvert as the shells were falling uncomfortably close. Within a few minutes, the German observer must have found more interesting targets. Bruno and I beat a hasty retreat from our exposed position back into the streets where the partisans and Fascists were busy shooting it out and moving their wounded in two-wheeled handcarts. The partisans were easily identifiable by the red kerchiefs they wore around their necks.

Florence was a city without water and food, and most of its inhabitants were trapped indoors. Long lines of men and women with wicker baskets stood at a little dam which crossed the Arno and like a column of ants walked across to the south shore to pick up whatever meager food supplies were available. Occasionally, as the men and women carefully threaded their way across the dam, German shells abruptly brought their progress to a halt. The Army had set up water purification stations at various points throughout the city. There, lines of women bearing all sorts of receptacles stood patiently to gather the precious liquid and take it home.

The incongruity of moving from the tumult outside into the salon of the Hotel Excelsior where the string quartet was playing Boccherini and Bach struck us all immediately and profoundly. With the whining of the shells overhead, the sounds of the string instruments sometimes created a tremolo where none was called for in the score.

After three days in Florence, we had completed our mission with several guerrilla leaders and the Galileo Laboratories. On our way back to Siena we began sifting through the intelligence material we had collected. I had hardly settled myself to look over the material when a phone call from AAI informed me that a foreign correspondent was waiting to speak to me. I immediately drove down to the G-2 tent, and to my surprise the correspondent turned out to be a good-looking woman with a note from our Rome office. Helen Hyatt represented an American news syndicate and had been covering Gibraltar since the early war years. The Rome office had told her that she could get in touch with me through the Company D Office. Over breakfast at the officers' mess the next morning, she told me that she wanted to write a series on the partisan warfare in Italy, and within security limitations about the work our organization was doing.

The presence of a pretty American female reporter caused a flurry of tie straightening and hair combing among the officers. After breakfast I drove her to Florence, where fighting was still going on in the outskirts of the city. Her close look at the damage which the city had suffered and the conditions under which the civilian population had been living provided her with a lot of material for her articles. I also gave her some background on the partisan warfare being waged in the Domodossola area. With this information she went back to Rome to do her writing.

Coming back to Siena, I went to work to complete the briefing on several tactical missions to be infiltrated through the lines. When I had finished Lieutenant Icardi took the missions back to the front to infiltrate them through enemy lines. The young men who had volunteered for this task came from the Romagna area and were part of the "Pricklypear" team. Craveri had recruited them as members of the ORI group. Sadly, both Tonino Chiarone and Giuseppe Alietti, who were infiltrated on August 15, were never heard from again after they crossed into German-held territory. When they failed to report, we searched the area for them but to no avail. They were presumed to have been captured and executed by the Germans who at this point were observing none of the niceties of war. As we knew well, the Sicherheits Dients (SD)—SS counter-intelligence—was thoroughly ruthless in its handling of refugees suspected of spying.

During this period, General Donovan was visiting the Italian theater and participated at numerous meetings. One reason why he was visiting was the impending invasion of France, but as usual, ever since the Sicilian campaign, whenever he came to Italy he would seek me out or would send for me.

It was during this visit that I suggested that we undertake a project that would immediately start the collection of intelligence material on Japan. This intelligence material was available in the form of studies and reports of the SIM files in Rome and in the offices of various companies that had done business in the Far East. I suggested that in view of the intransigent positions which Russia was assuming, we should include information about Russia that might become available from various sources.

Both Rodrigo and Donovan enthusiastically supported my proposal on Japanese intelligence with Donovan asking that it be costed out with a proposed budget. Rodrigo and I both agreed, however, that no additional funds were necessary and that the work would be done as part of the intelligence functions of Italian SI. We included the objectives as part of our functions, and Donovan gave the project the green light. As part of the discussion on the Japanese intelligence project, I briefed Donovan on the solid relationship that had been established with both SIM and its chief, Colonel Pompeo Agrifoglio. Lieutenant Colonel Ricca, our senior SI officer in Rome, also took the time to outline how helpful Agrifoglio had been since the early days when Marshal Badoglio set up his government in Brindisi.

To express his personal appreciation to the head of the Italian intelligence service, Donovan wrote a personal letter to Agrifoglio and entrusted its delivery to me. The letter was dated in Rome, August 11, 1944.

Dear Col. Agrifoglio:
   From both Max Corvo and John Ricca I have heard of the help you have given to our organization during the past ten months.
   I wish to express my gratitude and appreciation—I hope that within a short time opportunity will present itself for me to express my thanks to you personally.

                                             Sincerely yours,
                                             William J. Donovan [5]

I then briefed Donovan on the developments in Italian operations and Suhling's capable handling of the administrative details of Company D. I outlined the duplication of effort and confusion which existed with Switzerland, as well as my proposal to send a liaison mission to northern Italy to work in close contact with CLNAI and to counterbalance the secret mission of General Cadorna. Donovan approved the plan. As he planned to visit Siena before embarking on "Anvil," he suggested that we continue our discussion of Italian operations in Siena.

Briefly, among the many missions I had planned for the field, I had worked out the "Mangosteen" mission which would act as our official liaison with the command of the patriot forces in northern Italy. I had discussed this matter in depth with Bill Suhling who was in agreement. The original mission had been planned as a three-man SI operation with a mission leader, a W/T, and an assistant mission leader. [6] The SI officer was to be Lieutenant Icardi and the selection of the field officer who was to lead the mission was postponed. Plans called for dropping an Italian civilian who would act as a guide and later join Enzo Boeri, becoming Deputy CLNAI intelligence chief. This person was Tullio Lussi (codenamed "Landi") who had served as a reserve officer in the Italian Army and whose extremely tranquil nature made him one of the coolest agents in enemy territory. Landi was a close friend of Boeri; both had been recruited into ORI by Craveri.

While the "Mangosteen" mission was in the planning stage, an OG mission codenamed "Chrysler" was scheduled to jump into the same area to one of our reception committees. It had flown several times without success. The mission leader was Lieutenant Victor Giannino, assisted by two GIs, Sergeant Carl LoDolce, W/T, and Sergeant Ciarmicola. After consulting with Suhling, the scope of the "Mangosteen" mission was expanded to include personnel of the OG "Chrysler" mission so that all phases of OSS operations would be represented by the mission. Upon Donovan's arrival in Siena, we took up the matter of the "Mangosteen-Chrysler" mission and the selection of a field grade officer to command the liaison group. Sitting beneath the huge flowering magnolia in the garden at the back of the villa, we discussed the candidates for the job. Suhling finally suggested his executive officer, Captain Bill Hollohan. I interposed that Hollohan, who was still a captain, did not speak a word of Italian and knew neither the terrain nor the situation. Suhling countered with the fact that once in the field, the mission might come under political pressure, and that Hollohan could be counted on not to play any political games. As to Hollohan's promotion to field grade, this did not pose a problem as he could leave with major's leaves while his promotion to major was being processed. Donovan supported Suhling's thesis, and Hollohan was chosen to lead the mission, subject to his acceptance. Soon after the meeting, the general left to join the task force which was headed for the invasion of southern France. Hollohan and the other members of the mission were assembled for parachute training at Brindisi under Mim Daddario's direction. Toward the end of August, during one of my visits to the station, I briefed Hollohan, Icardi, and the rest of the personnel.

Another problem Donovan discussed with Glavin and Tom Early was the question of air lift for partisan resupply. During the month of August, the RAF's 334 Wing, which had been flying supplies out of Brindisi for SOE and OSS was practically destroyed over Warsaw. With fall coming and no prospect in sight that the weakened Allied forces in Italy could break through the Gothic Line (a line of formidable fortifications constructed by the Germans in the Apennines from the Adriatic to the Tyrrhenian), it became essential to replace the British loss of planes and pilots who had been shot down over Poland. The problem was assigned to Colonel Early, Glavin's executive officer. Early had excellent connections with the Air Force; moreover, his genuine affability could favorably influence decisions. On August 25, Early encapsulated the situation in the following memo to General Donovan:

1. As a supplement to the memorandum describing the restricted air lift to northern Italy, it is pointed out by the Chief of Operations Supply that the allotment of 142 tons to OSS for the resistance groups in northern Italy is based solely upon the British being able not only to provide the various supplies and containers, but also to pack them.

2. Major Lawrence points out that the procuring of one or two more squadrons of airplanes to carry supplies to northern Italy does not exactly solve the problem, since the British have already informed us that American operations in northern Italy were not included in their estimates of supply

requirements and that they have been able to meet the American requirements only at the expense of their October reserves.

3. The British have further stated that they could continue to meet American requirements only if definitely assured of replacement in the near future from American supplies. Since American supplies for Italy were included in the recent revision of the catalog only on the basis of 40 sorties or 200 tons per month, and since these supplies are not as yet available in the Theater in even that monthly quantity, the difficulty in meeting an additional air lift from purely American resources is apparent.

4. Since it is evident that further aid to the resistance groups in southern France will come to an end within the next few days, it should be pointed out that the supplies now on hand there will run around 800 to 1,000 tons, about one-half of which is food, and could be transshiped to Italy for packing and supplying to the Italian resistance groups. If this is to be done, however, it will necessitate our procuring the use of at least one ship large enough to transport 1,000 tons of supplies plus some 15,000 chutes, packing equipment, and 1,000 containers. Therefore, it is recommended that you procure the use of one LST boat to perform this job.

5. In order to assist OSS-MED to increase its air lift to the required tonnage the following firm commitment must be procured from the British; namely, that they supply 50 tons packed and ready for delivery for the month of August; 175 tons packed and ready for shipment for the month of September; and 100 tons ready for delivery for the first fifteen days of October. A further commitment should also be obtained from the British to continue to do all necessary packing for OSS until the first of the year.

6. In return for these commitments from the British, OSS will make a firm commitment to SOE to replace the previously stated tonnage at the rate of 50 tons a month beginning October 1. Furthermore, as soon as French operations cease, OSS will contribute 30 American personnel now in packing station in Algiers to a joint forward packing setup to be established at Piombino to carry as much of the British and American load as may be feasible.

7. If the British do not desire to continue packing for OSS, then it will be necessary to move from London 125 packing personnel to carry on packing in Italy.

> Thomas G. Early
> Lt. Colonel, AC
> Acting Operations and
> Training Officer[7]

As a result of the efforts of OSS headquarters and Donovan's insistence, U.S. Air Force planes were made available to carry on the job of resupply. This was hastened by the rapid advance of Patch's Seventh Army in southern France which freed up supplies no longer needed by the French Maquis and made them available to the Italian theater.

In early August 1944, OSS headquarters made another effort to close down Palermo's SI station. The reaction of the station's intelligence clients was swift. Alfred Nester, U.S. consul general in Palermo, immediately sent a letter to Donovan through Scamp (who had recently returned to Rome), contending that the SI station should be kept open.

The letter stated in part:

I have heard that there is a possibility that OSS will be withdrawn from Sicily, which I hope will not be the case. During the past months your Palermo office and the consulate have been working in closest cooperation, and I am deeply appreciative of the cordial assistance which OSS has given us. The effective team which you have working on the island had been the source of much important information which could not have been furnished to the Consulate or to our government by any other means, and should this service be terminated, the loss would be keenly felt.

At the same time, the ONI officer at Palermo Naval Base, Lieutenant Commander B. F. Murphy, Jr. sent a letter to Joe Russo, OSS station CO, stating:

during one year of difficult and complex conditions prevailing in a recently occupied country, you have provided much intelligence in the political, economic and security fields . . . .this information has frequently been the basis of specific security measures taken in conjunction with the operation of this base.

Consul General Nester, going one step further, wrote to the Secretary of State in Washington urging that the OSS be asked to reverse its decision.[8] He stated that:

OSS has had excellent coverage of Sicily, and the reports of their agents have furnished material which it would have been impossible for the consulate to obtain otherwise. Politics in this area are in a state of turmoil, due primarily to the separatist movement and the communist party and many people anticipate disorder of a serious nature. Due to the strategic position of Sicily, it is assumed that the department desires to be kept informed of developments, and if OSS is withdrawn, this cannot be done as efficiently as it should be.

The British government maintains active units of the field security system in Sicily which, it should be stated, also cooperate with the consulate, but I feel that it is essential for us to keep our own intelligence service here, not only to assist the consulate in gathering political and economic information, but also, such an organization would be most helpful in protecting American lives and property, should the need arise.

CC: Hon. Alexander Kirk
    Hon. Robert Murphy

This last effort to close out the Palermo SI station did not succeed because of protests from the State Department, ONI, and CIC. These agencies argued persuasively that the SI reports being produced by the station were important to the formulation of policy and dealt with highly credible information and sources.

There were few activities on the island which escaped our narrow scrutiny and few political leaders who were able to avert the influence of the Palermo station which had helped the democratic forces to reorganize themselves immediately after the invasion. Some of these individuals played leading roles on the national political stage, and we had been in contact with them even before the landing at Gela.

The director's office in Washington, which had been following the situation at Palermo, decided to keep the station open until the end of the war, when Italian SI was phased out of the theater.

With the forward movement of Company D to Siena and with Scamp's absence in the States, I had been constantly on the move from one station to another in order to coordinate the work of the section and to keep Company D abreast of events. The communications situation had not improved. In addition, contacts with Brindisi, which was still the most important OSS operational base in Italy, were still impossible. Finally, in late August, it was decided to set up radio contact between Brindisi and Siena, but instead of establishing the message center at SI headquarters, they chose 13 Via Roma, which was the air operations office to which Jiminez had been recently assigned.

On August 18, Daddario wrote to me bringing me up to date on what was happening in Brindisi. The letter indicated the daily trials of our operations and training center: constantly working with a skeleton staff, plagued by the lack of equipment, and still the object of intraorganizational bickering.

Dear Max:

I am sending along to you several ATF Forms with notations for your files and so that you can contact the field accordingly. I understand that the field has been switched around so that all the messages are going to come up front through you. That will help tremendously as you will then be able to keep in daily contact with me through the base station which is being opened here Monday under Jiminez. It is sort of a paradox that we should now be faced with a radio here when we had one and were told it was not necessary. Even more humourous is the fact that Garcia is running the show for #13. At any rate we shall keep them busy and you shall hear from me often via that means. (Garcia was one of our original operators.)

Last night Strawberry went off again and was forced to return. It was probably one of the most trying nights we have had here. After bringing the men to the plane and seeing them on board I drove around to the take-off end of the strip to see them off. Finally the plane came down and any damn fool could see that they weren't going fast enough to take off. The plane then suddenly swung over to the left with a tremendous roar, failing to tip over simply through a miracle. In talking to the pilot afterwards it seemed that a couple of the crew thought they saw a DC-3 towing a glider right in front of them, making his action necessary. The real story behind it, however, seems to be the lacing that they have taken here the last several nights. That fact was apparent immediately before take-off when their attitude was decidedly poor in comparison with the spirit of a month or so back. However that may be. . . .the mission was called off and I returned with the men to Hq. Immediately thereupon a telephone call was received and back to the airport we went. The boys then took off at about 22:30. . . .returning four hours later. They are on again tonight.

If you could have seen the reaction of the three boys you would certainly have been most proud. They were not at all fased by the first experience. . . .whereas all others aboard were. . . .and were more anxious than ever to take off in the same night at even that late hour.

I just wired you re Salem. Vic got over target and ready to jump when the signal pattern below was extinguished. It seems that a red flare was fired some two kilometers away and that it was a signal for the reception to douse the lights. The lights were put out and though the aircraft buzzed the field several times nothing else was seen. I am sure that the red flare was fired by one of Salem's look-outs. However, it would be wise if you would wire the field for the whole story so that we can be properly guided here before the operation is to leave for another attempt. Another pinpoint would probably be advisable. . . .as this one had been used several times already. That is, however, up to the field to decide upon your recommendation.

The parachute school has been arranged for six men on each of the following two weeks. I have had all the men examined and have drawn pen sketches for the British. That will be done in accordance with the discussion we had on that subject when you were last here. This will mean that you should have twelve men ready for work within two weeks. . . .plus those men that have already been through. That will give you six to seven teams for the field.

As the reports will indicate, Lt. Houston has been informed of the three teams for the Trieste area. . . .and we should have the radio equipment by the time the approval for the missions is received.

Still have those two sets for your front line activities. Let me know when you want them.

Vestri seems to be coming around lately. He has been on the ball. . . .and is being depended upon by the other members of his team. I think we should let him go along as he could do a good job. Please wire me confirmation of that as I will hold up that operation until I hear from you.

Mike just called and said something about the station being over here instead of at his place. That seems quite logical and seems to have been put over by a master craftsman. I wonder who intervened?????

That about does it, Max. Best to you Clem, Frank, et al.

With direct radio communications finally established, it was now possible to give more coherent direction to operations and feed Daddario timely information about the operational results and field activities. In the interim, the organization of Company D made it possible to delineate the responsibilities of the various units. The tactical intelligence responsibilities were turned over to the two units that were attached to the operating armies. These units often called on SI, SO, and OG for support in more complex operations. The Fifth Army unit was commanded by Captain James Abrignani who spent a good deal of time mastering the problems of line infiltration and working with partisan units near the front and became quite good at the work. The Eighth Army unit was commanded by Captain Alphonse Thiele who had helped Croze run line operations at the Anzio beachhead and was attached to the headquarters of the British Army whose intelligence people seemed to prefer his work to that of the SOE counterpart.

At this time there was also a tactical maritime unit in the Adriatic. This unit operated with the help of the Italian Marines of the San Marco Battalion and used the services of the Italian Navy MAS boats and other naval craft. The unit was commanded by Navy Lieutenant Richard Kelly.

The other branches of OSS such as X-2, MO, and R & A were represented at headquarters. The editing of the *Daily Bulletin*, which had started out as an SI initiative, was continued by Lieutenant Barnes of the Reports Board.[10]

During one of my visits to Agrifoglio's office during August, we discussed the probability that the war would continue until 1945. The guerrilla movement under the spur of CLNAI had grown by leaps and bounds during the summer. The cruelty and repression of Mussolini's Black Brigades and the German SS had provided the impetus for this growth. The fine summer weather added to attract many young city people to join the bands operating in the Alpine fringes of northwestern Italy, all the way from the Riviera to the Swiss border.

With the approach of the fall season and with losses suffered by the 334 Wing, we knew how tough it would be to get food and arms to the patriot forces in the mountains and the Po Valley. Frequently during the late fall and winter, the entire area is blanketed by a shroud of impenetrable fog for days at a time. At my request, Agrifoglio sent one of the officers to get several maps of the Franco-Italian frontier. He called in Captain Pico, an outstanding Alpinist and ski expert for a conference.

"Anvil" was already making phenomenal progress up the Rhone Valley, and in all likelihood the entire Alpine fringe would soon be cleared of enemy troops. Since General Patch's priority was to link up with the "Overlord" forces, there was no chance that the Fifteenth Army would receive any help from General Devers' Sixth Army Group. Thus, Piedmont, Liguria, and Lombardy would become a military pocket where the patriot forces could expect little help and comfort, and it was probable that they would be forced to scatter and disband.

Agrifoglio asked Captain Pico whether he thought it was feasible for teams of Alpinists to cross over in the winter months from France into Italy, bearing packs of supplies and arms. Pico replied that it was a feasible undertaking, and he estimated that the maximum load which an experienced mountain climber could safely carry was about 20 kilos. Captain Pico was in his late twenties or early thirties and had won a number of skiing and mountaineering competitions. If the project which we were discussing was approved, he would become one of the first members of the staff.

We concurred that a number of depots could be created along the frontier. These were to be located where Italian guerrillas familiar with the terrain could cross over into France, pick up supplies, and then return to their unit. In this manner, a minimum subsistence amount of food, medicines, and ammunition could be delivered to the Garibaldi and the Giustizia e Liberta formations (Justice and Liberty—partisans representing Action party) that were fighting the Germans and Fascists. I asked the colonel to have his staff prepare a list of equipment and clothing that would be indispensable for Alpine operations and to notify me when the basic plan and list were ready.

In order to secure the necessary approval, I went immediately to Caserta to discuss the proposal with Joe Rodrigo and Tom Early. They quickly approved the concept and suggested that details be worked out with Suhling and that all branches should participate in the project.[11] They also approved the participation of SIM, which was to supply us with a number of officers and special mountaineering equipment.

On August 6, tragedy struck Captain Bruno Rossoni, courageous leader of the "Pear" mission in the Padua-Venice area. Rossoni, during the six months that had passed since his landing from a submarine, had earned the reputation as one of our best secret agents in German-occupied Italy. His reports on military rail traffic, bombing damage, and enemy high-echelon military plans were prized at AFHQ and AAI. His information on counterespionage agents and organizations provided long lists for CIC, X-2, and other Allied counterintelligence organizations. He became one of the leaders of the Venice CLN. Through him, the patriot forces in the Monte Grappa area received their first supply drops and expanded in strength so that they could later provide safe reception committees for other OSS and Allied missions.

During the latter part of April when he became suspect by the enemy, Rossoni made several efforts to evacuate his radio operator and his family by sea, but enemy surveillance of the coast made it impossible. After repeated attempts, we had to give up the effort. Disregarding his own safety, Rossoni sent his family and radio operator away, and despite great personal danger, he continued to operate. Finally, on August 6 he was arrested by the Fascist police and turned over to the Germans.[12] Bruno Rossoni was executed by the SS on December 29, 1944 at Methausen. While at Methausen, he met another OSS/SI agent, Corporal Louis Biagioni, whom he recognized, having seen him at our Brindisi headquarters that January.

Captain Rossoni, a man motivated by the highest ideals, was remembered as a pleasant individual, a good conversationalist, and a superb bridge player. He had a remarkable devotion and dedication to the work he had undertaken. He died heroically, never betraying the trust of his colleagues. Posthumously, he was awarded Italy's highest decoration, the Gold Medal.

In conjunction with the "Mangosteen" mission, while Captain Hollohan was training in Brindisi, both he and Daddario were asked to attend a staff meeting at Bari to participate in the discussion of the Rankin Plan. This was a British plan which foresaw a vacuum in northern Italy in the event of a sudden collapse of German resistance or withdrawal. The plan proposed that Allied officers be "on the ready" to take over the administration of the towns and cities of the north so that a period of anarchy could be averted. It also sought to preempt a possible takeover by the Italian Communist brigades.

When Hollohan and Daddario returned from the meeting, after lengthy discussion, we came to the conclusion that "Rankin" had been conceived to give British policymakers an advantage to further Foreign

Office policies in support of right-wing and monarchist forces. In any event, the OSS did not have enough trained officers to participate on a co-equal basis with British intelligence.

SI and Company D were already committed to participate in the ICU City Team program which I felt had greater significance from an intelligence point of view. While we could and should collaborate in the execution of the Rankin Plan, to safeguard Italian patrimony, we did not foresee any Communist takeover of northern Italy, as we did not foresee any imminent collapse of German resistance on the Gothic Line.

I sent Suhling a memo on the matter, advising him of our participation in the meeting:

The matter of the Rankin Plan has been discussed with Major Hollohan and it would seem better to have the mission adhere to its original plan—strict military liaison.

4. I have discussed with Col. Rodrigo the matter of sending a group to the Franco-Italian frontier in order to establish direct contact with the SI teams at present operating in the area. The Colonel has expressed his approval and has asked me to get your opinion of the matter. Such a group would be led by Major Tozzi and would include a radio operator and one or two enlisted men. Their principal duties once in the area would be to direct activities and to be on the spot when the "Rankin Plan" is activated. It is planned that the mission which will be known as "Papaya" will also arrange courier service to bring tactical material across the 5th Army lines. Your immediate concurrence on this matter is asked and the departure of the mission from Siena to Brindisi should take place as soon as possible. Arrangements for transport will be made at Caserta.

5. Rankin Plan. Major Hollohan and Lt. Daddario attended the meeting at your request. After the meeting the three of us had ample opportunity to discuss the plan as well as what took place at the meeting. I had been aware for some time that S.O.E. had presented such a plan to the Allied Control Commission and the Allied Military Government in Rome, but assumed that you had been informed of the matter. Briefly, this is the way we see it: It is the British plan that the areas of northern Italy should come under immediate Allied control as soon as the Germans evacuate them. Since O.S.S. does not have an overabundance of officers in the field (behind enemy lines), it would be extremely advantageous (to the British) to have British officers take over major cities in northern Italy long before Allied troops reach them. As we are at the present time preparing to put our efforts in the ICU matter, it will be difficult to find officers to fill in these new spots. If there is any intelligence matter to be had in these respective cities, it will be gone by the time the ICU is activated. It is therefore our thought that some officers scheduled at present for ICU should be diverted for the use in "Rankin." It might be well worthwhile to have some officers join the "Papaya" group which will be operated at the Franco-Italian border so that they may sweep down to take over the various cities assigned to them. It is also considered possible that arrangements with the 15th Air Force or with TAC could be made to fly various groups to the specific zones assigned, providing airports in the area can be made available by the patriots. It has come to our knowledge that the British are training special groups of officers and men who may be intended to do this work.

Since our connections (contacts) with the patriots are at this time to be considered extremely good, I advise that a directive to the various OSS mission leaders should be issued. This directive would cover the basic points: a) Intelligence will continue to be transmitted til further notice from Hq. Co. D; b) All radio operators are to hold themselves at the disposal of occupation officers; c) All mission leaders will report to the nearest Allied officer, but are not to turn over any organizational or operational records until the arrival of competent organization officers . . . .

If I may suggest here, I understand that a number of OG officers are available at this time. These may well be held in readiness for the work to be undertaken in connection with the plan. From an intelligence point of view, participation in this operation is of utmost important.[13]

Chapter 15

A Winter of Great Discontent

Having spent its forward momentum with the capture of Florence, the Fifteenth Army Group, although substantially weaker because of the withdrawal of the divisions for the invasion of southern France, attempted throughout the fall of 1944 to break through the mountainous Apennine barrier into the Po Valley to bring a quick end to the Italian campaign. Not only did the stiff German resistance repulse every effort, but also the weather prevented the Eighth Army's breakthrough on the Adriatic coast where easily defensible rivers and canals, swollen by the autumn rains, brought the British advance to a halt. Obviously, any hope of successfully breaking the defenses of the Gothic Line had to be given up until spring, when a reinforced Fifteenth Army Group could storm through the Futa Pass and other Apennine routes, capture Bologna, and go on to Genova, Milan, and Turin, while pursuing Kesselring's forces in the Tyrol. This military stalemate placed an unusually heavy burden on the OSS, SOE, and the patriot forces operating behind the German lines.

Staff meetings at AAI indicated that General Alexander and his advisers were in favor of temporarily dismantling the guerrilla forces by issuing a proclamation for the volunteers to return temporarily to their homes. The rationale for this decision was based on the fact that it would be impossible to supply even the minimal needs of the irregular forces through air supply drops because of the shortage of aircraft and negative weather patterns prevailing during the winter months. Judged on both of these counts, the decision to tell the guerrilla forces to go home might have been correct, but Alexander's eventual proclamation did not take into account the impossibility of telling the men and women who had been proscribed to return home to certain persecution and jail. It also failed to take into account Donovan's persistence in securing a fleet of 30 U.S. planes and moving the packing station personnel into Italy to cope with growing demands for supplies from the CLNAI. Finally, Alexander's order also did not take into account the unusually favorable weather patterns that were to prevail in the winter and early spring of 1945.

Based on the most dour predictions we set to work shaping a program for OSS to follow in Italy. This program was based on stepping up the delivery of missions and supplies to northern Italy and an effort to better coordinate the command functions of the CLNAI over its irregular formations and to control their paramilitary activities in conjunction with orthodox military plans to be carried out by both Allied armies. During this period, SI provided drop zones and reception committees for a number of OG and SO missions and was itself busy preparing a number of missions to be dropped in all areas of northern Italy, including the tactical zones.

On September 4 Ennio Tassinari, leader of the "Apple" team who had been working in the Bologna area, came through the lines loaded down with information and details of the Gothic Line fortifications, which were immediately turned over to AAI and Fifth Army intelligence. Two days after he had returned, Tassinari was parachutèd back into the area as head of the "Medlar III" mission. This team was placed under Abrignani's tactical control and would operate in the area until December 27, 1944, when with his mission completed, Tassinari once again coolly walked through the German lines and reported back to SI headquarters, to head still another dangerous mission.

On September 9, the "Pineapple" mission headed by Louis Vestri, an Italian Air Force officer, was parachuted to a reception arranged by our "Orange" team in Piedmont. This mission worked very closely with Cino Moscatelli's First and Second Garibaldi Divisions in the Val Sesia and the Val d'Ossola. On the same night, the "Strawberry" team, made up of two Italian-speaking GIs and an Italian Army noncommissioned officer, operating in mutti, also successfully jumped to another "Orange" pinpoint in Piedmont. Both of these teams established radio communications with the base almost instantly and started transmitting important military intelligence. The "Pineapple" team obtained the supply drops for Moscatelli's formations, which were to play important roles in the guerrilla war against the German-Fascist forces in the Biella-Ossola area.

In preparation for the anticipated final phase of the Italian campaign, it was imperative that a high degree of coordination be achieved with the Swiss desk in Berne. An effort had already been initiated with the arrival of Homer Hall to set up the Swiss desk at Caserta. In mid-August, after having spent some time in Italy, Hall returned to the United States to report personally to Whitney Shepardson, chief of the SI Branch. He brought back such glowing reports on the work of Italian SI that Shepardson asked him to write a memo for the official record with a copy to Earl Brennan.

Homer's memorandum, dated August 14, 1944, and addressed to Brennan, stated:

After reporting to the Chief, SI Branch, Friday morning upon my return from Italy, my first act was to visit your office for the purpose of telling you personally that under your direction in Italy you have the finest damn group of men with whom it has ever been my good fortune to come in contact. This is not to be regarded in the light of an official report on the operations of your Italian units but, after expressing my purely personal opinion to Mr. Shepardson, he requested me to put it in writing 'for the record' and to send him a copy.

Prior to being assigned to the duty of setting up a Swiss Desk in Italy, I knew little or nothing concerning the activities of your section other than the Berne intelligence reports relayed to you. Furthermore, except for yourself and one or two others in the Washington office, I was not acquainted with a single individual connected with your outfit.

In the attempt to set up the Swiss Desk I discovered that its relationship to Italian operations overshadowed all its other activities. Headquarters, moving from Algiers to Italy, was paying little attention to the connection and in fact, had not been giving the hook-up between the two sections the cooperation deserved. I began working with Captain Jimmy Montante, the lad who keeps all ten fingers and both eyes and a keen brain on the pulse that makes Italian operations click like nobody's business. From there on I received courtesy and cooperation such as I have not been accustomed to in a long and checkered career.

I felt privileged to travel around various sections of Italy with such men as Captain Corvo (and his operations unit), Major Ricca, whose diplomacy in handling delicate matters connected with political factions rates him a place in the State Department; with Jiminez and his unit; Clemente, Bourgoin and a host of others too numerous to mention here. Your men put in twenty-four hours a day. From your highest ranking officers down to the lowliest G.I. Joe in their outfits your men, as a matter of routine, are performing hazardous acts, above and beyond the call of duty, that would rate them decorations in any man's army. As a whole, they are contributing more to the success of the campaign in Italy than many of the publicized divisions. The men in the field are constantly obtaining more information than the Brass Hats and G-2 are able to digest. You must be perfectly well aware of all this, as well as the fact that they keep a well ordered supply line to partisan units. There's no percentage in overdoing a word of enthusiastic praise.

If I am not sticking my neck out, permit me to ask why such deserving men as Pvt. Mike Contrastino (he should be a commissioned officer) left handling affairs back in Algiers, Major Ricca, Capt. Pasquale and others, have not been promoted? They're long overdue.

All in all, Mr. Brennan, were I in your shoes I'd be so damned proud I wouldn't speak to anybody else in OSS.

Events were reaching a climax, however. Donald Jones, who was running the Swiss-Italian operations for Allen Dulles in Lugano, Switzerland, was in contact with "Como," an agent who had been infiltrated by Captain Bourgoin and had taken refuge in Switzerland. "Como" plotted with a number of guerrilla leaders to take over the Ossola Valley, an area northwest of Lake Maggiore, contiguous with the Swiss border. Their plan to seize the area called for the seizure of the main Ossola Valley, together with minor valleys west of the lake and the setting up of a free enclave. Irregular forces operating in the area represented many political persuasions, ranging from tough Communist units to Monarchists and right-wing forces and democratic-inspired formations.

Jones, who used the code name "Scotti" in his meetings with partisan leaders, promised that there would be substantial Allied help from the military command in southern Italy. At no time, however, was the plan presented to Company D or to the OSS Caserta headquarters. If it had been, the advice would have been negative, because it is axiomatic that irregular forces should not attempt to hold terrain against orthodox forces. Furthermore, the area in question had no particular significance to impending AAI operations which were aimed ultimately in the opposite direction toward Austria and southern Germany. Part of the plan to take over the Ossola Valley envisaged the participation of thousands of interned Allied prisoners from Switzerland.

During July and August, the German-Fascist forces had mopped up the valley and driven the guerrillas to the mountains. At the end of the operation, the troops were pulled out and small garrisons were left to man the many villages dotting the area. Believing in the promises of Allied assistance, partisan leaders planned a series of surprise attacks against the light enemy garrisons.

At the beginning of August the Piave Division, by use of stealth tactics, isolated the garrison in the town of Orasso, which, seeing itself surrounded, retreated to the much better protected town of Cannobio on the west bank of Lake Maggiore. At the same time, four of the other major partisan units in the area, the Garibaldi Second Division, the Valdossola Division, the Beltrami Division, and the Valtoce, started taking up positions to carry out surprise attacks against the other German-Fascist garrisons in the area. Toward the end of August, a small group of internees crossed over from Switzerland.

Believing in "Scotti's" promise that thousands of prisoners would join them and the OSS would parachute arms and supplies, on September 2 the Piave Division attacked Cannobio. After vainly resisting a few hours, the German unit surrendered, whereupon the population of the town took to the streets, wildly celebrating their newfound freedom.[3] Other units of the Piave Division had captured the frontier station at Piaggio Valmara. Still others had liberated some 20 kilometers of the west bank of Lake Maggiore between the hamlets of Cannero and Oggebio. On September 5, formations of the Piave Division struck west and in rapid succession took over a number of towns. They were joined by countless volunteers from the liberated towns. The road to the city of Domodossola was opened. Somewhat earlier, on August 29, Moscatelli's Second Garibaldi Division had attacked Baceno and taken over the Formazza Valley as well as the towns of Creola and Varzo, commanding the northern approaches to Domodossola.

South of Domodossola, Alfredo Di Dio's Valtoce Division attacked the outskirts of Pie di Mulara. Meeting heavy enemy resistance, the attack was about to be called off when the enemy garrison decided to withdraw, leaving the road to Domodossola open. One of the units struck Vogogna, inflicting heavy losses on the enemy and starting a rout, which made it possible for the partisans to surround the city. As the partisan forces were preparing the final assault on the city, news arrived that a Fascist force had landed to retake Cannobio. Apparently, the enemy had been accurately informed that most of the guerrilla forces had been moved to Domodossola. The Piave Division command withdrew its forces to contain the threat of Cannobio, and the remaining partisan forces agreed to a truce negotiated by the local clergy. As a result, the fully armed German-Fascist forces were able to evacuate Domodossola which was immediately occupied by the patriot forces.

On the same day, Major Superti, commander of the Valdossola Division, published an order announcing the constitution of a provisional government junta in which all the democratic parties were represented under the presidency of Professor Ettore Tibaldi, a socialist who had recently returned from Switzerland. Major Superti, who had been one of the partisan leaders in direct touch with Donald Jones, realized the problems that the liberated "Ossola Republic" would face and immediately asked Jones for military supplies and assistance from OSS Italy.

In the liberated valleys, the logistical problems of bare subsistence for the population of the area and the expanding partisan forces became acute. With help from the Swiss authorities, however, with whom relaxed frontier procedures were worked out, some food supplies became available. Meanwhile, the local industries were reactivated, and the ranks of the paramilitary formations swelled as youthful volunteers from Milan and other cities joined up. The promises of the OSS Swiss desk to send hundreds of U.S. and Yugoslav internees across the frontier to join the Ossola partisans never materialized; nor did the delivery of airdrops from the south. The main reason was that the 334 Wing had been diverted to the emergency supply operation in support of the Warsaw uprising. In anticipation of Allied assistance, the partisans prepared two landing fields in the area, but they were never to be used. Because the various partisan leaders were motivated by their personal political leanings, the junta finally managed to impose on them a unified military command under Colonel "Federici," a professional Italian Army officer.

While this unfortunate situation had been precipitated by OSS/Berne without coordination with OSS/Italy, the "Mangosteen" mission, whose principal duty was to have been military liaison with the CLNAI and resupply of CLNAI pinpoints, was flown over its drop zone several times. Finally, it was transferred for delivery out of Maison Blanche, Algiers, where on the night of September 26, it was successfully parachuted to our Mottarone drop zone to a reception committee provided by Boeri's brother, Renato.

The situation in the zone was accurately described by Lieutenant Victor Giannino whose "Chrysler" mission had been combined with "Mangosteen."

September 26th we left Algiers in two planes for mission in Northern Italy. Two Sergeants and I were in the second plane which due to motor trouble arrived over the target area at 2400 hours. On proper signals we parachuted and were met by a group of partisans, also by Captain Hollohan and Lt. Icardi of the first plane. We were taken to partisan headquarters under orders of Captain Hollohan to a villa in Coiromonte, a partisan held town, where we established our HQ.

On the 28th, Lt. Icardi, Sgt. Ciarmicoli and myself left from Gravellona where we received word that the partisans were to attack the town on the morning of the 29th. . . .but the attack never took place due to a change of plans. . . .We returned to Coiromonte on the 30th to learn of a supply drop on the 29th (two planes).

With the reorganization of OSS Italian operations under Company D and the assignment of Tactical Intelligence to the Fifth and Eighth Army units, there was no longer any need for the SI tactical encampment in Siena. The tents were struck down, and the personnel were sent back to Brindisi where they were badly needed.

On September 7, Salvatore Amodio, the W/T of the "Fig" mission, had managed to cross the German lines and report back to our headquarters. Amodio, an Italian Navy noncommissioned officer, had been landed from the first submarine operation in January. The members of the mission had been harried by both the Germans and Tito's partisans. The Yugoslavs finally arrested De Basseggio and Bucalo, the mission leaders, on the ground that they were operating in the area without Tito's permission.

After being debriefed, Amodio was quickly assigned as a W/T to one of the segments of the "Papaya" mission which was being organized to go to the Franco-Italian border.

At about the same time Giansandro Menghi of our "Youngstown" mission which had been landed along the Ligurian coast in one of Captain Bonfiglio's maritime operations from Bastia on March 28, who had been picked up by the SD, managed to escape. He made his way to France via the Riviera and was able to carefully mark the defensive positions of the enemy in the area from Rapallo to Ventimiglia. The map, together with other vital information, was placed in a safe house in Nice; Bonfiglio and Menghi were sent to retrieve it, which they did after a hazardous journey. The information was turned over to the G-2, Seventh Army who had high praise for the meticulous manner in which it had been prepared. Upon his return to Brindisi, Menghi was debriefed and assigned to another mission in the Genoa area. Captain Bonfiglio was assigned an important role in the "Papaya" mission whose functions had now been expanded to set up a supply dump at the frontier.

The establishment of this supply depot was very much in the mind of the Italian General Staff. On September 12, I received a memo from Colonel Agrifoglio reminding me of the importance of the operation:

With the approach of the winter season we deem it advisable to speed up the delivery of skis and supplies to the patriot formations operating in Piedmont.

Of particular urgency is a request for 150 pairs of skis and 200 pairs of snowshoes which are available in our Italian army headquarters.

As previously agreed, I urge you to impress upon AFHQ the need to authorize the release of said material from our warehouses and the authorization of transportation of this material to OSS for transfer to the zone of operations.

The Chief of Service

Pompeo Agrifoglio

This would have to wait awhile as "Papaya" was still being put together with representative personnel from the various branches of the organization under our guidance. The operational scope of the mission was further expanded to cover a number of potential situations that could develop in northwest Italy, including the eventual liberation and temporary administration of Italy's industrial triangle.

A final decisional meeting was held at Caserta in order to discuss the objectives of the mission. Present at this meeting were Colonel Glavin, Lieutenant Colonel Bill Maddox, Lieutenant Colonel David Rosen, Lieutenant Commander Milton Katz, Lieutenant Colonel Weil, Major Norman Newhouse, Major Bill Suhling, and Major Max Corvo. The operational plan and goals were approved, and Colonel Davis was asked to arrange transportation to Annecy, France.

The plan was for the mission to establish a temporary base at Abries or Aguilles and then wait to establish contact with Renato who had been made aware of our plans.[6] Renato was the assistant leader of our "Orange" mission and he was also one of the foremost partisan leaders in the Val Pellice.

Papaya 1   Ensign Peck, leader; Private Berruti, Mr. Duro, W/T; Mr. Longo, Italian Army
Papaya 2:   Major Tozzi, U.S. Army, leader; Lieutenant Milton Wolf, Mr. David Colin, Sal Amodeo, W/T, and Sergeant LaGatta
Papaya 3:   Captain Bonfiglio, leader; Mr. Cosenza, Sergeant Maccaroni, and Sergeant DeTiberia
Papaya 4:   For infiltration for Lieutenant Goff's unit — Mr. Petroni, Mr. Rossi, and Mr. Dariot

Special agent for Switzerland: Mr. Raimondo Craveri and Corporal Peter Durante.

Prior to departure for France intensive training and briefing sessions were held, and I did final briefing in Siena. On September 28, the group departed under orders issued by General Lyman Lemnitzer and arrived at Annecy the same afternoon. Craveri was immediately taken to the Swiss border to take up his new station as liaison to CLNAI and to OSS/Switzerland, as well as to enable him to be close to the ORI missions in Milan and Turin. The Goff group, which was seeking to be infiltrated into Piedmont to join one of the Communist formations, was taken in tow by Lieutenant Milton Wolf, but when they decided to infiltrate in civvies he proceeded on to Grenoble. The other components of the mission were aided by the FFI (French Forces of the Interior) to reach their destination at Guillestres.

Because of the extremely cold weather, Captain Bonfiglio set to work to find winter clothing and rations for the members of the mission as the area was hit by early winter storms. Although OSS had a station at Annecy, it had not been advised of the arrival of the group, and Bonfiglio was forced to go to the supply depot at Lyon. Upon arrival there, he was informed that the depot had been moved some 200 miles away. By the time he returned to join the group, Major Tozzi and members of "Papaya 2" had left with four guides to enter Val Pellice. With him were Ensign Peck, Private Berruti, and the W/T, Sal Amodeo. Tozzi had made a number of inquiries about guides which Renato had sent to escort the mission. By chance, one of Renato's couriers (Guy Giovanni) who was in the area seemed to fit the description of one of the guides but he had been sent to deliver a pouch and not to act as a guide for the mission.

Tozzi's decision to proceed forthwith seemed strange in view of the fact that "Logan," his radio transmitter, had come on the air on October 2 and sent the following message:[8]

Arrived Aguilles. No Renato. Abries razed. All passes to Italy closed. Inform Renato our presence. He can reach us via French HQ. Have we contact in Sisteron? What is status of Youngstown team?

On October 3 we received another message:

Germans very active in vicinity. Moving to Guillestre. Need warm clothing badly.

"Logan's" first message was acknowledged by SI Siena on October 3:

Regret your present difficulties but glad all safe. Have wired Renato to arrange meeting at Aguilles. Have also instructed French desk to contact you and render assistance. . . .Keep us posted.

That day we transmitted the following order:

Do not attempt to cross border until Renato has contacted you. Should you be forced to move advise us immediately new location. Have wired Renato.

Unfortunately, that same day Tozzi decided to go ahead and cross the border, convinced that Guy Giovanni was Renato's emissary and not just a simple courier.

On October 16 a message from "Strawberry" mission advised us that "American mission of five captured. Mission had radio and ciphers." We alerted "Orange," cautioning them that the Tozzi group might have compromising documents. On October 18, "Orange" advised:

Courier and men with ciphers have at last returned. On crossing border into Italy met German patrol and had to fight. American sergeant accompanying them surrendered. . . .of the patriot force one was killed, courier himself was wounded.

Salvatore Amodeo recounted the whole story in his briefing report:

We went with a civilian car to Aguilles, from where we left on foot on the 7th of October, with the intention of crossing the border into northern Italy.

Snowfall, rain and heavily loaded rucksacks rendered our march particularly difficult and tiring. We were in proximity of the border when we decided to leave all of the excess equipment in a hiding place.

On October 9th at 0500 hours we crossed the frontier; we were walking through thick fog, hoping it would last as it would hide our tracks in the snow. The frontier was about two kilometers behind us when we heard voices speaking in German. A German artillery battery was about 500 meters from us. We hid behind a rock and tried to make a decision while the fog was rapidly dissipating. The situation became critical. We could not go back because we would have been spotted, and we could not go forward, so we decided to stay put, hoping that the Germans would not discover our tracks in the snow. At 1300 hours, the Germans opened fire with their machine guns against us, wounding one of the guides. Our only alternative was to fight, and we opened fire. One of our guides and one of the Germans were killed, and our ammo was almost finished. Our intention was to resist until nightfall and the guides went back in order to make sure that the Germans did not try to outflank us, but as they were not able to do this, they cut and escaped, while we fought on. By 1730 hours we were completely surrounded by the Germans who asked us to surrender, and because we had run out of ammunition, we surrendered.

The following day they took us to Saluzzo. During the trip the German convoy was attacked by Italian Partisans. Unfortunately, the attack was not successful.[9]

Papaya 2 was therefore in enemy hands facing a German tribunal for espionage, despite the fact that all the men were in proper military attire. Meanwhile, Papaya 1 and 3 continued to operate under the leadership of Captain Joseph Bonfiglio and brought the assigned (ICU) intelligence mission to a successful conclusion, helping to save the lives of many Allied soldiers and drive the Germans out of the area.

In connection with Allied psychological warfare operations, in late August, the MO Branch of OSS asked SI, Italy to help firm up its black and grey propaganda operation, "Sauerkraut," whose aim was to demoralize German soldiers in Italy through a disinformation program. In order to carry out certain phases of the operation, MO specifically asked for information regarding the morale of the German troops in northern Italy. Our teams immediately started gathering and transmitting this information.

Reports from the field indicated that German officers foresaw an early end to the campaign in Italy and that they had been instructed to sleep with their units. Many officers were reported to have packed their belongings to facilitate a hasty departure. On the basis of this information, MO began to print and distribute an order, ostensibly signed by Marshal Kesselring, that German officers must refrain from preparing for evacuation. The order had such a negative effect that Marshal Kesselring was forced to deny its authorship. The MO chief in Italy acknowledged our cooperation with the following statement:

on August 18th the S.I. Section at the request of the M.O. office, asked its agents for special reports on enemy morale. Some 20 successful items have been received to date. One of them formed the basis for the proclamation carried in the "Sauerkraut Operation" and contributed elements of timeliness and verisimilitude so necessary for effectiveness. . .

October brought good news as some 30 USAF C-47s were transferred from Algiers to Brindisi to undertake the heavy air lift we were projecting for Italian underground forces. These planes had been released at Donovan's behest from support of French operations in connection with the Seventh Army operations in southern France. Among the loose ends that needed to be straightened out were the relationship and coordination of Swiss-Italian operations which, in view of the northward drive of the Allied armies, had shortened operational distances and was compressing the geographic area of the battlefield, thus creating the need for greater military control of the unorthodox forces. Since November 1942, when he arrived in Switzerland, Allen Dulles had been cut off from physical control by Washington. His personal stature with Donovan and other OSS notables was so great that invariably his requests were quickly validated by the Hill, as the director's office was called. In late September we had already sent Raimondo Craveri to Switzerland where he had met with Don Jones and the representatives of the underground. Dulles was aware of the meetings and had the opportunity to exchange views with Mondo on a number of occcasions.

In furtherance of the effort to bring all activities under the operational control of OSS/AFHQ, I proposed to meet with either Dulles or Jones for face-to-face discussions and to hammer out a cooperative agreement that would restore control over duplication of effort and eliminate blunders such as the disastrous partisan occupation of Val d'Ossola. Colonel Glavin approved the trip, and two other officers were added to the mission: Lieutenant Robert Wauchope, U.S. Navy, head of the Swiss/MEDTO Desk; and Captain Andre Bourgoin of the French Army on detached service with OSS.

After travel orders were issued by regimental headquarters, we left on October 7 for the landing field at Annecy, France, which was located near the OSS base at Annemasse. On arrival at Annecy, I asked Captain Mathieu, the station CO, if he had any news about our "Papaya" mission to which he answered that he had been out of touch with them since the end of September when they had departed for the Italian frontier.

In order to cross the Swiss border, arrangements had to be made with the Swiss SR. It took Jones several days to make the arrangements through Captain Bustelli. Mondo had already established an excellent relationship with both Jones and Bustelli, having been given the status of a Swiss secret agent and placed on Bustelli's secret list of contacts. Finally, we crossed over as civilians and started a round of seemingly never-ending meetings which were interrupted only for a lunch with Jones at a downtown Geneva restaurant. After lunch, the meetings continued as we attempted to cut through a mass of detailed work and to straighten out the major problems that confronted us.[10] These critical meetings helped to set the stage for utmost cooperation between the Swiss and Italian desks until the end of the war. In addition to Mondo, it was agreed that I would send an officer from Brindisi to coordinate the military operations and work with Jones and Dulles.

The important events and decisions of October 14 were covered in three memos which I wrote on October 25, the circulation of which was restricted to the highest operational echelons. The intent of the memos was to provide for the setting up of a direct communications link between Lugano-Campione and OSS/Italy and the dispatching of an experienced military representative to Lugano who could direct and coordinate the work with the partisan formations.

While in Geneva, I had the opportunity to meet with many of the partisan leaders from the contiguous border areas who had come to discuss the plight of their units. Don Jones was particularly interested in the situation in the Val d'Ossola which had started to deteriorate under a concentrated attack by German-Fascist forces. The partisans had been forced to abandon the city of Domodossola and were fighting rearguard actions while falling back toward the Swiss frontier. Jones suggested that I make arrangements to take over the partisan situation and promised that he would get the Swiss to provide some light armored cars. This was tantamount to stopping the flood with a finger in the dike. Several days later, under a strong attack, the irregular formations of the Ossola Valley (or what remained of them) crossed over the frontier and sought refuge in Switzerland, thus bringing an end to the short-lived Ossola Republic. Some of the outstanding partisan leaders paid with their lives, while Cino Moscatelli pulled back his Communist forces into the high mountains in order to survive the onslaught. Among those crossing was Lieutenant Victor Giannino of the "Mangosteen" mission.

Without undue loss of time, I quickly left Geneva and traveled to Lyon where I met Pete Durante. From there we proceeded by car to Paris, via the Cote d'Or and then flew back to Italy to implement the Geneva agreement.

In some military quarters there was still hope that the German defense along the Gothic Line could be breached and that the Allies could fan out over the Po Valley. In anticipation of the fall of Bologna, Major Tarallo and his ICU team, which had been briefed and were still billeted in Siena, were alerted for possible movement.

Much to my surprise, on my return I found that Captain Christopher De Hartungen, leader of the "Fig" mission which had been infiltrated by submarine in January 1944, had worked his way back through the lines and reported to our headquarters. The area of Bolzano was of primary interest to the intelligence people because the Brenner Pass was the highway for German forces and equipment into Italy. De Hartungen, a native of the area, spoke fluent German. He was put to work immediately preparing a comprehensive report on the military situation, giving the location and identity of German units and commands. He outlined the strength of Fascist units and their officers, and provided an account of the partisan forces operating in the area. Before heading south, De Hartungen had set up an organization throughout the South Tyrol in anticipation of being sent back in with proper communications.

At the Eighth Army front, where a stalemate had been created, Captain Thiele's OSS unit was asked to step up its infiltration. In order to comply with this request, I ordered the Brindisi base to supply six trained tactical agents and one W/T operator. These men were familiar with the terrain and had operated there for some time. On the northwest frontier, in order to implement the program for the creation of Alpine depots, that segment of the Papaya which was in place under the command of Captain Joseph Bonfiglio was ordered to take charge of setting up a supply center at Bourg St. Maurice. In preparation for this task, Bonfiglio was recalled to be briefed on his tasks, which included the addition of expert Italian Alpine officers to his staff. This plan also called for the establishment of a secret intelligence base for the collection, processing, and dissemination of reports from the Liguria and Piedmont region.

On November 13, the radio program, "Italia Combatte," which had a wide audience in German-occupied Italy, broadcast an ill-advised but well-intentioned message to the Italian resistance movement from General Harold Alexander, commanding general, Fifteenth Army Group.[11] He thanked the Italian partisans for having rendered such effective assistance during the victorious summer campaign, and he pointed out that the season of rain and mud would slow down the advance of the Allied armies. The partisans would be facing a new enemy: winter. General Alexander's message also mentioned the difficulties of supplying the guerrilla bands from the air because of the meteorological conditions which usually prevailed in northern Italy during the winter months. The statement also recommended that the patriots not carry out large-scale operations against the enemy and that they conserve ammunition and supplies; wait for new instructions; take advantage of favorable opportunities to attack the enemy; and continue to collect military intelligence. Finally, the general thanked all formations for past paramilitary activities that assisted the Allied effort.

The reaction of the field missions and CLNAI to the general's message was instantaneous and negative. They construed it primarily as a message of abandonment of the resistance movement, whose underlying motives were political and represented the unity effort of the major political parties. This disappointment was aggravated by the fact that the message had been broadcast and provided the enemy with a psychological weapon. Now it could charge that the resistance movement had been abandoned by the Allied High Command and that the partisans should cease their activities and go home.

We attempted to counter the effect of General Alexander's message with explanations to the committee and our own missions in the field. It was not until the arrival of the CLN mission in Rome in December, however, that we had the opportunity to fully explain the gaffe of the officers who had prepared the general's statement.

That the aerial resupply of the patriot bands would be difficult during the winter months had been the subject of a number of studies we had made since late summer in concert with Bill Suhling, G-3 of AFHQ and Fifteenth Army Group, and the staff of Italian military intelligence. Action had already been taken to establish emergency depots, and the "Papaya" mission was already in place to help with the problem. The mission included a number of Italian "civilians," who were SIM officers operating in mufti. Despite everyone's best efforts, the summer of 1944 had not produced an adequate resupply program for the Italian underground forces inasmuch as the 334 Wing and supplies had been diverted. The truth of the matter was that General Alexander's message, phrased in so rational and matter of fact a way, was the kind of message that could be safely delivered to British troops in person. When delivered through the air waves to irregular troops, however, it was interpreted as an order to abandon the field of battle. What the authors of the message failed to comprehend was that in the conduct of irregular warfare when the field is abandoned, all is over. The field of battle is never static until the war is over either through victory or defeat. There were no lulls in partisan warfare—no rest—no respite.

The Rome Agreements between CLN and AFHQ, together with the visit of Parri, Pizzoni, and Pajetta, helped to overcome the negative effect of the Alexander message. The period between November 15 and November 30 saw the progressive buildup of supply drops to some of our SI pinpoints in selected areas of northern Italy. On the night of November 16, 30 planes took part in a massive air drop at the "Drupe" pinpoint that had been supplied by our team "Meriden," which was operating in the mountains of Liguria (Genoa). This supply drop, as well as smaller ones that preceded it, helped to arm the underground forces in the area. On the night of November 28, six planeloads of supplies were dropped to pinpoints of the "Meriden" and "Cromwell" teams. The cargo of these planes contained five SSTR-1 radios for SO and SI and OG teams operating in the area.

On November 24, the "Cherry" mission infiltrated by sea into German-occupied Italy. This mission was the first of a new SI type planned to operate in cities where cover was difficult. "Cherry" was a one-man mission. The agent was both a W/T and cryptographer and had to establish his own information cells with whom he would work through cutouts in order to achieve maximum security. "Cherry" was to work in the general Venice area. In the event the German resistance crumbled, he was to retreat northward with the enemy, providing details of the enemy's military moves. The agent had been selected for his expert knowledge of German.

During the latter part of November, OSS/AFHQ decided and Suhling concurred, that Captain Bourgoin's chain of SO missions was to be turned over to Italian SI. We started discussions on the transfer with Captain Bourgoin, who had moved his headquarters to a villa on the outskirts of Siena, several miles from Company D headquarters. For all of his feverish activity in over one year of operations, Andre Bourgoin had little to show for his efforts. He had been hampered primarily by his lack of philosophical commitment to his "metier." As a French colon from Morocco, he had no attachment to the United States, nor did he have much empathy for the plight of the Italians whom he really seemed to dislike. Andre had spent a lot of time in Morocco and had developed a callous attitude toward his subordinates. I did not find out why he was leaving Italy and the OSS, nor did I ever inquire—even after the war when I visited him briefly in Casablanca during one of my trips there. We parted company on amicable terms after he had turned over control of the following teams: "Lobo," "Maria Giovanna," "Piroscafo," "Lancia," and "Republica." Of these, "Maria Giovanna's" operator had been captured by the Germans, and we were continuing to work the circuit in order to keep the operator alive, without letting him know we were aware of his plight.[12] Occasionally, in answer to some inquiry from the field, the Germans were thrown some valueless items. (Later, we agreed to work this circuit jointly with X-2's Jim Angleton, Jr., who had been transferred from London to Italy late in 1944).

We set to work to reorganize the agents of these missions who were available, and with a bit of attention and retraining, some of the stations came back on the air. Agents were recalled and rebriefed, and a number of them were turned over to Abrignani and the Fifth Army Tactical Unit.

In compliance with the August agreement worked out with General Donovan, during the months of October and November, the Rome office under Vincent Scamporino, began to put together a special subsection that specialized in gathering information about Japan. I had discussed the matter with Agrifoglio whose office had returned to SIM's headquarters in Via XX Settembre after the fall of Rome. SIM regained most of the archives which had been hidden during the German occupation.

During my frequent visits to Rome, I stopped in and discussed various situations of common interest. During one of these visits Scamp and I discussed ways and means by which SIM might collaborate in the Japanese intelligence project, calculating that once the war in Europe was over, Italy might provide OSS with some specialized Far East intelligence people for the penetration of Manchukuo, Japanese-occupied China and the Japanese home islands.

Agrifoglio, having foreseen the benefits of ongoing Italian collaboration, agreed to assign three SIM specialists to the section, which also included a professor from the University of Rome and two of our own people from Rome. At the same time, a meeting was arranged with Italian Air Force Colonel Nerio Brunetti, who had been the last Italian Air Force attache' in Tokyo. Brunetti, with whom I met privately on various occasions and who was one of the few Westerners who had even been allowed to fly over the Home Islands, had authored a Japanese-Italian dictionary of Air Force terminology. He had a complete set of air charts of Japan and was one of those rare intelligence finds who was happy to work with the United States.[13] Delighted at having his services, we made arrangements to ship him surreptitiously to Washington where his knowledge would be useful to the U.S. Air Force program to bomb strategic targets in Japan.

At the same time, Agrifoglio also made arrangements for me to interview merchant marine Captain Pardo who had commanded an Italian blockade runner which he had successfully sailed back to Europe from the Far East. Pardo, every inch a seafarer, gave an account of his adventures in the Far East and South China Sea. He had good knowledge of the mined coastal waters off Japan, and he also had maritime charts which we judged would be very useful. Both Brunetti and Pardo were shipped to Washington in November with Colonel Rodrigo, who personally took 150 pounds of Japanese intelligence material and studies back to the States with him.

As 1944 was drawing to a close, the SI/OSS position in Italy was reaching a state of peak performance. At this time, our missions covered all parts of Italy and were bearing much fruit. The "Apricot" and "Citron" missions not only directed CLNAI intelligence, but also constituted the only direct communications link with AFHQ and AAI through Company D; the situation with the OSS/Swiss desk had been resolved through the October Geneva accords; SI/Italy was in a position to provide drop zones for SO and OG missions; the major guerrilla forces were in contact with our missions, and air resupply was affected at our designated pinpoints; a courier service effectively functioned from Milan to Switzerland and thence to Siena; and an important radio transmitter "Boston" was set up at Lugano and moved to Campione d'Italia at the border.

After examining a number of alternatives, I asked Mim Daddario if he would like to go to Switzerland and work with Don Jones, Dulles, and Craveri. It made a lot of sense to send Mim to Lugano to handle the coordination of operations because he had been working with me since we set up the Brindisi base and he was acquainted with all of the missions and personnel operating behind enemy lines. Mim also knew the problems we faced in the south and was attuned to my handling of them at the various OSS and Allied headquarters since he was my closest collaborator.

In late November, an event that had been in the planning stage for about six months finally came to pass. Through Allen Dulles and John McCaffrey in Berne, we managed to arrange the dispatching of a mission from CLNAI to meet with the Allied High Command in liberated Italy. It was not easy to arrange the transit of such a mission without obtaining the consent and participation of SOE, which was extremely wary of CLN's political intentions. The SOE feared that left wing forces were altogether too powerful and would attempt to take over the areas evacuated by the Germans and Fascists, once the war came to an end. The president of CLNAI, Alfred Pizzoni, who was a banker and a conservative, was close to the British, but he was a patriot who was convinced that no such unhappy event would take place. He believed that the CLN needed to work in unison in order to be of military value to the Allied and Italian cause.

The British were suspicious until Colonel Roseberry flew in to Berne from London to participate in the discussion. Craveri, who was on the spot, quickly alerted us to the situation. Finally, a meeting was held by Allen Dulles, McCaffery, and Pizzoni, and the mission to the Allied High Command was approved by the British.

The members of the mission were Alfredo Pizzoni (code name Pietro Longhi); Ferruccio Parri (code name Maurizio); Gian Carlo Pajetta (code name "Mare"); and Eddy Sogno, an Italian officer who worked closely with SOE.[14] Thus, the mission represented all political currents of CLN from the extreme right to the communist left. Parri had asked for such a meeting since spring, but for one reason or another, it had been impossible to organize the trip.

With the passing of time, the position of OSS in Italy had gained strength as the number of clandestine missions increased, air resupply became more frequent, and the strength of the CLN and the guerrilla forces increased. The CLNAI mission was seeking Allied recognition and financing for its operations, as well as official recognition from the Italian (Badoglio) government as its agent in enemy-occupied territory. Soon after its arrival, we arranged a series of meetings with Pizzoni, Parri, and Pajetta during which we discussed the situation of their underground forces.

I had ordered Craveri to accompany the mission so that he could spend time with Parri, who already was acquainted with the OSS position, to obtain recognition and financing without asking too many questions and without creating any unnecessary roadblocks. We felt confident that OSS would soon dominate the intelligence and unorthodox warfare operations in Italy and that with the arrival of additional aircraft and the transfer of the packing station we could look forward to dropping increased tonnage.

As our relationship with the three members of the mission became solidified, we participated in a number of meetings at AAI and in Rome for the signing of the so-called Rome Agreements. The language of the agreements was worked out jointly by SOE, OSS, AAI, and CLNAI, and was reviewed and approved by AFHQ. The agreements covered the acceptance of the military authority of AAI over the resistance operations; spelled out the exercise of authority stemming therefrom; and apportioned the sum of 160 million lire a month to the various areas of northern Italy as follows: Liguria, 20 million; Piemonte, 60 million; Lombardy, 25 million; Emilia, 20 million; and the Veneto, 35 million. The signatories of the memorandum of agreement between CINCMED and CLNAI were Pietro Longhi, Maurizio, Mare, Eddy Sogno, and General Maitland-Wilson.

Both Longhi and Maurizio were anxious to get back to Milan to continue the clandestine struggle against the Germans, but Mare was left in Rome to work out the details of the CLNAI as the Italian government's agent in northern Italy. Craveri, who had been most helpful during the mission's stay in the south, returned to Switzerland to further implement SI plans for the coming months.

Many of the meetings took place at Company D headquarters in Siena; Major Suhling, Major Cagiati, and other members of the staff participated in the discussions. The results of the Company D meetings covered the following subjects on November 29, 1944:

Unity of CLNAI Command
Recognition of CLNAI
Financing of CLNAI
Communications problems
Attitude and relations with Switzerland, Yugoslavia, France, and Italy vis-a-vis Allies
OSS missions
Anti-scorch activities
Controls

Thus, eleven months of patient and highly dangerous work were finally rewarded with the recognition of the Supreme Allied Commander. The result was a chain of command coordination of resistance paramilitary activity which turned out to be one of the best models of collaboration in any theater of wartime operations. This had been achieved despite the off-repeated opposition of individuals within the OSS organization in the theater and in Washington. This opposition never abated, continuing until the end of the war in Italy.

The CLN had maintained close contact with our "Mangosteen" mission, and through the mission had provided many pinpoints to supply the partisans. Parri had arranged to meet with Hollohan through "Landi," who had been one of the original members of the mission. Landi, who had originally been designated to lead a mission to Trieste, was asked to remain in Milan as a backup to Boeri, the underground intelligence chief. However, he still kept in touch with Icardi and Hollohan and sometimes met with them to discuss pending operations.

In December we received news that the villa where the Hollohan mission was quartered had come under enemy attack. In the confusion created by the shooting, the members of the mission scattered in different directions. Sometime later, when they reassembled, Major Hollohan did not turn up. It was assumed that he was still hiding and would turn up later. When he failed to show up, it was thought that he might have been captured by the enemy. In order to find out what might have happened, several priests were asked to search the area to see if there was any sign of the major. Using school children to allay enemy suspicions, the priests searched thoroughly but failed to find any trace of him. The following day Landi came into the area to confer with Hollohan and Icardi and was told that the major was missing. In his debriefing report, dated May 28, 1945, Landi recalled the event:

The contacts with the Chrysler Mission during the many months of its operational activities were my responsibility. Both Major Hollohan and Lt. Icardi were most helpful whenever we requested any help. From the very beginning the collaboration between Chrysler and CLNAI had been excellent. At the end of December, 1944, while on a visit to confer with Major Hollohan, I was informed that the day before my arrival, the villa where the American officers were quartered, had come under attack by unknown elements and the group had scattered in separate directions, and while they later were reunited at Pella on Lake Orta, the Major was missing and there was no news of him. I remained in the area for a day to conduct an exhaustive investigation, but I failed to come up with any positive elements.

This was a hard blow to our plans to establish a prestigious military mission headed by a field grade American officer. Hollohan had been promoted to major in October, after leaving on mission, so that he would have field grade status.

For some inexplicable reason, Major Suhling's personal relationship with me, which had been consistently very friendly to this point, seemed to change after this incident. As time went on, despite the outstanding work of the Italian SI Section, the relationship even became confrontational.

Despite Hollohan's disappearance and Giannino's return via exfiltration through Switzerland, the work of the "Chrysler-Mangosteen" mission continued under Icardi and played an important role in tying down German-Fascist forces in the area. These forces would otherwise have been used to strengthen the German positions along the Gothic Line. At this very same time, German and Fascist counterintelligence services were busy in the area, trying to locate the "Apricot," "Citron," and "Mangosteen" transmitters. Boeri sounded the alarm, which was confirmed by the fact that radio transmission was shortened in order to make it difficult to triangulate the radio signals. In his debriefing report, Gelindo Bertoluzzi, one of the original members of "Mangosteen," who was a W/T, reported:

I remained with my friends, the W/Ts of "Apricot" and "Citron" until December 1944, helping their radio transmissions. By now the zone had become highly dangerous as the Nazi-Fascist forces were constantly in action. As a matter of fact, on October 20, we had to stop operating our radios for a number of days because the Germans were close by, looking for our transmitters; however, the members of the Stefanoni Brigade were guarding us. On November 15, they captured four Germans who had strapped portable radio direction finders under their raincoats. This equipment was used to triangulate our location. During the search of their personal effects they found a map on which the precise location of our radio was marked.

On orders from Dr. Boeri and Lt. Icardi and the OSS base, we stopped all transmissions until new cipher plans were delivered.

Obviously, despite the protection of the Stefanoni Brigade, the mission was fraught with danger because its presence was known to the residents of the nearby villages, its transmissions could be heard by the enemy, and its movements were hampered by the fact that its personnel was operating in U.S. military uniforms.[15]

In the semimonthly report dated December 22, covering the section's activities from December 1 to December 15, 1944, it was reported of "Mangosteen": "This team recently was forced to suspend contacts because of enemy action in the zone. It is believed that this mission is moving to a safe zone." The report covering the period December 16-31 simply noted: "Mangosteen—no intelligence since December 17th."

Major Hollohan's disappearance was to have particular reverberations in the early 1950s when it became a celebrated case. Even today, it is the subject of research, with several authors writing books about it. In wartime, many strange things happen, particularly in the conduct of unorthodox intelligence operations that flaunt international rules in order to outwit the enemy. When anyone volunteers to operate behind enemy lines, death is an ever present reality, and so at the time, the disappearance of Bill Hollohan was viewed simply as an unfortunate incident.

Chapter 16

The Rome Station

With the fall of Rome, the Italian SI's political, economic, and industrial intelligence section moved up from Naples. With Scamp leading the way, part of the Naples staff had entered the Eternal City with the S-Force which had been organized to swoop down on targeted areas and buildings in search of documents and intelligence. When Scamp was recalled to the United States, Major Ricca who had been our liaison with the Italian government, temporarily took command of the SI office.

During Major Torrielli's attempt to dismember and take over our section as described earlier in the book, I visited Rome frequently both to joust verbally with Torrielli and to keep abreast of developments.

After Torrielli had been transferred out of the Italian theater and Scamporino returned from the States in late August, Scamp expanded the section. He placed Captain Joseph Caputa in charge of the Reports Section. This section had at its disposal the necessary staff to do technical translations, gather vital political intelligence, maintain unofficial liaison with certain Vatican monsignori, keep in touch with SIM headquarters, and establish contacts with the highest levels of the Italian government.

Among the members of Scamp's Rome staff were Major Ricca, Captain Caputa, Major Felix Pasqualino, Lieutenmant Bruno Bisceglia, Sergeant Salvatore Accampora, Sergeant Al Spera, civilians James Franklyn, Martin Carney, Lawrence Battistini, Joe d'Amato, Sam Prete, Umberto Galleani, Nick Olds, James St. Lawrence O'Toole, Martin Quigley, Vincenzo Vacirca, and, for a while, Serafino Romualdi, Vanni Montana, and a number of Italian civilians. The rear echelon at regimental headquarters included Captain James Montante and Sergeant Mike Contrastino.

The basic reports were compiled at the Rome office and were distributed to the various Allied offices in the Rome area, AFHQ, AAI, and

Washington. Pouch material, which in the fall of 1944 was starting to come through Switzerland from Milan by special underground couriers, was processed by the Rome SI Reports Board, which was designated the official Rome Reports Board. It incorporated some of the other OSS personnel which had been assigned to the "Camilluccia," a luxurious villa that OSS had requisitioned for its Rome headquarters. The Camilluccia was located on Monte Mario overlooking the entire city of Rome which majestically spread out below with its ancient landmarks. In the distance rose the Alban Hills with their quaint villages overlooking Rome and Nettuno and Anzio, the site of the long, drawn-out, bitter winter of the Allies' agony.

The extraterritoriality of Vatican City was one of Rome's many fascinations. During the German occupation, many anti-Fascists, Jews, and escaped prisoners of war found refuge in the various Vatican properties covered by the protocol of neutrality. But when the city fell to the Allies, some Fascists and Germans also sought refuge in the same Vatican properties and found it. Among them was the former head of SIM, General Giacomo Carbone, who had been in command of the Italian Mobile Armored Group which was to have defended Rome and who, instead, failed to effectively oppose the Germans. When the Germans took over the city, Carbone went into hiding and became a target of the Italian government and the new SIM organization as well as the Allies.

It was General Carbone who had met General Maxwell Taylor during his secret trip to Rome to finalize Italian and Allied military collaboration in connection with the projected use of the U.S. Eighty-second Airborne to bolster the Italian defense of Rome.[1] (Italian SI had been assigned the task of capturing Ventotene Island to set up an air directional beacon for the Eighty-second.) Carbone's defeatist attitude during his meeting with Taylor brought about the cancellation of the operation.

Carbone continued to be the Vatican's unwelcome guest even after the city was occupied by Allied forces; only after the war did he emerge and then to face a court martial which in the end exonerated him of any wrongdoing. At the time, SIM was interested in obtaining an accounting of its secret funds. His military trial aroused a storm of controversy, for he had powerful friends among the communists whom he had armed to defend Rome against the Germans when the Badoglio government fled from the city.

Our Major Pasqualino, who was well connected to the Vatican, was assigned the task of maintaining a strict surveillance of Carbone during his stay in the Vatican. He did so through friendly prelates who obliged him from time to time by agreeing to move the general and his luggage from one place to another, thus providing OSS with the opportunity to keep track of his whereabouts and his visitors, including a mistress, who used to visit him quite frequently.

Notwithstanding his exoneration by the court martial, many responsible people in the armed forces considered his behavior unpardonable. In

In his book *Generals, Intelligance Services, and Fascism* (Mondadori, 1978), Carlo DeRisio has this comment on Carbone's comportment:

It is difficult to absolve the General, who while his troops were facing the Germans, could do nothing more than discard his uniform, empty out the SIM treasury of currency and valuables and go underground. The lack of sense of responsibility in a soldier and an authentic moral and physcial flight, is incompatible with even the elementary rules of military honor.

The political section of the Rome office was in touch with events at every level of government. Scamp and the men who worked with him were on a first-name basis with the leaders of all parties, and their reports accurately reflected the events that took place in the back rooms where the decisions were made. Scamp was in an enviable position, for he could talk authoritatively about political events on both sides of the battle lines.

The political parties in Italy were cut in two by the Gothic Line, and those politicians who operated in Rome had their counterparts in Milan CLN. The OSS often provided the only link of communications by which the north and the south could carry on a limited dialogue. SI's political and economic reports on both German and Allied-occupied Italy were distributed to policy-making Allied agencies in Italy and Washington and often helped to shape both wartime and postwar policies. These contacts helped build a sense of confidence and trust between Italy and the United States which remains the basis for their relationship to this day.

Chapter 17

Backstairs Diplomacy

Earlier, when the relationship between the United States and Italy was still based on an insecure co-belligerent status imposed by the Armistice terms, a close rapport was established between Major Ricca and Marshal Badoglio. This rapport was made possible by the empathy which the old Marshal felt for Ricca who spoke his own dialect. In those early days, Italy was under Allied military rule and had no diplomatic relations with Washington. Badoglio, after inviting Ricca to lunch in Brindisi on November 10, 1943, asked him if he would carry a secret personal message to Algiers. Ricca informed me by radio the same day, and I urged him to reply affirmatively. From this relationship developed a secret channel of communications which for months saw OSS serve as the unofficial link between the Badoglio government and Washington, with Ricca traveling to Washington as the go-between.

In mid-January 1944, Badoglio met with Ricca and expressed a desire to meet General Donovan. Ricca sent me the request by radio, and a meeting was arranged during Donovan's visit to Naples in connection with the Anzio landing. Badoglio refers to the meeting in his book *Italy in the Second World War* (Mondadori, 1946). He wrote:

I was informed that General Donovan, who was very close to President Roosevelt, was in Naples. I had met him in Buffalo in 1921 and had seen him again at Macalle (Ethiopia) where he had come as observer to make a report to President Roosevelt. He sent word to me that he would very much like to see me but that at the moment he could not move from Naples. So I went to see him. I arrived just at the time he was returning from the Anzio beachhead. I conveyed my thoughts on our situation to him and he insisted that those thoughts should be expressed in a letter which he would deliver to the President.

I wrote a letter in which I requested the President to take the initiative for a change in Allied policy toward Italy and proposing an Alliance.

. . . .

... the reply to the letter which Donovan delivered to the President arrived. The President thanked me as an old soldier who spoke his mind frankly. This permitted him to reply in terms of equal frankness. He said that he had been following our government's efforts to aid the Allied effort and he was ready to acknowledge our loyalty and cooperation, but in his opinion, only a broad based and democratic government in which all anti-Fascist parties were represented would be in a position to marshall all of the country's efforts for a broader participation in the war. Roosevelt promised to re-examine the Italian situation only after the creation of such a government.

In late April, the first unofficial emissary of the Italian government was smuggled into the United States by Jack Ricca when he surreptitiously flew with Professor Guido Pazzi to Washington, bearing a personal letter to President Roosevelt. Pazzi, a socialist, had walked through the lines from Rome bearing messages from the CLN and Pietro Nenni which allowed the democratization of the Badoglio government, a move that the president had recommended.

The contacts with the White House and State Department were maintained through Jonathan Daniels, one of the most influential members of President Roosevelt's staff, and Adolph Berle, Jr., assistant secretary of state. In his book, *White House Witness, 1942-1945*, Daniels recalls the event:

Thursday, May 18, Major George Watts Hill and Earl Brennan of OSS came in to see me this morning. It seems that the chief of the Southern European section of OSS abroad arrived at Presque Isle, Maine this week with a "gentleman." He had no passport except his OSS travel orders. After phoning Washington, Brennan assured the State Department that it would be all right to admit the man. He came to Washington by plane and is at the Statler Hotel under the name of Michele Rossi. He is actually Prof. Guido Pazzi, who was assistant professor at the University of Messina and was never promoted because he was not a member of the Fascist Party. He is a native of Bologna. He has considerable experience in the labor field. He is a socialist and worked with the International Labor Office of the League of Nations and also before the war he had some relationship with the Russians.

He comes to this country with plenipotentiary powers from Badoglio. Apparently the British are unwilling that there be any Badoglio representative in this country. OSS feels that the State Department's representatives in Italy are dominated by the British. In essence it seems to me that OSS, which says it has the confidence of Badoglio while the British and other Americans have not, has smuggled an ambassador or potential ambassador into the U.S. under the guise that he is coming to give political or economic advice to OSS.

Hill and Brennan asked my advice as to what to do. I told them that I did not think it a good idea to bypass the State Department and agreed to discuss the thing with Adolf Berle.

Pazzi is living at the Statler Hotel with a young officer in OSS and it is regarded as very important that nobody know in advance the facts about this matter.

I talked to Berle who is going to see Brennan.

Guido Pazzi was a guest of the Italian Section until October when he returned to Italy escorted by Lieutenant Pompey Orlando, Brennan's executive assistant in Washington. The letter which Pazzi bore from Marshal Badoglio was a plaintive appeal to the president to change the status of relations between the two nations. Rather than treat Italy as a vanquished nation, deprived of all possibilities of internal decision-making, he pleaded for a status that would give hope to the Italians in their recuperation attempt and help the nation recover its self-respect.

Dear Mr. President:

On April 2nd I wrote to say that I confidently hoped to be able in a very short time to form a truly national government, including all the major organized parties. What was then my hope, has today materialized, without any exception, all the parties which, since the fall of Fascism have again taken up their free activity, are cooperating today, with all their best men, in a new government representing the largest possible concentration of democratic forces, and which is exclusively bent on galvanizing the country in its fight against Germany, and the bringing of it on the road to material and moral rebirth.

Men such as Benedetto Croce and Count Sforza, notwithstanding any past vicissitudes, are today unreservedly sharing with me this great national task.

Professor Pazzi is leaving within the next few days for the United States on an unofficial and secret mission, the practical execution of which has only been made possible through the generous understanding of North American channels, to whom I am most indebted.

I am therefore entrusting this letter of mine to Professor Pazzi if—as I hope— you shall see fit to consent it—will be in a position to explain in person what is actually our present situation, through what developments the formation of the present government has been reached, what are in fact the purport and significance of this event.

Prof. Pazzi will, above all, be in a position to explain that the rebirth of a democratic and liberal Italy, is beyond any doubt, already under way, and how and why in order to give to the country a moral strength and impetus which alone can enable it to proceed with ever greater resolution along the road which it has started, it is today absolutely necessary and at the same time invaluable to the common aims, that the internal regeneration of the country, of which the new government is the expression, should be accompanied by a parallel and synchronic revision and revaluation of its international situation.

You are well aware, Mr. President, which is this internal situation today. A continued imprisonment within a humiliating and demoralizing armistice; a minute and daily control, which allows of no breathing space and no initiative; an atmosphere of diffidence and suspicion which stifles and stultifies every possibility of durable recovery; Italian military participation measured out and contained within the narrowest possible limits, etc.

This iron ring, in which we are constricted for the last eight months, can only be broken by a generous word on your part, by a human gesture which, implementing the assurance given to us at Quebec, may serve at last, through the Alliance, to bring back a free Italy, almost to the family of free nations.

This is, today, what I would like to report, the most favorable occasion and the most timely contingency for such a word and such a gesture; and this is why I take it upon me to write to you once more on the subject, and notwithstanding your present grave tasks, to ask you to give your favorable attention to what the bearer of the letter will have the opportunity to explain to you more fully in detail.

I would like to add (though it is a detail of too personal a character, for which you will forgive me) that I am writing under stress of what is for me a particularly painful moment. I have just learned in fact that my only remaining boy, who was waiting for me in Rome, was trailed and arrested by the German police the day before yesterday. I have no news as to his state. You will understand what this means.

I venture to mention to you this circumstance merely because I am confident that it may serve, better than any other argument, to explain to you that I am alone supported by the hope of being able to bring back my country in the powers of recuperation and recovery of which I have unflinching trust, provided your generous help will not fail—on the side, above all, of the United States, whose friendship for us is essential.

Believe me, Mr. President, with heartfelt and devoted friendship.

Badoglio[1]

Guido Pazzi remained in Washington over five months under the watchful eyes of Lieutenant Bisceglia who was given the difficult task of security, taking care that "Mr. Rossi" (Pazzi's code name) would not attract undue attention from the counterespionage organizations in Washington. "Rossi" was an extrovert and was quite attracted to the pretty women who seemed to abound in the Statler's lobby and Washington's restaurants. He also liked to get up late in the morning and, to the astonishment of other guests, to loll around in his pajamas, walking around the corridors of the hotel. Bisceglia had his hands full and was quite happy to relinquish the task when he returned.

The words of encouragement for Italy did not come until Badoglio had relinquished the reins of government and was succeeded by Premier Ivanhoe Bonomi, a pre-Fascist parliamentary leader. The occasion was the annual Columbus Day observance on October 12, 1944, staged by the Italian-American Labor Council in New York, when the Four Freedoms Award was presented to President Roosevelt. The award was accepted for the president by Attorney General Francis Biddle[2] who assured Italian-Americans in the audience that "it is the settled determination of President Roosevelt to bring the provisions of the Atlantic Charter to bear upon Italy's problems. This policy was stated by Mr. Adolf Berle, Jr., Assistant Secretary of State, and reaffirmed at Quebec four weeks ago."

In a special message delivered by telephone to the over 2,500 guests gathered at the Hotel Commodore, President Roosevelt addressed a number of questions Badoglio had posed in his letter, stating that "the American Army—including thousands of Americans of Italian descent—entered Italy, not as conquerors, but as liberators. Their object is military, not political. When the military objective is accomplished . . . the Italian people will be free to work their own destiny under a government of their own choosing." Then the president announced a series of changes relaxing restrictions on delivery of mail and packages to Italy and lifting the prohibition of the transfer of limited funds. The president completed his telephone address by saying "to the people of Italy, we have pledged our help—and we will keep the faith."

Thus, through Italian SI activities the problems which the Italian people were facing were brought to President Roosevelt's attention through the back door of the White House and the State Department. The delivery of Badoglio's succinct letter analyzing the problems of the fledgling democratic government, helped relax the harsh terms imposed by the long armistice and laid the groundwork for the postwar collaboration and friendship between the two nations.

In mid-November of 1944, the Italian Section SI was redesignated as the Italian Division SI MEDTO. This change had been made necessary by the creation of a Reports Board Section which was headed by Captain Caputa.

The personnel for the division were constantly bolstered by the arrival of new people from Washington. In October, Martin Carney, who spoke Italian fluently and studied voice and had sung in opera productions in Italy, had reported for duty at the Rome office. On the same day, Joseph D'Amato, a Boston school teacher, whose Italian was also fluent, also signed in for service in Rome.

On December 24, Martin Quigley, Jr., reported to undertake a special assignment in Rome. Martin, whose family published a number of outstanding publications connected with the New York stage and the Hollywood film industry, had been sent under cover to Ireland and was assigned the difficult task of using Vatican connections to bring the war in the Far East to a quick finish.

The workload of the Italian SI and Reports Board became heavier daily as it embarked on the Japanese intelligence project, which had been approved by Donovan in August, and as operators from the section established close ties at the highest levels of the Vatican secretariat, where the nerve center of Vatican communications with its worldwide network was located.

This "penetration" made it possible to get a close look at the various diplomatic chanceries in the world. Thus, a number of persons were assigned to maintain relations with the various monsignori who constituted the mainstay of the Vatican's administrative and decision-making bureaucracy.

The sources that produced this wealth of intelligence were collectively codenamed "Vessel" and immediately in the postwar period gave rise to a heated controversy between Scamporino and the newly arrived X-2 desk chief, James Angleton, Jr.[3] The quality of the political reports produced by SI Rome was rated highly according to a memo from Dr. Sterling A. Callisen to General Donovan, dated September 22, 1944. In the memo,

Dr. Callisen compared an Italian SI report (A-38815) with a political report emanating from Rumania (A-38846) which was produced by another branch of OSS:

Two reports are attached to illustrate the point. The first report (A38815) from Italy, fulfills the conditions of an ideal report on a political subject. In this case the reader is left in no doubt as to the political leanings of the sources and can satisfy himself as to the reliability of the material. In the case of the second report (A38846) from Roumania, a fairly sweeping statement is made in the first sentence regarding the reaction of the Roumanian population towards Russia. Without a further statement as to the qualifications of the source, it is difficult for anyone outside O.S.S. to evaluate the information adequately.[4]

In this connection, the Rome SI office had a wide and appreciative clientele for its intelligence product and when R & A needed help in preparing a report on Argentina, the desired information was provided by the Rome office of SI.

Dr. William Langer, the chief of the R & A branch in Washington, wrote:

The Latin American Division would like to express its deepest gratitude for the assistance rendered by the Italian outpost in securing documents for our emergency project on Argentina. Two of the documents were of capital importance and were transmitted to State Department, which immediately forwarded them to the American delegation in Mexico City. The other documents all contained valuable background information.
    I should appreciate it if you could inform Gen. Magruder and the Italian outpost of the extreme usefulness of the latter's efforts in our behalf.[5]

"Vessel" and other Rome intelligence sources provided information from all corners of the globe. Much of this information was quickly relayed to Brennan and Donovan, and from there it found its way to the White House. The Rome office did not neglect its contacts with the highest political levels in the Italian government. Scamporino established a friendly relationship with the key political leaders of Italy, who often sought him out for advice on how their positions on important matters would be viewed in Washington. Obviously, the fact that Italian SI also played a prominent role in the underground activities of the political parties in northern Italy helped to create confidence in our Rome contacts.

During its operations in Rome from June 1944 until its closing twelve months later at the end of June 1945, the Rome SI Reports Board produced some 2,000 reports that were distributed to all key American political and military offices in the theater and in Washington. Another 1,000 reports were processed from October 1943, when the political and economic section was set up in Palermo, until June, when the office moved up from Naples to Rome. The intelligence produced was so valuable that our government representatives had advance knowledge of events and were therefore in a position to make good use of it in preestablishing their policy positions.

Chapter 18

Reap the Whirlwind

The return of Parri and Pizzoni to Milan at the end of December signalled the Allies' preparation of a massive spring offensive to break the German defenses along the Gothic Line. In the latter part of December, two members of the Appuania-Massa CLN crossed the Fifth Army lines and reported to SI with messages and information from which we were able to reconstruct the enemy's positions in the area. They outlined the situation of the partisans and asked for help for the families of the underground. Their arrival was given the full attention of the Rome office and Fifth Army detachment. They returned to Massa with the promise of full Allied assistance to prepare stepped-up operations against the German lines of communication.

On December 16, the "Cherry" team made the first radio contact, and on the ensuing nights, a number of successful supply drops were made to the teams in enemy territory. On December 27, "Date II," an agent with radio, was dropped in the northeast. The entire mission could not be dropped since two other members had become ill and would have to be dropped at a later date.

As the year drew to a close, the following missions were fully trained and awaited transportation to the field:

1. MITRAGLIA—one agent and one W/T destined to be dropped in the Veneto.

2. DIANA—two agents and one W/T to operate in Val Camonica and the Stelvio Pass and Tonale area.

3. NORMA—one agent and one W/T north of Brescia to work under the "Diana" leader.

4. MORRISTOWN—two agents and W/T for the Langhe area of Piedmont.

5. DICK—two agents and W/T for the Valtellina and Valsassina.[1]

In the field, a vast network of intelligence agents had been created in less than a year through the tireless work and perseverance of the under-staffed Brindisi station, which despite the opposition of many influential officers in both Algiers and Naples, had been kept open and even expanded. Brindisi had served all of the OSS branches and sections by making its communications and other facilities available to all who needed them. Through its establishment of vital communications links with the German-occupied north and its close rapport with the Committee of National Liberation, its operations made it possible for OSS to assume an authoritative position in the miltary campaign in Italy.

In December 1944 there were seventeen SI secret radio transmitters operating in northern Italy, daily supplying intelligence, tracking enemy movements, order of battle information, military industrial production figures, bombing damage reports, psychological warfare data, counter-intelligence information and drop zones to supply the armed groups.[2]

Although it was realized that hard fighting lay ahead and that Ameri-can and Allied casualties would mount, it was obvious that the war in Europe would soon come to an end. This was in everyone's mind until the desperate Germans attacked in the Ardennes with the Fifth and Sixth Panzer Armies on December 6. Their surprise breakthrough set the Allied timetable back, creating a state of total alarm throughout the European battle fronts. The fierce German attack was spearheaded by special units trained and parachuted by Colonel Otto Skorzeny, the officer who had rescued Mussolini. It created fear that surprise attacks would be made on many of the Allied headquarters, including those in Italy. OSS headquarters in Caserta and Rome were placed on total alert, but nothing happened.

I happened to be visiting the Camilluccia headquarters in Rome at the time the alert signal came in. The CO in Rome was Lieutenant Colonel George Van der Hoef, a corpulent, ineffectual man who was an expert mainly in wielding knife and fork at the dinner table. When the alarm sounded, Van der Hoef, in a nervous, excitable voice, immediately suggested that we place antipersonnel mines around the property, whereupon Major Felix Pasqualino, who served as major domo at Rome headquarters, invited him to have a cup of coffee and a piece of cake with a mountain of whipped cream to calm him down. And so ended his panic.

By the end of 1944, the coordination achieved through the operation of Company D and Suhling's businesslike administrative approach to the problem provided the necessary conditions that would allow operations to move smoothly. It also made it clear that the central point of control for Italian operations must be Company D headquarters.

The long-postponed unification of all OSS Italian paramilitary activities, which should have taken place a year before at Naples, had finally occurred, with all branches of OSS making their contributions through a single administrative entity. The Rome station would continue to operate under the jurisdiction of regimental headquarters. The branches there had a good deal of autonomy in developing their own programs. Concurrently, the Italian battlefronts had been stabilized along the length of the high ridges of the Apennines which Marshal Kesselring had dubbed the Gothic Line. This compressed enemy-occupied Italy between the northern slopes of the Apennines and the southern slopes of the Alps—the Po Valley—within which Italy's major cities and industrial centers were entrapped. This area became the scene of violent conflicts between highly organized clandestine forces and ruthless counterinsurgency forces made up of German and Fascist units that threw the rule books away in order to stamp out the guerrillas.

In the west, the French border was secured by the U.S. Seventh Army forces and the French Maquisards, so that the German forces were bottled up except in the northeast through the South Tyrol and the Brenner Pass. The German-Fascist forces were powerful enough to contain Allied attacks against the Gothic Line; fighting along the entire front dwindled down to company- or battalion-level skirmishes. In this situation, the Fifteenth Army Group headquarters started evaluating the help of the Italian guerrilla forces in a more favorable light.

In order to shorten the distances of the drop zones, the packing station was moved under OSS jurisdiction to the Cecina-Leghorn area, and flights to deliver supplies were moved near the packing station. The necessity of making several other moves also became evident. Company D headquarters was scheduled to move to Florence, where it could be housed in larger headquarters and could be near Fifteenth Army Group headquarters. The Italian SI planned to move from its Brindisi base and use the Siena headquarters to house its staff, whereas the Serraglio installation was to be used as an agent-holding and training area to replace our facilities at Fasano and Ostuni, which were to be closed down at the same time as Brindisi.

In the interim, until a definite date for the move was set, the training and dispatch of SI teams was to continue as scheduled under Mim Daddario who was himself scheduled for transfer to Lugano, Switzerland. There he was to represent OSS Italy and end some of the confusion that had been created by the lack of proper and rapid communications with Allen Dulles and Don Jones.

Company D's move took place in the early part of January 1945. Suhling expanded his staff to cope with the greater workload created by the stepped-up operations. Again, the chronic problem of communications arose as the clandestine traffic from the field increased and new circuits came on the air. In the first week of January, our SI stations transmitted a total of 17,823 five-letter cipher groups, and a large number of courier pouches started arriving via Switzerland and France. This pouched intelligence was immediately processed and translated at Rome; the most important material and maps were rushed by courier to the Company D Reports Board for distribution.

Among the intelligence staff at Company D headquarters provided by SI were Captains Clemente and Uberti as well as several enlisted men. Marcel Clemente attended the Fifteenth Army Group staff meetings as the Company D representative. During this period, the Florence staff was augmented when Captain Arthur Latina, Air Force, was transferred from OSS London. Arthur Latina was to remain at Company D headquarters when Clemente and Uberti would eventually move out to the field to join the Trieste ICU team.

On January 16, in a daring daylight drop, an OG team was parachuted together with supplies to a pinpoint and reception committee provided by SI team "Lobo." Several nights later (January 18), two radios were dropped to "Lobo" for use by other SI teams that had lost their radios as a result of enemy mop up operations. These two circuits quickly came on the air. On the same night of January 18, our SI team "Morristown" was dropped in Piedmont at a pinpoint supplied by "Orange." By January 23, "Morristown" was already transmitting valuable intelligence from the zone.

Major Joseph Bonfiglio of "Papaya," who assumed command when the first segment of that mission was captured by the Germans, started the overland supply of Italian partisan groups during January. With the help of Lieutenant Colonel Carlos Baker, OSS station chief at Annecy, France, some supplies and arms were made available and the first partisan formations from the Bardonecchia Valley, composed of expert mountaineers on skis, came over to France to pick up the supplies. Bonfiglio also sent out a patrol with French troops to meet personnel from the "Orange" mission, which, unfortunately, could not keep the rendezvous. On the return, the French patrol and our "Papaya" personnel got into a firefight with a German patrol, capturing several prisoners and killing six Germans. Our unit suffered no casualties.

In order to reinforce Bonfiglio's unit in the Alps, Colonel Agrifoglio of SIM agreed to provide me with two Alpine officers who knew the terrain well. In January, these two officers were flown to France where they were placed under Bonfiglio's command.

At the request of the chief of MO Italy, SI Operations agreed to distribute MO materials to its teams out in the field. The various missions were asked to monitor the results of the propaganda and provide periodic reports for MO headquarters.

The weather, which is usually at its worst in the Po Valley in winter, suddenly and miraculously cleared during the second half of January, providing us with the rare opportunity to drop 41 planeloads of supplies and arms to the beleaguered guerrilla formations between January 18 and 29. But we also had bad news. In the latter part of January, our "Apricot" team reported that the W/T of "Citron" and one of the key agents of the team had been captured by the SD. However, the enemy failed to find the radio, which continued to be operated by a volunteer recruited by Boeri.

A significant addition to our intelligence operations was made when we finally managed to track down Gastone Famos, a courageous operator who had been originally sent to northern Italy by Andre Bourgoin. Famos, though he had lost his communications equipment and other members of his team, had managed to keep in touch with OSS/ Italy headquarters through other OSS missions. He was finally tracked down by Dr. Boeri, and we began to train and brief a W/T to join him in northeastern Italy.

After a year of operating underground under the very noses of the German and Fascist secret police, it was decided that we should change Dr. Boeri's signal plan. In cooperation with the communications branch, we substituted the "Salem" plan with the "Jolliet" plan in order to maintain the security of our communications. We felt that security might have been endangered by the SD's constant monitoring service and by German cryptographers who carefully followed the clandestine transmissions to break the codes. Dr. Boeri, whose physical description was unknown by either the Germans or Fascists, was one of the most sought-after agents in Milan. A price of one million lire was offered to anyone who could provide information leading to his arrest. This did not deter Boeri from his work in one of the most responsible positions in the entire Italian underground.

The signal from "Wildcat," a new circuit which was to replace our "Lancia" station, was heard for the first time on January 22. "Wildcat" had been sent to take some of the strain from its sister station and immediately started transmitting railroad information which provoked very favorable comments in Fifteenth Army Group intelligence circles. For that matter, Italian SI clandestine field traffic from its active transmitters during the period of January 16 to January 31 had reached the robust proportions of 27,000 cipher groups, with a veritable treasure of highly classified information, operational messages, and military instructions. The total number of operational teams during this month was twenty, four of which were sleepers and sixteen were active.

Thus, by the end of January 1945, with the help of an improved weather pattern, increased field operations, and Company D's improved handling of operational and command functions, the stage was set for the final act of the Italian campaign. OSS could now bring into play the various facets of its hard-learned expertise. Our section would be called on to exert every ounce of effort to guide policy and operations, and anticipate the military needs of CLNAI, AFHQ, and Fifteenth Army Group. A part of this problem was the nagging question of what would happen once German military authority collapsed. Would the left-wing forces agree to stack arms, or would they use those arms to take over the government?

The problem was magnified by two factors that worried Allied planners:

1. Would the Nazis retreat and defend their vaunted Alpine redoubt in Bavaria and the Tyrol?
2. Would the Russians continue their massive westward drive into Yugoslavia and possibly Italy's eastern frontier and Trieste?

If either of these two conditions took place, Fifteenth Army Group could not delay the pursuit of the retreating German forces. Thus, Anglo-American troops could not be spared to handle the occupation of northwestern Italy.

Our intelligence confirmed the fact that the Germans were creating a series of formidable fortifications which they had already designated as the "Veneto Line" to defend the approach of the South Tyrol. This was an indication that Marshal Kesselring, the master of the fighting retreat, intended to take his armies into the redoubt. Our missions sent detailed photos, sketches, and maps of the area as well as its defenses which were immediately delivered to superior headquarters.

The politico-military problems had been discussed in depth with Parri during his visit and were being followed closely by Craveri at Lugano. Although we had absolutely no control over the thinking of the communist apparatus in Italy, we considered it an integral part of Italian political life. I recalled only too vividly President Roosevelt's initial answer to Marshal Badoglio's first appeal. The president advised that Italy must broaden its government to include all colors of the political spectrum. I also recalled Donovan's dictum that all patriot formations which showed a willingness to fight the enemy must be armed without discrimination. I personally believed that Palmiro Togliatti, Luigi Longo, and Giancarlo Pajetta, who had spent years in exile in Russia and to whom Russian was a second language, would follow whatever order Moscow gave, particularly if the Soviet forces gained a window on the Adriatic. Since Tito had his eyes set on Venezia Giulia and Trieste, I did not believe it likely that the Russians would do anything to embarass the Yugoslavs and prevent them from grabbing the main port in the Adriatic and Italian territory. This being the case, I supported the thesis that CLNAI would take over the civil administrative functions of the liberated industrial triangle and that Italy's political future would be decided once the war was over. The agreement recognizing CLNAI as the agent of the Italian government in enemy-occupied Italy had been negotiated by Giancarlo Pajetta (Mare), the communist representative of the mission, who had remained in Rome for this specific purpose.

The polyglot forces that made up the Fifteenth Army Group at this juncture of the Italian campaign constituted an incredible mix of many nationalities and contingents from various parts of the globe. On December 16 General Mark Clark had been promoted to General Alexander's Fifteenth Army Group command, while Alexander had been promoted to Maitland-Wilson's post at AFHQ.

The command of the Fifth Army was entrusted to General Lucian Truscott, a tough commander who had led the Third U.S. Infantry Division's attack on western Sicily and who was highly regarded by the troops he commanded. Clark brought many of his Fifth Army Staff officers with him to his new command, so that the composition and points of view of the Army Group Staff became sympathetic to the U.S. point of view, particularly as General Clark had a high regard for OSS.

By early February, the time had come to close down the SI operations base in Brindisi. Captain Clemente was sent down to make the preliminary preparations and to evaluate the remaining teams being trained. Daddario, who had been left in charge of Brindisi, was preparing to leave for his new assignment to Switzerland and needed a hand in making the arrangements since operations were to continue until the last possible moment.

On February 8, after several months of waiting and intensive training, the "Pomegranate" (Portland) team was parachuted into the strategic Belluno area and on February 13 "Dick" (Anita), composed of three bodies and two transmitters, was dropped to a reception team together with 2,000 pounds of supplies. That same night (February 13), "Franconia" (Elinor), with 4,000 pounds of special supplies, was dropped into the Valtellina area. The CO of the team, an Italian officer, had a multiple assignment and was to prepare a number of pinpoints and receptions for OG missions; contact the important Fiamme Verde guerrilla formations; and obtain intelligence on German defenses in the area that could be used to impair the planned retreat of the German forces to the Tyrol.

February 13 was a busy night, for SI managed to drop "Betty" (Apple II) which consisted of four men and equipment. Between February 1 and February 15, fourteen planeloads of supplies were dropped to our pin-points for a total of 22,226 pounds of supplies to the underground formations.

During the same period, SI agents transmitted a total of 37,000 cipher groups, an increase of 11,000 groups over the preceding fifteen-day period. This was encouraging for the guerrilla formations, which only several months before had been disheartened by General Alexander's glum message.

The skies literally opened up during the last thirteen days of February as, night after night, the Po and Alpine valleys experienced ideal meteorological conditions. Company D's operational personnel worked feverishly as a massive air supply program was carried out to beef up the CLNAI formations to get them ready for the coming rising against the enemy. All operational branches of Company D (SI, SO, OG, and MO) were able to parachute a staggering 778,900 pounds of supplies behind enemy lines in 135 separate sorties.[3] Out of the total, 648,500 pounds were delivered to SI pinpoints, while the rest, 130,400 pounds, were dropped to SO and OG pinpoints. SI Italy accounted for 124 out of 134 sorties. During the same thirteen-day period, radio traffic with the SI teams increased to 41,500 cipher groups, adding vital intelligence to the planning of the spring offense which was underway at Fifteenth Army Group.

On February 19, Mim Daddario arrived at Lugano to take up his new duties as representative of Company D. He and Don Jones, Allen Dulles' assistant, worked in concert to straighten out many of the problems that had plagued the Swiss operations in Italy. A total of 29 SI missions were in radio contact with the base by the end of February.[4] They covered the most important areas of the country north of the Gothic Line, maintaining the only Allied radio communications link between the Allied High Command and the CLN in Milan, as well as the individual partisan formations scattered in both mountain areas and the cities. These radio communication links made it possible to rapidly relay Allied military orders.

On the very same day that Mim Daddario arrived at Lugano, I closed down the Brindisi station and led a long convoy made up of 2½ ton trucks, which had been loaned to us by the Fifteenth Air Force, to Naples and then Rome and finally to our destination in Siena which was to become our final operational headquarters until the end of the war.

SI Command headquarters was located at Villa Poggio in Pini, whereas the training headquarters and staff, which included Captains Sam Fraulino, Seb Passanisi, and Lieutenant Peppino Puleo, were set up at "Serraglio." Puleo was one of the men who had participated in the "Bathtub" operation against Sardinia, and he had recently been commissioned as a second lieutenant. The security of the two villas was assigned to our Italian military guard detachment, whom I had transferred from their post at Ostuni, Fasano, and Brindisi headquarters.

Siena was a relatively short ride from Company D headquarters in Florence, which would make it possible to confer with Suhling and the staff more frequently, as we planned our participation in the final phase of the Italian campaign.

During this period my personal relations with Bill Suhling seemed to deteriorate further, with the respect and trust of the past vanishing. I attributed part of this change to Hollohan's disappearance. Another factor may have been the influence of several southern staff members whom he had brought into the organization and who made no secret of their dislike for Italo-Americans and people of other ethnic backgrounds. Among the group was his right-hand man, Major Judd Smith.

I suspect that Suhling may have believed that I had been somehow responsible for what happened to Hollohan, but he had absolutely no reason for such a belief. But we both realized that the work ahead of us was too important to allow the deteriorating personal relationship to matter. So we met frequently considering that SI was carrying the lion's share of Company D's operational load.

In order to set the stage for the proposed armed uprising, a number of our mission leaders were scheduled to be exfiltrated, debriefed, rebriefed, and then returned to their missions behind the German lines. A number of situations at the French border had to be discussed with Colonel John Riepe of G-3 Special Operations AG, so that policies could be formulated to smooth out relations with the French authorities on the Alpine border.

With the weather in March still holding, we were able to continue our aerial supply program with the dropping of some 175,000 pounds of supplies between March 1 and March 15. Intelligence traffic from our transmitters in the north also increased dramatically as our secret agents and the CLN intelligence services stepped up activities to provide full coverage of the enemy's plans and movements.

OSS operations were increasingly successful: our radio circuits often transmitted messages from Allied intelligence missions that had lost communication with their bases. On March 4, SI provided reception committees for the OG missions "Santee" and "Spokane." The OG unit was designated as Company A 2671st Recce Bn and had established its headquarters near Company D. Their work was detailed and was coordinated with ours. Their operations officer was Captain Albert Materazzi.

Lieutenant Colonel George A. Stapleton, CO, Company A, acknowledged our assistance in a letter:

Both Santee and Spokane missions were dropped to the "Beet" pinpoint on March 4th. Both stations have contacted the base and reported that all personnel had arrived safely.

We wish to extend our gratitude for the splendid cooperation given us by your section in the preparation of reception for these missions. Please extend our thanks to the field stations involved.[5]

The advanced proficiency of our intelligence operations was demonstrated by a request from "Dick" mission on March 8. The call was for a bombing strike against the railroad yard at Lecco, where freight trains were carrying supplies to the German armies at the front. The supply trains were switched at this yard.

On March 10, we received the following message from A-2MATAF:

Regarding S.I. radio "Dick's" request for a bombing of the freight yards in the RR station at Lecco, it has just been reported that these cars were attacked, sixteen of them were destroyed and damage was inflicted on two others and three locomotives.

The following day "Dick" reported that during the February 9 bombing of the Lecco railroad station, one locomotive and twenty-two cars loaded with material had been destroyed. The operation clearly demonstrated the great value of ground spotting and confirmation by on-the-spot agents and the close collaboration between the Air Force and OSS.

On March 1, the "Boston" mission, which was selected and briefed by Mim Daddario in Lugano, came on the air for its first contact with the base. It was planned to move this mission in the area of Verona where some key German commands were located. On March 5, the "Montreal" team made its first contact via its own radio. This team had originally been infiltrated as team "Locust" by boat from Corsica, but, owing to the loss of its radio, had been reporting with its own ciphers via Dr. Boeri's facilities in Milan.

One of the most important events of early March was the arrival of the "Orange" mission leader Marcello DeLeva ("Leccio"). DeLeva was an Italian Air Force officer who was also a first-class engineer with wide and important connections in the industrial community in Piedmont (which included Fiat).[6] The intelligence he transmitted had been given the highest rating by AFHQ and Fifteenth Army Group whose G-2 and G-3 officers were very anxious to talk to him in person. Accordingly, conferences were arranged with both headquarters and the Twelfth U.S. Air Force. During one of these meetings, Colonel John Riepe discussed the patriot situation in the Piedmont. When the meeting was over, Riepe assured him that supplies would be made available to all patriot formations that were sincerely willing to fight the enemy.

One of the priority items discussed at Twelfth Air Force was Fiat's probable manufacture of jet-propelled fighter turbines and the possibility of securing plans and prints of the top secret and revolutionary engine. DeLeva had excellent connections at Fiat, whose management collaborated with the Italian underground. The work on the turbines was reportedly under the strict supervision of the German military.

DeLeva's assistant, Italian Air Force Lieutenant Riccardo Vanzetti (codenamed "Renato"), was also an engineer and, since parachuting behind enemy lines, had shown a superior aptitude for irregular warfare.[6] Renato had assumed command of the Fifth GL Alpine Division in the Monferrato area. He revolutionized the pattern of irregular warfare by creating a fluid pattern of action whereby many nuclei composed of 20 to 30 men would come together at a given moment to attack a target while other units created diversions. In one single attack led by Renato, almost all the stock of ballbearings, valued at 100 million lire, was destroyed by his unit at the RIV plant (Italy's most important ballbearing manufacturer).

The Action party of Piedmont, which rated Renato's unit as one of the best in northern Italy, pointed out that the 5th Division was constantly at work sabotaging the enemy's communications lines. Renato was later given operational control over all units in the area and organized the First Mobile Operational Group which undertook large-scale operations against the German-Fascist forces in a major city.

A serious problem which we inherited when we began our work on the Franco-Italian frontier was the French officers' resentment of the Italians. This strain was the result of Mussolini's attack against France and the Italian occupation of southern France and Corsica which followed the Franco-Italian armistice. The feelings were most discernible in the border area between France and the Aosta Valley—a beautiful Alpine area of majestic mountains and lovely valleys at the extreme northwest frontier.

We had sent an officer from the Italian General Staff, Major Augusto Adam, to the OSS station at Annemasse to help Colonel Baker deal with the situation involving about a thousand Valdostian partisans who had been driven out of the valley by German troops and had sought refuge in France. There the DGER (Direction General des Etudes et des Recherches) assumed a revanchist attitude because the DeGaulle representatives had presented a petition from the people in the valley to have the territory annexed to France. The CLN delegate, Dr. Eugenio Dugoni, went to Annemasse in an attempt to handle the question on the diplomatic level with the help of Colonel Baker. Parri and Pizzoni, who at this time were returning to Milan via Switzerland, stopped at Annemasse and left instructions that a policy of friendship was to be followed with the French, despite the fact that the DGER might be tempted to send in French forces in the event of a German withdrawal. Their orders were that, in the event the French Army attempted to occupy the valley, the partisan formations should withdraw to the Canavese region rather than risk armed confrontation.

Major Adam was sent into the valley with autonomist leader "Mesard" (Captain Cesare Olietti) as part of the mission; the French objected preferring that "Mesard" head the mission. We thereafter recalled Major Adam to SI headquarters to discuss the situation. Mesard volunteered to come south with Adam. Mesard's position was clear. He was not seeking independence for the Aosta Valley, nor was he seeking French annexation. He wanted autonomous status for the valley within the framework of the new postwar Italian state.

Eugenio Dugoni, the CLN delegate, was also invited to come to Siena to discuss the situation. On the arrival of the group in Siena, a conference was held at Fifteenth Army Group, and the entire situation was reviewed. With Colonel Riepe's concurrence, Major Adam, Mesard, and a W/T were to be sent as a mission to assume the command of the partisan forces in the entire Aosta Valley for CLNAI. The mission was codenamed "Mohawk."

Although the preparations and training for the mission were left to SI Italy, the mission was not to come under the OSS's jurisdiction. This decision was designed to eliminate any possible diplomatic pitfalls when the Germans withdrew from the area and the territory's administrative jurisdiction might become a matter of Franco-Italian contention. The "Mohawk" team was to be parachuted to a pinpoint and reception committee provided by Lieutenant Aldo Icardi, who had already been behind the German lines for many months.

At the beginning of March, word out of Milan, Switzerland, and headquarters indicated that elements in the German High Command were making serious efforts to negotiate a peaceful retreat or surrender.[7] This news was not surprising in view of the almost untenable situation which the ever expanding, ever bolder operations of the underground forces and the massive supply drops carried out by SOE and OSS in February, had created in northern Italy.

The sudden evacuation of most of the Po Valley had received priority consideration in our intelligence plans for some time. It served as the basis for the formation of special city teams that could be ready at a moment's notice to be dispatched and help to take over the administration of the cities evacuated by the Germans. "Papaya" had been dispatched as one of the advance groups in September 1944, and part of the mission was successfully operating under Bonfiglio's command.

In my reports to Suhling and Glavin, I had covered our plans extensively, and on various occasions I had discussed the details with them. One report stated:

Extensive plans are being drawn up to cope with an eventual German withdrawal or collapse in northern Italy. These plans provide for the immediate dispatch of competent officers and men to the larger Italian cities. Their principal objects were:

    a. The seizure of important documents and arrest of suspects;
    b. Regrouping of teams now operating in the field;
    c. Preparation for groundwork for intermediary intelligence phase.

. . . .

Teams will be sent to Genova, Venezia, Torino, Trieste, Milan and Bologna . . . it is anticipated that some S.O. personnel will be made available in case of German collapse . . . the bulk of the personnel will be provided by S.I. . . . the future relations between S.I. and X-2 have been considered. With the advance movement into northern Italy, S.I. will, at the request of X-2, undertake some of its work . . . it is being planned to drop 2 X-2 agents to an S.I. reception committee to be provided by "Baldwin" [Dr. Boeri].

Two S.I. missions are being prepared for the Bolzano area: Lorelei and Brunhilde, both being led by German speaking mission leaders. Since this area is under a German gauleiter, the population is German-speaking and is considered the core of Austrian revanchism, both teams will have radio communications with headquarters.[8]

The report then went on to list the personnel that would be assigned to each city team, their targets and their logistical supplies. These missions would be bolstered by our personnel who were already on mission in various areas of northern Italy, together with their nets of agents and subagents.

In preparation for such a quick move, I issued orders that the briefing and training of the city units should proceed under the direction of Captain Passanisi and Lieutenant Puleo at the Siena station. I then notified Scamporino in Rome to send some of the Italian democratic political leaders to Siena by April 2 to be integrated into our teams. Because these men (such as socialist leader Giuseppe Romita and communist Giancarlo Pajetta) were part of the CLNAI underground, it was essential that they rejoin their colleagues. It would make the OSS task a little easier to have their support.

I made provisions for an SI rear echelon unit that was to remain with Company D in Florence under the direction of Captain Arthur Latina.

Captain Passanisi was to remain in charge of the Siena station and prepare quarters and debriefing facilities for the teams returning from the field.

During the period from March 1 to March 15, field transmissions increased to 59,458 cipher groups, of which 51,383 were incoming intelligence and 8,075 were outgoing military orders and operational messages. The tempo of our aerial supply drops was maintained with a total of 174,944 pounds of arms and equipment being dropped to SI pinpoints and reception committees. Active SI key teams responsible for intelligence and operational activity totaled 29 separate missions and transmitters. News of our teams that were no longer active was received from various sources and their files were updated.

The questioning by X-2 of a recently captured SD agent who had been operating in liberated Italy shed some light on the whereabouts of Captain Rossoni, the courageous leader of our "Pear" mission. The SD agent revealed that Rossoni was arrested by Zanni of the SS, who upon searching Rossoni's house found his radio. Rossoni refused to incriminate anyone and accepted full responsibility. Although he was the only one who knew the code, he would not use it to save his life. Rossoni's wife and sister were also arrested. Zanni, evidently much impressed by Rossoni's courage and patriotic convictions, rather than having him tried by a military tribunal assigned him to forced labor at Bolzano. Upon hearing this news, we made an attempt through Daddario and Don Jones in Switzerland to negotiate his release in exchange for some important German prisoner. Unfortunately, the effort got nowhere. We later learned that he had been transferred to Methausen where he was seen by Corporal Biagioni, whom we were also attempting to exchange.

Among the many reports which Dr. Boeri transmitted during March were a number of messages from Major Max Salvadori of SOE who had recently been sent to Milan but did not have a radio to communicate with his headquarters. Salvadori used the nom de guerre "Major Max." These messages were duly delivered to No. 1 Special Force (SOE's designation in Italy) and continued to be transmitted through our facility for some time.

By early March then, OSS Italy was ready not only to continue its intelligence work and coordination of the activities of the underground forces, but also to provide the personnel and expertise to guide the smooth transfer of power from the enemy's control to the interim Allied and Italian governing authorities.

Chapter 19

The Arrival of Spring

With the arrival of spring, the twilight of the vaunted Nazi military power was reaching its final phase as Allied armies hammered from the west, the east, and the south, and rained death, fire, and destruction from the heavens over the German homeland. There would obviously be no letup in OSS operations if U.S. and Allied casualties were to be kept to a minimum.

Our troops, which had dug into the sides of the Apennines in order to survive the harsh winter snows and cold, were coming out of their lairs and preparing to attack the last strongholds of the Gothic Line. From their mountain positions they could readily see the medieval city of Bologna and the Po Valley.

In order to exert greater pressure on the enemy, we continued to drop supplies to partisan bands, changing the composition of the container contents to reflect the immediate medicinal and food needs of the bands and the villagers who supported them. Between March 16 and March 31, we managed to drop 170,000 pounds of supplies to SI pinpoints, despite the bad weather.

Resistance was mushrooming in all parts of Italy as more arms became available and the youth of the land were caught up by patriotic fervor to liberate their land and bring German and Fascist atrocities to an end. The collection and transmission of intelligence continued apace, with some 800 messages being received from the field missions, totaling some 75,000 cipher groups in less than two weeks.

On March 21 our "Franconia" mission received the ALO (Allied Liaison Officers) team "Offense" and a British mission at the "Chard" pinpoint. Both teams were extremely impressed by their efficient reception. The patriots had used a field which was crossed with high-voltage wires. The wires had been taken down for the drop, and afterward they were restrung on the poles.

" 'Offense' wired the base . . . may plan to leave a member of our team when we go south. Send a few submachine guns on next trip . . . we have high regard for 'Franco' (the Franconia mission leader)."

The quality of the intelligence transmitted by Dr. Boeri demonstrated that he had managed to effectively penetrate the German command.[1] On March 17, he reported that Marshal von Runsted was about to be replaced by Marshal Kesselring. The official announcement of the change was not made public until March 22 by the headquarters of the German Twenty-first Army Group in France. This announcement clearly indicated that Hitler was nearing the end. Boeri also advised us of the appointment of Colonel General von Vietinghoff as supreme German commander in Italy some days before the official announcement was made by the Oberkommando der Wehrmacht (OKW).

Our activities report covering this period noted that much of the intelligence material coming through pouches from Switzerland and bearing a Berne code number originated with our own SI sources in German-occupied Italy. These sources simply found it less dangerous and more expedient to pass the material over the Swiss border rather than through the lines. Some of the sources identified were Citron, Apricot, Locust, Sauk, Gastone, Feltre, Como, Savio, and Zucca.

Comments from the field about our activities were always of great interest, such as a note sent by a Captain H. Boutigny, British SOE, who was attached to one of the guerrilla formations in Piedmont, complaining to his headquarters that "regretted Americans lavishly supplying Renato who distributed only to GL formations at the moment. This and the fact that American teams in general do not seek to work through Committees, as we do, produces comment and impression that GL is backed up by Americans. This is another fact weakening the power of central authority." What Captain Boutigny obviously did not know was that we were responsible for fully supporting the CLNAI and then helping it to extend its control, and that we were carrying out Donovan's orders to supply any unit that was willing to fight the enemy. Captain Boutigny just happened to be working in one of the areas where our people dominated the situation.

At the end of March, Dr. Boeri, our key agent in Milan and director of the underground intelligence, was accidentally arrested by the enemy security services. Luckily, they did not identify him as the person on whose head they had placed a million lire reward. Our contingency plan immediately was activated. Tullio Lussi ("Landi"), whom we had sent with "Mangosteen," automatically took charge of the operations at CLN with Professor Maiga ("Cassini"), another SI agent, as his deputy.

Boeri's arrest was of only short duration: his brother, Renato, who led one of the bands in the Mottarone area, effected his release on April 7 through an exchange of prisoners with the Fascists. All the same, Dr.

Boeri could not go back to Milan; for security reasons he had to remain with his brother's guerrilla band until the uprising in Milan.

In spite of the extremely heavy security measures, I surmised that some high-level meetings were being held in Switzerland. For a long time I had known that one of Allen Dulles' goals was the negotiation of a possible German surrender through some of his German contacts, but Donovan had applied the brakes against such unilateral action for fear of possible repercussions from both Britain and Russia—not to mention the White House.

Had a surrender in Italy been broached with the proper military authorities even in early March 1945, it might have shortened the war in Europe by several crucial months, saving thousands of lives on both the eastern and western fronts. There was never any German military consensus for such negotiations, however, even though Himmler, Kaltenbrunner, and other SS elements had sent out unsuccessful feelers. General Cadorna himself had received offers from SS General Karl Wolff to negotiate.

Thus, military plans forged ahead, and the top Allied command proceeded with meticulously crafted plans to take Bologna, break out in the Po Valley, and destroy Vietinghoff's forces before they could withdraw to prepared defensive positions protecting the southern approaches to Hitler's national redoubt. Disregarding all rumors and reports, we went ahead with plans to carry out a series of missions considered vital to the concluding military phase of the war in Italy. We continued to drop supplies from the air, with our own pinpoints receiving another 135,000 pounds of medicines, foodstuffs, and ammunition between April 1 and April 15.

On April 1, Scamporino and I met with General Cadorna and Ferruccio Parri in Rome. They had come south through Switzerland and France in order to determine the role CLNAI would play in the final phase of the military operations. They had already met with Marshal Alexander and AFHQ officials at Caserta, including Colonel George King, chief of special operations, G-3. Parri, who had been arrested in Milan soon after his return from his mission to liberated Italy in December, had not, at first, been recognized by the Germans. While searching his house, however, they found all the evidence they needed to identify him, and they decided to hold him for safekeeping against a rainy day.

Through a number of intermediaries, General Wolff got word to CLN that a deal to free Parri was possible, but the organization, afraid of negative Allied reaction, turned the offer down without officially submitting it to us.[2] In early March, when the same offer to negotiate the surrender of German forces in Italy was made to Allen Dulles by Baron Parilli, an Italian businessman, Dulles requested that Wolff, who was the SS chief in Italy, free Parri and Major Toni Usmiani as a gesture of good faith.

Parri and Usmiani were freed and were brought to Switzerland on March 7 and 8, when a preliminary secret meeting took place between General Wolff and Dulles. This meeting had the tacit approval of AFHQ, which kept in touch with the situation through OSS Caserta headquarters, which, in turn, relayed information to Fifteenth Army Group through Suhling and Company D in Florence. These negotiations, which seemed to have a life of their own, with ups and downs on both sides and in which AFHQ representatives participated, were almost abandoned and were the subject of terse exchanges of notes between Stalin and Roosevelt.

General Cadorna and Parri were the guests of our headquarters in Siena during their stay. I took them to Company D for a round of meetings with Suhling and the staff. Later, we proceeded to Fifteenth Army Group together with Major Alex Cagiati and a representative of SOE, where a long conference was held with Colonel Riepe for approval of the plans the partisan bands were to implement. The two CLN representatives were then taken for a personal conference with General Alfred Gruenther, Mark Clark's chief of staff.

The following day, April 5, Cadorna and Parri were guests of SOE for most of the day. According to reports of the meeting, Major Vincent, one of the key SOE officers, indicated that SOE was miffed that we had monopolized the guests for most of their visit and conferences. (This situation must have been particularly galling since the SOE had originally sent General Cadorna on mission in an effort to counterbalance our own influence in CLNAI.)

With the essential meetings over, Parri and Cadorna were in a hurry to get back to Milan, for one of the key individuals left in charge had been caught by the Germans and events were rushing to a climax. On April 6, they left to return to Rome and German-occupied Italy.

This same urgency to get back into action convinced Dr. Eugenio Dugoni, the CLN delegate, to get back to Piedmont by the shortest possible route: via parachute. Dugoni, without the benefit of any parachute training, decided that he would jump in. Though no youngster, he was a man of undisputed courage and dedication. His mission was code-named "Doughnut" and was flown for the first time on April 9 to a reception by our "Orange" team, but unfortunately there were no light patterns or signals on the ground and the aircraft had to return to the base. A few nights later, the operation was put on the board again, and Dr. Dugoni jumped into the dark to carry out the directives to handle the Franco-Italian relations in the most diplomatic manner. He had been preceded by the "Mohawk" mission on April 6, which also jumped with little or no training into Val D'Aosta. Adam and Mesard had been joined by a third Italian General Staff officer, Major Pistocchi. Their communications link to our headquarters in Company D were to be later provided by our "Strawberry" mission.

Two other critical SI missions were dropped into their operational zones early in the month. On April 4, "Grape II" was parachuted to a pinpoint provided by "Franconia" in the Friuli region, right in the contested area on the Yugoslav border. The mission leader, Santini, had done an outstanding job leading previous SI missions.

On April 5, Christopher de Hartungen and his "Norma" mission were parachuted into the Trento-Bolzano area, one of the most dangerous operational zones through which the German armies were to withdraw into the proposed redoubt. At the same time, we parachuted the radio for the "Lorelei" mission which was to operate under the direction of Gastone Famos. De Hartungen was an Alpini captain who had led our "Fig" mission in January 1944 and had returned through the lines in October. I spent a lot of time discussing the situation in the Bolzano area which had been incorporated as part of the Greater Reich and which was a hotbed of Austrian annexationist agitation, as well as anti-Italian feeling.

De Hartungen was one of the officers whom SIM had early on made available to us, and he had created a network that was placed at the disposal of CLNAI. While Cadorna and Parri were in Siena, they met with him to discuss ways of handling the situation in the area as there was a possibility that the pro-Austrian groups were planning to eliminate the leaders of the Italian minority. The captain also had an opportunity to confer with Colonel Agrifoglio and Lieutenant Colonel Massaioli of SIM to give them his appraisal of the situation.

On April 9, with the arrival in Florence of "Giorgio" (Aminta Migliari), the partisan to whom the immediate security of the "Mangosteen" mission had been entrusted by Major Hollohan, I had my first opportunity to talk to someone with firsthand knowledge of the major's disappearance. Giorgio, a lean man with a razor-sharp profile, thin drawn lips, and piercing black eyes, would certainly not have been my choice for such a delicate assignment. He obviously had the cleverness to operate in a clandestine environment and the ability to survive in enemy-occupied territory. He had assisted the mission through the establishment of an intelligence chain known as SIMNI, which sent its voluminous reports through Lieutenant Icardi's "Diana" and "Westwood" circuits and pouched its reports through the Lugano office.

Before debriefing Giorgio, I carefully studied the reports which Icardi had pouched through Switzerland. In addition to the written reports, there was a map of the Lake Orta area where the attack that led to Hollohan's disappearance had taken place. After studying the documents, I asked Giorgio to write a report on the events that had transpired. He set to work immediately so that when I returned to the villa from Florence that night, I found his report ready. The report included a map of the area, which was similar to the one we had received from Switzerland. After reading the text and comparing the map, there was no doubt that both reports were written by the same person. This fact was not in itself remarkable since Giorgio was in charge of the safety of the mission. When I mentioned the similarity of the reports, he readily admitted having written the first report and drawing the map.

After the report was translated, I gave a copy of it to Suhling with the suggestion that a request be made through the International Red Cross to find out whether Holohan had been captured and was in a prisoner-of-war camp. My own impression was that the security of the mission had been lax and that inasmuch as the mission had operated in military uniforms, it should have been attached to one of the partisan bands in the area. Several of these bands were operating nearby in the Domodossola and Valsesia area. This would have minimized radio transmission exposure, and there would have been no need to move the mission in a thickly inhabited area.

I do not know if Suhling ever attempted to get any information about Hollohan through the Red Cross, or how Hollohan's absence was recorded in the regimental records, but I do know that as a result of the incident the relationship between Suhling and myself kept deteriorating. When the rift finally came to the attention of Colonel Glavin and General Donovan, the general talked to me about it during my visit to the Florence headquarters. Shortly thereafter, they informed Suhling that he was being promoted and that they would send him as a military advisor to Allen Dulles.

The impending offensive to break the Gothic Line was imminent, and events remained at a standstill as we prepared the city teams, awaiting the German collapse. On April 11, the SI detachment in Siena participated in the formal presentation of decorations to four of our GIs who had performed outstanding work behind enemy lines as members of the "Date" and "Arctic" missions. Colonel Glavin traveled from Caserta to personally decorate Sergeant Albino Perna, W/T of "Date"; Corporal Carl Bova, W/T of "Arctic"; and Corporal Chester Maccarone, mission leader of "Arctic." Three of these men participated in the ceremony in which Captain Donato Petruccelli, adjutant of Company D, read the citations and Colonel Glavin pinned the Legion of Merit on them. The fourth man, Corporal Maccarone, was on mission.

Through radio "Brutus" and by pouch, I gave Captain Daddario instructions to cross the frontier once the uprising of the patriot forces got underway. These orders were to move to Milan and take Mussolini as a prisoner of war and then to set up headquarters and immediately establish a liaison with General Cadorna and CLNAI as the official U.S. Army/OSS representative. Instructions were sent by radio to Lieutenant Icardi, who was in touch with Cino Moscatelli's Valsesia Division, to be ready to move with this important Communist unit to Busto Arsizio, Novara, and from there to Milan where he could join forces with Daddario.

It was clear that only meager Allied forces could be diverted to northwestern Italy. The preponderant strength of the Fifteenth Army

Group would be concentrated to cut off German forces south of the Po, capture Verona, Venice, and Trieste, and drive up the Brenner and into Austria to deliver the final blow to Nazi Germany. The military vacuum in the Piedmont, Liguria, and Lombardy areas would have to be filled by the guerrilla forces under Volunteers of Liberty Corps (CVL), the regional committees of the CLN, and the OSS and SOE missions and officers operating behind the lines. Instructions were prepared for all mission leaders to continue intelligence transmissions until the city teams arrived to take up their positions. At that point, the teams were to make themselves available to the OSS senior officer in the city. In view of the necessity to be on the spot as soon as possible, I planned to parachute into the San Siro race track, together with some of the younger members of the Milan city team.

While pressure was building up for the final phase of the campaign, the preparation of further paramilitary and offensive intelligence operations was put on hold. The entire effort of OSS/Company D was concentrated on conducting a massive antiscorch campaign designed to prevent the Germans from destroying the country's industrial establishments and hydroelectric and power-generating facilities; to preserve its art and cultural patrimony; to end unnecessary destruction; to secure enemy stay-behind agents; to arrest war criminals; and to locate documents vital to future intelligence operations.

These objectives were outlined in a briefing paper which I prepared and which was distributed to all members of Company D missions scheduled to be sent to the field.[3] The basic instructions and objectives of the organization would therefore be uniform. The briefing papers also sought to establish facts regarding the economic needs of the various areas and to provide information on which long-range Allied plans for the postwar reconstruction of the country could be formulated.

While the city teams awaited their call in the Siena area, a group of select political leaders convened at our Serraglio training station. They were to undergo a training program so that they could join the teams and help to administer and pacify the regions evacuated by the enemy. These men were dressed in U.S. uniforms so as not to arouse the curiosity of the neighborhood or attract the attention of the enemy's counterespionage people.

By mid-April, some members of the SI teams who had been operating behind the lines started filtering through the battle lines on the way to our headquarters. As they crossed the lines, X-2 and CIC were alerted and were sent to Siena for debriefing. On April 21, after a sharp attack by the U.S. Fifth Army forces, the Poles and strong partisan formations, the city of Bologna fell. On the right flank, in the Lake Comacchio area, the Eighth Army struck hard and debouched through the strategic Argenta gap in a pincers movement that was coordinated with the Fifth Army's assault on the city of Massa, thus trapping large numbers of the Germany Army Group C before it could cross the Po River. The operation was eminently successful, and the bulk of the Fifteenth Army Group headed for Verona and Trieste.

Major Tarallo and the Bologna city team followed, making their way through the almost totally demolished villages of the Futa Pass. On arrival in Bologna, he quickly set up our headquarters on the outskirts of the city.[4]

Reports from the field indicated that the various regional committees had given the signal for a mass uprising and that the German and Fascist units were reacting in a confused manner while withdrawing from the western regions of northern Italy. Many of the units were out of touch with their headquarters at Fasano, while the scarcity of fuel hampered the movement of their motorized equipment.

The entire German military position was disintegrating before our very eyes. I requested permission to carry out my jump into the San Siro racetrack so that I could render immediate assistance to the CLNAI, but Caserta had changed its mind and felt that for security reasons I should wait for the situation to stabilize and then proceed overland.

After sending the signal to Daddario at Lugano to move south to Milan, I left Siena at the head of an armed convoy for Bologna to join Tarallo and try to get to Milan as soon as possible. We stopped briefly at Company D headquarters in Florence to read some of the incoming "traffic" from the various SI missions in the field.[5] We also sent out last-minute instructions to the mission leaders who were moving with the partisans to interdict German troop movements and take over the towns and cities. I instructed Captain Latina to transmit all priority messages to our field radio which would keep us in touch with headquarters during our trip to Milan, where, on arrival, we would set up a regular communication schedule. Latina was also instructed to transmit priority intelligence to Caserta and Washington without delay.

Soon after our arrival in Bologna, a delegation from the family of Leandro Arpinati came to our headquarters seeking help.[6] Arpinati had been a minister in Mussolini's first government in 1923, had dropped out of Fascist politics in 1932, and had been sentenced by them to forced residence. Signor Arpinati had been gunned down in cold blood by unknown partisans shortly after the Allied forces passed his property. He had been sprayed with machine gun bullets fired from a motorcycle sidecar. The members of the execution team had threatened to shoot anyone who helped the family to bury the body. The family did not know whom to turn to for help, so they came to us. Tarallo and I left immediately in two jeeps with an escort. When we got to the farmhouse, we found the body of the heavyset Arpinati lying covered on top of an improvised pallet. Lifting the cover, I could see that he had been dead for some time and that he had been peppered with machine pistol bullets. The body needed burial without further delay, and we got word to the CLN to provide protection for the family.

It was ironic that Arpinati had been killed in such a manner after he had refused to collaborate with Mussolini and, according to the family, he had actually provided a hiding place on his farm for several Italian officers from SIM who had been working with British intelligence. The crime could only be attributed to personal vendetta rather than political motive. In the confusion and lawlessness of the moment, there were many such cases in Italy.

After returning to our Bologna headquarters, I decided to lead the convoy with the Milan, Turin, and Genoa teams as soon as possible through the battle lines. Meanwhile, our radio station was receiving the most critical news from our various teams in northern Italy. On April 25, all of the major cities were up in arms hampering enemy troop movements and blocking Fascist troops within their own compounds. The best German divisions were disintegrating under the blows of the combined Allied attacks and guerrilla onslaught.

On the morning of April 26, I was advised that Daddario had crossed the Swiss frontier into Italy with a small armed group and was heading for Como. I had no way of reaching him until he arrived at Milan and he contacted our mission there. Having completely briefed him on the objectives of his mission, we knew that unless something unforeseen happened he would carry out his important assignments, chief among which was the capture of Mussolini.

Mussolini's own indecision sealed his doom when, at a meeting held on April 25 at Cardinal Schuster's office, a meeting called to negotiate with General Cadorna and the CLNAI, he found out that General Wolff had been negotiating behind his back with Allen Dulles in Switzerland for the surrender of the German Armies in Italy. Crying out that the Germans had betrayed him, he left the meeting in anger, promising the Cardinal that he would return within an hour. From that moment on, he committed one error of judgment after another until finally he decided to leave the city with a number of his ministers and take refuge in the Valtellina near the Swiss border. There a large number of Fascist troops were supposed to converge to put up a last-ditch battle. The Duce's convoy left Milan and headed for Como, where it arrived the same evening. Seven hours later Mussolini decided to proceed to Menaggio, while Marshal Graziani remained in Como and penned a message authorizing the Germans to represent him in surrender negotiations with the Allies.[7] Daddario's official report detailed his important mission:

My reasons for going there were to discuss the segregation of German troops which were garrisoned there, to prevent Partisan and German activity from commencing at a definite hour which had been set by the partisans, and to take Graziani, Bonomi and Sorrentino with me as I had received information that they were hiding there. My reasons were to prevent open conflict and needless loss of life at a time when there was no further need for combat since such a conflict, if commenced, would probably continue until the arrival of Allied troops and would necessitate the need of their action and expenditure of life. My desire to take Graziani prisoner was that he still was of intelligence value, being in command of the Ligurian Army.

I approached the Villa Locatelli with Lt. Bonetti of the Partisans under a white flag and was admitted, stating that I was an American officer. The villa was well armed and all men were at their posts waiting for the Partisan attack which was momentarily expected. I had previously told the local CLN what my plans were and the reasons behind them and they agreed to back me to the limit. Captain Felter who was C.O. at the Villa stated to me that he would not surrender to them, and that he had received strict orders to that effect. After a long discussion it was agreed that:

A. All German troops would remain segregated until Allied troops would arrive, at which time they would be completely disarmed and brought to the rear;

B. That they would consign immediately three-quarters of their arms (this was requested as I could not ask them to be completely disarmed as I could not guarantee them protection from Partisan attacks);

C. That Graziani and party were to be my prisoners;

D. That the hospital at the villa would continue with German personnel, would not be attacked, and the 200 wounded at the station would be moved to the hospital with Partisan protection.

During all this time the German troops in the Villa had direct telephone communications with General Leyers in Como under whose command they were.

I left Cernobbio with a convoy of five cars and about ten armed men. Graziani was in the lead car with Lt. Bonetti and myself. The other prisoners were disposed through the other vehicles. We stopped at Como where another tempestuous situation presented itself as German armed soldiers were about to provoke a general disturbance. I went to the Committee and told them that I was going to see General Leyers, if possible, for the purpose of segregating all troops in the city until the arrival of Allied troops and they agreed to give me all the help necessary. I went to the main entrance of the stadium in Como and there I stated that I wanted to see Leyers. After some delay I was admitted and conferred at length with him. It was agreed that:

a. All troops in Como would remain in the stadium until the arrival of Allied troops;

b. Three-quarters of their arms would be placed immediately in trucks for delivery to Allied troops;

c. Partisan guards would be regularized and would properly patrol at a certain distance from the stadium so that no undue incident would occur;

d. That all troops under Leyers in the Como area would likewise remain segregated until the arrival of Allied troops.

The hospital situation was again gone over in detail and Leyers agreed that such action on the part of the Allies was to be appreciated. As I was not able to be present when Allied troops arrived, I left Larry Bigelow to explain the situation to the first American forces that arrived in town. On arrival of these troops everything went off as planned according to a report received by Bigelow a few days later. A report on this situation is now being prepared by the Committee of Liberation of Como and will be forwarded when received.

With the convoy now composed of six cars we headed for Milan at about 2300 hours of the 26th. All road blocks were successfully negotiated and Milan was entered without incident. Upon entry, however, we were immediately attacked by unknown elements with automatic fire and though we passed, three cars were lost. All three cars that broke through were hit in several places; however, no one was wounded. The other three cars were recovered next day with all hands safe.

Since it was known that all Fascist groups had not as yet been eliminated, I decided to form a barricade so that we could resist any attack until daybreak when we would surely be able to explain our situation to the Patriots in case we were being attacked by them, or to expect assistance from them in case our attacks were from Fascists. The three cars were then drawn into a secluded area and all men were placed at strategic posts. A new development immediately presented itself, however, when we were challenged by someone who spoke German. I immediately replied in Italian that I had come to talk to his commanding officer, if he were a German soldier, as I figured that Germans were in a talking rather than fighting mood, which was not the case with the Fascists. After a great deal of haranguing, I was asked to wait a reply, and shortly afterward was conducted to the Hqs. of Colonel Rauff, C.O. of all SS and Police troops in Liguria, Lombardy, and Piedmont and part of Emilia, at the Albergo Regina.[8]

The situation in Milan at that moment was one in which all German troops were barricaded in several establishments in Milan where they had orders to resist all Partisan activities. The main German installations were at the Albergo Regina, Piazza Brescia and the telephone exchange. General Vening was technically in command of all Wehrmacht troops while Colonel Rauff commanded the SS and police units. These Germans were at the time of my arrival faced with a systematic activity on the part of the patriots of neutralizing the smaller German strongholds. Because of this, their position was precarious as they had orders to surrender only when ordered by Allied troops and not to Partisans.

At the Albergo Regina I spoke to Colonel Rauff in the manner as I had with General Leyers. I told him that I would do everything possible to keep conditions in the city at a status quo until the arrival of Allied troops. If I could so arrange matters he would come to terms immediately with such troops so that there would be no resistance whatsoever. He stated that he could not at the time give a definite answer because he had orders to fight and would follow those orders until he received notification from General Wolff, who, he said, had gone to Switzerland to discuss peace terms with Mr. Dulles. Since he had received no word, and because Wolff had said that he would return to Northern Italy immediately, Rauff felt he could not act. It was therefore agreed that I would return the next day for further discussion.

I went immediately from the Albergo Regina to the Commando Generale of the Committee of Liberation and discussed the whole situation with General Cadorna. He agreed that everything possible should be done to prevent fighting within the city but felt that it would be difficult to accomplish this as various Patriot leaders had already planned attacks on the larger German installations. He said that the only terms could be immediate surrender on the part of the Germans to the Partisans. He agreed that further fighting would be disastrous since the Germans were extremely well armed and since the fighting was not necessary at the time. The only danger which presented itself was notification that various German troops were converging on Milano from Torino and that these troops would certainly give assistance to the Milano garrisons if they ever arrived in the city. It was agreed however that General Cadorna would come with me the next day to the Albergo Regina to speak with Colonel Rauff.

The next morning I was called on the telephone by Colonel Rauff who requested that I come to the Albergo Regina immediately. When I arrived a long general discussion followed wherein it was agreed a meeting be arranged that afternoon between Col. Rauff, General Vening, General Cadorna and myself at the Albergo Regina. I immediately contacted Cadorna and went over the whole situation with him. At that time the Partisan leaders were terribly worried about the German troops outside the city of Milan, and wished to take immediate action against all German troops in the city so that there could not be help given from within. It was agreed however that the German forces outside Milan had very little chance to reach the city since they were facing resistance in every sector by both Allied and Partisan forces, yet, there was an element to be considered and a solution to counteract these forces was necessary. It was finally agreed to present Col. Rauff and General Vening with the following proposal:

a. Col. Rauff would go with me outside of Milan to stop all German forces which were pointing towards Milan. If Col. Rauff agreed to this, Partisan activity against German forces in Milan would cease immediately. The Partisans would then set up a guard to prevent escape of individual Germans, if attempted, until the arrival of Allied troops. On the arrival of our forces the Germans would immediately give up all arms and come to terms.

b. If Col. Rauff and General Vening did not agree to the first proposal they would then give up all arms immediately and become prisoners of the Partisans.

c. If they did not agree to either of the above proposals they would immediately be attacked by Partisan forces then situated in Milan.

After a great deal of discussions, Col. Rauff and General Vening agreed to aid in whatever manner possible the proposal as outlined in (a) above. In short, to attempt to neutralize German forces then converging on Milan and to remain isolated within their present establishments until Allied troops arrived, at which time they would surrender without any resistance. The agreement was reached just before Moscatelli arrived in Milan with 1500 Communist Partisans for the purpose of reducing the Albergo Regina and other German installations. The result of such an action would have been general German resistance in the whole city with loss of life, destruction of public property, including the telephone exchange, and, most likely, control of Milan by Communist forces. The accord which had been reached had the approval of the Committee of Liberation, including the Communists, and was strictly adhered to from that moment until the arrival of Allied troops.

11. On the afternoon of April 28th, Col. Fisk representing Gen. Grittenberger of the 4th Corps, arrived at the Albergo Milano. I explained the situation then existent in the city and he officially accepted the surrender of all SS troops from

Col. Rauff. We then went to Piazza Brescia where Gen. Vening officially surrendered all Wehrmacht troops.

12. During all this time Marshal Graziani, General Bonomi and General Sorrentino had presented difficulties of their own. I had kept them under strict guard at the Albergo Milano and had utilized a Matteotti brigade headed by a Partisan friend. All had gone well until the bodies of Mussolini and the other Fascist leaders were brought to Milano. Immediately thereupon the cry arose in the city for Graziani. As he was my prisoner it was my duty to protect him until he could be turned over to the proper Allied miltary authorities. I had in fact received a wire over the Brutus radio that he was wanted by the 15th Army Group and that I should deliver him to a bomber which they were ready to send. Since the Albergo Milano was not protected enough I desired to have the three men brought to San Vittore, where protection could be guaranteed. Another reason for my desiring this was that the Matteotti brigade then guarding Graziani for me had issued an ultimatum that I turn him over to the Committee of Liberation for their action. I went to see General Cadorna and explained the situation to him. I requested his aid and told him that I could not turn Graziani over to anyone but Allied authorities. He agreed to do everything possible to help me. A conference was then called of all the representatives of the CVI and it was decided that they would allow Graziani and the 2 Generals to be brought to San Vittore. General Cadorna agreed to go along with me for the protection that his personal presence would give.

The group of 3 was then transported from the Albergo Milano to San Vittore under the protection of the Matteotti brigade and a unit of the Val Toce Division. The only undue incident was an explosion which occurred within the car which was assigned to transport Graziani to San Vittore. As a result of this explosion Lt. Bonetti was badly wounded and has lost the sight of one eye and is in danger of losing that of the other.

13. When Col. Fisk came to Milan he brought with him orders to evacuate Marshal Graziani. The imprisonment of Graziani had occurred on the morning of the day in which Col. Fisk had accepted the surrender of the German troops in Milan. I told Col. Fisk that the situation was very delicate but that I would do everything possible to deliver Graziani to him. I also requested that he take Gen. Bonomi and Gen. Sorrentino with him if it could be arranged since they would suffer if Graziani were withdrawn and they were not. Again I went to General Cadorna for assistance. When I arrived he was in conference and when I explained my situation he told me that the meeting he was then attending was to form a tribunal for the adjudication of Graziani. He agreed that this was irregular and told me that I had his approval to take Graziani and the other two Generals out of San Vittore, but that I had better do it immediately. I then went to San Vittore with a closed car and the three jeeps which Col. Fisk had brought with him to Milan. Col. Fisk had agreed to let me handle the whole situation and gave me his entire cooperation. At San Vittore I went to the warden and told him that I was taking out my prisoners and that I wanted him to come with me for assistance. He fortunately had not received orders to the contrary and did not object. Graziani, Bonomi and Sorrentino were in 3 separate cells and I went to each of them and advised them to get dressed immediately as we were leaving the prison. I then brought them from their cells to the closed car which was backed into the main entrance of the prison and with the 3 jeeps as escort drove towards

the Autostrada for Bergamo. Several kilometers outside of Milan the prisoners were transposed to Col. Fisk's jeeps and were brought safely to 4th Corps Headquarters then situated near Bergamo.

14. On April 30th the evacuation of German prisoners in the city of Milan began. At 4 o'clock in the afternoon I was asked by Col. Fisk to meet General Crittenberger together with General Cadorna at the outskirts of Milan, before the entry of American forces. General Cadorna and I were thus presented to General Crittenberger who thanked us both for the conditions which Col. Fisk had found in Milan. He stated that the work done in the city before the arrival of the troops was greatly appreciated by him. It was on that afternoon that American troops came to Milan for the first time in force.

Leaving Bologna in the armed convoy early on the morning of April 29, we took the Via Emilia northward to Modena and thence to Reggio Emilia. As we drove through the villages and cities, we could see groups of partisans who had been left in control by the rapidly advancing Allied armies. Many of the guerrillas, boys in their early teens, were busy rounding up stray German soldiers who had been overlooked by the advancing Fifth Army units. The youthful age of these partisans did not portend well for the prisoners of war, for these kids had itchy trigger fingers.

As we passed Parma and headed toward Piacenza, we knifed through German units which were moving aimlessly, fully armed, making their way to prisoner-of-war areas. The people of the villages whom we met en route came out in force to welcome us with flowers and huge signs. They cheered us in great jubilation as we were the first U.S. troops they had seen. By the time we got to Piacenza, the partisan units became more numerous, the welcoming crowds more vociferous, and the damage from aerial bombing heavier. We knew that our engineering battalions had passed us as we crossed one Bailey Bridge after another. These bridges temporarily replaced the permanent ones that had been blown up either by the partisans to impede the German withdrawal or by the Germans to impede the Allied advance.

When we crossed the Po at Piacenza on a long pontoon bridge, we saw that both banks of the river were pockmarked by innumerable bomb craters, indicating the effort the U.S. Twelfth Air Force had made to knock out the important bridges before the Germans could get across. They succeeded. While we were making our way to Milan, a great deal had happened. We were apprised of events through our contacts with the base and through the Milan radio which the CLN had taken over.

On April 26, Mussolini left Como and made his way to Menaggio. Then on April 27, he was stopped at Musso, where a German unit was obstructing the narrow road that followed the steep banks of Lake Como. The delay led to the recognition and arrest of Mussolini and his chief ministers by the partisans. He was taken to Giulino di Mezzagra for safekeeping where he and Claretta Petacci spent the night in a humble farmhouse. On the morrow, April 28, Walter Audisio and Aldo Lampredi representing the CLNAI, arrived on the scene and in the afternoon executed both Mussolini and Petacci, carrying out the orders they had received. The rest of Mussolini's party was executed en masse in the town square of the village of Dongo. The electrifying news soon spread to the populace which had been subjected to the extreme cruelty and bloody abuses of the SS, the Black Brigades, and other repressive Fascist organizations for over eighteen months. They rejoiced that their long ordeal was finally coming to an end and that peace was only a few days away.

On April 27, Daddario was already in Milan and had established contact with General Cadorna. When Walter Audisio was sent on the special mission to pick up Mussolini, he used an identification document that was signed by Daddario to facilitate his mission. Since Daddario was the Allied officer officially accredited to CLNAI, he had been asked to sign numerous documents of this type. He was not aware, however, that Audisio had received orders to execute Mussolini or that Lampredi, who was vice chief of the communist Garibaldi Brigade, was going along with him.[9] The National Liberation Committee had been told that Mussolini was to be captured alive and turned over to be tried by a high Allied Tribunal.

On April 29, the bodies of the executed Fascist leaders, including that of Claretta Petacci, were brought to Milan and placed on display before thousands of Milanesi at Piazzale Loreto—strung up by their feet at a gas station. Thus, in the same metropolis where in 1922 he had successfully thundered his challenge to the constitutional monarchy, his body went on display suffering the abuses and mockery of a people that, following years of anguish and its own abuse at Fascist hands, had lost its civility.

For us, the last 30 miles to Milan were like the triumphant entry of an army. Hundreds of people gathered at the side of the highway and through the streets of the various towns, believing us to be the vanguard of the Allied forces. I could see Giancarlo Pajetta, standing upright at the back of one of the jeeps, giving the public the clenched fist salute of the Communist party. I could also see the broad smile on Giuseppe Romita's face as the people greeted our motorcade in a wild display of exuberant applause and shower of flowers, as though our convoy were the advance guard of a newly found freedom.

In the afternoon of April 29, we entered Milan and drove to Via Manzoni, to the staid old Hotel Milano—a landmark of Milanese life, where Giuseppe Verdi lived the last days and hours of his life. Mim Daddario had requisitioned the hotel as the OSS headquarters. It was guarded by the members of a socialist Matteotti Brigade, some of whose officers had come from Switzerland with him. Within its walls were many distinguished and infamous involuntary guests who had fallen into our hands. With the thirst for revenge not quenched in the ranks of the underground, they constituted a serious security problem.

Daddario and Icardi greeted us enthusiastically with a joyous hug in the very middle of Via Manzoni. We quickly went into the hotel to review the situation with Scamporino, who had decided to join our party at Bologna, and Lieutenant Colonel Ricca, whose mission was to proceed to Turin. We went over the most immediate problems and reviewed the roster of prisoners who were being held in the various rooms. I also made plans to interrogate the key prisoners without losing time. Scamp and Mondo immediately set to work to review the political events that were shaping up and to evaluate some of the problems AFHQ had foreseen about the political and economic instability of the north Italian industrial triangle. They scheduled meetings with Romita, Parri, Longo, and other political leaders.

One nagging question that remained was what to do about the Communists who had played a key role in the armed uprising and whose leaders, Palmiro Togliatti and Luigi Longo, were considered tough negotiators. The British had always believed that the Communists and left-wing forces would take over the government by force and that the Garibaldi Brigades would not give up their arms when called on to do so. Although there were hard-core Communists who thought in such terms, they were isolated by the Moscow-trained leadership which was content to bide its time. They were not ready to have an armed confrontation with the Allied troops in Italy, especially the American forces.

Although the major crisis had passed, sporadic fighting was still occurring in various areas of Milan. To the west of the city there was a powerful German force whose armored units were reported to be moving on Milan to retake it from the partisans. Within the Hotel Milan, it had been necessary to post guards to watch the partisan guards, because outside pressures were being exerted to kill or kidnap some of the prisoners who were considered war criminals. As a matter of principle, we did not want to be a party to summary judgments that would lead to execution by firing squads. There was enough of that activity going on outside of our jurisdiction, and the cemeteries were full of unidentified bodies—a product of the lawlessness that is an inevitable part of any popular rising.

In between tending to more pressing problems, I started to look over the lists of prisoners who were under our protection. Among the names was that of Fascist Minister of the Interior Guido Buffarini-Guidi, who had been caught at the Swiss border with a big satchel of cash. The cash had been turned over to the Como CLN, and the minister had been turned over to our custody. He had barely missed the shooting party at Dongo. Buffarini-Guidi, the head of the repressive police system of the post-Armistice puppet Fascist regime, had refused to lift a finger to aid the 335 patriots and victims who were killed by the SS at the Ardeatine Caves as a reprisal for the March 23, 1944 bombing of the German mess hall at Via Rasella in Rome.

When I asked the guard to open the door to his room, Buffarini was busy talking to his roommate, Angelo Tarchi, the industrial production minister. Both men stood at attention when I entered the room, wondering who I was, and what was going to happen next. Both were nervous, but Buffarini was almost to the point of a nervous breakdown, aware that he was a first-class candidate for a partisan firing squad and that the CLN was clamoring to get its hands on him.

Both prisoners were perceptibly relieved when, in Italian, I explained why I was there. After sparring with them for a while, I assured them that nothing would happen to them as long as they were under our protection. I did not minimize the danger or pressures that were being exerted to secure their release to Italian government justice.

Next, I had the guard bring in paper and pencils, and I asked them to write reports covering the last 30 to 40 days of their ministries. Relieved at being given something to do that might help their case, they immediately set to work to write lengthy reports. From my short stay with them, I judged Tarchi, a professor, to be a gentleman of even temperament and dignity, whereas Buffarini seemed to be disturbed by his past. He apparently felt that he was close to meeting his Maker—and found the prospect terrifying.

During the day members of the SI teams that had been operating in the area kept coming in to report and receive temporary assignments in the Milan area. John Ricca and his Turin city team, which was made up of several enlisted men and noncoms and four civilians, left to set up their headquarters and help the Committee of Liberation in Piedmont which was having problems with the French in the Alpine valleys connecting Italy with France.[10]

As night fell on Milan, we began to shore up our defenses in the hotel in the event one of the partisan units should attempt to force our hand to give up the prisoners under our protection. Our information was that certain people wanted us to give up Buffarini, Tarchi, Count Thun und Taxis, Max Knipping, and several officers of the French Blue Legion and of the Guardia Nazionale Republicana (GNR).

Among the prisoners were a number of German women and an elegant French woman who had followed a Vichy minister. When she asked to share the minister's room, I assented, knowing no good reason why I should say no, considering the difficult days that lay ahead for them. (Finally, they were destined to be turned over to the Free French.) Among the German women, most of whom were civilians, was one who had been living in Como and had been caught by the rising in Milan. She claimed to be the wife of a Hamburg industrialist and to have come to Italy for reasons of health. She spoke English and Italian fluently and was of a superior cultural level to the other German girls who had come to Italy for reasons of work.

Around nightfall, a dispatch rider from one of the partisan units defending the western approaches to Milan, came to our headquarters with the alarming news that a major German Army unit was threatening to move and take over the city as they did not want to surrender to the partisans. Since the German general had asked to parley with the Allied command, CLNAI asked that we send an officer to negotiate with the Germans.

Daddario and I left immediately with a small escort of partisans toward Porta Magenta. The city was enveloped in darkness, and no one dared to move about the streets for fear of being ambushed. Suddenly, at the intersection before Porta Magenta, all the overhead spotlights went on and a score of heavily armed partisans jumped out of the darkness pointing their Sten guns at us. We stopped. When they were finally convinced that we were U.S. officers, they pointed the way to Magenta and described the partisan command post that we were looking for as a schoolhouse. We continued on our trip until another partisan patrol stopped us and directed us to the schoolhouse up a side road.

When we got there, we were met by the partisan commander, a young bearded giant, who told us that the German unit, which was of divisional strength, was surrounded by his men. When I asked how many men and what kind of armaments he had, it became obvious that there was only a thin line of irregulars between us and the enemy. Thus, if the Germans wanted to move towards Milan there was little in the way to stop them—especially with their superior armor and firepower.

We asked the commander to send out scouts under a truce flag to inform the Germans that U.S. officers were on hand to negotiate their surrender. We waited in the schoolhouse for a reply. In one of the classrooms under the watchful eye of several partisan guards were about 20 or 30 teenagers locked up as prisoners of war. Some of them could not have been any more than ten years old. They had been members of a Fascist Black Brigade and had been rounded up after a firefight with the partisans.

In another room were several officers of the Black Brigades, pacing back and forth in the confinement of their classroom prison.[11] Since the door to the classroom had glass window panes, you could see what was going on inside the classroom. Suddenly we heard a loud thump coming from the room. Hearing a second thump, we ran to see what was happening, and looking in we quickly discovered the reason. The Black Brigade commander, a middle-aged, balding man with a rodent-like profile, was attempting to commit suicide by running from one end of the room and banging his head against the stone wall, which was now splattered with blood. Finally, a couple of other prisoners held him down until the guards could enter the room and restrain him. The man kept muttering and shouting to let him alone as he preferred to die this way rather than face the partisan firing squad that was awaiting him.

The Black Brigades had been used primarily as a repressive force and had themselves carried out hundreds of summary executions against members of the underground. Now that their roles were reversed, the

Black Brigades commander could expect little mercy from the guerrillas, especially since he was an officer. Rules of war do not stand up well in the conduct of guerrilla warfare or in the extraordinary defensive measures that have to be adopted to carry out counterinsurgency.

The return of the truce emissaries called our attention to the problem that had originally brought us to the outskirts of historic Magenta.[12] The Germans had received the partisan truce team courteously and had assured them that they had no intention of moving from their positions until a unit of the Allied armies arrived. They would keep their arms and would surrender them to the American forces, after which they would march off to the prisoner-of-war camp. After admonishing the partisan commander that the truce should not be violated unless the Germans started moving toward Milan, we promised that we would urge the Milan CLN to immediately send reinforcements to hold the position.

On our return to the Hotel Milano, I reviewed our situation with Scamp, Daddario, Icardi, and some of the civilian experts we had brought to Milan.

Industrial leaders were already putting in requests for coal and other raw materials to keep industry moving and people working, but little could be done about that problem at the moment. Since the head of AMG, Colonel Charles Poletti, was in Milano, some of the information was turned over to his office, including Tarchi's analysis of the industrial situation and a list of raw materials needed by Fiat which had been prepared by the office of Ing. Vittorio Valletta, general manager of Fiat.

Poletti had arrived in Milan shortly after our convoy. The gruesome scene at Piazzale Loreto had now been cleaned up, and the bodies been given a hasty (and secret) burial. Charlie was still accompanied by Lieutenant Colonel Orfeo Bizzozerro, who was the sanitarian and health officer of the AMG District. They set up shop and started to work with city and provincial officials designated by CLNAI to restore order.

An important part of our mission was to lay the groundwork for the smooth transition of power. This task necessitated that we keep in touch with all the partisan armed units and provide for their eventual disarmament. It was not easy, for at both the western frontier with France and the eastern frontier with Yugoslavia, partisan forces were close to blows with the French Army and Tito's partisans.

The "Secret Surrender" negotiations between Allen Dulles and General Wolff in Switzerland were by now an open secret. Our "Norma" mission in Bolzano was transmitting appeals from General Vietinghoff to General Clark to send emissaries to Bolzano to accept the surrender of the German Armies in Italy. The negotiations between Vietinghoff and DeAngelis, the CLN president, at Bolzano were being assisted by our mission leader Captain Chris De Hartungen, who kept headquarters advised of all the events taking place in Bolzano and the Alto Adige area. The situation was all the more astounding because the secret negotiations between Wolff and Dulles and AFHQ had been going on since early March.[13]

It was obvious that Wolff's ideas had been thwarted only by the fact that, by the time the Germans got their act together, the war in Italy was practically over and organized German military resistance had totally disintegrated.

Why had it been necessary for Dulles and OSS/AFHQ to waste time sending a radio operator codenamed "Little Wally" to Wolff's Bolzano headquarters, when we already had "Norma" in place? It was incomprehensible.

The Bolzano area, where most of the German forces that had not been immobilized or forced to surrender had retreated, was still considered part of Germany and was ruled by Gauleiter Hofer. In addition, the area had a strong anti-Italian movement propelled by Austrian nationalists.

On May 1, "Norma" transmitted its message No. 15:

Have established contact with DeAngelis and Franco of the Alto Adige CLN who have just arrived bringing priority message for General Clark rpt Clark from Gen. Vietinghoff rpt Vietinghoff. DeAngelis and Franco awaiting reply at our CP. Will be on the air every hour. For Gen. Clark: We have been negotiating with Gen. Vietinghoff C.O. South Tyrol Army GP. We have agreed in principle on the control of Bolzano and Merano. The reason for our initiative is to avoid conflict between Italians and Alogeni (German-speaking native population). We believe that it is absolutely necessary to have your designated plenipotentiary present. Please advise CLNAI and Gen. Fiore. Let us have your answer. Your representative can reach an understanding with Vietinghoff. A plane can land at Bolzano airport at 2100 hours. Signed Bruno DeAngelis, Pres. CLN, Alto Adige.

A little later in the day another message arrived:

Our mission has been officially recognized by the Bolzano CLN and the German Command. This evening a preliminary agreement with SS Brigadier Fuhrer General Brumer has been reached that there will be a cease fire tomorrow morning at 5 a.m. until such time as General Clark's representative arrives to negotiate unconditional surrender with South Tyrole Army GP. You can transmit through us the name of General Clark's representative.

These messages continued to arrive from "Norma" in Bolzano to Company D headquarters and OSS Caserta, but those in command paid little attention. [14] Busy with the extraneous details of the "secret" surrender, they failed to effect the linkage, and I was not informed.

In Milan, we had our work cut out for us as we started implementing the counterespionage phase of our mission. From the beginning, we had attempted to give X-2 a hand in the theater, realizing that they were short of personnel. During the Sicilian campaign, we had been instrumental in getting X-2 representatives admitted to Seventh Army jurisdiction, despite the active opposition of the CIC people who claimed to have overall responsibility for counterintelligence work. After our transfer from Palermo to Brindisi, we had little contact inasmuch as we were away from the front which, in the early days, was in the Cassino area. Gradually, as the OSS buildup in Italy developed and more X-2 personnel became available, we started security clearances for our prospective agents through X-2.

With the fall of Rome, our advance parties with the special Intelligence Collection Units were constantly on the lookout for counterintelligence material that could be operationally useful to X-2 and CIC. We continued to cooperate wholeheartedly with CIC because its presence was pervasive on both the combat fronts and in the rear echelon areas. Our X-2 had been patterned somewhat after MI5, which had also provided X-2 with some training as well as a part of its registry information bank.

In setting up the intelligence service for CLNAI, a great deal of attention was paid to counterintelligence work. Our "Apricot" team, which for a long time provided both the direction and the sinews of the partisan information networks, issued a weekly *Counter Espionage Bulletin* covering all enemy-held territory and including lists of defensive and offensive school trainees and agents. Copies of these bulletins were immediately made available to X-2, so that it could add the names of hundreds of enemy agents to its files and could work with CIC, the British, and Italian counterespionage organizations to apprehend enemy agents operating behind our own lines. At one point, we even offered to drop X-2 agents with our teams in northern Italy, but no such combined operations were ever carried out.

When Lieutenant Jim Angleton was transferred from Britain to Italy in charge of X-2, he broached the idea of some cooperative undertakings. I was gratified by his intense interest in the work. I had known his father from the early days in OSS Washington and had seen Jim himself on and off since his stay at our headquarters in Palermo. From the elder Angleton I had learned about their long residence in Italy, where the father had been the head of the National Cash Register operations until Italy entered the war.

At one point, young Jim asked if any of our teams had been captured and were being worked by the enemy. I told him that one of the missions we had inherited from Bourgoin was still being operated by the SD and that we were continuing the contacts in an effort to prolong the life span of the operator whom the Germans had coerced into collaboration. When he asked to handle the traffic with the "Maria Giovanna" mission, I agreed on condition that I continue to review incoming and outgoing traffic. He agreed and was given a free hand.

With the Italian campaign coming to an end, he came to see me at the Hotel Milan where I placed him in contact with the counterintelligence section of the CLN headquarters. I spoke to Boeri about having his people collaborate fully with Angleton and X-2 and turning over any material of value to X-2. I also told Jim that I was starting to interrogate some of our prisoners and that when I had completed the report I would give him a copy.

That same day I talked to Buffarini about his written report, pointing out his neglect of several areas of interest. When I asked him point-blank where the files of the Internal Affairs Ministry of the Fascist Social Republic at Salo were located, he immediately drew me a map of where they could be found. Then, to my surprise, he voluntarily disclosed the location of the files of the Armed Forces Ministry and the Ministry of Foreign Affairs. Without wasting any time, I sent "Ike" Icardi in charge of a truck convoy to Lake Garda to pick up and return the documents to our Milan offices. Within two days we had the files in our possession whereupon we transferred them to our Rome office which started to process them. (Angleton later claimed the credit for the intelligence haul as one of his great coups.)[15]

By now, Buffarini was gaining confidence about his future. During one of the interrogation sessions, he implied that if I would help him escape to Switzerland, he would make it worth my while, for he had a lot of money in Swiss banks.

Answering that his proposal was an error in judgment on his part, I also told him that the CLN was intent on trying him for war crimes. As long as he was our prisoner, however, the rules of war would be observed, although I could not guarantee his ultimate fate.

I also carried out long interrogations of some of our other "guests," including the first secretary of the Japanese Embassy in Berlin and his assistant, who claimed they had come to Milan to buy rice. Both of them would spend their time relaxing in their pajamas. As soon as the guard opened the door to their room, they would both jump up and bow deeply and reverently. One of them had brought along his violin and was often heard entertaining himself and his roommate. I suspect that their move out of Berlin was permanent because the temperature in that city was too hot—why else bring the fiddle on a rice-buying trip? To their ultimate relief, since both of them were diplomats they were turned over to the Army, which quartered them in the diplomatic holding area at Chianciano, Tuscany.

One of the partisans who had joined Daddario on his trip from Switzerland to Milan was a frail youth, Johnny Segre-Reinach, a surviving member of a distinguished Jewish family in Milan that had been practically exterminated by the Nazis. Johnny was about twenty years old and had been active in the resistance movement as a courier between Lugano and Milan. Since the age of six, he had been afflicted with diabetes and needed insulin injections daily. Even though the danger of diabetic shock was ever present, adding to the already dangerous risks he was taking, he pursued his work with the resistance.

The Segre-Reinach family had a lovely villa atop the mountains overlooking the Swiss border in the village of Lanzo d'Intelvi. Johnny therefore had a thorough knowledge of the border. This knowledge was extremely useful in establishing the courier route that kept vital information moving between Milan, Switzerland and AFHQ.

In the first few days we were in Milan, some of the resistance units were given a free hand because of military priorities. Many innocent people were killed in personal vendettas; some partisan leaders had become so accustomed to living in a climate of lawlessness that their own version of justice was allowed to prevail.

On the day of the uprising, the cemetery in Milan was full of unidentified corpses, as were the cemeteries in the neighboring towns. Youthful firing squads meted out "justice" rapidly. Due process had no meaning for people whose families and comrades had fallen prey to the "justice" meted out by the SS and the Fascists. Some notorious Fascist officials were reported to have been executed as many as five times in various areas of the country—obviously all of them innocent victims of mistaken identity. Fortunately, this state of affairs ended when the CLNAI and AMG began to function smoothly, and normalcy was rapidly restored.

Word came from Turin that the French, whose forces were penetrating the Val d'Aosta, were making life difficult in other areas for the CLN and other Italian government officials. We therefore sent Icardi to Turin on a special counterpenetration assignment which would give us foreknowledge and help avoid a showdown between the Italian and French. "Ike" Icardi, who had done some outstanding work for OSS during the Italian campaign, created an intelligence network in the Val d'Aosta which kept AFHQ and our State Department fully informed of events days in advance of their occurrence. The intelligence he uncovered helped to avoid a clash with our French allies and put to rest any French revanchism for the Aosta Valley.

We did not do as well in the Trieste area where the British Thirteenth Corps, spearheaded by Fryeberg's New Zealanders, had tactical control over the territory.[16] Our mission, denied entry into the city, was forced to set up at Udine. This mission was headed by Marcel Clemente, whose brother Egidio we had transferred to the MO branch where he had done an outstanding job. Both brothers had been born in Trieste when that city was part of Austria, and they belonged to an ardently irredentist family who favored annexation by Italy.

Marcel had worked for one of the large New York international banks, and, although he was old enough to have a son in the U.S. Army, he himself had volunteered for dangerous service in the OSS. Marcel had handled traffic from our field agents, most of whom he had personally known. Later, as our operations grew, I had appointed him intelligence officer to Company D in Florence, where he had attended the G-2 staff meetings at Fifteenth Army Group as OSS representative.

Despite our pressure at AFHQ, the British absolutely refused to have our OSS teams enter the Trieste city area which was being hotly contested by Tito's Fourth Yugoslav Army. The Yugoslavs, went on a rampage, disarming all Italian patriot forces and occupying practically all of Venezia Giulia. They also made life miserable for the British forces which held only strong points within the inner city.

Our Trieste team also included Captain Bruno Uberti, a U.S. Medical Corps officer whom I had recruited in Washington and who had worked with Clemente for many months over the interpretation of field messages from our agents. Bruno, whose original family name was Huppert, was born in Trieste and graduated from the Medical School at the University of Bologna. Because both of his parents were of Jewish extraction, he left Italy in the late 1930s when the Fascist racial laws were promulgated. Clemente and Uberti, with the other members of our team, could have made substantial contributions to the problems that plagued the Anglo-American command in Trieste. But perhaps British intelligence did not want to precipitate a confrontation between OSS and Tito.

Italian SI recalled only too well the intransigence of the Yugoslav Partisans in mid-1944 when U.S. Sergeant Albino Perna and Corporal Valeriano Melchiorre from our "Date" team were detained, arrested and threatened with execution for operating in Italian territory. "Date" operated behind enemy lines for a number of weeks until the personnel were taken prisoner by the Partisans from Primorsko Korpus, held incommunicado, mistreated, threatened with execution, and finally became the subject of heated exchanges which reached the highest military and diplomatic levels. At that time, since Tito considered all territory east of the Tagliamento River to be under his jurisdiction, he was adamant that Allied secret missions operating in the territory could function only with his absolute sanction. Being aware of the edict, early in January 1944, I attempted to obtain Marshal Tito's permission to put teams in their drop zones with his help by infiltrating them through Partisan-controlled territory.

Together with one of my officers, Captain Edward Baransky, I made several trips to Bari to talk to Makiedo, Tito's commissar in Bari. I had met Makiedo when he first arrived in Brindisi in November 1943 and had put him in touch with the OSS Balkan desk in Bari. During our discussions, I asked his assistance in getting the missions through Yugoslav territory. He replied that he would send a message to Tito's headquarters to ask that permisssion be granted. The route worked out was through the island of Vis from where the partisans could help the agents reach their destination. Toward the end of January, after having waited three weeks for an answer from Tito, we gave up on getting his help with the projected infiltration. I thanked Makiedo for his cooperation and went on to work out plans for direct infiltration of the three teams destined to be dropped into the northeast area.

Why the British kept our OSS City team out of Trieste was never fully or satisfactorily explained. It was an action that rankled a long time with Major Clemente, who wrote me several months later

I guess you learned by now the story of my city team and the swift kick in the pants we got from our cousins. Was and still am very much upset about the matter, more so as we had our heart set and prepared for two years to do a first class job in standing with S.I. tradition. The latest developments, however, are to a certain extent vindicating us from what I consider an unjust and arbitrary action on the part of our "pals."

The confrontation between the Italian and Yugoslav partisans; the takeover of the territories at Italy's eastern frontier; the international tangle over the port of Trieste, all are part of the historical record. And all could have been avoided if wise policy decisions had been made (notably, united Allied action instead of dissension).

OSS had earned the right to expect the minimum collaboration from Tito in order to carry out its work of assisting the various underground movements in areas bordering on Yugoslavia. In fact, this was one of the items of discussion during General Donovan's talks with Tito and Brigadier Fitzroy McLean, the head of the British mission to Tito on August 10 1944, when it was agreed that a U.S. mission would be sent to the island of Vis (Tito's headquarters). Heading the mission was Colonel Ellery Huntington who, in the early days, had commanded the Fifth Army unit at Salerno. Donovan asked that the U.S. mission have parity standing with the British and Russian missions. One of the specific items on the agenda was Yugoslav assistance to enlist "the Marshal's aid in the penetration of enemy countries in furtherance of intelligence activities." (2677 memo #J-010-815, August 11, 1944).

The "Date" and "Plum" missions provided prima facie evidence of what the democracies could expect from the old-line Communist leaders who were coming into power in Eastern Europe.

Major Clemente's final report as leader of the Trieste mission was made on June 16, after the team was recalled from Udine. It was brief and to the point:

C. Trieste (Udine) Base Report
1. This team was assigned to the Venezia Giulia and Trentino areas of North Eastern Italy. It was briefed to collect documents and intelligence and to report and appraise the political situation there. The personnel included two U.S. officers, natives of the region, fluent in the local dialect, thoroughly familiar with the political and economic situation and having several important Italian and Slav contacts. The team was attached to "S" Force and was to enter Trieste.

2. On May 2 it arrived in the suburbs of Trieste. The British military authorities, however, would not let the team enter the city except for 3-12 hour passes granted between the 10th and 29th of May. In the meantime, the British intelligence teams and Italian teams, under British control, were operating in the city of Trieste. Our team was ordered to remain west of the Isonzo River. Overcoming these difficulties, the team did

establish contact with the numerous Italian and Slav political leaders in Trieste, Udine, Monfalcone and Gorizia. Reports were made on the political, economic and sanitary situation in Trieste and Friuli. Battle order data was furnished at the request of 15th AG and II Corps (US). The G-2 of II Corps was highly pleased with the intelligence furnished and formally expressed his appreciation.

3. On the 14th of June, the team received telegraphic orders to return to its base and on the 16th it reported to Siena.

The Genoa team, under the guidance of Major Bonfiglio, tackled the work with the assistance of all the teams that had been dropped into the Liguria area. Bonfiglio had originally infiltrated several of these teams by PT boat from Bastia. Some of the personnel had been exfiltrated and then been parachuted back in.

Johnny Menghi, the leader of "Youngstown/Melon," had been captured by the SS, but, fortunately, he was able to escape and make his way across the border at Ventimiglia at about the time of the "Anvil" landings in southern France. He had hidden maps showing the Axis defenses of the Ligurian coast. Upon meeting Bonfiglio, they both went back to the area and, at great personal risk, retrieved the maps he had left behind. Copies of the maps provided to G-2 Seventh Army and to Fifteenth Army Group were found to be highly useful. Air photos confirmed all of the fortifications and gun emplacements marked on the maps.

Genoa had been the first great city to signal the rising of the anti-Fascist forces in the north. The Germans were planning to blow up the important port infrastructure and to sink ships in the harbor before they evacuated the city. The CLN not only made it impossible for the German troops to carry out their program of destruction by having shipyard workers disarm many of the carefully laid charges, but it also prevented the German troops from moving about the city by laying siege to the barracks and buildings in which they were quartered. Finally, they were forced to surrender.

The advance nucleus of the "Gamble" mission (Genoa Team), made up of enlisted men equipped with radio, arrived in Genoa on April 30. Major Bonfiglio, who was at Station 'F' in France, arrived in Genoa on May 2. The station closed down on May 17.

On May 5, Luigi Longo, leader of the Communist forces in northern Italy, whose position in the CLN was parallel to Ferruccio Parri, invited all of the SI staff to a dinner at the Garibaldi Brigade headquarters in Milan. On hand for the occasion were Lampredi, Giancarlo Pajetta ("Mare"), who had come with our convoy to Milan; Cino Moscatelli, the commander of the Valsesia and the Valdossola Garibaldi divisions which had successfully fought both the Fascist and German forces and had prevented them from destroying the vital hydroelectric installations in the area; and other Garibaldi Brigade commanders and officers, many of whom had been fighting for the better part of two decades in foreign battlefields and in the Italian underground.

The dinner was Longo's way of expressing his thanks to OSS and the United States for the arms and supplies they had been receiving during the many months of guerrilla warfare when the odds seemed impossible. Some of our missions had worked for long periods with the Garibaldi units, and we had arranged OG personnel drops in various areas to work with their units.

Captain Icardi's mission in the Novarra-Busto Arsizio area had worked closely with Moscatelli, whose units were outfitted and disciplined almost as well as regular troops. During the victory parade held on April 30, they had made a tremendous impression on both the military and civilian population in Milan.

Despite the misgivings of some of the top brass at AFHQ and at Whitehall, at war's end, the Italian Communists did not attempt to take over the government, nor did they refuse to turn over the bulk of their weapons once the war was over. In fact, from the time of Togliatti's return to Italy, when Badoglio was still premier, their policy in Italy was one of conciliation to the status quo. This approach fit in with their long range plans of strengthening their party through control of the labor organizations, cementing their pact with the Socialists through Nenni, and biding their time for the takeover of the government once the Allies had left Italian soil.

The early postwar schism within the Socialist party raised havoc with these long-range plans and made it possible for DeGasperi's Christian Democrats to win the 1948 election and exclude the Communists from active government participation. (The schism was financed by Luigi Antonini's labor organization, ILGWU Local 89, to break the Socialist-Communist Unity Pact.) In 1945, however, the Communist party boasted of controlling the most powerful partisan formation in the Italian underground. Had it chosen to follow a path of resistance and refused to stack arms, it could have created a grave problem. This is not to say that a percentage of the weapons and ammunition were not squirreled away in some mountain hideouts for possible future use, but theirs were not the sole partisan formations that resorted to hiding some of their armaments.

The wisdom of the long-range policies which Italian SI had formulated and implemented in working with a number of top political leaders paid handsome dividends for the long-term plans of the democratic political forces. They created the favorable climate for the ascendancy of U.S. influence in postwar Italy. In addition to Italian SI contacts with the Italian democratic parties, within the OSS Fifth Army unit a small cadre made up of former members of the Lincoln Brigade had been created. These men, who had earlier fought in the Spanish Civil War, had participated in early OSS operations in Tunisia and had established a working relationship with Donald Downes who took some of them with his detachment to Salerno.

In the ensuing internal OSS struggle for control of Italian operations, Lieutenant Irving Goff, the leader of this group, was tabbed by Captain Andre Pacatte to form an intelligence chain, with manpower provided by the Italian Communists. When Pacatte was recalled to Washington, Goff's group continued its work with the Fifth Army detachment. Goff even made several trips to our base in Brindisi, and we dispatched some of his agents in one of our submarine missions.

General Donovan though aware of the political leanings of these men, was appreciative of the work they were doing to help build up the resistance and to procure intelligence through their contacts. While they may have used their communications links to transmit some messages from Togliatti to Communists in the north, their communications channels and ciphers were controlled by OSS headquarters. If standard monitoring procedures had been exercised, the radio messages could have been sanitized in order to avoid violations.

The work of this group produced good results and may have helped to tranquilize Togliatti and the Italian Communists as to the sincerity of Donovan and the OSS to singularly pursue the Allied goals of defeating the enemy. Donovan placed no restrictions on Goff and his companions, considering them just another segment of the OSS operation in Italy.

Upon the liberation of Milan, General Donovan, in gratitude for CLNAI's assistance to OSS, ordered two planeloads of scarce medical supplies flown to Milan. The supplies arrived on May 3, and I presented them to a grateful committee. The receipt of the gift was acknowledged in a letter from Pizzoni, president of CLNAI, to Donovan on May 4, which was transmitted by radio to Donovan: "The CLNAI wishes to express its gratitude for your precious gift and for your recognition of the effort and sacrifices of the Italian people in the common fight against the common enemy.   Pizzoni."

Later in the day the following radio message was received from Fifteenth Army Group:

For Corvo. It is requested that you pass the following message from Field Marshal Alexander to Chairman CLNAI. Quote: "Now that the campaign in northern Italy has ended victoriously I would be pleased if you could convey to General Cadorna and all the subordinate patriot commanders and units my admiration and gratitude for the successful part which they have played both in the destruction of the enemy and the preservation of the installations and plants vital to the future life of Italy. I have noted also with particular pleasure the efficiency and speed with which the CLNAI has been able to turn from these military achievements to the equally important task of restoring in conjunction with my AMG officers civil administration in liberated Italy." Unquote Gen. Mark Clark.

With the end of the war, the various teams we had sent to the field began to report to our Milan office where emotional welcomes became the order of the day. The mere sight of the survivors of the missions whose every moment of life among the enemy, while working for OSS, had been fraught with mortal danger, was reason for rejoicing.

Our sense of relief was somehow tinged by sadness now that the entire brutalizing experience was over. None of us would emerge from the experience unchanged. We knew that nothing in our future experience could ever even approach the victory parades, and the adulation of the demonstrative throngs. Somehow this sudden realization made us all feel a little down. Something had happened to the Army too. Everyone was in a rush to wrap things up, pack up, and go home.

As the teams reported, the men were sent to our headquarters in Siena where debriefing facilities had been set up, after which each agent would be sent home to pick up where he had left off in civilian life—if he could.

Meanwhile, Scamporino and I were discussing the implementation of the intermediate phase of intelligence operations which had been the subject of a good deal of planning in both Washington and the field. While discussing these plans, a phone call came from the downstairs reception desk informing us that Allen Dulles was on his way up. Surprised that he had not sent word he was coming, we were still talking when he came in, leaning slightly on an elegant cane for support from an attack of gout.

Both the fact that Dulles had come to Milan without informing us and his autocratic and patronizing attitude in his discussion of some juris-dictional matters provoked Scamp to express his opinions with undiplo-matic bluntness. The infuriated Dulles, who had come to us fresh from his euphoric participation in "Sunrise," left, threatened that the matter under discussion was not over and muttering that he had never been so humiliated in his life. He left for Switzerland immediately.

Dulles was especially insufferable during this period of time because he was riding the crest of a wave of favorable publicity in connection with the "secret armistice." In all fairness, too, his gout was causing him genuine pain. The incident was regrettable, but the fault was not one-sided. I knew that he would probably immediately inform Donovan about the incident. Considering the exaggerated credit he had been given for ending the war—which had already ended in Italy before the "surrender" was signed, we knew that we would soon hear from Washington.

We had no time to worry about it, however, for other pressing matters needed our attention, among them the mounting pressure being exerted on us by certain elements of the CLN to turn Buffarini over to them for trial. The situation became so tense that, fearing a possible attack from some partisan unit, we had to double our guard both inside and outside the hotel. Finally, after a conference with General Cadorna, we decided that Buffarini would be turned over to the committee and placed in con-finement at San Vittore Prison to await trial by a Special Tribunal of the Milan Assizes. After being taken to San Vittore, Buffarini still managed to get a message to me by bypassing the prison's maximum security measures.

On June 16, the Milan court found Buffarini guilty of war crimes, and he was scheduled to be executed on July 10 by a firing squad. Early in the morning of his scheduled execution, he tried to cheat justice by ingesting a huge overdose of barbiturates. The partisan guards revived him, and while semiconscious he was carried and tied to a chair with his back to the firing squad. He was given the last sacraments by a priest just before being shot in the back. I was not in Milan at the time of his sentencing and execution. I saw the photographs of his last moments, kissing a crucifix, in a Washington newspaper. Buffarini's extensive report was classified and made available to X-2 and Jim Angleton. A copy was sent to the office in Washington.

The OSS mission in Milan played a very important role in the transition period. We gradually moved our operations out of the Hotel Milano to a private building at Piazza Fiume in order to regain some of our more confidential functions. We placed the counterintelligence chief of CLN in contact with Angleton's X-2 section, and eventually we turned over to CLN a number of enemy agents, including Count Thun and Max Knipping.

Our office at the hotel had become a veritable Mecca for Milan officials, representatives of the major industrial establishments, and most leading politicians of the key political parties.

Out of the chaos of revolutionary Milan, order was finally being established when a radiogram arrived from Washington. The message, which bore Donovan's name, ordered that Scamporino, Corvo, Ricca, Pasqualino, D'Amato, Bisceglia, and "Sgt. Mike" should forthwith return to Washington.[18] The radiogram also asked that Scamporino and I designate who would continue the work in Italy until the various stations were phased out and/or replaced by peacetime operations.

We all agreed that Allen Dulles and some of our "friends" in Washington had finally prevailed. With the war over, there was no further need to tolerate people who spoke their minds and were willing to fight for their beliefs. We decided that Dick Mazzarini, who had recently arrived from the London office, should replace Scamp. Mim Daddario should take over Italian SI operations in Milan and Icardi should replace Jack Ricca in Turin. With little ceremony and little time to bid goodbye to some of our close friends and collaborators, we packed our bags and left Milan for Siena and Rome.

We retraced our steps southward through the Po Valley; Bologna; through the shambles of the villages of the Futa Pass; and Florence, where we stopped briefly and ordered the consolidation of the section at our Siena base.

When we arrived in Siena, the old DeVecchi villa was humming with activity as debriefing teams were still at work putting together the history of each team, its casualties, its accomplishments, and its failures. Documents and files were being boxed under prodding from Caserta,

which was anxious to ship personnel back home, to the China/Burma/
India theater and the Far East. The OSS's priorities were now being
realigned to concentrate on the battle against Japan. I gave Captain
Passanisi instructions as to how the historical files of our section should
be shipped back to the states and how each returning city team should be
debriefed. At the same time, I took care of procedures for compensating
the families of individuals who had been killed by the enemy while they
were on mission for OSS. On May 19, I drove to Rome to meet the other
members of the homeward-bound party. When in Rome I met with
Agrifoglio to inform him that Donovan had suddenly recalled us to
Washington. I urged him to give our successor the same kind of support
and assistance he had given us.

As an old army man, such orders did not seem strange to him, but he
wondered aloud what would be done with our acquired expertise in
Italian affairs and the conduct of clandestine operations.

For my part, I asked him whether it would be possible to put together a
task force of experts on the Far East who could work as a unit with OSS
in an effort to penetrate Japanese-held territory and the home islands.
He liked the idea and said he would immediately look into assembling
such a mission. I promised him that I would keep in touch with him and
would submit the idea of a joint Far East Intelligence Task Force to
Donovan when I arrived in Washington.

On May 24, exactly two years after leaving Washington to begin
operations against the Fascist government, I was back in Washington.

Chapter 20

Retrospective

Brennan was livid over the general's action in recalling us and even more furious at the summary dismantling of the SI's leadership overseas. He accused a number of people of having conspired against the Italian Section because it had managed to hold together through three years of internecine warfare within OSS and because it had been eminently successful in accomplishing what it had set out to do. I saw clear evidence that our Washington office had failed to carry out any positive public relations and that Brennan had, at times, become surly in his relationship with other branch chiefs.

There was also a feeling within the organization that there were too many Italo-Americans in the Italian SI Section. This ran against the grain of some people who genuinely believed that first-generation Americans and foreigners should not be entrusted with highly classified secrets. Fortunately, people like David Bruce and General Donovan rejected such wrong thinking. If this had not been so, the story of OSS might have been totally different.

The recent declassification of OSS documents at the National Archives has shed light on some of the events that preceded Donovan's decision to ring down the curtain on the Italian SI operations in Italy. The recall order had been preceded by a meeting held in Paris in early April 1945 in which Whitney Shepardson, Bob Joyce, Allen Dulles, and representatives from MEDTO participated. It was at this meeting that it had been decreed that Italian SI should be dissolved.

On April 17, Bob Joyce, who had been named senior staff officer for Rear Zone Intelligence (liberated territories) in December 1944, prepared and made recommendations regarding the political and economic operations of Italian SI.[1] The study was forwarded to General

Magruder and Whitney Shepardson in Washington. Joyce was a former State Department Foreign Service officer and had been head of the Balkan SI desk at Bari. In his new position, he was charged with the task of reviewing SI, R & A, and X-2 operations in Italy, but he concentrated on the Rome station. He came to a series of facile conclusions that were prefaced in a bucksheet, dated April 17, 1945, and sent to Shepardson and Maddox. Joyce's annotated comment was:

> I am attaching hereto a memorandum (first draft) which I dictated to cover certain thoughts I have in regard to Italian S.I. I hope that you will understand that the general conclusions I have reached are in no sense intended to detract or to criticize in a captious way the unquestionable useful and sometimes brilliant work which has been accomplished by Italian S.I. By the same token, my remarks should not be interpreted as a reflection of the loyalty or efficiency of the men who have worked in Italy for the S.I. Branch. I feel that most of what I have to say in my memorandum presents nothing particularly new and will probably be considered pretty self-evident.

The memorandum, addressed to Magruder and Shepardson for action, attempted to analyze the Italian situation by describing Italian officials as falling over each other to provide U.S. officials with information, thus obviating the need for Italian SI personnel and leaving the field to the State Department and the news media. It further attempted to point out that, with the anticipated end of the war, consideration should be given as to "whether the non-military activities of the S.I. branch in Italy are performing are to the best interest of O.S.S."

The memo also reported discussions with U.S. Ambassador to Italy Alexander Kirk and the secretary of the Embassy, Walter Dowling, as to the further need of Italian SI.[2] They were said to have been negative to SI and more condescending to R & A.

Joyce's conclusions were as follows:

> 1. The personnel of Italian S.I. was primarily recruited and trained for the purpose of conducting secret operations directed against military forces. Its record in this field is characterized by solid performance, and S.I. coverage in northern Italy, behind enemy lines at the present time is most impressive and of inestimable value to the Allied miltary forces. It is my opinion, however, that the present personnel of Italian S.I. is not by background, education and training prepared to cope with entirely new problems of secret intelligence of a non-military nature. In other words, I feel that the time has now arisen with regard to Italian S.I. operations where we must consider matters of general policy in preparation for the post-war period. The officers and civilians of Italian S.I. have unquestionably performed brilliantly in their field, but that field is ceasing and will soon have ceased completely to exist.
>
> . . . .
>
> Attention should be given at this time to the reorganization of Italian S.I. and plans be undertaken now to meet the situation which will arise after Italy has been entirely liberated.

. . . .
It is, of course, understood that the present operations in Italian S.I. in Rome, which readily fall into the category of Secret Intelligence work, should be continued on as at present.

Only twelve days later, the final draft of Joyce's memo with a new buck slip was submitted for transmittal to Washington and for action by Colonel Glavin, CO, 2677 Regiment, through chief SI. In it, Joyce commented: "It will be noted that the first draft was submitted to Mr. Scamporino and Lt. Colonel Maddox, both of whom agreed that it would go forward to Washington."

The routing slip with comments was declassified on October 17, 1986, by the National Archives and the CIA, and contains the following notations:

Endorsement 6. From S.I. to C.O. 7 May 1945, "Forwarded." W.P.M. (Maddox
Endorsement 7. Intelligence to C.O. through Exec. Off. "It was my
understanding that the decision was made in Paris to wind up Italian S.I."

Endorsement 8. E.G. (Ed Glavin) to Intelligence. "1. Right. 2. Have Col. Maddox study and advise us. Close out S.I. . . . Endorsement 9. Secret to Col. Maddox. 8 May 1945. Your action in accordance with endorsement 8. Countersigned EG."

Thus, the end of the Italian Section was decreed and assented to by the top people in the 2677th regimental chain of command, without any second thought ever given to the consequences of the action which they in turn required from Donovan.

Replacing the leadership of the section overseas was not easily done. Commenting on Washington's efforts to send new bodies to the field in a letter addressed to Shepardson on July 18, Colonel Maddox was outspoken:

It would seem extremely doubtful whether any new organization will be instituted on the basis of these recommendations in time to meet the needs of General McNarney. *This* is the crucial period, and also the next few months. It is a great pity that all our work had to cease before the new phase can possibly start.

For the record, I should like again to express my regrets that the decision was made, first to withdraw Scamporino et al in May, and second, to shut down all of Italian S.I. in July. Scamp had his detractors (in other branches) but I still maintain, that with the admitted faults, he would have been capable of providing valuable intelligence for six months after V-E Day. Even now I would have liked to have seen Mazzarini and a dozen others remain for some months.[3]

No encomium to the work of Italian SI could have spoken more eloquently or more clearly to the glaring error of pulling out the top overseas leadership of the section than Maddox's indictment of the decision. Only recently has this information seen the light of day, 41 years after they were penned and conveniently overlooked by the compilers of the official OSS history.

Within a month after our return to the United States, I prepared an 18-paragraph summation of the Section's achievements during the final phase of the Italian campaign. I presented the memo to Donovan at a meeting held in his office on June 19. The meeting was attended by Whitney Shepardson, Commander Milton Katz, Lieutenant Tom Beale, Earl Brennan, Scamporino, Ricca, and myself.

As a result of the meeting, on June 25, Donovan sent Glavin the following radiogram:

1. Please have the following matters undertaken in connection with SI Italy debriefing activities. They were suggested by Scamporino:

   a) Have Captain Passanisi forward to Washington copy of all debriefing reports. S.I. Washington also wishes communications files of teams in field and other documents pertaining to these teams. Scamp suggested Captain Fraulino be designated courier to bring these back.

   b) You should write a letter of appreciation to Lt. Col. Massaioli of S.I.M. who was last located in Siena for help he and his staff gave us.

   c) Letter of thanks should be written to Lt. Saverio Calo for services rendered since October 1943.

   d) Scamporino recommends a letter of appreciation be forwarded to Major Adam.

   e) Special letter of commendation and sympathy should be hand delivered to Spazzoli family in Forli whose two sons, Arturo and Antonio, were killed in the town square along with others of our service, including the partisan leader Silvio Corbara.

   f) A similar letter to the family of Captain Rossoni should be delivered at Venice. He was executed at Methausen at Christmas. I understand he rendered outstanding services.

   g) Similar letter to family of Lt. Pelli executed in Autumn 1944 at Fossoli concentration camp.

   h) Letters to the families of Ciclone and Marchi, missing in action and presumed dead in battle of Gothic Line who rendered valuable service.

   i) Following should be sent letters of appreciation for services: Dr. Dugoni, CLN representative to French military authorities; Raimondo Craveri; Giorgio, Chief of SIMNI who worked with Pineapple team behind lines; Captain De Leva, chief of Orange Mission which was instrumental in organization of Patriot movement in Piedmont; Dr. Enzo Boeri, Chief of CLNAI intelligence.

   j) Should send letter of appreciation to S.I.A. (Air Force Intelligence), C.I.S. (Naval Intelligence) and S.I.M. (Military Intelligence Service, General Staff), for their collaboration with us.

   k) Letter of thanks should be sent to General Cadorna for courtesies extended while he was commanding general of (CVL) Patriot forces of northern Italy.[4]

On that same day, June 25, Whitney Shepardson followed up the Italian SI memo with a memo to Bill Maddox, SI chief, MEDTO, asking him to check the claims made in the memo. The intent of his letter was clear.

The statement is concrete and impressive, and the facts, when duly authenticated, should become part of the record of Italian S.I.

Will you therefore examine the statement with very great care, indicating whether you agree with it, or in what respects it should be added to or subtracted from.

My sole purpose in this connection is to establish the record in the approved manner, by having it proceed through the chain of command OSS MTO, and thus carry the weight which attaches to that procedure.

If there are any commendations from Allied military or political authorities which touch on the work of this section please forward them with the necessary or appropriate explanations.

Colonel Maddox's reply was dispatched from Rome on July 16, 1945 with a three-page, point-by-point comment on all claims.

Maddox did not like the format of our memorandum, which he felt "read like the output of a second rate advertising agency. It cheapened the product . . . Italian S.I. has no need to pound its chest or burst its lungs in a frenzy of vainglory. Its sound achievements are well known here and are in the record of OSS Washington to see." (Obviously, Shepardson had not bothered to look at the record.) Maddox concluded, "If there are any detractors and skeptics, the record should be prepared and exhibited as history, not as sales talk." (Evidently, even the editors of the long-classified OSS War Report failed to consult the record and buried it under a pile of rubbish.)

It was not until July 18 that I finally managed to have a long talk with General Donovan who had been busy with many important matters. He invited me to lunch at his home where we discussed the past as well as the future, carefully skirting the subject of our sudden and unexpected recall from Italy. He asked me how quickly the Italian Section could be phased out, and I told him that I would discuss the matter with Brennan and prepare a timetable for him. At this point, I asked directly why he had decided to recall Scamp and me at such a crucial moment. I could see that the question disturbed him. I had seen this same reaction before when I asked a question with unpleasant connotations. He finally answered to the effect that "you Italians have politics in your blood . . . . and you and Scamp were getting mixed up in Italian politics." He then concluded with the remark, "someday you will thank me for having recalled you to Washington."

The minor unpleasantness over, I explained that before leaving Rome I had discussed with Agrifoglio the creation of a joint SIM/OSS Far East intelligence unit to penetrate Japan. He liked the idea and asked that I outline my plans in a memo and discuss the matter with Major Duncan Lee. With regard to the liquidation of the Italian Section, he asked me to write him a note and let him know how it would be done and how many persons would remain. It was agreed that I would put together my plan for the Far East operation and that I would lead a mission to China after having assembled the personnel in Italy with Agrifoglio. Next day, July 19, I sent him the following memo:

1. As outlined in our conversation of yesterday, the personnel to be retained by the Italian and Albanian S.I. sections for the purpose of liquidation, participation in Far Eastern activities and for the compilation of the section's historical record in the field will be limited to twenty persons.
2. 101 men and women constitute the present strength of this section, including the local staff and overseas personnel. Eighty-one of these will be reassigned either to other branches of OSS, the Army, or be returned to civilian status.
3. Notice has already been given to civilians of termination of their services. Mr. Scamporino and Mr. Mazzarini are being retained to settle various problems arising out of liquidation.
4. In view of your impending departure and to avoid any misunderstanding in your absence, it will be appreciated if the above to brought to the attention of the appropriate officials.

                                        BMC

My luncheon conversation with Donovan had made it eminently clear that Italian SI, despite its yeoman work in the war, would have no role in the development of the intermediary-phase intelligence operations, let along the long-range phase. Too many powerful influences within OSS had coalesced against us, and these influences were secretly militating for our immediate liquidation now that the war was over, using the excuse that new people should be brought in. These forces resented the fact that for almost three years we had managed to stay together, carrying out plans developed in the early days in Washington. Our plans had been carried out sometimes with little or no support from field headquarters; sometimes over objections from superior headquarters; but always with the objective of advancing U.S. interests and OSS expertise in the intelligence struggle and the coordination of special operations.

Scamporino's incident with Allen Dulles added to the complaints voiced by some people who had returned from Italy to Washington and found the willing ears of Whitney Shepardson, chief of SI, an old friend and associate of Dulles, who was having difficulties dealing with Earl Brennan. One of the returnees was James St. Lawrence O'Toole who had been sent to Rome to work under Scamporino to gather political intelligence and work with contacts in the Vatican. O'Toole was supposed to be an undercover intermediary agent. Prior to the war, he had carried on a lucrative art business between Italy and New York and was married to a Venetian woman. He arrived in Italy on New Year's Day 1945 and for reasons of work had to live by himself. He had limited contact with other members of the SI staff. His mission had been set up by Brennan and Orlando with whom he carried on a continuing correspondence. Somehow, events did not work out as foreseen, and his interest in paintings may have taken precedence over his assigned mission. He was sent back home where he may have joined other discordant voices, including that of Mrs. Hawkins who had been a member of the Rome Reports Board. On returning home, Mrs. Hawkins wrote a scathing and highly critical "report" on the Italian Division SI (Her report covered the Reports Board in Rome as she knew nothing about the section's military intelligence operations.). Mrs. Hawkins was a diminutive, wide-eyed woman, who had apparently taken a dislike to the way Scamp ran SI, Rome, or to the way she may have been treated. Her "report" to Whitney Shepardson (a copy of which came to my attention) showed extreme bias against Italo-Americans and, in view of the achievements of our office, should have automatically become suspect to any objective superior. Whitney Shepardson added fuel to the fire by writing a memoradum to General Donovan to which he attached the Hawkins "report." In his memo he synthesized her views and added his own comments.

The obvious prejudice against the Italian Section's esprit de corps culminating in Donovan's sudden recall radiogram was discernible in early 1944, prior to the general's initiating his inspection trip to Italy. On April 2, 1944, Donovan wrote to Brennan, suggesting that he had yielded to pressure to revamp the Italian SI show in Italy. The letter stated the intent clearly:

Dear Earl:
I do not want to leave without expressing my appreciation for the fine work you have done for this organization and the splendid results which that work has achieved.
Recent developments will necessitate certain modifications in the organization's work abroad which I would like to discuss with you when I return, however I want to let you know that I am certain the job could not have been accomplished without your energy and unswerving devotion to this task.
Sincerely,
William J. Donovan[5]

Before sending Brennan the letter, the subject had obviously been discussed with Whitney Shepardson. A note from Donovan to Shepardson on the subject forecast what was planned. The note which was in the general's handwriting stated:

Sunday morning,
Dear Whitney,
I have explained to you the reason for doing in Italy what I have already done in France.
Specifically it will next appear in a cable I intend to send to Glavin.
You know what a good job I think has been done by Brennan, Scamporino and Corvo and their teams, but we now have a new problem which must be met in a different way.
Donovan[6]

In retrospect, it was apparent that radical changes had long been contemplated in the top personnel and operational jurisdiction of Italian SI and that, because of the section's past achievements, Donovan had not tackled the changes with his usual zest. In fact, while a number of changes were made in the relationship between OSS/AFHQ and OSS/Fifth Army, the only significant change finally made in the field SI was Scamporino's recall to the United States at the end of May 1944. By the end of August, however, we had prevailed on the general to send him back to Italy. Once in Italy, Donovan had first-hand knowledge of the situation. A review of the successful operations and achievements of our section changed his mind about doing any surgical work. However, surgery was done elsewhere.

In the interim, the Goodfellow Board was visiting the various bases in MEDTO and in the Middle East looking into the use and fitness of personnel. Many of the members of our section who had already participated in various missions were earmarked to be returned to the States, whereas others were to be transferred to other branches and still others to be returned to Army replacement centers.

After looking over the situation, the board could find only that there was an excess of personnel. This oversupply was due to the radical changes in the situation wrought by the Italian surrender in September 1943, which opened the door to the full collaboration of the Badoglio government and made available to us a large number of potential intelligence operators who needed little training in order to work in their own familiar environment.

The 2677th Regiment's June 15, 1944, semimonthly report covering activities between May 15 and May 31, signed by Colonel Glavin, included the following segment:

The Director has ordered that a thorough investigation be made of Italian S.I. activities. . .orders were secured for Col. Glavin and Major Chapin and the inspection began on May 26th. The results of the visit are the subject of a separate report which, if not completed, will be held for the General's arrival on June 22nd

The most important results, however, can be mentioned briefly now. They are: first: The responsibilities of the Chief Italian S.I. desk were defined as were the responsibilities of the Chief Intelligence Officer. Second: The relations between these two were thoroughly discussed and defined. Third: a complete survey of all intelligence activities was made, including an exhaustive survey of all individuals engaged in the activities, with the result that all activities were coordinated and approximately 50% of the personnel were relieved from current assignment and scheduled for return to the United States.

A comprehensive report covering MEDTO operations dated July 25, 1944, stated unequivocally that

The Brindisi and Pozzuoli areas are being closed and a good part of its personnel is being returned to Washington. Mr. Scamporino has already come back and his return to the field is problematical. Major Ricca is acting SI chief in his absence. The tightening of administrative control over S.I. activities which began in May is being continued and SI units and SI operations accompanying forward groups will be integrated with the work of Italian SI branch. During the early part of 1944 forward operations and long range intelligence teams were independent of each other and the results were not entirely creditable to OSS. Captain Corvo is remaining in Italy, but he is no longer S.I. operations officer.[7]

This report was based on anticipated events and was classified secret by someone who was out of touch with the Italian situation, for I continued to head SI operations throughout the Italian campaign and Scamporino returned to the field to continue as chief of Italian SI until we left the theater in May 1945. Brindisi remained open until I decided to move the facility to Siena in February 1945. The real reason for the recall must be attributed to the pentup animosity of a number of OSS operators who from the beginning had sought to take over Italian intelligence operations and had failed in their effort to enlist the support of Italian SI.

Mrs. Hawkins' memo, to which Whitney Shepardson had penned his remarks, was meant to conjure up the worst of all possible scenarios by referring to the section as being "largely of Sicilian origin" and displaying "peculiar group loyalty."[8] It even went so far as to try to exploit Italian regional sectionalism by implying that the "north Italians and Romans despised all southern Italians and Sicilians" and that "they (Italian SI) were both despised and laughed at, and much of the information given them was done with tongue in cheek, precisely because of their origin."

Both Whitney Shepardson and Mrs. Hawkins made common cause in their denigration of our section and obviously did not understand that many of the key people in the Badoglio government were southern Italian and Sicilian, as were many of the leaders of the anti-Fascist movement. Don Luigi Sturzo, widely recognized as the dean of anti-Fascism and the leader of the Christian Democratic movement; Professor Giuseppe Borgese, Guido Jung, Ugo LaMalfa, Professor George La Piana, Mario Scelba, Giuseppe Lupis, Vincenzo Vacirca, to mention a few of the top political leaders of that period and the postwar era, were Sicilians and close friends of the SI Section.

Vittorio Emanuele Orlando, Italy's prime minister during World War I, was adviser to Marshal Badoglio, and Dr. Giuseppe Caronia, rector of the University of Rome, were both Sicilians and were in frequent touch with Scamporino and other members of the staff. The head of SIM, Agrifoglio, was from Palermo, and his deputy, Lieutenant Colonel Massaioli, was from Potenza in southern Italy. If there had been wholesale prejudice against southerners and Sicilians, it was hardly likely that so many of the key positions would have been occupied by them.

The unfortunate attitude of the Shepardson-Hawkins memo spilled over into the official history of OSS which was edited by Kim Roosevelt and Peter Karlow. When the galleys covering the history of the Italian campaign were ready in 1949, General Donovan sent me a copy for review of their historical accuracy. He asked me to get in touch with Peter Karlow in the event I should find inaccuracies or omissions.

After reading the galleys, on August 15, 1949, I wrote to Karlow as follows:

I have looked over the original historical report covering the Italian campaign and have accordingly made such corrections or additions as I could recall.

I have not made such corrections or additions insofar as the political reporting of the section is concerned, but am relying on your sense of fair play and judgment for such corrections.

You may recall that when Gen. Donovan first asked R & A to take to the field that we were the first to invite its representative, Rudy Winnacker, to join us and that we provided for him all of the assistance he needed at that time. You may recall that in several of my rare visits to Algiers, I extended to you an invitation to come to the field. Are these examples of a section that is supposed to have operated as a "closed operation?"

I have noted with deep interest on page 194 of Volume 4, the following paragraph:

This policy tended to compromise the semi-official atmosphere essential for political reporting, in addition to Italian sectionalism, the Sicilian ancestry of several of the S.I. officers was deprecated by the Italian political leaders from Central and Northern Italy. . . .

I wonder just what this statement was based on. For the information of the writer of the original draft, the Rome political section was made up of the following key persons: Scamporino, Sicilian background; Caputa, Central Italian; Battistini, Tuscan; Bisceglia, Calabrian; Galleani, Lombard.

The facts do not bear out the charge, and to the Rome staff you must add such names as Quigley, O'Toole, Carney, etc., who were also members of the political section.

On pages 194 and 195 I found the following statement:

"Furthermore, informed or semi-official contact with foreign political elements entailed an overt intelligence procurement function clearly in the province of trained R & A personnel. Political reports forwarded by S.I. Italy might more aptly have been classified as unevaluated propaganda."

I find little reason to include this type of a broad statement in the official history of the organization. For the evaluation of SI political reporting I should like to refer the writer of the above paragraph to the record. AFHQ and State Department were more than amply satisfied with both the political reporting and economic reports of S.I. These reports were in the main based on undercover information of highly placed agents and though contacts were maintained with Italian political elements, only information of important pending events was included in reports covering such contacts.

Political information emanating from behind enemy lines provided the United States Armed Forces and the Department of State with the only accurate picture of the situation in northern Italy and served as a basis for guiding U.S. policy in the area. These facts are attested to by the fact that S.I. Italy was called upon to participate in all of the meetings involving the negotiations between CLNAI and AFHQ.

I sincerely hope that you will take time out to correct some of the things which I have pointed out. I hope that you can find the time to look at the record and I am sure that you will be convinced of the sincerity with which this work was tackled by the section and of the outstanding job that was done in both political and military fields. I feel, as I am sure you do, that history must be based on facts and all that I ask of you is that you incorporate such facts in the record of our work. . .such work was accomplished under the most difficult conditions and the length of Italy is covered with the blood of men who lost their lives to write a glowing page in the history of the American secret service.[9]

Appended to the letter was an additional memo highlighting the key achievements of Italian SI behind enemy lines for the period January 1, 1944, to the end of May 1945. No modifications were made to the original text, and the history was published as a classified document, marked secret.

It was not until 1976 that the two-volume history was published, but again without corrections to the text regarding Italian SI operations. Thus, when other works based in part on *The War Report of the OSS* were written, they continued to repeat the gross historical inaccuracies and distortions. The fact is that the relationships established by Italian SI in Italy during 1943-1945 were to be the determining factors for four decades after World War II. A succession of politicians whom we had befriended came to power in Italy and placed the Italian Republic smack on the side of the United States in the era of the extreme Cold War.

In the summer of 1945, General Donovan and OSS were busy dismantling the European assets and transferring their attention to the Far East, where the gap in intelligence and special operations had to be filled by OSS Detachments 101 in Burma and 202 in China.

While waiting to liquidate our section as the men came back from their assignments in Italy, I put together the plan of the Far Eastern operations by the proposed OSS/SIM task force. I gave a copy to Duncan Lee, but the probabilities that it could be activated grew less likely every day and evaporated with the dropping of the first atomic bomb on Hiroshima on August 6 and Nagasaki on August 9. Japan surrendered, and World War II came to an end on September 2.

I immediately saw Donovan and suggested that Scamporino and I be allowed to go back to Italy to personally thank Parri and other political and military leaders who had worked with us in the war effort and to establish the supremacy of the democratic institutions in Italy. In addition, we wanted to visit the families of the men who had fallen in the line of extraordinary duty, while serving with the OSS.

As I anticipated, he immediately approved our return to Italy and asked to be particularly remembered to Parri and Agrifoglio. On August 30, I flew to Casablanca. As luck would have it, at the airport I bumped into Mim Daddario and Icardi who were on their way home. In the limited time we had to talk, they brought me to up date with events in Italy and suggested that I keep in touch with Colonel Maddox who was now in charge.

I remained in Casablanca several days. I looked up Captain Andre Bourgoin whom I had not seen since he had turned over his missions to me in the preceding fall. Andre was ensconced in a comfortable home on the outskirts of the city and bore little resemblance to the person I had known in Italy. Gone was the uniform and the military bearing; in their place was a portly man in a flowing native robe with a red fez atop his head. He talked of the past—the Spanish Civil War, when as a representative of a petroleum company, he sold gas to both the Loyalists and the Franco forces. Then we talked about the Italian campaign.

The next day I continued my trip to Italy. It was early morning when our plane flew over the Sicilian channel and Sicily. The atmosphere was clear, and from the great height I could see the entire island. It seemed like a copy of my relief map in Washington. On arrival in Rome, I reported to Colonel Maddox who was genuinely glad to see me. Both he and his wife Louise were very kind to me during my stay in Italy.

Scamp had left the States on another flight and had stopped in Algiers to get married to a lovely French girl whom he had met there. Now he was faced with the problem of getting her into Italy at a time when official Franco-Italian relations had not yet been reestablished. When I caught up with him in Rome, we decided to have her fly from Algiers to Marseilles and then sneak her across the frontier at Ventimiglia. When we arrived in Milan, we were met by Gianni Segre at whose apartment I was a guest, while Scamp went on to Genoa to keep his rendezvous with his wife Lucienne. It all went off without a hitch, and no one was the wiser that a French citizen had entered Italy without a visa.

I remained in Milan to visit with many of the men and women who had distinguished themselves during the German occupation. I visited the border area around Lanzo d'Intelvi where the comfortable Villa Reinach was located and where I talked with some of the men who had been part of the brigade that had captured Mussolini.

After I had finished paying my official visits to the families of some of the men who had fallen and after I had the opportunity to talk at length with Enzo Boeri about the arrangements to pay some compensation to the families, I decided to return to Rome. There Scamp was arranging a small dinner for Ferruccio Parri who had become premier of Italy. The arrangements were made by Raimondo Craveri ("Mondo"), and among those invited were a small group of resistance co-workers. Parri, always serious, was particularly subdued by the enormity of his responsibilities as prime minister. The country was in shambles, having suffered enormous destruction, and had few resources with which to rebuild. Parri was working endless hours to fit the pieces in the economic jigsaw puzzle, but there were not enough hours in the day to satisfy him. His was an almost hopeless task, but he was heartened that the United States was once again coming to the aid of the Italian people. A scrupulously honest man, he found it difficult to accept an engraved pocket watch which we presented him as a token of appreciation from OSS.

Ferruccio Parri was not cut out to be a politician. His moral standards were so rigid that there was little flexibility in his makeup. He possessed enormous energy: All work papers and decisions landed on his desk, and he would pour over papers until the early morning hours. His self-imposed work schedule and meticulous standards caused his early burnout. His stewardship was of short duration, as was the lifespan of his dynamic Action party, which finally splintered and provided brilliant talent for many other democratic parties.

Another individual high on our list to see was Colonel Pompeo Agrifoglio who was still head of Italian military intelligence. Agrifoglio had taken over the service at its lowest ebb. Fresh from a prisoner-of-war camp in the United States, Agrifoglio came to Brindisi to reorganize the service. Slowly in the first several months, as various General Staff officers crossed the battlelines to join the legitimate Italian government, he put together an organization that worked closely with No. 1 Special Force (SOE) and ISLD. When Scamp and I established contact with him for OSS, we found the door open to honest collaboration.

Though a member of the losing side which had surrendered unconditionally, Agrifoglio was a man of such rare honesty and candor that he earned the rights of a close ally. He expected and received the military respect due to his high office, as Allied officers would find out. His able assistant, Lieutenant Colonel Giuseppe Massaioli, his chief of offensive operations, was equally straitlaced and dedicated to his intelligence activities. During the postwar era, Massaioli went on to occupy some of the most prominent military positions in the Italian armed forces, concluding his career as chairman of the Italian Chiefs of Staff.

Agrifoglio's dedication to duty was all the more astounding given the fact that his wife and some of his children were caught behind German lines and that the Fascist and German police were constantly searching for them because they knew he was the head of SIM. He angrily and proudly turned down all Allied efforts to corrupt him with lucrative offers. He died prematurely in 1948, leaving his family in serious economic straits. His devotion to the rebirth of his country and his high standards of both honor and morality were the legacy he left his children.

The preliminary work of recommending awards and decorations for the members of the SI field teams had been done in Italy by the debriefing teams. In addition, Colonel Glavin had written personal letters to the families of the men who had fallen in the clandestine war against the enemy. The finance officer had prepared the paperwork to compensate the families, and compensation sometimes took a long time. In December 1948, Enzo Boeri wrote:

Dear Max:

I should give you very good news. Mrs. Palmira Campanelli, the widow of Bruno, informs me that she has received from the Federal Security Office of

Rome the sum of 1,388,374 lire for herself and 940,985 for her daughter. You can imagine how glad I was for it. I soon wrote a letter to the American Embassy in Rome. And now I'm thanking you very much for what you have done for poor Palmira. I shall not forget it. (Bruno Campanelli was the W/T of the "Apricot" mission who was captured, tortured, and killed by the German SD.)

Among the matters to be squared away was the regularization of Italian armed forces personnel who had been working for OSS since the surrender of Italy in September 1943. Some of these personnel had volunteered to work for OSS during the Sicilian campaign; some had been enlisted from units that had disbanded after the landing at Salerno; and others had been officially loaned to OSS through SIM, the Italian Navy, and the Air Force. These personnel, unless regularized within the framework of the Italian armed forces, would have been listed in the official records as deserters, despite the fact that they had participated in hair-raising missions fraught with personal risk.

When I sat down with Agrifoglio and Massaioli and went over the histories of each individual, we arranged for each survivor to be credited with his service and for the families of the dead to be given pensions.

That done, on September 28, I headed for Sicily with Scamp and his wife. We visited Palermo, Catania, and some of the other centers to thank those who had helped us in our work from the inception of the Sicilian campaign. On November 2, my work completed, I headed back to Washington to finish my tour of duty.

On my arrival there General Donovan was already gone, and to all intents and purposes OSS was out of business, replaced by something called the Strategic Services Unit (SSU) which was under the control of the War Department, with Colonel William Quinn, former G-2 of Seventh Army as CO. Quinn had worked with OSS during "Anvil," and he appreciated the type of intelligence the organization had provided during the campaign.

On September 20, President Truman signed an order liquidating the Office of Strategic Services and dispersing some of its people to other government agencies and departments. This was a tragic error. The reasons why Donovan lost personal prestige at the White House are not the silly assumptions drawn in Cave Brown's biography of the general. Those assumptions attributed the coolness to a series of "failed" OSS operations. The truth is that some people at the White House blamed Donovan for the leakage of classified foreign policy information to the Republican National Committee in 1944. The GOP presidential candidate, Thomas Dewey, ostensibly used the information in the 1944 presidential campaign. Without looking more closely into the matter, these White House advisers placed the blame on General Donovan, conveniently forgetting that Dewey's foreign policy adviser was John Foster Dulles, whose brother Allen had a direct pipeline into the heart of the OSS and thus had unlimited access to policy-making intelligence in the highest military and diplomatic circles in Washington and London.

Before leaving OSS, Donovan took time to warmly attest to Italian SI's contribution. In a letter to Earl Brennan dated September 27, 1945, he stated:

Dear Earl,

At the time of the termination of the Office of Strategic Services I desire to express to you my thanks for the contribution you have made to the work of this Agency over a period of more than three years.

The plans you made, and the men whom you sent to the combat areas to direct hazardous missions and to participate in them, contributed importantly to the success of Allied arms in the Mediterranean theater.

I wish you the best for the future.

William J. Donovan, Director

At Brennan's request I remained in SSU to tie up any loose ends that remained and to expedite recommendations for awards to those who had rendered outstanding services during the campaign in Italy.

My friendly rapport with General Donovan continued until his death in 1959. I was a frequent visitor at his law office on Wall Street and his home on Sutton Place. His interest in intelligence and policy-making continued to the end and was often the topic of our conversations.

While intelligence continued to be one of my interests after the war, I did not pursue it as a career. The peacetime collection of intelligence, particularly the high tech collection methods in use today, might have obviated the need for many intelligence missions during World War II, but it is equally true that there is no substitute for a motivated intelligence agent relying solely on his wits to carry out his mission. This is a lesson we should have learned at Pearl Harbor, Kassarene Pass, the Ardennes, and Arnhem, where our possession of Magic and Ultra failed to save us from almost irreparable intelligence failures.

Notes

Chapter 1

1. "Sicily: Her Role in the Mediterranean Conflict," A paper on the Sicilian people and their island by Private Biagio M. Corvo, S-2 Section, Camp Lee, Va. Sent to Assistant Chief of Staff, G-2, Headquarters Third Corps Area, Baltimore, Md., June 18, 1942. Author's files.

2. Letter from Senator Danaher to Private Corvo, June 30, 1942.

Chapter 2

1. Colonel Whelms was appointed the first postwar U.S. military attache to Italy.

2. The original copy of War Department Red Border Letter ordering the tranfer of Private Corvo, dated August 5, 1942. Author's files.

3. Secret instructions to report to Training Center, Sparks, Md.

Chapter 3

1. The Royal Decree 529, March 26, 1926, read as follows:

The loss of his Italian citizenship, together with the confiscation of all his possessions is inflicted on Vincenzo Vacirca by King Victor Emanuel II of Italy . . . for holding public conferences and having written articles which have denigrated the Italian nation and for having incited violence and disorder among our immigrants abroad . . . we unanimously decree the sentence imposed under the law of January 31, 1926, Special Tribunal . . . Signed Mussolini-Federzoni. (A photocopy is in the author's files.)

2. Letter from Lieutenant Colonel Sweet-Escott to Earl Brennan dated September 2, 1942. Author's files.

3. Copy of Special Military Orders No. 11, issued by Colonel McDonnell, January 16, 1943, authorizing Private Biagio M. Corvo to travel to any place within the continental United States.

4. The mission undertaken by Special Prefect Cesare Mori is covered in a meticulously documented volume by Salvio Porto entitled *Mafia e Fascismo* published by Flaccovio, Palermo, Sicily, 1977.

5. As a result of the incident, I was asked to file a report of the events leading up to my apprehension by CIC in order to clear the record. A summary court martial was held at which a Captain White was the hearing officer, and the incident was closed with a lesson learned. Copy of the original report in author's files and OSS archives at National Archives.

Chapter 4

1. Article by Earl Brennan in *La Parola*, July 1976, covering the history of the Italian SI Section of OSS and including the background of the relief map of Sicily, p. 269.

2. Copy of two letters of introduction provided by Pacciardi to SI for delivery to North African contacts in April 1943. Author's files.

3. Subject discussed with Ernie Cuneo during OSS Symposium, September 19 and 20, 1986, Hotel Mayflower, Washington, D.C., and subsequent telephone calls initiated by Cuneo who planned to write about the effort to establish an Italian government in exile. See Giorgio Pisano, *Storia della Guerra Civile in Italia* (Milan: Edizioni FPE, 1965), Vol. 1, p. 9.

Chapter 5

1. In his book *The Secret Surrender* (New York: Harper and Row, 1966), pp. 13-18, Allen Dulles recounts that his documents were examined by the Gestapo at Annemasse and that he prevailed on a French officer to look the other way while he crossed the frontier to Switzerland. However, other versions of the story that circulated in OSS at that time indicated that the Gestapo meticulously perused his papers and then went for a long lunch while he crossed the frontier.

2. Original copy Washington Planning Board files, OSS files at National Archives, and copy in author's files.

3. "Italian Prisoners in East Africa," Inter-office memo. An assessment of the use of Italian prisoners of war and proposed repatriation of Italian nationals, by the author. Italian SI files and author's documents.

4. Eddy's proposal to have Pacciardi commissioned in the U.S. Army and the negative reaction of the State Department were communicated by General Marshall on June 24, 1943, to Eisenhower and are documented in official State Department and War Department files and in copies of those communications in the author's files.

5. Donovan personally signed the overseas duty orders of the first Earl Group on March 13, 1943. The group included Privates Luigi DiMaggio, Louis S. Timpanaro (Louis Trunk), Gaspare Salerno, Nato DeAngelis, Giovanni Di Montis, John Ballato, Peppino Puleo, Vincent Paia, Louis Fiorilla, and Lieutenant Frank Tarallo. Author's files.

6. Letter from I. D. Shapiro, OSS North African Theater Officer, to Colonel Buxton, April 5, 1943, urging that B. M. Corvo be commissioned. National Archives.

7. War Department Orders, April 28, 1943, appointing author as Second Lieutenant, AUS, and assignment to duty with SI, North Africa, JCS-170. Entry 110, Box 46, Folder 476, National Archives.

Chapter 6

1. Radiograms sent by Eisenhower to War Department; Donovan to Eddy; Eddy to SI; SO from Eddy; SO from Exedet. These messages, as well as other communications, stressed the need for Italian-speaking personnel in order to live up to the OSS commitment to Eisenhower and AFHQ. Original messages at National Archives. Copies in author's files.

2. June 14 order from Eddy to Colonel John Weaver giving priority to QXR schedules and codes for Earl Group, June 14, 1943. Author's files.

3. ISLD message regarding Sardinia, June 13, 1943, from Major Adams to Scamporino. Protocol No. 1039. Author's files.

4. AFHQ travel orders for Second Lieutenant Biagio M. Corvo, June 19, 1943, "to Bizerte and such places in the North African Theater as may be necessary." Author's files.

5. Letter of introduction to Rear Admiral Connally from Colonel Eddy to discuss Special Operations of OSS. Author's 201 file.

6. Reports on the "Bathtub" mission. Article in Anthony Camboni, *La Parola del Popolo*, Chicago, June 1976; Debriefing Report of Private Vincent Pavia to Lieutenant Corvo, National Archives and author's files; Report on Sardinian Mission by Anthony Camboni at the time of debriefing, October 22, 1943, National Archives, Box 38, Folder 319.

Chapter 7

1. Later (August 1944) Bruce sent Lieutenant William J. Casey to Algiers to report on the methods used by 2677 Regiment in preparing, controlling operations, and reporting and distributing intelligence gathered in the field. Casey wrote a glowing report on his observations and suggested that OSS/London adopt many of the same procedures. A copy of Casey's report was forwarded to General Donovan through E. J. Putzel by Colonel Tom Early on September 9, 1944. Entry 99, Box 33, Folder 163a, National Archives.

2. "Husky" included the first massive Allied parachute operation of the war. It was led by some of the most prominent officers who were to emerge during World War II. The shooting down of many C-47s by our own invasion fleet and over the beachhead is accurately recounted in William B. Breuer, *Drop Zone Sicily* (San Rafael, Calif.: Presidio Press, 1986).

3. Colonel Cummings' letter of introduction to CG British Eighth Army. Author's 201 file.

4. Professor Carleton S. Coon vividly describes his experiences in Tunisia in his book *A North African Story 1941-1943* (Ipswich: Gambit, 1980). Some of the OSS activities are also described by Colonel Jerry Sage in his book *Sage* (Wayne, Ind.: Miles Standish Press, 1985), and are corroborated in tapes by Irving Goff who served with Sage in Tunisia. These tapes were prepared for the OSS Symposium, September 19 and 20, 1986, Washington, D.C.

5. "Garibaldi" communications file, messages to "Yankee," Algiers. Messages 1-50 incoming and outgoing, July-August 1943. OSS Communications files, National Archives, author's files.

6. Rudolph Winnacker, R & A "Report for Period of August 5 to August 15" to William Eddy and W. A. Langer, National Archives, Field Reports Entry 99, Box 31, Folder 151. Copy author's files.

Chapter 8

1. "Garibaldi/McGreggor" communications file.

2. Yankee to Garibaldi: Eddy to Scamp. Assignment of Italian SI personnel to Fifth Army OSS Unit under Donald Downes.

3. Downes wrote an account of his "Banana" mission and his Fifth Army activity in his book *The Scarlet Thread* (London: Verschoyle, 1953). Thereafter, the story is repeated in Harris Smith, *OSS: Secret History of America's First Intelligence* (Berkeley; University of California Press, 1972); and Kermit Roosevelt, *The War Report of the OSS* (New York: Walker, 1976).

4. The 38° 40′ Naval Operational Restriction was enforced for security reasons in order to avoid alerting the enemy of the anticipated Allied landing in mainland Italy.

5. The CIC officer operating at Petralia Sottana was Lieutenant Mario Brod, with whom we kept in touch throughout the Italian campaign.

6. The San Fratello mission report was written as part of the debriefing of Sergeant Anthony Ribbarich. National Archives, Entry 99, Folder 195A, Box 39.

7. General Giuseppe Castellano covers all phases of his negotiations in his book *Come Firmai L'Armistizio di Cassibile* (Milan: Mondadori, 1945). I have discussed the details of the negotiations with Attorney Vito Guarrasi of Palermo, who was Castellano's chief aide, and with General Castellano himself, whom I saw during the war and occasionally during postwar trips to Italy.

8. Lieutenant James Russo was from Middletown, Conn., and had been recruited in the OG. He was sent to Salerno and was wounded when a booby trap blew up the Naples Post Office. On his return to Washington he transferred to Italian SI.

9. The landing at Brolo is described in several books, including Admiral Morrison's *Sicily, Salerno and Anzio* (Boston: Little, Brown, 1964), pp. 203-205; and *U.S. Army History in World War II: Mediterranean Theater of Operations—Sicily and the Fall of Fascism.*

10. Lipari Island Operational Report by Captain Frank Tarallo. Author's files and National Archives.

11. "Garibaldi" to "Yankee," July 22, 1943. Arthur Roseborough, chief, SI North African theater, was "sacked" because he favored U.S. backing for General DeGaulle. He was a highly skilled international lawyer with expertise in French affairs and even though he was associated with the Dulles law firm of Sullivan and Cromwell, he was unjustly purged from the OSS. See National Archives files; copy author's files.

Chapter 9

1. Pantaleoni was never aware of his designation as CO of Palermo OSS Station. He was captured and listed as missing in action during the San Fratello mission.

2. "Yankee" to "Garibaldi" from Eddy outlining the assignment of OSS/SI support missions for "Avalanche" with Naval Task Force 80.4.

3. General Maxwell Taylor gives an account of the plans for the dropping of the Eighty-second Airborne in the outskirts of Rome and his recommendations that the operation be canceled, as a result of Rome conference with General Carbone and other officials. *Swords and Plowshares* (New York: W.W. Norton, 1972).

4. Tarallo Report of the Ventotene Mission. National Archives, Entry 165, Box 36, Folder 354, and author's files. Report of Task Force 80.4 by Captain C. L.

Andrews, U.S. Navy, to Commander and Chief, U.S. Fleet, declassified 843089, author and National Archives, including copy of unconditional surrender. Entry 165, Folder 354, Caserta S. AD-2.

5. Account of Ventotene and other insular operations by E. Clemente, *La Parola Del Popolo*, Chicago, July/August 1973 issue.

6. Report by Lieutenant Andre Pacatte to Vincent Scamporino covering activities during September 9-26. National Archives, Entry 99, Box 31, Folder 156.

7. De Angelis, Activities of the Special Detachment No. 7 at the Salerno Salient, G-2, Fifth Army, September 23, 1943. Author's files; National Archives. Also, report to Donovan by Scamporino, Operations of the Seventh Detachment, National Archives.

8. "Greenbrier" operation. Radio File, "Greenbrier to Garibaldi," incoming and outgoing messages. Author's files.

9. Cianca and Tarchiani, among others, were landed at Salerno by SOE. This party had been taken in tow by Dino Gentili, who had played a leading role in attempting to organize an Italian government in exile with the approval of President Roosevelt. Leo Valiani mentions "Dino" a number of times in his book, *Tutte le Strade Conducano a Roma* (Florence: La Nuova Italia, 1947). Gentili's background is referred to on p. 9, Item 20, of Pisano's *Storia della Guerra Civile in Italia 1943-1945*.

Chapter 10

1. The details of Donovan's visit to the Salerno beachhead and the changes in the command structure which he made are detailed in Downes' book, *The Scarlet Thread*; Peter Thompkins' *A Spy in Rome* (New York: Simon and Schuster, 1962); Harris Smith *OSS*; OSS Fifth Army Files in the National Archives; "Pacatte Report," Entry 99, Folder 42, Box 30, National Archives; Roosevelt, *The War Report of the OSS*; Anthony Cave Brown, *The Secret Report of the OSS* (New York: Berkely, 1976).

2. Radio Files, "Concord" to "Yankee." Donovan's messages to Eddy announcing decision to consolidate operations in the Fifth Army area with Huntington as CO. OSS files; National Archives.

3. Eddy to Huntington and Eddy to Corvo, citing orders and AFHQ radio message No. 8866 by Eisenhower. Author's files; OSS communications files at National Archives.

Chapter 11

1. Cables 112136A to CG Seventh Army from CINCMED.

2. The basic OSS/SIM agreement was activated after having been approved by Algiers and was honored by both sides until totally implemented.

3. The report of the Giglio mission is filed with the National Archives and the author's files and was prepared by Wayne Nelson, November 3, 1943. "Paternoster" mission, November 23, 1943.

4. Minutes of meeting at OSS Algiers Headquarters, December 8, 1943. 2677 regiment AFHQ Files at National Archives and author's files. Letter from Scamp to Corvo, December 9, 1943. Author's files.

5. No contact was established by SI Italy with Colonel Dodds-Parker to clear the planned missions, as I construed that such a contact would have hampered our freedom of action in conducting our SI operations in enemy territory.

6. "Garibaldi" to "Yankee," OSS radio communications files. National Archives and author's files.

7. General Castellano, *Come Firmai L'Armistizio di Cassibile* and Dodds-Parker, *Setting Europe Ablaze* (Windlesham, Surrey: Springwood Books, 1983).

8. Pacatte Report to Huntington, Entry 99, Folder 142, Box 30, National Archives; author's files.

9. Commanders Log, Royal Italian Navy Submarine *Askum*, CO Sorrentino. Mission report by Andre Pacatte, author's files.

10. Raimondo Craveri, *I Servizi Segreti e la Campagna d'Italia* (Milan: La Pietra, 1980).

11. Memo from Donovan to Major General Alfred Gruenther, September 24, 1943. National Archives, OSS Fifth Army files; and author's files.

12. Memo from Brigadier J.M.W. Martin to Fifth Army OSS, October 23, 1943. National Archives, Fifth Army OSS files, and copy author's files.

13. Message from John Shaheen to Mike Burke. Author's personal files made available by Shaheen before his death.

14. Personal report by Colonel Huntington to Donovan, "Personal and Confidential by Pouch," November 17, 1943. Subject: "Interference with OSS Activities." National Archives, Fifth Army OSS files, and copy author's files.

Chapter 12

1. Radio orders from Glavin. "Yankee" Radio File, National Archives.

2. Log of voyage by Italian Royal Navy Submarine *Platino* kept by OSS escorting officer, Peter Durante, author's files.

3. SI Brindisi memo regarding assignment of Italian SI personnel in MEDTO, SI, OSS files, and author's files.

4. Anzio report by Lieutenant Croze, Box 31, EQ-5, Folder 279. National Archives and copy author's files.

5. Proposed plan to bring guerrilla involvement under military supervision, February 19, 1944. Author's files.

6. Durante log. Second mission by submarine *Platino* to land "Banana," "Raisin," and "Lemon" missions. Author's files. Note: This "Banana" mission should not be confused with Downes' mission in Spain.

7. Radio message from "Yankee" to "Garibaldi" and repeated to "Concord." Author's files and National Archives.

8. Radio message from "Yankee" to "Garibaldi" and "Concord" from "Gamble" to Corvo and Reutershan.

9. General Order No. 92 issued by Brigadier General B. F. Caffey. National Archives and author's files.

10. Mission "Ginny" sources include the files of the Operational Groups (OG); Roosevelt, *War Report of the OSS*; and Anthony Cave Brown, *Wild Bill Donovan: The Last Hero* (New York: Times Books, 1982); Courts Martial Proceedings Against General Dostler.

11. Francesco Aurello DiBella, *Un Aviatore Racconta le Sue Battaglie* (Palermo: Renna, 1950).

12. Memo from SBS, Bari, Commander Edward Green. National Archives, Declassified NND 843099.

13. Thompkins, *A Spy in Rome*; Brown, *The Last Hero*.

14. Report on Theater Personnel and Reorganization by Colonel Vanderblue. National Archives, OP-23, Entry 99, Folder 164, Box No. 33.

15. Glavin to Director, OSS, and Shepardson. Encomiums to SI Intelligence, Memo. National Archives.

16. Two orders from Torrielli to Corvo. Author's files, Caserta files, and National Archives.

17. Allied meeting to discuss plans for the disposition of partisan armaments and groups. Rome Area Command AAI. National Archives.

18. Designation of units of the 2677 Regiment; Roosevelt, *War Report of the O.S.S.*, Caserta files, and National Archives.

Chapter 13

1. The Parri message was sent out under his codename "Franco" through the SI team "Apricot" of which Boeri was the mission leader. Author's files, National Archives, OSS/ISI files.

2. Raffaele Cadorna, *La Riscossa* (Turin: Bietti, 1965).

3. Report on the "Kingston" mission. National Archives, OSS Bastia files.

Chapter 14

1. OSS Review of meetings on the Island of Capri. Minutes and notes taken by Bob Joyce. National Archives.

2. Communication from Swiss SI desk, Washington, to Homer Hall and memo from Reginald C. Foster re Italian-Swiss operational plan. August 2, August 4, 1944. Author's files; National Archives, Box 37, AD-3, Folder 373.

3. Original note in author's 201 file.

4. Report on the infiltration of "Pricklypear" team by Aldo Icardi. National Archives, Box 35, Entry 165, Folder 331.

5. Copy of the original Donovan letter from Donovan to Agrifoglio. Author's files.

6. "Mangosteen" mission plan for liaison to CLNAI. Author's files, National Archives, COD, SI Files, Siena/Florence.

7. Memorandum from Colonel Tom Early to General Donovan. National Archives and copy author's files.

8. Communications from Consul General Nester to Secretary of State, to Alexander Kirk and Robert Murphy. State Department Files re Consulate General, Palermo, Italy. Author's files.

9. Letter from Daddario to Corvo. Author's files.

10. Company D Intelligence Bulletins. National Archives, Box 3, Entry 165, Folder 226.

11. Memo from Major Max Corvo to Major William Suhling re creation of Alpine supply depots on the French Alps. National Archives, Co. D/SI Correspondence, Box 37, File 3, Folder 374; National Archives, Box 2, File OSS-2, Folder 24; author's files.

12. Debriefing report of the W/T Gaetano Neglia of the "Pear" mission. National Archives, SI Reports, Box 34, File AD-1, Folder 303.

13. Memo/Letter to Suhling from Corvo regarding Rankin Plan. National Archives, CO. D/SI Correspondence, Box 37, File 3, Folder 374; copy author's files.

Chapter 15

1. Letter to Earl Brennan, author's files. Other communications may be found in the National Archives, Box 37, AD-3, Folder 373.

2. References and facsimiles of messages are included in Pietro Secchia, *Storia della Resistenza* (Milan: Editori Ruiniti, 1963).

3. Ossola Campaign Debriefing of Lieutenant Giannino's "Chrysler" mission, Co. A, 2671, Sp. REC. Bn; National Archives, Box 36, Entry AA, Folder 186. Marco Fini, R. Pesenti, and M. Ponzo, *Guerriglia nell'Ossola* (Milan: Feltrinelli, 1975).

4. Ibid. National Archives. Giannino Report, including Report of Sergeant LoDolce and other components of mission.

5. Memo from Colonel Pompeo Agrifoglio. Author's personal files.

6. General Plan for "Papaya" mission, September 1944. Letter and memo, Corvo to Suhling. Reply from Suhling, September 23, 1944. National Archives, Box 24, AD-6, Folder 25, Siena, July-October 1944.

7. Travel Orders for members of "Papaya" mission, September 27, 1944. Headquarters Allied Armies in Italy by command of Major General Lyman Lemnitzer.

8. "Logan" radio messages and "Fratello" radio messages reproduced in October 27, 1944, report by Corvo to CO Company D, 2677 Regiment. National Archives, OSS/SI Siena; author's files.

9. Debriefing of radio operator Sal Amodei, May 31, 1945. SI Files, "Papaya" mission. Amodei was a petty officer from the Italian Navy who had participated as a volunteer in a number of dangerous missions. At the last minute, because the team was operating in U.S. uniforms, I borrowed a dog tag from one of my U.S. sergeants, Mario Mussi of Brooklyn, New York, and put it on a chain around Amodei's neck. When he was captured by the Germans the dog tags saved his life because they listed him on their prisoner-of-war records in Stalag 7A as U.S. Sergeant Mario Mussi from Brooklyn, New York. Amodei insisted that he had emigrated to the United States just before the outbreak of the war. That provided the explanation for his poor English. Author's files and National Archives, OSS/SI Debriefing of Teams.

10. Three memos of Geneva Conferences held on October 14, 1944. Written by Max Corvo on October 25, 1944, for CO 2677 Regiment and CO Company D. (1) "Future Plans and Correlation of S.I. Activities with Switzerland; (2) "Meeting with Partisan Leaders"; (3) Meeting with 807." (All future policies with Switzerland were thereafter based on these documents.) National Archives; author's files.

11. Marshal Alexander's radio message to the Italian partisans is fully reported in Secchia, *Storia della Resistenza*, and a number of other books covering the underground war in Italy.

12. Debriefing report of survivors of the "Maria Giovanna" mission, including radio files. OSS/SI files at National Archives, Box 39, File Ad-14, Folder 394, and copy author's files.

13. Semimonthly reports of Italian SI Section 2677th Regiment OSS/AFHQ; Caserta file at National Archives; copy author's files.

14. The work of the CLNAI mission has been amply chronicled in various books and publications, including General Cadorna's *La Riscossa*; Craveri, *I Servizi Segreti e La Campagna d'Italia*; Company D 2677 Regiment Records, National Archives.

15. The debriefing reports of Tullio Lussi and other members of the "Mangosteen" mission are part of the Italian SI, Company D Records, available at the National Archives in various boxes and folders. Several books on the subject are reported to be in preparation; Aldo Icardi, *American Master Spy* (New York: University Books, 1954) covers the incident and history of the mission. Confirmation of the fluidity in the area is provided in the debriefing report of Gelindo Bertoluzzi, one of the original members of the mission.

Chapter 16

1. An accurate accounting of the meeting with General Carbone is included in General Maxwell Taylor's *Swords and Plowshares*.

Chapter 17

1. A copy of Badoglio's original letter to President Roosevelt was among the Brennan Papers. Author's files.

2. Attorney General Francis Biddle's speech was fully reported in the *New York Times*, October 13, 1944.

3. All "Vessel" reports were classified "Secret/Control," and their distribution was highly restricted. Cave Brown's *The Last Hero* makes a number of erroneous assumptions; Father Graham, a Jesuit, prevailed on the CIA to declassify a number of original documents in 1978-1979. R. Harris Smith in his *OSS* printed erroneous information which was repeated in Cave Brown's *The War Report of the OSS*. Many of James Angleton's assertions regarding "Vessel" were rebutted in a special analytical article which I wrote and which appeared in the *Middletown Bulletin* in its December 1984 issue.

4. Copies of Dr. Callisen's letter to Donovan were found among the Brennan papers, and a copy is in the author's files.

5. Dr. Langer's communication appears in the Italian SI semimonthly reports of 2677th Regiment, Caserta. National Archives, Box 34, File AD-1, Folder 303.

Chapter 18

1. Italian SI semimonthly report, December 1-15, 1944. National Archives, Box 34, File AD-1, Folder 303. These missions were primarily designed to cover any stragetic retreat to the reported redoubt which the Nazis were said to be creating in Bavaria and the Tyrol.

2. Ibid. Italian SI Report listing the active radio-equipped missions in the field. At this time, some of these missions had already been operating for ten months in enemy territory.

3. Ibid. Italian SI Report, February 16-28. Comparative charts of supply drops by the three operational branches of Company D. The code names of individual pinpoints appear as part of these same reports.

4. Ibid.

5. Letter from Colonel George Stapleton to SI. Copy in author's files.

6. Debriefing reports of the "Orange" mission, Co. D SI files, National Archives, Box 37, AD-3, Folder 374. Craveri, *I Servizi Segreti e la Campagna d'Italia*.

7. Early in February 1945, the "Rosetta" mission in Piedmont started to transmit a series of intelligence reports indicating that certain elements in the German Army were attempting to start serious negotiations to effect a surrender. These messages outlined the necessary steps that needed to be followed. The scenario proposed was the same one that Baron Parilli eventually offered Allen Dulles, including the release of Ferruccio Parri. National Archives, "German Attempts to Negotite Armistice," Box 34, File AD-1, Folder 307, copy in author's files.

8. Plans for the city teams and intelligence briefing material were sent to both Suhling and Glavin and are stored, in part, at the National Archives, Box 34, File AD-1, Folder 298. Copy author's files.

Chapter 19

1. Dr. Enzo Boeri had many friends and managed to penetrate the German High Command. The radio files of "Apricot/Jolliet" and "Citron/Baldwin," April 1944/May 1945, reveal that Boeri transmitted key strategic intelligence as well as order of battle (OB) and tactical information.

2. See Note 7, Chapter 18, above.

3. Briefing Papers, City Teams. National Archives, Box 34, File AD-1, Folder 298.

4. Report of the Bologna Team, CO Major Frank Tarallo. National Archives, Box 34, File AD-1, Folder 304.

5. Messages from "Brutus/Daddario," Milan, gave an account of the situation. National Archives, Box 39, Pers. 23, Folder 297.

6. Leandro Arpinati served as undersecretary of Interior during 1929-1933. Of socialist background, he was one of the founders of Bologna Fasci di Combattimento in 1919. He was the undisputed leader of the Fascists in Bologna. He was accused of complicity in Zaniboni's attempt to kill Mussolini and was reported to be incorruptible and uncompromising. Despite Mussolini's respect for him, he was asked to resign in 1933. He rejected service with the Fascist Social Republic when he turned down Mussolini's personal appeal in 1943. Cannistraro, *Historical Dictionary of Fascist Italy* (Westport, Conn.: Greenwood Press, 1982).

7.   "April 26, 1945
"With this letter, I, Rodolfo Graziani, Marshal of Italy, in my capacity as Minister of the Armed Forces, give full powers to Gen. Karl Wolff, Supreme Chief of the SS and Police and General Plenipotentiary of the German Forces in Italy, to conduct, on my behalf, negotiations under the same conditions as he may obtain for the German Armed Forces in Italy. Such terms to be binding on the Regular Armed Forces of the Italian Army, the Air Force and the Navy, as well as the Fascist military formations.

                                                            Marshal of Italy
Author's files.   (s) Rodolfo Graziani"

8. Colonel Walter Rauff was the second highest ranking SS officer in Italy and was in charge of the Milan area as deputy to General Karl Wolff. Prior to being transferred to Italy, Colonel Rauff was accused of being the inventor of the gas wagons used to exterminate the prisoners and of killing 96,000 Jews. After the war he managed to escape, and he settled in South America. While he was sought for war crimes, he was never brought to justice. He died in Santiago, Chile, in May 1984.

9. On March 19, 1947, in a communique issued by the components of the CLNAI, the decision to execute Mussolini was assumed by all of the parties represented on the committee. The powers to make the decision were attributed to the agreement which the CLNAI and the Italian government had negotiated in 1944. The statement was published in *Il Momento* and in other papers in Italy. Prior to the issuance of the statement, Longo had been accused of having personally given Valerio the execution orders.

10. Lieutenant Icardi was later sent to Piedmont to organize an intelligence operation that could observe and report accurately French military moves to annex some Alpine valleys, particularly the Aosta Valley. His reports are filed with the SI Caserta files at the National Archives.

11. The Black Brigades were organized by the Fascist Social Republic to

counter the patriot underground formations. It was to be used in the cities for counterpartisan work and to spread fear and terror among the populace. These forces were often used to conduct operations to retake areas under partisan control. They were known for their extreme cruelty and merciless execution of prisoners.

12. Magenta was the site of an impressive victory of the French Army during the War of Italian Liberation.

13. Caserta Office: Operation Sunrise/Crossword. Surrender of Axis Forces in North Italy, Box 1-2, Folder 11-19.

14. It seems inexplicable that AFHQ and Fifteenth Army Group should have disregarded the messages being transmitted by SI mission "Norma," which was in direct contact with the German High Command. Just as inexplicable was the Dulles/2677 operation to set up communications through "Little Wally" when radio contact was already available. Some would attribute the eror to excessive secrecy, but Suhling and Glavin were already aware that we were in contact with Vietinghoff, Brumer, and the Committee of Liberation in Bolzano.

15. These files were later turned over to the Fifteenth Army Group at the request of the British who made representations to the effect that we had unilaterally secured them.

16. On May 6 we received a message from OG team "Battle" informing us that the OSS Trieste City Team had been kicked out and advising us not to get involved with the Yugoslav "matter" in the slightest degree. National Archives, Box 40, Entry 165, Folder 417.

17. We had received a radiogram from Glavin regarding entry of OSS personnel from Switzerland into the Milan area. The message revealed that relations between Berne and Caserta seemed to be strained. The radiogram stated: "110 (Dulles) from Glavin and Maddox, info Donovan, in accordance with established principles OSS organizational responsibility, no OSS personnel from Switzerland may enter AFHQ area under control Caserta without explicit permission 2677 Regimental Headquarters." National Archives, Box 40, Entry 165, Folder 414.

18. The radiogram from Donovan asking for the liquidation of the Italian SI Section was answered by Glavin on May 14, giving the schedule of liquidation and making a series of suggestions calculated to mitigate the situation. National Archives, Box 39, Pers. 23, Folder 404.

Chapter 20

1. Copy of Bob Joyce memo to Magruder and Shepardson regarding postwar SI operations in Italy and the Balkans. National Archives.

2. Walter "Red" Dowling had been in close touch with Brennan in Washington and had been briefed constantly about the Italian situation. When he joined the U.S. Embassy Staff in Rome, he became antagonistic and later was reported to have made negative comments according to Marco Fini, *Americans in Italy* (Milan: Feltrinelli, 1976).

3. Letter from Maddox to Shepardson, July 15, 1945. National Archives; author's files.

4. Radio from Donovan to Glavin. National Archives, Box 40, Entry 165, Folder 414; copy author's files.

5. Handwritten note by Donovan. Author's files.

6. Handwritten note to Shepardson from Donovan.

7. Memo: "Mediterranean Reorganization," July 25, 1944. Page Six, Washington Historical Office, 6P, 23, Entry 99, Folder 164, Box 33, National Archives.

8. Memo from Shepardson to Donovan relating to Mrs. Hawkins' report. Author's files.

9. Letter from author to Serge Peter Karlow, August 15, 1944. Author's files.

Biographical Sketches of the Leaders of the Italian Resistance

In order to have a better understanding of the Italian situation, the readers should be given a brief background of the principal players of the dramatic events that culminated with the rise en masse by the North Italian resistance movement.

While some resistance leaders were forced by circumstances to seek asylum abroad to avoid the relentless persecution of the OVRA and the Special Tribunals, others continued their fight against Fascism in Italy or from the penal colonies in which they were condemned.

Some, like Giacomo Matteotti, outspoken member of the Italian Parliament, paid for their opposition to Fascism with their lives.

Don Luigi Sturzo

Born in Caltigirone, Sicily, in 1871, from parents in comfortable financial circumstances, Don Luigi together with his brother Mario were ordained priests. Mario went on to be appointed bishop of Piazza Armerina, Sicily, whereas Don Luigi became the social conscience and founder of the Christian Democratic movement.

He early displayed his sociological bent while a student at the Gregorian University in Rome. After graduation he returned to Caltagirone where he championed the cause of the sulphur miners and peasants. While there he taught at the Seminary. His work to resolve social problems led him into politics; he was elected mayor of the city, a position he held until 1920.

With the election of Benedict XV, who was a more liberal Pontiff, Sturzo was called to Rome to assume the position of secretary of Catholic Action. This appointment marked the beginning of his political activism and led to the foundation of the Popular party, forerunner of the Christian Democratic party.

Sturzo's position in Catholic Action gave him the opportunity to visit all the regions of Italy and to set up Catholic workers committees. In November 1918, he announced the formation of the new Democratic party in a famous speech delivered in Milan. He was elected secretary of the new party, and in the elections of November of 1919, the party elected 111 deputies out of a total of 508 seats.

The post-World War I years saw the gradual deterioration and destruction of Italy's democratic parliamentary system, and on Mussolini's march on Rome in 1922, Sturzo led his party in opposition to Fascism.

In 1923 at the Party Congress in Turin, Sturzo forced the issue, and the democratic ministers abandoned the government. This action earned him Mussolini's total enmity. Sturzo was forced to retire to a convent, and in November 1924, left Italy to go abroad. Until the beginning of World War II, he commuted between London and Paris. In 1936, he founded a Demo-Christian group in London, and in 1940 he created the International Christian Democratic Union.

Sturzo was considered the moral and spiritual leader of the Italian antiFascist movement. His books and articles became compulsory reading in the free world which was yearning to see Italy liberated from the Fascist yoke.

With the fall of France and in failing health, Sturzo moved to Brooklyn, New York, where he was frequently sought out by the U.S. State Department and by Allied government representatives who considered him the leader of the opposition to Mussolini. From his pen he poured advice and encouragement for the repressed people of Italy.

Sturzo reentered Italy in 1946, and he lived in the convent of the Connosian Sisters at 53 Via Mondovi, Rome. His office became the mecca for the leaders of the Demo-Christian party, from Alcide DeGasperi who had worked with him in 1919 and who now headed the government, to Mario Scelba, a fellow townsman who became prime minister in 1953.

Sturzo died on August 8, 1959, in the same convent where he had taken up residence in 1946.

I last saw him in the summer of 1953 busily at work in his studio with a desk filled with towerlike stacks of books and manuscripts he had carefully laid to one side for future reading.

Ferruccio Parri

If the Italian underground had a "Scarlet Pimpernel," his real name was Ferruccio Parri who was born in Pinerolo, Piedmont, in 1890 and who devoted a good part of his adult life to actively fighting Fascist repression in Italy.

A graduate of the University of Turin, Parri embarked on a teaching career which was interrupted by Italy's entry into World War I in 1915. Serving as an officer, he was highly decorated for bravery and was promoted to a staff position where he demonstrated outstanding qualities in military strategy. At the end of the war, he was named director of veterans' affairs, a position he left to embark on a career as an editor, eventually working as an associate to Luigi Albertini at Italy's largest daily, *Corriere Della Sera*.

Because Parri opposed Fascism, he was dismissed from *Il Corriere*, followed by Albertini.

In order to continue militating against Mussolini after the murder of Matteotti, Parri, Bauer, Arpesani, Basso, and Mira started an opposition paper called *Il Caffe*, but it was soon closed down.

With his friends Parri began to build an organization that helped many of the prominent antiFascist political leaders escape from Italy. Among the escapes carried out were those of Nenni, Sarragat, Trevis, and Turati. In this work, he also had the help of Carlo Rosselli and Sandro Pertini. He was arrested and sentenced for antiFascist activities, and in 1927 he was sent to the penal colony on the island of Lipari until 1929. Free for a few months he was again picked up and sent to the island of Ustica until 1933. Upon his liberation, with the help of friends, he found a position on the research staff of the Edison Company.

The founding of Giustizia e Liberta, an activist organization created by Carlo Rosselli and Emilio Lussu during the mid-1930s, was welcomed by Parri who chose to remain in Italy to fight the Fascist regime. Both Rosselli and Lussu, who were with him in Lipari, were aided in their daring escape to France while he went on working underground and finally was sentenced to forced residence in Vallo della Lucania, a small desolate town in southern Italy.

In 1942 Parri was briefly arrested by the OVRA but released, after which he set to work in earnest to help organize the Action party, a dynamic political grouping of men and women endowed with unusually outstanding cultural backgrounds.

With the advent of the September 1943 armistice, Parri led the CLN in the serious organizational work of creating a central command point for guerrilla warfare. He and Communist Luigi Longo teamed up to create a unified command of The Volunteers of Liberty, the military arm of CLNAI. In the summer of 1944 General Cadorna was parachuted into northern Italy and took over all command with Parri and Longo as his deputies.

In the fall of 1944, Parri led a CLN mission to southern Italy to negotiate with the Allies and the Italian government for the official recognition of the partisan movement. Other members of the mission who were exfiltrated through Switzerland with the help of OSS and SOE were Alfredo Pizzoni, president of the CLNAI; Giancarlo Pajetta, representing Longo and the Communist Brigades; and Eddy Sogno, an Italian officer who was assigned to the British SOE. The mission visited General Maitland-Wilson at AFHQ and General Alexander at Fifteenth Army Group, and attained both its military and political goals with the signing of the so-called "Rome Accords."

Unfortunately, not long after his return to Milan, Parri was captured by the German SS, but General Karl Wolff, who had been angling for an armistice, saved him as a possible future bargaining chip with the Allies.

Released as part of Wolff's effort to negotiate an armistice with the Allies, Parri, joined by Cadorna, came south for a final military conference with Alexander and Clark and with OSS and SOE. He returned to Milan in time to take part in the popular rising in northern Italy of which he had been one of the principal architects.

In June Parri was called to head Italy's first postwar government in which were represented all the parties in the country's political spectrum. Members of his cabinet included DeGasperi and Togliatti, but the government was short-lived and its mandate ended in December 1945.

Following the collapse of his government and the dissolution of the Action party in 1963, Parri was nominated to the Senate with lifelong tenure.

He died at the age of 91 in December 1981.

General Raffaele Cadorna

A native of Pallanza in Piedmont, Raffaele Cadorna was born in 1889. He represented a third generation of military men who had devoted their lives to the Italian Army. He graduated from the Military Academy at the age of twenty, whereupon he was assigned as a lieutenant to the Florence Lancers, a cavalry outfit that was sent to Libya in 1911 where he distinguished himself by recon-coitering behind enemy lines and was awarded a bronze medal.

Cadorna took part in World War I and fought on many fronts as a captain, winning three silver medals for outstanding bravery. By the end of the war he had won promotion to Major, and soon after the end of the conflict he was named military attache to Prague Czechoslovakia. When he had finished, he was promoted to colonel and given the command of a crack cavalry unit, the Savoy Cavalry.

During World War II he commanded an armored division and was in command of the Ariete Division at the of the Armistice. This was part of the Mobile Army Group that was supposed to defend Rome. His was the only division that opposed the German Army as it attempted to invest Rome. He refused to surrender, and his division fought the Wehrmacht until its ammunition ran out.

Cadorna's name was placed on the black list of both German and Fascist secret services. He went underground and eventually made his way south to join the Badoglio government.

Parachuted into German-occupied Italy in a joint SOE/SIM operation, Cadorna was named commander of the Volunteers of Liberty—the military arm of CLNAI. His deputies were Ferruccio Parri of the GL formations and Luigi Longo of the Communist-controlled Garibaldi Brigades. The command structure, despite the various political currents, worked with outstanding courage and success. He moved about northern Italy under a series of noms de guerre.

Cadorna was part of the second CLNAI mission to southern Italy where he, Parri, and Giancarlo Pajetta attended a series of high-level meetings to work out miltary strategy with AFHQ and Mark Clark's Fifteenth Army Group.

Immediately after the war, Cadorna was named chief of the Italian General Staff where he was handed the task of rebuilding the armed forces. He held that position until 1947. He was elected to the Italian Senate in 1948 and retired from politics in 1963. He died at his villa in Pallanza on December 20, 1973.

Cadorna was decorated with three silver medals for his direction in the underground battle against German-Nazi forces. His father was the commander and chief of the Italian armed forces in World War I, Marshal Cadorna, who had made no secret of his dislike for Fascism. Raffaele Cadorna followed in his footsteps.

Luigi Longo

Luigi Longo, Communist leader of the Garilbaldi Brigades, was born in the Monferrato area of Piedmont in 1900 to a family of small landowners and completed technical studies at the age of 20 when he joined the Italian Socialist party.

Together with Togliatti, he helped found the Communist party at age 23. Upon the rise of Fascism, he followed Togliatti into exile in Russia where he attended Communist political and military schools and made Russian his second language.

Despite the fact that he was a founder of the Italian Communist party, he was relatively unknown both in Italy and abroad until the Spanish Civil War where he turned up as political Kommissar of the International Brigades upon recommendation of Togliatti and Dimitrov, the two most influential members of the Comintern.

Using the nom de guerre "Luigi Gallo" Longo gained a reputation as a hard-line administrator and disciplinarian in the Russian Communist style.

Described by those who knew him as a cold and ruthlessly motivated person, he also displayed unusual personal bravery and disdain for personal danger.

With the defeat of the Loyalist forces, Longo crossed the frontier into France and was interned in the camp at Vernet. In 1941, at the request of the Fascist government, he was extradited and was sentened to serve five years at Ventotene. The Fascists overlooked the fact that they had sentenced him to death in absentia.

Longo was freed from Ventotene in 1943 and adhered to the unity pact with the socialists. He took charge of partisan activities in Rome and later in Milan where he become commanding general of the Garilbaldi Brigades and vice commander of the Volunteers of Liberty. He gave the orders for the execution of Mussolini.

Upon Togliatti's death he succeeded him as general secretary of the Italian party.

Colonel Pompeo Agrifoglio

The man who played a primary role in the rebirth of the Italian Military Intelligence Service was Colonel Pompeo Agrifoglio who was born in Palermo, Sicily, in 1888 and attended the Military Academy.

Agrifoglio served with distinction as a junior officer in World War I, seeing action on various fronts and receiving a number of decorations. Later, he also saw service in Africa and in Spain.

A man of high moral purpose, as a professional army officer, Agrifoglio never joined the Fascist party but was treated by the Fascists with deference. He entered the intelligence service and was assigned to North Africa in World War II. When Axis resistance collapsed, he went underground and gathered and transmitted data on the Allied OB with the counterintelligence people hot on his trail. He gave himself up to the U.S. forces and was sent for confinement at a prisoner-of-war camp in the United States.

With the signing of the armistice, AFHQ was asked to return Agrifoglio to Italy so that he could reorganize the SIM. He did this, winning the respect of the former enemies, by showing rectitude and professional pride and his incorruptibility in his dealings with the Allies.

Agrifoglio retired from the service after Umberto di Savoia went into exile. He was one of the last to see the monarch before his departure into exile to Portugal.

Agrifoglio worked under extreme pressure for many months as his family was in German-held territory and the Fascists were constantly searching for his wife and children.

He died suddenly in Palermo in 1948.

Professor Enzo Boeri

Born in Milan in 1914 to an outstanding democratic family, Boeri graduated cum laude in Medicine and Surgery in 1938. He enrolled in the Italian Navy where he served as medical lieutenant and won a War Cross for valor.

In 1942 while he was stationed in Naples, Boeri became an assistant of the Institute of Human Physiology at Naples University in which he remained as a researcher until 1954.

While serving with the Navy in Naples in October 1943, he participated in the insurrection against the Nazis, and after the liberation of the city he joined Craveri's ORI group of volunteers. He was trained and parachuted by SI/OSS as leader of the "Apricot" mission to CLNAI. He was SI's key agent in northern Italy and was appointed by CLN to head its intelligence section. His radio transmitter provided a communications link between AFHQ and the northern patriot commands. He was instrumental in helping other OSS and Allied missions behind enemy lines.

Boeri transmitted over one thousand messages during the long period that he operated behind the German lines. He was captured by the Fascists who had been looking for him, but fortunately he was not recognized and was exchanged for Fascist prisoners who were held captive by his brother. He was awarded the Silver Medal for valor by the Italian government and the Bronze Medal by the U.S. government.

In 1948 Boeri returned to his academic career at the university. From September 1951 to March 1953, he was a Rockefeller Fellow to the Institute of Chemical Biology of the Nobel Foundation at Stockholm. From 1954 to 1960, he was a researcher at the University at Ferrara and with the Johnson Foundation in Philadelphia. He was provided with a Rockefeller grant in 1956 with which he set up the Institute of Human Physiology at Ferrara. He published many papers on the subject which gained worldwide recognition.

Boeri died at Ferrara on October 28, 1960 at the age of 46.

General Giuseppe Massaioli

Born in Vietri di Potenza in 1901, General Giuseppe Massaioli entered the Italian Military Academy in 1923 and was commissioned a second lieutenant in 1925. He was attached to the Twenty-sixth Infantry Regiment and later sent to East Africa to serve on the Command Staff in Italian Somaliland and afterwards in Eritrea. Massaioli was promoted for exceptional service to captain in 1934, and in 1941 he was advanced to the grade of major. In 1942, he was assigned to the Russian front as chief of staff of the "Cosseria" Infantry Division; he fought on the Don where he earned a field promotion and several decorations for military valor.

When the Italian expeditionary forces retreated from Russia during the winter of 1942-1943, Massaioli was among the few who made it back to Italy. With the advent of the September 1943 Armistice, he made his way through the German lines, and he reported for duty at Badoglio's headquarters in Brindisi. There he was assigned to SIM and he became head of the offensive intelligence division under Colonel Agrigoflio. In this position he worked very closely with SOE and trained and briefed many of the missions that were dispatched into enemy terrain.

In 1948, Massaioli was named military attache to Tito's government in Belgrade, and in 1950 he was promoted to full colonel and given command of the Fortieth Infantry Regiment. Soon thereafter he was placed in command of the security forces in Italian Somaliland.

At the end of this assignment he was given command of the "Friuli" Division with the grade of brigadier general; promoted to major general he was given command of the "Aosta" Infantry Division.

As a lieutenant general, his next assignment was that of commanding general of the Sicilian territorial forces, and thereafter he was given command of the southern Italian territorial forces.

Called upon to assume the delicate post of commanding general of the Guardia di Finanza, he aquitted himself with distinction and integrity. His last assignment was that of chairman of the Italian Joint Chiefs of Staff, and at the termination of his term he retired from active service.

Massaioli represented the best traditions of the professional Italian officer corps and was motivated solely by selfless patriotism.

Giuseppe Romita

A militant socialist since his early youth, Giuseppe Romita was an engineer by profession. Born in Tortona on July 1, 1889, he early rebelled against the monarchy. He later graduated from the Turin Polytechnic Institute and then entered politics as a member of the municipal council of Tortona and later Turin.

A lifelong member of the Socialist party, motivated by centrist tendencies, Romita early joined the ranks of militant antiFascists. In 1926 he was sentenced to serve five years on the island of Ustica, from which he was released after two years. Although placed under special surveillance by the OVRA, he managed to keep in touch with Parri, Rosselli, and other key antiFascists.

In 1931, together with other Socialist party members, Romita was sentenced to two years of forced domicile at Vercoli, where he remained two years after which Mussolini allowed him to take up residence in Rome.

In 1940 Romita established contacts with his socialist friends, and the party was secretly reconstituted. Romita was elected secretary. A day after the fall of Mussolini, he surfaced to support the Unity Pact with the Communists, and he helped unite the two socialist currents in Italy of which Pietro Nenni became the party secretary (PSIUP—Partito Socialista Italiano di Unita Proletaria).

Romita was minister of public works in the government formed by Ferruccio Parri and minister of the interior in the first deGaspari government in which he played a key role during the referendum that established the Italian Republic.

Romita joined the antiCommunist wing of the Socialist party and eventually joined the wing of the Social Democrats founded by Giuseppe Saragat as a result of the party schism of 1947. He continued to serve various governments, providing strong support for the Christian Democrats. On February 2, 1952, he became secretary of the PSDI. He died in Rome on May 3, 1958. Among his close collaborators were Giuseppe and Filippo Lupis.

Giuseppe Lupis

On December 19, 1979, Giuseppe Lupis, one of the founders of the Italian Social Democratic party, died in a Rome clinic after a few weeks of illness. Though 84 years old, "Peppino" Lupis was active until the very end.

As a young officer in the Italian Army during World War I, Lupis was wounded on two occasions and the last time was left for dead on the battlefield. He was picked up by an Austrian patrol, hospitalized, and released at the end of the war— to the surprise of his family, which had been notified of his death and had already celebrated a Requiem Mass in his memory.

Born in Ragusa, Sicily, Lupis studied and briefly practiced law until he joined the Socialist party of which he became the secretary for the Province of Syracuse. With the advent of Fascism, he was forced to seek asylum abroad. He settled in New York in 1926 where, for over two decades, he was a distinguished journalist, editor, and one of the leaders of the antiFascist movement.

Lupis edited a number of Italian-language newspapers and still later the monthly magazine, *Il Mondo*. Conbributing editors to this publication included Don Luigi Sturzo, Nitti, Salvemini, Ferrero, Sforza, Nenni, Saragat, Silone, and a host of other leading antiFascist exiles.

Lupis returned to Italy in 1945 and quickly became active in the political life of the country. In 1946, when the Socialist party split up into two currents, Lupis joined the right-wing faction headed by Giuseppe Saragat, a close friend of the Lupis family. This faction favored close ties with the United States and opposed the Popular Front with the Communists. Nenni was the leader of the left-wing group favoring the Front.

Lupis was elected to the Chamber of Deputies from the District of Catania, Sicily, in 1948 and served until 1976.

Glossary

"A" Force	Organization to facilitate the escape of Allied prisoners of war behind enemy lines
A-2	Air Force Intelligence
AAF	Army Air Force
AAI	Allied Armies in Italy
Abwehr	German military intelligence
ACC	Allied Control Commission: Agency for guidance and supervision of the Italian government in areas no longer directly under AMG
ACMF	Allied Central Mediterranean Force
AFHQ	Allied Force Headquarters for operations in the western Mediterranean
ALO	Allied Liaison Officer
AMGOT	Allied Military Government Occupied Territory—later changed simply to AMG
ATC	Air Transport Command of the Army Air Force
BBC	British Broadcasting Corporation
"Broadway"	Code name for SIS
CIC	Counter-Intelligence Corps (G-2)
CINCMED	Commander-in-Chief—Mediterranean
CIS	Italian Naval Intelligence

CLNAI	Committee of National Liberation Upper Italy
COI	Coordinator of Information—precursor of OSS
COMNAVNAW	Commander—United Stated Naval Forces, Northwest African Waters
CVL	Volunteers of Liberty Corps: Fighting forces of the CLNAI
DGER	Direction General des Etudes et Recherches
DSM	Direction des Service de Securite Militaire.
ETOUSA	European Theater of Operations
FBI	Federal Bureau of Investigation
FFI	French Forces of the Interior
FOTALI	Fleet Operations Italy (British)
G-2	Army Intelligence
G-3 Experimental Detachment	OSS unit attached to AFHQ
GESTAPO	Geheime Staten Polizei (Nazi Secret Police)
HMS	His Majesty's Ship
ICU	Intelligence Collection Unit
ISLD	Interservice Liaison Department (SIS)
JCS	Joint Chiefs of Staff
JIC	Joint Intelligence Committee
JICA	Joint Intelligence Collection Committee
MAAF	Mediterranean Allied Air Force
MATAF	Mediterranean Allied Tactical Air Force
MATS	Mediterranean Air Transport Service
MI5	British Counter Intelligence
MIS	Military Intelligence Service (G-2 War Department General Staff)
MO	Morale Operations—OSS Psychological War Unit
MU	Maritime Unit—OSS Maritime Training Unit
NATOUSA	North African Theater of Operations—U.S. Army
NKGB	Russian Secret Service
NOB	Naval Operations Base
OG	OSS Operational Groups (Commando Units)
OKW	Oberkommando der Wehrmacht

ONI	Office of Naval Intelligence—U.S. Navy
ORI	Organization for Italian Resistance
OSO	Office of Special Operations
OSS	Office of Strategic Services
OVRA	Opera Volontaria Repressione Antifascista
PTB Ron 15	Motor Torpedo Boat Squadron attached to U.S. Mediterranean Fleet.
PWB	Psychological Warfare Board
RAF	Royal Air Force
R & A	Research & Analysis Division, OSS
R & D	Research & Development Division, OSS
SA/B	Special Activities/Bruce—COI intelligence
SA/G	Special Activities/Goodfellow—COI operations
SBS	Special Bari Section (OSS Balkan Operations)
SCIU	Special Counter Intelligence Unit
SD	Sicherheits Dienst—SS counterintelligence
SI	Secret Intelligence Branch, OSS
SIA	Italian Air Force Intelligence
SIM	Servizio Informazioni Militare—Italian Intelligence Service
SIS	Secret Intelligence Service (British)—MI6
SO	Special Operations Branch, OSS
SOE	Special Operations Executive (British)
SR	Service de Renseignments (French)
SS	Schutz Staffel (Nazi Secret Police)
SSU	Strategic Services Unit (Successor to OSS)
2677 Regiment	OSS Mediterranean Command
2677 Regiment	Company A—OG Operations
2677 Regiment	Company B—French Operations
2677 Regiment	Company C—Balkan Operations
2677 Regiment	Company D—Italian Operations
X-2	Counter Intelligence Division, OSS

Bibliography

Allen, William L. *Anzio: The Edge of Disaster.* New York: W.W. Norton, 1978.

Alsop, Stewart, and Braden, Thomas. *Sub Rosa: The OSS and American Espionage.* New York: Reynal and Hitchcock, 1946.

Antonini, Luigi. *Dynamic Democracy.* New York: Eloquent Press, 1944.

Attanasio, Alessandro. *Gli Italiani e la Guerra di Spagna.* Milan: Mursia, 1974.

———. *Sicilia Senza Italia.* Milan: Mursia, 1976.

———. *Gli Anni Della Rabbia.* Milan: Mursia, 1981.

Badoglio, Pietro. *L'Italia Nella Seconda Guerra Mondiale.* Milan: Mondadori, 1946.

Bennett, Ralph. *Ultra in the West.* New York: Scribner's, 1979.

Blumenson, Martin. *Mark Clark.* New York: Congdon-Weed, 1984.

———. *Kasserine Pass.* New York: Tower Books, 1966.

Bocca, Giorgio. *Storia dell'Italia Partigiana.* Bari: La Terza, 1966.

Bradley, Omar. *A Soldier's Story.* New York: Henry Holt and Co., 1951.

Breuer, William R. *Drop Zone Sicily.* San Rafael: Presidio Press, 1986.

Brissaud, Andre. *Canaris.* New York: Grosset and Dunlop, 1974.

Brown, Anthony Cave. *Bodyguard of Lies.* New York: Harper and Row, 1975.

———. *Secret War Report of the OSS.* New York: Berkely, 1976.

———. *The Last Hero: Wild Bill Donovan.* New York: Times Books, 1982.

Burke, Michael. *Outrageous Good Fortune.* Boston: Little, Brown, 1984.

Byrnes, James F. *Speaking Frankly.* New York: Harper and Brothers, 1947.

Cadorna, Raffaele. *La Riscossa.* Turin: Bietti, 1965.

Campbell, Rodney. *The Luciano Project: The Secret War Time Collaboration of the Mafia and the U.S. Navy.* New York: McGraw-Hill, 1977.

Cannistraro, Philip V. *Historical Dictionary of Fascist Italy.* Westport, Ct.: Greenwood Press, 1982.

Carcaci, Duke of. *Il Movimento per l'Indipendenza della Sicilia.* Palermo: Flaccovio, 1977.

Carver, Michael. *Tobruk.* London: B.T. Batsford Ltd., 1964.

Castellano, Giuseppe, Gen. *Come Firmai L'Armistizio di Cassibile.* Milan: Mondadori, 1945.

Constantinides, George C. *Intelligence and Espionage: An Analytical Bibliography.* Boulder, Colo.: Westview Press, 1983.

Coon, Carleton S. *A North African Story 1941-1943.* Ipswich: Gambit, 1980.

Corson, William. *The Armies of Ignorance: The Rise of the American Intelligence Empire.* New York: Dial Press, 1977.

Craveri, Raimondo. *I Servizi Segreti e la Campagna d'Italia.* Milan: La Pietra, 1980.

Daniels, Jonathan. *White House Witness, 1942-1945.*

Darby, William, and Baumer, William H. *We led the Way.* San Rafael: Presidio, 1980.

Deacon, Richard. *A History of the British Secret Service.* London: Frederick Muller, 1966.

Delzell, Charles F. *Mussolini's Enemies: The Italian Anti-fascist Resistance.* Princeton, N.J.: Princeton University Press, 1961.

DeRisio, Carlo. *Generali, Servizi Segreti e Fascismo 1940-1943.* Milan: Mondadori, 1978.

DiBella, Francesco Aurelio. *Un Aviatore Racconta le Sue Battaglie.* Palermo: Renna, Ed., 1950.

Djilas, Milovan. *Memoir of a Revolutionary.* New York: Harcourt, Brace, Jovanovich, 1973.

Downes, Donald. *The Scarlet Thread.* London: Verschoyle, 1953.

Dulles, Allan W. *Germany's Underground.* New York: Macmillan, 1947.

——. *The Craft of Intelligence.* New York: Harper and Row, 1963.

——. *The Secret Surrender.* New York: Harper and Row, 1966.

Dunlop, Richard. *Donovan: America's Master Spy.* Chicago: Rand McNally, 1982.

Eisenhower, Dwight. *Crusade in Europe.* New York: Doubleday, 1945.

Faenza, Roberto, and Fini, Marco. *Gli Americani in Italia.* Milan: Feltrinelli, 1976.

Farago, Ladislas. *Patton: Ordeal and Triumph.* New York: Dell, 1965.

Fini, Marco, and Faenza, Roberto. *Gli Americani in Italia.* Milan: Feltrinelli, 1976.

Fini, Marco, Pesenti R., and Ponzo, M. *Guerriglia nell'Ossola.* Milan: Feltrinelli, 1975.

Ford, Corey. *Donovan of OSS.* Boston: Little, Brown, 1970.

Ford, Corey, and McBain, Allistair. *Cloak and Dagger.* New York: Random House, 1945.

Garlinski, Joseph. *The Enigma War.* New York: Scribner's, 1980.

Gehlen, Reinhard. *The Service: The Memoirs of Gen. Reinhard Gehlen.* New York: World Publishing, 1972.

Geraghty, Tony. *Inside the SAS.* New York: Ballantine Books, 1980.

Goralski, Robert. *World War II Almanac 1931-1945.* New York: G. Putnam's Sons, 1981.

Graham, Dominick, and Shelford, Bidwell. *Tug of War.* New York: St. Martin's Press, 1986.

Graziani, Rodolfo. *Ho Difeso La Patria.* Milan: Garzanti, 1948.

Gunther, John. *D-Day: Inside the First Great Invasion of Hitler's Europe - Sicily.* New York: Harper and Row, 1943.

Harpor, Brian. *The Impossible Victory.* New York: Hippocrene Books, 1981.

Hessame, H. *Patton.* New York: Scribner's, 1974.

Hyde, H. Montgomery. *Room 3603: The Story of the British Intelligence Center.* New York: Farrar, Straus and Giroux, 1963.

——. *Secret Intelligence Agent.* London: Constable, 1982.

Hymoff, Edward. *The O.S.S. In World War II.* New York: Ballantine, 1972.

Icardi, Aldo. *American Master Spy.* New York: University Books, 1956.

Jackson, W.G.F. *The Battle For Italy*. New York: Harper and Row, 1967.
———. *The Battle For Rome*. New York: Charles Scribner's, 1969.
Kahn, David. *The Code Breakers*. New York: Macmillan, 1967.
———. *Hitler's Spies*. New York: Macmillan, 1978.
Katz, Robert. *Death in Rome*. New York: Macmillan, 1967.
Kent, Sherman. *Strategic Intelligence for American World Policy*. Princeton, N.J.: Princeton University Press, 1951.
Kirkpatrick, Lyman. *The Real C.I.A.* New York: Macmillan, 1973.
———. *The Intelligence Community*. New York: Hill and Wang, 1973.
Leslie, Peter. *The Liberation of the Riviera*. New York: Wyndham, 1980.
Lewin, Ronald. *Ultra Goes to War*. New York: McGraw-Hill, 1978.
Lewis, Flora. *The Red Pawn: The Story of Noel Field*. New York: Doubleday, 1965.
Long, Garvin. *Greece, Crete and Syria*. Canberra Australian War Memorial. 1953.
Mackey, Kenneth. *Kesselring*. New York: David McKay, 1978.
Macksey, Kenneth. *Bede Fomm: The Classic Victory*. London: Ballantine's Illustrated History Battle Book, No. 22.
Martin, David C. *Wilderness of Mirrors*. New York: Harper and Row, 1980.
Masterman, Sir John. *The Double Cross System*. New Haven, Conn.: Yale University Press, 1972.
McCoy, Alfred W. *The Politics of Heroin and S.E. Asia*. New York: Harper-Colophan, 1972.
McDonald, Elizabeth. *Undercover Girl*. New York: Macmillan, 1947.
McLean, Fitzroy. *Tito the Man Who Defied Hitler*. New York: Ballantine Books, 1957.
Mercurio Magazine. *Miscellaneous stories of the Italian Resistance*. Milan: December, 1945.
Michel, Henri. *The Shadow War: Resistance in Europe 1939-1945*. London: Andre Deutsch, 1972.
Mikssche, F.O. *Secret Forces*. London: Farber and Farber, 1948.
Montgomery, Viscount of Alamain. *El Alamain to the River Sangro*. New York: St. Martin's Press, 1974.
Morris, Eric. *Salerno: A Military Fiasco*. New York: Stein and Day, 1983.
Morrison, Samuel Elliot. *History of the United States Naval Operations in World War II*. Vol. Nine, "Sicily, Salerno, Anzio." Boston: Little, Brown, 1964.
Mosley, Leonard. *Dulles: A Biography of the Dulles Family Network*. New York: Dial Press, 1978.
Nicholson, G.W.L. *The Canadians in Italy 1943-1945*. Ottawa: Roger Duhamel, 1967.
Nicolson, Nigel. *Alex, The Life of Field Marshal Alexander*. New York: Atheneum, 1973.
Obolensky, Sergei. *One Man In His Time*. New York: McDonald-Obolensky, 1958.
Office of the Chief of Military History, United States Army. *Salerno to Cassino*.
———. *Sicily and the Surrender of Italy*.
Origo, Iris. *A Need to Testify*. New York: Harcourt, Brace, Jovanovich, 1984.
Padovani, M. *La Lunga Marcia del P.C.I.* Milan: Mursia, 1976.
Page, Bruce, Leitch, David, and Knightly, Philip. *The Philby Conspiracy*. New York: Signet Books, 1969.
Paine, Lauran. *German Military Intelligence in World War II*. New York: Stein and Day, 1984.
Patton, George. *War As I Knew It*. Boston: Houghton Mifflin, 1947.
Peis, Gunter. *The Mirror of Deception: How Britain Turned the Nazi Spy Machine Against Itself*. London: Weidenfeld and Nicholson, 1977.

Peniakoff, Vladimir. *Popski's Private Army*. New York: Doubleday, 1980.
Persico, Joseph. *Piercing the Reich*. New York: Viking, 1979.
Pertini, Sandro. *Sei Condanne: Due Evasioni*. Milan: Oscar Mondadori, 1974.
Pesce, Giovanni. *Quando Cessarono Gli Spari*. Milan: Feltrinelli, 1977.
Philby, Kim. *My Silent War*. New York: Grove Press, 1968.
Pinto, Oreste. *Spy Catcher*. New York: Harper and Brothers, 1952.
Pisano, Giorgio. *Storia della Guerra Civile in Italia*. Milan: Edizione F.P.E., 1965.
Popov, Dusko. *Spy/Counterspy*. New York: Grosset and Dunlap, 1974.
Porto, Salvo. *Mafia e Fascismo*. Palermo: Flaccovio, 1977.
Prouty, Fletcher L. *The Secret Team*. New York: Prentice-Hall, 1973.
Rado, Sandor. *Codename Dora*. London: Abelost, 1977.
Read, Anthony, and Fisher, David. *Colonel Z*. New York: Viking, 1985.
———. *Operation Lucy*. New York: Coward, McCann and Geoghan. 1981.
Ricchezza, Antonio & Giulio. *L'Esercito del Sud*. Milan: Mursia, 1973.
Romita, Giuseppe. *Dalla Monarchia Alla Republica*. Milan: Mursia, 1959.
Romualdi, Serafino. *Presidents and Peons*. New York: Funk and Wagnalls, 1967.
Roosevelt, Kermit. *The War Report of the OSS*. New York: Walker, 1976.
Rosengarten, Frank. *The Italian Anti-Fascist Press 1919-1945*. Cleveland: 1968.
Sage, Jerry. *Sage*. Wayne, Ind.: Standish Press, 1985.
Saini, Ezio. *La Notte Di Dongo*. Rome: Casa Editrice Libreria Corso, 1950.
Schellenberger, Walter. *The Labyrinth*. New York: Harper, 1956.
———. *Hitler's Secret Service*. New York: Pyramid Books, 1958.
Secchia, Pietro. *Storia della Resistenza*. Milan: Editori Riuniti.
Smith, F. Bradley. *The Shadow Warriors*. New York: Basic Books, 1983.
———. *Operation Sunrise*. Written with Elena Agarossi. New York: Basic Books, 1979.
Smith, R. Harris. *OSS: The Secret History of America's First Central Intelligence*. Berkeley: University of California Press, 1972.
Smyth, Howard McGaw. *Secrets of the Fascist Era*. Southern Illinois University Press, 1975.
Solari, Fermo. *L'Armonia Discutibile della Resistenza*. Milan: La Pietra, 1979.
Spriano, Paolo. *Storia del Partito Comunista Italiano*. Turin: Einaudi, 1970.
Sweet-Escott, Bickham. *Baker Street Irregular*. London: Methuen, 1965.
Taylor, Maxwell D. *Swords and Plowshares*. New York: W.W. Norton, 1972.
Thomas, Hugh. *The Spanish Civil War*.
Tompkins, Peter. *A Spy in Rome*. New York: Simon and Schuster, 1962.
Toscano, Mario. *Designs in Diplomacy*. Baltimore: Johns Hopkins University Press, 1970.
Tosi, Michele. *La Republica di Bobbio*. Bobbio: 1977.
Tregarskis, Richard. *Invasion Diary*. New York: Random House, 1944.
Trepper, Leopold. *The Great Game*. New York: McGraw-Hill, 1977.
Troy, Thomas. *Donovan and the CIA*. Frederick: University Publications, 1981.
U.S. House Committee on Armed Services. *Testimony and Confessions Relating to the Disappearance of Major William Hollohan*. Washington, D.C.: U.S. Printing Office, 1953.
Valiani, Leo. *Tutte le Strade Conducano a Roma*. Florence: La Nuova Italia, 1947.
West. Nigel. *MI 6*. New York: Random House, 1983.
———. *MI 5*. New York: Stein and Day, 1981.
Wilson, Hugh R. *Diplomat Between Wars*. New York: Longmans-Green, 1941.
Winterbotham, F.W. *The Ultra Secret*. London: Weidenfeld and Nicholson, 1974.
Zevi, Bruno. *Quaderni Italiani, Vol. II*. Boston: 1942.
Zingale, Gaetano. *L'Invasione della Sicilia*. Catania: Crissafulli, 1962.

Index

The names of Earl Brennan, chief of the Italian Division SI, and that of Vincent Scamporino, chief Italian SI, MEDTO, have not been included in this index as they are an intrinsic part of this account of historic OSS events, almost from the beginning to the end.

About the Author

MAX CORVO has been publisher of the Middletown *Bulletin* since 1947. He presided over the O.S.S. Symposium Committee in a two-day session held in Washington, D.C., in September, 1986.